The Murde

Colin Wilson was born in Leicester in 1931. He left school at sixteen and spent several years working in a wool warehouse, a laboratory, a plastics factory and a coffee bar before *The Outsider* was published in 1956 to oustanding critical acclaim. Since then he has written many books on philosophy, the occult, crime and sexual deviance, plus a number of successful novels. His work includes *The Mammoth Book of True Crime*, *The Mammoth Book of the Supernatural*, *The Mind Parasites*, *New Pathways in Psychology*, and *The Occult*. Mr. Wilson is well known as a lecturer and radio and television personality. He lives in Cornwall.

Also by Colin Wilson

NON-FICTION
The Outsider
Religion and the Rebel
The Age of Defeat
Encyclopaedia of Murder (with Patricia Pitman)
Origins of the Sexual Impulse
Beyond the Outsider: The Philosophy of the Future
Voyage to a Beginning (autobiography)
A Casebook of Murder
The Occult
Order of Assassins: The Psychology of Murder
Strange Powers
Mysterious Powers
The Craft of the Novel
The Geller Phenomenon
Science Fiction as Existentialism
The Search for the Real Arthur
Starseekers
The Quest for Wilhelm Reich
Lord of the Underworld: Jung and the Twentieth Century
A Criminal History of Mankind
The Misfits
The Mammoth Book of True Crime
Written in Blood
The Mammoth Book of True Crime 2

FICTION
Ritual in the Dark
The World of Violence
Necessary Doubt
The Glass Cage
The Killer
The Schoolgirl Murder Case
The Janus Murder Case
The Mind Parasites
The Space Vampires
Spider World

The Murder Casebook

Edited by Colin Wilson

Magpie Books, London

For Denis Hocking
last of the great pathologists

Constable & Robinson Ltd
3 The Lanchesters
162 Fulham Palace Road
London W6 9ER
www.constablerobinson.com

This edition published by Magpie Books,
an imprint of Constable & Robinson Ltd 2005

Previously published separately as
Murder in the 1930s and *Murder in the 1940s*
by Robinson, an imprint of Constable & Robinson Ltd, 1992 and 1993

A copy of the British Library Cataloguing in
Publication Data is available from the British Library

ISBN 978-1-84529-181-5

Printed and bound in the EU

3 5 7 9 10 8 6 4

Part 1

Murder in the 1930s

Contents

Acknowledgements

The publishers would like to extend their grateful thanks to the following authors, publishers and others for kindly granting them permission to reproduce the copyrighted material included in this book. Every effort has been made to secure and clear copyrights and the publishers trust that their apologies will be accepted for any errors or omissions.

'Misapplied Ingenuity of a Bigamist: The Rouse Case' by F. A. Beaumont. Originally published in *The Fifty Most Amazing Crimes of the Last 100 Years*, Odhams, 1936.

'Man Hunters: The German Rouse Case' by F. A. Beaumont. Originally published in *The Fifty Most Amazing Crimes of the Last 100 years*, Odhams, 1936.

'The Otterburn Mystery' by Val Gielgud. Originally published in *Great Unsolved Crimes*, Hutchinson, n.d. Reprinted by permission of the author's estate.

'The Murder of Julia Wallace' by Dorothy L. Sayers. Originally published in *Great Unsolved Crimes*, Hutchinson, n.d. Reprinted by permission of David Higham Associates and Lloyds Bank PLC.

'The Vera Page Case' by George Cornish. Originally published in *Great Unsolved Crimes*, Hutchinson, n.d.

'Winnie Ruth Judd' by Geoffrey Homes. Originally published in *Los Angeles Murders*, Duell, Sloan and Pearce, 1947. Reprinted by permission of John Hawkins & Associates Inc.

Introduction

From our age of sex crime and serial murder, we look back with something like nostalgia on the less complicated crimes of the 1930s. Some crimes – like Wallace, Rouse and Ruxton – have become gruesome classics; others – like Winnie Judd, Frau Marek and Georges Sarret – have hardly achieved the celebrity they deserve. One of the aims of this collection is to restore the balance.

Let us try to place the decade in some kind of criminological perspective. One of the most interesting things about the 1930s is that crime detection was becoming so efficient that the period has rather less than its fair share of famous cases. In earlier decades, the careful criminal had a far better chance of getting away with murder. In fact, even as late as the 1880s, there was virtually nothing that could be called a science of crime detection. When Conan Doyle created Sherlock Holmes in *A Study in Scarlet*, which appeared in *Beeton's Christmas Annual* in 1887, real crime detection was a hit-and miss affair; detectives did not crawl on the floor with magnifying glasses, or even sprinkle fine dust on polished surfaces to reveal fingerprints – for although the uniqueness of fingerprints had been known for about ten years, no one had yet discovered how to classify them, and it would be another ten years before the police learned to make practical use of them.

But by the early years of the 20th century, fingerprinting, ballistics (the study of guns), blood-grouping and the use of the microscope were turning crime detection into a formidable science. Poison, the favourite method of murderers since Roman times, was now as dangerous to the killer as to the victim. In 1910, Crippen was sentenced for the murder of his wife on the evidence of the hyoscine found in her body, and on Bernard Spilsbury's identification of the mutilated remains – largely through an operation scar on the stomach. In 1917, Louis Voisin was convicted of murdering and dismembering his mistress, again largely on the evidence derived from Spilsbury's painstaking forensic study. In 1923, two professional burglars named Klauss and Doelitzsch were found guilty of the murder of an Alexandrian merchant because of an ingenious chain of deduction on the part of forensic expert Sidney Smith. Even the famous "St. Valentine's Day massacre" of 1929 was solved by a ballistics expert – Calvin Goddard – who was able to identify the tommy guns used to shoot down seven men in a Chicago garage.

So by 1930, murder had become a highly dangerous method for the solving of personal problems. Sidney Harry Fox learned this the hard way after strangling his mother in a hotel room in Margate, Kent, and then setting the room on fire top make it look like an accident. Doctors decided that her death was due to asphyxiation and shock, and a death certificate was issued without question. But the insurance company who had to pay Sidney Fox £6,000 was suspicious. Examination of the hotel room revealed that although the blaze was supposed to have originated in the gas fire, there was a six inch patch of unburnt carpet between the fender and Mrs. Fox's burnt chair, which was directly in front of the fire. And when charred fragments of paper were discovered in the room, and a bottle containing petrol, Fox was arrested (on a fraud charge – he and his mother had never been known to pay their hotel bills), and Mrs. Fox's body was exhumed. Again, it was Spilsbury who discovered that she had been dead before the fire began – proved by absence of smoke in the lungs – while a bruise on the throat pointed to strangulation (although the hyoid bone was unbroken.) But it was finally Fox's own damaging admission that led to his conviction. He described going into the room and finding it full of smoke, then rushing out again and closing the door. Asked why he had closed the door, he explained that he did not want the smoke to spread into the hotel. In short, said the prosecution, he preferred to allow his mother to suffocate rather than let smoke into the hotel . . . Fox was hanged on April 8, 1930.

It might seem that the Fox case would have made an ideal opening chapter for this book. But then, it was necessary to choose carefully, in order to achieve the right balance between well-known and lesser known cases, and for me the deciding factor was that I could find no account of the case that seemed a good anthology piece. I felt equal regret in having to exclude one of America's most famous murder trials of the 'thirties – the case of Albert Fish. Born in 1870, Fish was one of the worst, as well as one of the earliest, serial killers of the 20th century. A sado-masochist who loved to drive needles into his scrotum, he also had an obsessive need to castrate boys and kill – and eat – girls. It was in 1928 that this mild-looking old man persuaded a New York family named Budd to allow him to take their ten year old daughter Grace to a birthday party. When they failed to return, the Budds discovered that the address of "Frank Howard's" sister was non-existent. A long and exhaustive police search produced no result. But in November 1934, Fish wrote a letter to Grace's parents, admitting that he had strangled her in an abandoned cottage, then cooked and eaten parts of her body. The envelope carried a set of printed initials that had been blacked out; a spectroscope revealed them to be the initials of a Chauffeurs' Benevolent Association. Detective Will King questioned employees at the Association, and finally persuaded one of them to admit that he had occasionally borrowed envelopes for his correspondence. He went to the boarding house where the chauffeur recalled leaving some of the envelopes in a cupboard, and described Grace Budd's kidnapper to the landlady. "That sounds like Mr. Fish." Albert Fish had occupied Room 7 after the chauffeur. After keeping a watch on the place for three weeks, King was finally able to arrest Fish – although the little man tried to attack him with a razor in both hands.

Fish subsequently claimed to have committed 400 child murders over the years. Although clearly insane, he was sentenced to death and electrocuted in January 1936. At least his masochism made him look forward to his execution as "the greatest thrill of my life".

These, then, are the two main omissions. Otherwise, I trust that this first volume of famous crimes of the decade will be regarded as reasonably complete.

Colin Wilson

Misapplied Ingenuity of a Bigamist: the Rouse Case

The Rouse case has always held a special interest for me because it is possible that, had things turned out differently, Alfred Rouse might have become my father. In 1930, my mother – then a nineteen year old named Hattie Jones – was working for a garment firm called Rudkin and Laundon in St. Saviours Road, Leicester. Rouse, a commercial traveller in braces and garters, visited the factory periodically. One day, my mother was looking in the window of a shop that sold coats when Rouse came and spoke to her. He had seen her in the factory and asked her if she would like to go for a meal. My mother had already eaten, and said that in any case, her father would probably object. When she told him her father was on the telephone, Rouse rang him and asked if he could take her out, promising to bring her straight home.

It seems to have been an odd "date", for my mother said she would prefer to wait in the car while he had a meal. He brought her a box of chocolates, and she ate some of them as she waited. After this, Rouse took her for a short drive and then, as he promised, drove her home. I asked her to repeat the story just before writing these words – she is now 81 – and she confirmed that Rouse behaved like a gentleman and took her home as promised. She never saw him again. From this I deduce that the episode took place not long before the murder (her memory on the subject is now poor). That he behaved "like a gentleman" is probably one of the reasons of his remarkable success with women. For seducers of the Rouse type, the pursuit is just as enjoyable as the capture; they enjoy the courtship procedure. If Rouse's life had been less complicated, he would probably have taken her out again next time he came to Leicester, and in due course, my mother might have succumbed to his charm. (I was, in fact, conceived about a month before Rouse murdered the unknown tramp.)

I first read about the case some ten years after it happened, in a book called *The Fifty Most Amazing Crimes of the Last Hundred Years*, published by Odhams Press in 1936. This volume was, as far as I can recall, my first encounter with the subject of true-life crime – my reading had so far been confined to boys' weeklies and tales like Ballantyne's *Coral Island* – and no doubt it was this early introduction that explains why I continued to be interested in the subject twenty years later when, together with Pat Pitman, I produced the first encyclopedia of murder that had ever appeared. But although I wrote an account of the case in the *Encyclopedia*, and have written about it several times since then, I have preferred to use here the account by F. A. Beaumont from *The Fifty Most Amazing Crimes of the Past Hundred Years*.

An aeroplane burst into flames, hung poised, before crumpling and diving earthwards through a spiral of black smoke. The blaze in the sky held the eyes of Private Alfred Arthur Rouse during the moment in which he waited for six inches of cold steel to plunge into his belly. He was in a bayonet mêlée in Northern France in 1915, and had just missed his man . . .

Then there was a terrific explosion, and everything went black. A shell had burst near Rouse, stunning him into merciful oblivion. He was severely wounded in the head and thigh, and was immediately evacuated to England. And he did not regain consciousness until the train conveying him to hospital was passing through the station of Bedford, where he was to be executed fifteen years later.

After the wound in his temple healed, the medical reports on its condition and effects were "scar irritable . . . patient unable to wear a hat of any kind . . . memory very defective . . . sleeps badly . . . easily excited . . . talks and laughs immoderately at times."

Sweating with terror, Rouse would often awaken in the small hours waiting for that bayonet thrust, seeing again the blaze in the sky that was as the angel of death to him.

Eventually Rouse was discharged with "capacity reduced three-quarters." Anxious to regain his health by an outdoor job, he became a commercial traveller for a Leicester firm, motoring up and down the country. Cars fascinated him, and he bought one after the other, quickly becoming not only a superb driver, but a highly skilled mechanic. With his "gift of the gab" and his cheery manner, it was not long before he had built up a wide and lucrative connection.

He was also very popular in the neighbourhood of his little home in Buxted Road, Finchley, which he was buying through a building society. He could tell a good story, and shone on the local tennis courts. His easy ways, lack of "side," good looks and charm made him well known and popular in the neighbourhood, but there seemed no reason why the world at large should hear anything more of him.

Until one night in 1930, when he fled from another blazing horror . . .

William Bailey and Alfred Thomas Brown, two young cousins, were returning at 2 a.m. from a Bonfire Night dance at Northampton, to their homes in the little village of Hardingstone. They had to walk along the main road

3

from Northampton to London and then turn to the left down Hardingstone Lane.

Just as they reached the corner, a motor-car flashed by them on the main road to London. It had scarcely passed when a man scrambled from a ditch. At first he did not seem aware of the cousins, who had indeed been momentarily hidden behind the advancing car.

It was a bright moonlight night, and they had a clear view of the stranger. He was bareheaded, agitated and breathless. He wore a light mackintosh and carried an attaché-case in his hand. The cousins wondered first why a respectably dressed man should be without a hat in winter, and then why he should be jumping out of a ditch at two in the morning.

They looked past him and saw a bright red glow about two hundred yards down Hardingstone Lane.

"What is the blaze?" Bailey asked his cousin.

Hurrying away from them, the hatless man gasped over his shoulder, as if he thought the question had been addressed to him. "It looks as if some one has had a bonfire."

The cousins began to walk swiftly towards the glare. They had to pass it in any case on their way home, but by now their curiosity was awakened. Once or twice they glanced back in the direction of the hatless man. He was still behaving queerly. He took a few steps towards Northampton, then turned towards London, and finally stood hesitating, as if undecided which way to go. The last the cousins saw of him was that he was watching them as they broke into a run towards the huge bonfire.

Through flames that were leaping fifteen feet high from a furnace so dense that scarcely anything else could be seen, they glimpsed the outlines of a motor-car. They ran on into the village. Bailey called out his father, the village constable, and he brought with him Police Constable Copping.

By this time the flames had dropped to a height of five or six feet, and they could go nearer. With the aid of Brown's torch, a black "ball" could be seen, and as the

4

flames lowered it was realised that this was the head of a huddled, shapeless body.

Twelve minutes later the fire had been extinguished with buckets of water. The car was almost completely burnt out. And slumping face downwards in it, like some horrible effigy that had been left behind by the revellers of the night before, was a charred and shrivelled corpse. Its trunk was lying across the passenger's seat and its face was in the driver's seat. The right arm was burnt off at the elbow, but it appeared to be stretched as if over the passenger's seat towards a petrol can in the rear, burst in on one of its seams, and with handle and screw missing.

The left arm could not be seen until the body was taken from the car. The left leg was doubled up underneath the trunk. The right leg was burnt off below the knee, but it was extended where the running-board had been, and was sticking out eight inches from the remains of the chassis.

Near the running-board was found a charred boot heel, and fourteen yards in front of the car a mallet with three or four hairs adhering to it, one of them human . . .

Wrapped in sacking, the corpse was removed to Northampton General Hospital. At first it was thought to be that of a woman, for every external evidence of sex had been destroyed by fire. Police inquiries were made in Northampton, including visits to every hotel and inn, but no woman in the town was reported missing.

The car was a Morris Minor, and its registered number, MU 1468, enabled the police to trace it to the home of Alfred Arthur Rouse, in Buxted Road, Finchley. Two plain clothes officers called on Mrs. Rouse during the afternoon of November 6th, 1930, and requested her to go to Northampton. There she was shown "brace buckles and pieces of clothing" which she thought might have belonged to her husband, though she was not allowed to view the charred body. Later it was discovered that Rouse had taken out an insurance for £1000, to be paid in the event of the accidental death of the owner-driver of the car.

Impressed by the information given by Brown and Bailey about the mysterious stranger they had encountered, the police circulated a statement that they were anxious to get into touch with a man aged between thirty and thirty-five, height five feet ten inches to six feet, with a small round face and curly black hair, wearing a light mackintosh, dark trousers, no hat, and carrying an attaché-case.

Tongues began to wag. It was hinted that the body found in the car was that of an unknown man, murdered by Rouse, and intended to be mistaken for himself, in order that Rouse could start life afresh under a new name.

On the face of it, such a suspicion appeared wildly absurd to every thinking person – in the early days of the case. Rouse had an excellent job, a comfortable home, and plenty of friends. If he disappeared, he would become a destitute vagrant, liable to be recognised at any moment and charged with murder. No man in his senses would even contemplate such a step. But the tangled forces of character and circumstances can impel towards strange hells . . .

Rouse was born on April 6th, 1894. There was discord in his home, and when young Rouse was only six years old, the children were separated from their mother, and committed by their father to the care of his sister.

Arthur Rouse was educated at a local Council school, and was remembered there as a keen, bright lad, fond of athletics. When he left he attended evening classes, and learnt to play the violin, piano and mandoline. His first job was as office boy to an estate agent. Then he worked for five years in a soft-furnishing house in the West End. During this time he became a sacristan at a church in Stoke Newington.

Only four days after the declaration of war in 1914, he enlisted as a private in the 24th Queen's (Territorial) Regiment. And before being drafted to France, he married on November 29th of that year, Lily May Watkins, a young woman clerk, at St. Saviour's, St. Albans. He was twenty then, and she three years older.

After his discharge from the army, Rouse found during his roving life as a commercial traveller that his really good looks, ingratiating air and plausible tongue appealed irresistibly to many women. He began to "pick up" attractive girls – waitresses, shop assistants, probationer nurses, and others – and take them for a ride.

In 1920 he met a fourteen-year-old Edinburgh girl. By the time she was fifteen she was in a home for unmarried mothers. The child died when only five weeks old. Rouse posed to the girl-mother as a single man, and in 1924 persuaded her to go through a ceremony of marriage, which she believed to be valid, at St. Mary's Church, Islington. A second child was born to her, and later it was arranged, after a meeting with Mrs. Rouse, that the boy should be reared in the Rouse home.

A young domestic servant, aged seventeen, and living in Hendon, met Rouse in 1925. She believed he was a single man with rooms in Victoria. Soon he was taking her with him on his journeys, and promising to marry her "when trade improved." A girl was born to her in 1928, and she obtained a maintenance order against Rouse.

A week before the fatal Bonfire Night of 1930, she gave birth to a second girl child by Rouse at the City of London Maternity Hospital, London. She did not know that at that time another young girl was lying very ill in her parents' home in Gellygaer, where she was expecting a child by Rouse.

This girl in distant Monmouthshire believed she was already married to Rouse. He had visited the home as her husband, and persuaded the family that he had paid £1,250 for a house at Kingston, which he had furnished sumptuously for the bride. Her sister was to stay with them during their first three months in their Kingston home.

But for once Rouse realised he had gone too far. The girl

7

he betrayed had a devoted father and brother. If Rouse failed to keep his promises he would have to answer to them. During these ominous days before November 5th, he racked his brains in vain to discover some way out of the net of lies and intrigues in which he had snared himself.

He was earning about £10 a week. He was paying £1 12s. a week on his car, and £1 7s. 6d. to the building society. He gave his wife £2 a week for housekeeping, and another 10s. when the Edinburgh girl's boy was with them. His outgoings and expenses in connection with various women throughout the country were ruining him. There was a child in Paris, and another in an English county . . . And strong grounds exist for believing that Rouse, bragging of his conquests on the road, was also being bled white by blackmailers. Finally there was the nightmare dilemma of Gellygaer.

If he could only vanish away from it all, start life again in some place where he was unknown! If every one thought, for instance, *he had died in a car accident*?

And out of the morass of his worry and despair rose a hellborn inspiration. A few days before, outside The Swan and Pyramid public-house in the Whetstone High Road, an unemployed man had accosted him. Rouse stood him a drink. The man told him he had been to Peterborough, Norwich, Hull and other places trying to get work, obtaining lifts on the road from passing motorists. "*I have no relations*," he added. And as he said so, Rouse suddenly perceived that the man was about his own height and build, and looked fairly respectable.

On the evening of November 5th, Rouse was sitting with the domestic servant previously mentioned. She noticed that he was very depressed and preoccupied. He seemed annoyed on hearing how soon she was leaving the maternity home, as if he feared he might have to find accommodation for her earlier than he had expected.

"Are you meeting any one?" she asked, noticing that

8

he kept an anxious eye on the clock all the time he was with her.

He stared at her vacantly and said, "No." Then he left, muttering that he had so many things to pay that he hardly knew where to turn.

Shortly after eight o'clock Rouse met the unemployed stranger by appointment outside The Swan and Pyramid. It had been arranged that Rouse should give him a lift as far as Leicester. Rouse was a strict teetotaller, but he bought a bottle of whisky for his passenger to drink on the journey. Near St. Albans, the stranger switched out the lights by mistake, and a policeman spoke to Rouse. The rest of the journey is best told in the grim confession he made just before his execution.

> "He was the sort of man no one would miss, and I thought he would suit the plan I had in mind.
>
> "He drank the whisky neat from the bottle and was getting quite fuzzled. We talked a lot, but he did not tell me who he actually was. I did not care.
>
> "I turned into Hardingstone Lane because it was quiet and near a main road, where I could get a lift from a lorry afterwards. I pulled the car up.
>
> "The man was half-dozing – the effect of the whisky. I looked at him and gripped him by the throat with my right hand. I pressed his head against the back of the seat. He slid down, his hat falling off. I saw he had a bald patch on the crown of his head.
>
> "He just gurgled. I pressed his throat hard. The man did not realise what was happening. I pushed his face back. After making a peculiar noise, the man was silent.
>
> "Then I got out of the car, taking my attaché-case, the can of petrol and the mallet with me. I walked about ten yards in front of the car,

and opened the can, using the mallet to do so. I threw the mallet away and made a trail of petrol to the car.

"Also, I poured petrol over the man and loosened the petrol union joint and took the top off the carburettor. I put the petrol can in the back of the car.

"I ran to the beginning of the petrol trail and put a match to it. The flame rushed to the car, which caught fire at once.

"Petrol was leaking from the bottom of the car. That was the petrol I had poured over the man and the petrol that was dripping from the union joint and carburettor.

"The fire was very quick, and the whole thing was a mass of flames in a few seconds. I ran away."

No murder in the annals of British crime was more fiendish and callous. And certainly none was ever planned with such ingenuity to defeat even the finest scientific methods of detection.

Rouse was infinitely more cunning than Sidney Fox, for example, who murdered his mother and then lit the fire that he thought would perfectly explain her death. The postmortem examination of Mrs. Fox conducted by Sir Bernard Spilsbury, however, showed that she had not breathed in smoke or carbon monoxide gas, and proved, therefore, that she must have been dead when the fire broke out.

But Rouse left his victim unconscious. He was actually burnt to death. Spectroscopic tests of his blood, and microscopic examination of the lining of his air passages revealed beyond all doubt that the man had been alive when the car burst into flames.

Nor could it be proved that the origin of the fire had not been accidental, even though the loosened petrol union joint and the open carburettor might afterwards arouse suspicion.

Petrol union joints are often left slack by careless garage mechanics, and, in the opinion of many experts, are nearly always found loose after a car has been burnt very badly. And the carburettor top might easily have been blown off during the fire.

The body of the unconscious man had been placed with such devilish skill that its identity was bound to be destroyed. The left leg was doubled up in such a position that the continuous drip from the leaking petrol union joint would fall on it just at the knee, feeding an intense flame which would rise from the floor of the car to shrivel the features of the face, turned downwards to meet it. The soaked cuff of the right arm reached backwards to the petrol can in the rear, so that another source of flame would travel from the can up the arm and shoulder to the face.

Rouse had planned it as a flawless murder. And if he had kept his head after the crime, probably all the legal, medical and engineering evidence in the world would not have sufficed to convict him. But at the sight of that roaring inferno, something must have snapped in his brain. Perhaps the flare of the aeroplane at Givenchy was before his eyes again, reviving that awful second when he awaited death.

His nerve broke and he stumbled down Hardingstone Lane in a panic to get away, anywhere, from that blazing, snarling horror. Once, he saw through a gap in the left hedge "a ploughed field," rushed towards it, then, with terrified animal cunning, thought of the footprints he would leave, and kept to the road. It was a meadow he could have crossed to safety without leaving a trace!

Nevertheless, he still had a million to one chance of "getting away with it." Yet that one chance defeated him. Rouse had almost as much reason to believe he would be struck by lightning as that two people should meet him just at that very moment in a quiet country lane during the small hours of the morning. If ever the hand of Fate caught a murderer, it was when the lighthearted young cousins stepped from behind the motor-car at the corner of Hardingstone Lane. Yet Rouse could still have saved his skin, in all probability, if a shred of reason had remained to persuade him to go back with them, and help to put out the fire.

Instead, the ruin of his original plan left him baffled and helpless. As he watched the two young men run towards the blazing car, he realised, too, the awful plight in which the encounter with them, and his impulsive remark about a bonfire, had placed him. And like a bewildered, hunted creature, he made instinctively for home.

He got a lift on a passing lorry, arrived at his house in Finchley at about 6.20 in the morning, and stayed there nearly half an hour. He ate nothing and did not even change his clothes. His own explanation was that he wanted "to tell my wife not to be worried," though actually he did not tell her anything. Mrs. Rouse said afterwards she thought he had returned at 2 a.m. – a mistake in time easy to make on a dark November morning – and that she thought the fire had occurred after his departure.

Rouse now behaved as if his mind had been shocked by another shell explosion. The cool, implacable murderer was once again the garrulous case who had been invalided home from Givenchy. He made no attempt to disappear, or to reason a way out of his predicament.

In his pocket was a telegram urgently summoning him to the bedside of the girl in Gellygaer. He went to a motor-coach company near the Strand and booked a seat to South Wales, joking with the agent, and telling him, quite unnecessarily, that his car had been stolen on the Great North Road while he was drinking coffee at a drivers' stall. On the journey he sat beside the driver, and told him that his car had been stolen near St. Albans, and that he was going to see his wife, who lived near Cardiff.

He opened a newspaper at Gellygaer, and saw *a full account of the car tragedy, a description of himself, and a report of the police visit to Mrs. Rouse and her visit to*

Northampton. It was a terrific blow to the murderer. He had expected at the most a line or two about a burnt-out car, and later perhaps a paragraph about an inquest. He was not a journalist or he would have realised before the crime the immense news value of such a discovery as that of a man burnt to death in a car.

After seeing the girl who had summoned him so urgently to her bedside, he went downstairs to supper. A Mr. Reakes called in with a newspaper displaying the car story, showed it to Rouse, and remarked, "Is this your car?"

Rouse answered, "It is not my car," and said nothing more about it that night.

Realising now the danger that the girl's family would see the paragraph about his wife, Rouse resolved to leave for London next morning. But before he left, the girl's sister showed him a paper with a photograph of the burnt-out car, with his name and registration number, and a statement that the Northampton police wished to interview the man seen near it at the time of the fire. Rouse put the paper in his pocket.

A Mr. Brownhill gave him a lift to Cardiff, asking him on the way if he had reported the loss of the car to the police. Rouse replied that he had done so, and also informed the insurance company. Mr. Brownhill asked how the accident had happened, and Rouse said that the matter was too long and complicated to go into.

They stopped for a few minutes at The Cooper's Arms Hotel, and Rouse told the proprietor, Mr. Morris, that his car had vanished after he had gone into a restaurant in London for a meal. A butcher's assistant entered and said that the body of a woman had been found in the burnt car.

"Oh, dear, dear," exclaimed Rouse, "I cannot bear to hear about it."

Then he went to a coach depôt and booked a seat for London.

The coach was met at Hammersmith by Detective-Sergeant

13

Skelly of the Metropolitan Police, at 9.20 p.m., on November 7th, and Rouse said to him:

"I am glad it is all over. I was going to Scotland Yard about it. I was responsible. I am very glad it is over. I have had no sleep."

At the Hammersmith police station, Skelly informed him that the Northampton police wished to interview him, and Rouse at once began a rambling statement.

"I suppose they wish to see me about it. I don't know what happened exactly. I picked the man up on the Great North Road; he asked me for a lift.

"He seemed a respectable man, and said he was going to the Midlands. I gave him a lift; it was just this side of St. Albans. He got in and I drove off, and after going some distance, I lost my way. A policeman spoke to me about my lights.

"I did not know anything about the man, and I thought I saw his hand on my case, which was in the back of the car. I later became sleepy and could hardly keep awake. The engine started to spit, and I thought I was running out of petrol. I pulled into the side of the road. I wanted to relieve myself, and said to the man, 'There is some petrol in the can; you can empty it into the tank while I am gone,' and lifted up the bonnet and showed him where to put it in.

"He said, 'What about a smoke?' I said, 'I have given you all my cigarettes as it is.' I then went some distance along the road, and had just got my trousers down when I noticed a big flame from behind. I pulled my trousers up quickly and ran towards the car, which was in flames. I saw the man was inside, and I tried to open the door, but I could not, as the car was then a mass of flames. I then began to tremble violently. I was all of a shake. I did not know what to do, and I ran as hard as I could along the road where I saw the two men. I felt I was responsible for what had happened. I lost my head, and I didn't know what to do, and really don't know what I have done since."

Skelly asked him if he had rescued the attaché-case he then had with him and Rouse explained that he had seen the man's hand on it when it was in the back of the car, so he took it with him when he got out.

The Northampton police officers arrived at one in the morning, Rouse was cautioned, and gave a statement substantially the same, except that now he said he met the man half a mile past Tally Ho Corner, in Finchley, and added:

"I thought his breath smelt of drink."

Then he mentioned a wooden mallet which he carried for beating out dents in mudguards, and was "practically certain" that when he last saw it it was in the well of the car. He was asked to explain how a human hair had got on the mallet, and replied:

"I cannot account for the fact in any way whatever, excepting that I may have rubbed it over my own hair."

"Can you explain how the car caught fire?" asked Inspector Lawrence, of the Northampton police.

Rouse answered: "First of all, I gave the man a cigar, which he would naturally light in some way or other. I presume he would have a match. Presuming he filled up the tank, he would put the petrol can back in the car, and he might not have put the cap on, and may have upset some petrol in the car, and then if he had lit his cigar the car would have caught fire."

Rouse was then taken to Northampton. And in Inspector Lawrence's office, he made an observation which, when published later by the press, was enough to condemn him, whether murderer or not, in the eyes of millions of respectable citizens.

> "She is really too good for me," he said. "I like a woman who will make a fuss of me. I don't ever remember my wife sitting on my knee, but otherwise she is a good wife. I am very friendly with several women, but it is an expensive game. I was on my way to Leicester on Wednesday when this happened, to hand in my slip on Thursday morning to draw some money from my firm. I was then going to Wales for the week-end. My harem takes me to several places, and I am not at home a great deal, but my wife doesn't ask questions now. I was arranging to sell my house and furniture. I was then going to make an allowance to my wife. I think I should clear between £100 and £150 from the sale."

"The man is easily excited and talkative," stated a medical report on Rouse in September, 1918. If Rouse could only have kept his mouth shut, he might have been alive to-day.

After further sensational evidence about his private life given before the County of Northampton Bench, Rouse was committed for trial and brought up at Northampton Assizes on January 26th, 1931, before Mr. Justice Talbot. Mr. Norman Birkett, K.C., M.P., and Mr. Richard Elwes were Counsel for the Crown, Mr. D. L. Finnemore and Mr. A. P. Marshall, Counsel for the Defence.

Rouse recovered some of his old composure during the trial. He knew that his case was a strong one. The story he had told was one that would convince the average motorist. He had been in a hurry to relieve himself, and it takes more than a few seconds to fill a petrol tank from a two-gallon can. And nearly every motorist had met the type of passenger who does not realise the danger of smoking when handling petrol. Besides, this man was in a stupor of drink and drowsiness.

So it was with a jaunty and self-assured air that he made answer to the deadly cross-examination of Mr. Birkett. His smile suggested to more than one observer that he knew a cleverer way of arranging a murder than that suggested by the prosecution.

For instance, Mr. Birkett suggested at one point that Rouse had thrown the man in an unconscious position, face forward, into the car that he was to light.

"Most decidedly not," answered Rouse. "I should not throw a man. If I did a thing like that, I should not throw him down face forward. *I should think where I put him, I imagine.*"

"You would imagine what? – Hardly that I would throw him down like nothing. That is absurd.

"If you rendered him unconscious, would you have a delicacy about his posture? – No, but I think if I had been going to do as you suggest, I should do a little more than that.

"Would you? – *I think I have a little more brains than that.*"

When Colonel Buckle, an expert on car fires, and a leading witness for the prosecution, was giving evidence, he watched Rouse closely, and noticed that he seemed unperturbed, and even amused, when Colonel Buckle assumed that the carburettor top had "melted" or "fallen off." After Colonel Buckle left the box, this carefree reaction of Rouse led Buckle to wonder if Rouse had deliberately removed the top.

And suddenly, without any warning, at a later stage of the trial the actual carburettor from the burnt car was placed in Rouse's hands. Every one noticed that, while he had remained unmoved by the evidence about the loosened petrol union joint, he now blanched visibly. He tried to mask his nervousness by a show of technical knowledge that produced exactly the opposite impression to the one he intended. He knew too much, he was far too clever, in the eyes of the now intent Court.

"If the cap of that (carburettor) is wrenched off by hand as it could be—? Yes, it could be. *It is not a wrench; I think you simply turn a clip.*"

And again: "The petrol from the carburettor could be lit from a person standing in the road? – Yes, but you would get a flash in any case, and a very bad flash with the amount of petrol in there . . . I have never lit a quantity of petrol. *When I light the blowlamp, I always do it with a rag.*" (Rouse had a blowlamp at home.)

The most damning clue against Rouse was that brought forward by Sir Bernard Spilsbury and Dr. Eric Shaw, a Northampton pathologist. The body of the victim had been burnt almost to a cinder, but strangely enough one tiny piece of cloth in the fork of his trousers had not been burnt. The doubling up of the left leg against the trunk had prevented air and fire from getting to it.

When this fragment of cloth was examined, it was found to be soaked in petrol, showing that Rouse, as he afterwards confessed, had emptied petrol over the man. But even this evidence was challenged by another witness, who declared that it was quite possible that the man, lurching drunkenly as he handled the petrol can, had spilt some of the petrol over himself.

Stolidly the jury listened to one great expert after another. It is doubtful if their findings, either for or against Rouse, were sufficient in themselves to sway them. One bucket of water fetched by Rouse, even one word of sympathy – "that poor man in my car," for instance – would have probably counted more with them than all the technical evidence in the world.

They might even have forgiven his flight from the fire, his lies to every one he met. People do queer things when they are panicstricken. What they could not forgive or forget was that Rouse never for one moment showed afterwards the slightest concern about the unknown wretch who had perished in his car. "He was the sort of man no one would miss," said Rouse. But this fiend had yet to learn that the awful might of British justice will protect and avenge even the humblest and lowest in the land.

On January 31st, 1931, Mr. Justice Talbot sentenced Alfred Arthur Rouse to death. His appeal against this judgment was dismissed on February 23rd. And on March 10th, 1931, Rouse was hanged at Bedford. Thus ended the career of one of the most loathsome murderers of modern times.

F. A. Beaumont

Man Hunters: The German Rouse Cases

In Germany at the same period there were two cases in which a random victim was burnt to solve the financial problems of the murderer. The first of these took place five weeks before the beginning of the 1930s, but since it inspired the second case – and possibly the crime of Alfred Rouse – I feel that it should be allowed inclusion in a book of cases of the thirties. It is also from *The Fifty Most Amazing Crimes of the Last Hundred Years*.

A week after Alfred Arthur Rouse was hanged at Bedford, another young commercial traveller, Kurt Erich Tetzner, stood in the dock at Ratisbon, Germany, while the Public Prosecutor accused him of burning to death in his car an unknown tramp whose body he had tried to pass off as his own.

But Tetzner had been arrested nearly a year before Rouse was taken to Hammersmith police station. Indeed, the Public Prosecutor at Ratisbon referred to Rouse as "just a pupil of Tetzner." But he paid a tribute to the efficiency of British law by emphasising that Rouse had been tried, found guilty, and executed only five months after the murder, whereas it had taken the Germans fourteen months to bring Tetzner to trial, after his arrest at Strasbourg on December 5th, 1929.

Tetzner's car had been found burnt out near the village of Ettershausen, Bavaria, on November 25th, 1929. A charred body was at the wheel. The police of Leipzig, where Tetzner lived, were notified, and Frau Tetzner was sent for. She identified the body as that of her husband.

The corpse was buried with great pomp, and Frau Tetzner, in deepest mourning, wept copiously as she followed the coffin. But the insurance companies with whom Tetzner had insured his life for 145,000 marks (£7250) were not convinced so easily. They got in touch with the Leipzig police, who began to shadow Frau Tetzner.

She had no telephone in her flat. Twice in the next few days she was summoned to the flat of a neighbour to answer calls from a Herr Stranelli, ringing up from Strasbourg, Alsace. The Leipzig police telephoned the French police at Strasbourg, giving them a detailed description of Tetzner, and asking them to take a good look at Stranelli. A Leipzig detective-officer set off by plane to Strasbourg. When he arrived, the French police had already arrested Stranelli, who was soon identified as Tetzner.

And now Kurt Tetzner, thick-set, with a fat white unhealthy face, and small beady eyes, stood in the dock, and licked his dry lips nervously as the Public Prosecutor thundered at him.

"First of all, after your arrest by the police, you confessed that you had murdered your passenger, then burnt his body in your motor-car in order to lead insurance companies, with whom you had insured your life, to believe you had been killed in a motoring accident. Later, you withdrew this confession and made, instead, a fresh statement, in which you declared the man whose body was found burnt in your car was a pedestrian, whom you had accidentally run over, and who had then died in the car. You said you had burned the body later in order to commit the fraud on the insurance companies. Which of these two statements," demanded the Prosecutor, "do you wish to put before the court to-day?"

Tetzner hesitated.

"The second," he replied, almost inaudibly.

The Prosecutor then referred to the death of the prisoner's

mother-in-law a few months before the burnt car was found. Tetzner had first dissuaded her from undergoing an operation for cancer. Then he had recommended it, after insuring her life for 10,000 marks (£500). She died three days after the operation.

"The ease with which you obtained those ten thousand marks was your undoing, was it not?" asked the Prosecutor.

Tetzner refused to be drawn.

"It was a great misfortune," he answered.

"Is it true your wife suggested to you that you should dig up a newly-buried body from the cemetery instead of murdering a man, and that you said to her, 'Don't be a fool. There must be blood about'?"

"I may have said something of the sort," replied the prisoner.

Tetzner then described two attempts he had made to lure a victim into his car. At first he advertised for a travelling companion, but a young man who got in touch with him grew suspicious and refused at the last moment. Then one day, while driving along the highway near Ingolstadt, he met a motor mechanic called Alois Ortner, who was seeking work, and who wanted a lift to Munich.

"I at once realised," Tetzner went on, "that this young man would be ideal to leave in the car. Passing through the town of Hof, I gave him some money, and told him to get a shave and buy himself a collar. I wanted him to look as respectable and as much like me as possible.

"Later, I asked Ortner to crawl under the car and look at the oil valve. While he was under the car, I seized a hammer and a pad of ether. When he emerged I fell on him, but he fought back powerfully and succeeded in escaping into the forest.

"On my return I told my wife of a new plan I had formed. I now intended to pick up a man in my car, blind him by throwing pepper in his face, then burn him alive while he was helpless."

The Public Prosecutor interrupted him with a gesture of loathing:

"What a fiendish idea!" he cried. "Don't you realise this is the most cruel form of death a man can devise?"

Tetzner stared at him blankly.

"It didn't seem so bad to me at the time," he muttered.

Then he went on with his grim story.

"On the night of November 25th, 1929, I ran over a man shortly after passing Bayreuth. I placed him on the seat beside me and drove on until he died. Then I put him in the dickey.

"While having supper in an inn, it occurred to me that here was an opportunity to carry out my scheme without murdering anybody. I drove on, and, shortly before reaching Ratisbon, I ran the car into a tree to make it appear as though an accident had happened. Then I sprinkled the car with petrol and set it on fire."

The Prosecutor riddled this account with sarcasm.

"How do you explain, Tetzner," he snapped, "that a man of your intelligence could for many months accuse himself to the police in his own statements (Tetzner had at first made a confession, then, after five months in prison, repudiated it) of a terrible murder in order to cover up a case of manslaughter?"

But Tetzner could not explain.

Alois Ortner was called into the witness-box. He told a horrified court how he had staggered from the car, with his face streaming with blood, and had collapsed a few moments after Tetzner had driven on. Later, in hospital, he could not remember the number of the car. The Ingolstadt police would not believe his story, said it was fantastic, and suspected him of an unsuccessful attempt to rob a passing motorist.

The chief witness for the defence was Dr. Kockel, postmortem expert of Leipzig University. He was convinced Tetzner was telling the truth when he said he had run over a man, killing him, and then burnt him in his car. The internal organs of the corpse, he argued, bore no traces of smoke or soot, as they would have done if the man had been alive when he was burnt. There were injuries to the body which showed that it had been violently maltreated, in a manner that suggested it had been run over by a car. Dr. Molitoris, of Erlangen University, another post-mortem expert, gave counter-evidence on behalf of the prosecution, and a long and wordy duel ensued between these leading witnesses.

Tetzner was condemned to death. Before he was executed at Regensburg, on May 2nd, 1931, he made a full confession. On the night of November 25th, 1929, he had given a lift to a travelling journeyman, aged twenty-one, whose name he did not know. The thinly-clad youth complained of the cold. Tetzner wrapped him in a heavy rug, pinioning his arms to his body. Then he strangled him with a piece of rope. Outside Ettershausen he crashed the car into a tree, opened the petrol tank, laid a petrol trail from the tank over the mudguard and right footboard to the back of the car, which he then set on fire.

"Gentlemen of the jury, think of my terrible position. I was leading a double life. At home I had to appear cheerful and contented, while my heart was breaking. At night I was forced to go out hunting for men to murder." And Fritz Saffran, fighting for his life in the Court of Bartenstein, East Prussia, spread out his hands with an appealing gesture, in an attempt to convince his hearers that he had played an unwilling part in one of the strangest crime dramas of the century.

Six months earlier, few men were so popular as Fritz Saffran in the little town of Rastenburg, only thirty miles away from the court in which he was to face his trial on the capital charge. He was young, good-looking and successful. Business men admired the acumen of this thirty-year-old manager of the Platz Furniture Store, who had made it a flourishing concern during the worst years of the depression.

His keen grey eyes and tight, determined lips impressed them with the feeling that here was a "warm" man. Customers thronged the store, enjoyed chatting with the affable young manager, who was never too busy to advise them regarding the choice of furniture, and always easy-going and ready to waive a clause or two in the hire purchase agreements. There was something about his confident smile and high intellectual forehead (he was formerly a schoolmaster) that made them trust him instinctively.

Herr Platz, the owner of the store, could never speak too highly of the brilliant young fellow who had enabled him to retire a few years before, leaving the direction of the business entirely in Saffran's hands. And when Fritz respectfully asked him for the hand of his daughter in marriage, the old man readily consented. Many a woman in Rastenburg envied Frau Saffran her handsome and distinguished young husband, whose devotion to his wife was a byword in the town.

On the evening of September 15th, 1930, a terrific explosion shook the store, and it burst almost instantly into a mass of flames. Thirty people were at work inside the inferno, and it was afterwards regarded as a miracle that every one of them managed to escape from it alive. The fire brigade arrived within a few minutes of the outbreak, but so fierce was the blaze that nothing could be done, and the firemen could only stand by helpless while the building was razed to the ground.

Wild-eyed, Erich Kipnik, chief clerk of the store, rushed into the home of Herr Platz and stammered hysterically that Saffran had perished in the fire. He and Saffran had spent the evening in a café, he said, and on their way home they had noticed a glow in the sky coming from the direction of the store. Saffran broke into a run, and when he saw that the store was indeed ablaze he had shouted to Kipnik that he was going inside to rescue the ledgers.

"Without a second's hesitation," sobbed Kipnik, "he dashed into the heart of the burning building. I have never seen anything so brave in my life."

And only a few hours later searchers among the ruins found the charred remains of a body, round which the tatters of a suit identified as Saffran's were still clinging. On the fingers of the corpse were rings belonging to Saffran, and in the waistcoat pocket was discovered his monogrammed silver watch.

Saffran had always been well liked by all his employees, but one in particular, Ella Augustin, grieved so much over his death that two days after the fire she collapsed sobbing in the street. She was not a pretty girl, but her vivacity and unruliness had already earned her a reputation as a "character" in the firm. Her resolute mouth and strongly marked eyebrows suggested that here was a woman who usually got what she wanted.

But a great disappointment had clouded her life. It was no secret that ever since she came to the firm, six years ago, Ella had fallen madly in love with the handsome young manager. Every one in the firm knew that she had been throwing herself at him ever since. What did she care if he were already married? She loved him, and that was all that mattered. Sooner or later she would make him respond to her passion.

Saffran tolerated for a time her open and unashamed advances with an air of pleasant good-humour. But soon he realised that her conduct was arousing comment among people who came to shop in the store, besides undermining the respect of his employees. She must stop this nonsense. And one day when he found she had made an error in her books, he seized the opportunity to upbraid her severely before the rest of the clerical staff. She cried with shame and humiliation, and Saffran almost regretted his unusual sternness. But afterwards, when he saw her going about her work with a subdued and chastened air, he decided that the lesson had been worth while. She would cause him no more embarrassment.

Two days after the fire Ella Augustin called at several garages in Rastenburg. Her mother was seriously ill, she

explained, and she wanted to hire a car to take her to
Königsberg. Eventually a chauffeur named Reck offered
his services. By arrangement with Ella, he called at the
Augustin home at three the next morning. To his surprise,
instead of the ailing mother a man came out of the house
and stepped into the car. Reck recognised him instantly as
Saffran.

The chauffeur drove Saffran as far as the village of
Gerdauen, then refused to go farther. Saffran walked
off towards the village, and Reck turned back towards
Rastenburg. The chauffeur was often employed by the
Platz firm. Later the police charged him with aiding and
abetting. It was never proved that he was a member of the
conspiracy. What is certain is that he opened his mouth to
some one about that mysterious night ride, for the very next
day the police began to make inquiries.

They discovered by persistent examination of reluctant
clerks formerly employed in the Platz store that the firm,
which every one thought so prosperous, had been since 1928
in serious difficulties. The customers whom Saffran had so
easily persuaded to hire furniture were not paying their
instalments. Unknown to Platz, Saffran had begun to obtain
large credits at high interest, and soon the firm was staggering
under a huge load of debt. Then Saffran raised money by
submitting the same hire purchase contracts to two different
financing houses, one in Berlin, the other in Königsberg. As
the struggle to keep the firm afloat became more and more
arduous, the desperate young manager forged nearly four
hundred sale contracts, and raised money on these in Berlin
and Königsberg. Finally he had been forced to falsify the
balance sheets. The assets on the firm's books were stated
to be 285,000 marks, when actually there was a bare 25,000.
The police also learnt that Ella Augustin had been carrying
on a liaison with Saffran, and had helped him to falsify the
ledgers.

Ella was arrested and put in prison. She tried to smuggle
out a note to Saffran. It was intercepted, but it told the police

little more than that Saffran was staying with one of her relations at an unknown address, somewhere in Berlin.

This man was a poor carpenter in the Lausitzer Strasse. Saffron hid for seven weeks in his tiny lodging, never daring to stir out until after dark. When he left Rastenburg, he had only three hundred marks with him. He was tired of living like a hunted beast, his money was ebbing fast, and he decided that his only hope of escape was to get out of the country. With the carpenter's identity papers, which he did not hesitate to steal, he thought he could make his way to Hamburg and there take a boat to Brazil.

Saffran bought a ticket to Hamburg at a Berlin travel bureau. But he was too clever to risk capture at the terminus station in Berlin, which he knew would be watched day and night. Instead, he went by the town railway to the suburb of Spandau, and there, at one o'clock in the morning of November 7th, he boarded the train for Hamburg. And had it not been for a stroke of almost incredible bad luck he would soon afterwards have been safe at sea.

Kipnik swore that Saffran had murdered the man whose body was found in the store. But it was not until Saffran addressed the court, and vainly tried to save his skin by denouncing his associates, that the full amazing story of their desperate crime came to light.

"When I realised that the store would soon be engulfed by a flood of unredeemable obligations," he began, "I insured my life for 140,000 marks (£7000). It was my intention to commit suicide, so that my wife would be provided for, but Ella dissuaded me from taking this step. I asked Kipnik for his advice, and he said we ought to get a body from somewhere and burn it in the store.

"At first it was our intention to obtain a corpse from a graveyard. But later we decided this would not be good enough for our purpose. So we established a murder camp in the Nikolai Forest. The girl stayed behind in the camp while Kipnik and I, each in his own car, roved the countryside for miles around, looking for a likely victim, then reported to

28

the camp at evening. After a time we all three began to go out on these man-hunts. During one of these drives, after passing the village of Sorquitten, we overtook a man and asked him if he would like a lift.

"He got in the car, and I drove off at a furious pace. Then suddenly I jammed on the brake, while Kipnik struck the man three blows on the head with his life preserver. Ella lost her nerve, however, and held Kipnik back, so that the man escaped. We then decided it was no good murdering a man and burning him in the car afterwards. Instead we decided we would take the body to the store to burn. In this way it was to appear as if I had committed suicide.

"On the night of September 12th, 1930, between eleven and midnight, Kipnik and I drove out in the car once more. In the dickey we had put a carpet in which to wrap the man whom we murdered. When we got to the village of Loetzen my courage failed me, and I said to Kipnik, 'Let us drive home.' Kipnik, however, declared that the crime had to be carried out that night or never.

"Near Luisenhof we met a pedestrian. Kipnik got out of the car, and I drove on at a furious speed for about one and a half miles, hoping against hope that Kipnik would not succeed in killing the man. When I returned Kipnik stopped me, tore open the dickey, pulled out the carpet, and said to me, 'I have got him down there in the ditch.' I was paralysed with horror. I remembered nothing more until I heard Kipnik shout to me, 'Now, drive for your life!'

"Something heavy seemed to bump into the back of the car as I pressed the accelerator and we got away. We took the body to the store, dressed it in my clothes, put my rings on its fingers and my watch in the waistcoat pocket. Then we poured twenty-five gallons of petrol over the floor of the store and set fire to it. There was a big explosion."

Whether Saffran or Kipnik shot the man will never be known, as each carried pistols. Saffran's story was not in accord with some of the established facts. For instance, he referred to the victim as a pedestrian, whereas he was actually a cyclist. He also stated that the body was dressed in one of Saffran's suits. Frau Dahl, on the other hand, identified the clothing as similar to that worn by her husband. Though most of the truth came to light in the combined accounts given by the accused, not much reliance can be placed on each separate statement, since each was trying to win the clemency of the court by a version that was obviously distorted in his or her own favour.

Saffran fell on his knees and cried like a child when Frau Dahl, the widow of the victim, a frail little woman wearing a heavy black veil, entered the witness-box.

"Frau Dahl, I share the responsibility for the death of your husband," he sobbed. "I beg you, I beseech you on my bended knees to forgive me for what we have done. And if you cannot grant me your forgiveness to-day, perhaps at some time in the future you will be able to sympathise with me."

Kipnik, too, made a great show of repentance, shouting to Frau Dahl, "It is terrible to me when I think of my own poor wife and our boy, and imagine what they would have suffered if what we did to your husband had happened to me."

But the public prosecutor cut short his display of remorse by snapping:

"Enough of this play-acting!"

Kipnik revealed under cross-examination that one night the three man-hunters got a pedestrian in their car and had decided to murder him when the man told them that he had six children. Moved by compassion, he added, they let him go. He also mentioned another occasion when the three of them were scouring the roads around Sensberg in their car and saw a man walking along a lane. Saffran shouted to him, but either the man did not hear, or was afraid, for he paid no attention and went on his way.

Night after night, continued Kipnik, they lurked in wait for their prey. Sometimes they would leave the car in a wood and hide behind a nearby hedge, watching for a man to come along the road. But it was Saffran who actually killed Dahl, protested Kipnik, with three shots fired through the head. They hid his cycle and leather bag afterwards in the forest bordering the highway. Kipnik admitted he had wrapped the body in the carpet they had brought with them. When they arrived in Rastenburg, he added, they carried the bundle into the Platz store, and Saffran said, "Now it can burn." It was Saffran, too, according to Kipnik, who forced his rings on the dead man's fingers, and also put his own gold collar studs into the man's shirt.

But the court put no more trust in the terse quiet statements of the cool and contemptuous chief clerk than they had in the hysterical blabbings of Saffran. Kipnik began to lose his nerve, made wild and incoherent charges against his accomplices, and finally, raising his hands in appeal, shouted a supreme protest:

"Saffran has ruined my life! I place my fate in the hands of the court. I wish I could prove to them that I am really a decent man!"

A scream rang out through the densely-packed courtroom. The astonished spectators turned to see Ella Augustin on her feet, her eyes blazing, her face livid with rage as she pointed an accusing finger at Kipnik.

"And yet you are the murderer!" she yelled.

Saffran and Kipnik were condemned to death. Later, however, the Prussian Government commuted their sentences to penal servitude for life. Ella Augustin was sentenced to five years' penal servitude. Such was the end of the man-hunters, inspired by modern greed, not ancient superstition, for this strange murder drama seems to belong more fittingly to those far-gone days when bands of savage priests roved the countrysides of primitive Europe in search of a human sacrifice to offer up on their altars.

F. A. Beaumont

The Otterburn Mystery

The theme of death by fire continues in the next case, the unsolved murder of Evelyn Foster – if, indeed, it was a murder. The story is to be found in a collection called Great Unsolved Crimes, *published by Hutchinsons in the 1930s (the volume bears no date.) The idea was to ask various policemen and writers of mystery stories for their accounts of various unsolved crimes, and for their suggestions for solutions. It is a classic compilation, with writers like Mrs. Belloc Lowndes, A. J. Cronin, G. B. Stern and J. D. Beresford – all names, I suspect, that have been totally forgotten by the present generation, but who, in their day, formed part of England's literary establishment. (I see that I picked up my own copy for four shillings; I saw one in a bookseller's catalogue the other day for £30.) Val Gielgud, the author of the present piece, was the elder brother of actor John Gielgud, and known to a generation of radio listeners during the Second World War as head of BBC sound drama.*

In spite of the book's title, the case is certainly not one of the great unsolved mysteries; yet it is oddly puzzling and disturbing. After I read this present account in the 1960s, it stuck in my mind, until I exorcised it by putting it into a novel called Lingard *(in England,* The Killer*) more than ten years later.*

To a writer of sensational fiction there can be few cases more fascinating than the story of what came to be called "The Otterburn Mystery."

Both as regards its environment and its circumstances, the story might so easily be judged to have sprung from the slightly morbid imagination of the novelist, rather than from cruelly hard fact. But once again fact proved stranger than fiction.

About half-past nine during a night in January of 1931, a bus belonging to a garage proprietor of Otterburn, Northumberland, was returning along the road from Otterburn to Newcastle, driven by a Mr. Johnson.

At a desolate spot on the moors, known as Wolf's Neck – the name of the place immediately brings to mind some chapter heading – he saw a motor-car about seventy yards away from the road. The car had been on fire and was still smouldering.

On investigation, Mr. Johnson and his conductor were amazed to find that the car belonged to the firm by which they were employed – that is to say, by Mr. Foster, the garage proprietor, of Otterburn. Not far from the car they made a hideous discovery.

Miss Evelyn Foster, Mr. Foster's twenty-seven-year-old daughter, was lying moaning on the grass, crying out for water. Below the waist all her clothes had been burned off, her hands were black from the effects of a hard frost; her face was severely discoloured.

Mr. Johnson wrapped the girl in his overcoat and took her home as quickly as possible. Most of the way she kept on muttering about "that awful man – that awful man." During intermittent periods of consciousness she told a long and detailed story of the incidents that had preceded and accompanied the tragedy, and shortly afterwards she died.

Her story in brief was this:

Miss Foster was in the habit of driving cars about the country for her father, and on the previous day she had driven three passengers to Rochester, a village in the neighbourhood. At Ellishaw, a village two miles away from Otterburn, she was accosted by a stranger, who told her that he wished to go to Ponteland in order to catch a bus to Newcastle.

About 7.30 in the evening she picked him up on the bridge just below the hotel at Ellishaw and drove him as far as Belsay. It must remembered that when she made her statement Miss Foster was in great pain, and was, in fact, dying.

But of what happened at Belsay no satisfactory account emerged. In reply to the urgent questionings of her mother, Miss Foster's words seemed to imply that her passenger made advances to her; when she resisted him he struck her in the eye; that she lost consciousness, and that the man finally drove the car away with Miss Foster inside along the road to Otterburn as far as the Wolf's Neck.

At that point her car was turned off the road and run down a 3-ft. bank on to the moor for 70 yards or so.

She described her assailant as rather a small man, wearing a bowler hat and a dark coat and speaking like a gentleman, although he had a Tyneside accent.

As to what happened at Wolf's Neck Miss Foster was unhappily, though not unnaturally, vaguer still. According to her story she recovered consciousness owing to the jerking and jolting of the car as it passed on to the moorland. The passenger then got out, took something from his pocket and applied a light to it.

There followed a small explosion and a blaze. Miss Foster, in horrible agony and feeling that she must be suffocated, struggled to get the door of the car open. This she finally succeeded in doing, and she crawled out and fell on to the grass where she was found. She seemed to remember seeing the man go back to the road, hearing another car coming along the road, hearing a whispered colloquy, and the other car drive away.

The only other significant item that the victim could add was the fact that the man had told her that he had been picked up at Jedburgh by a party of motorists on their way to Hexham, and had had tea with them – the party consisting of three men speaking with a Scottish accent in a saloon car, probably an Essex.

The B.B.C. broadcast a police message containing a

description of this party. The men were found and interviewed by the police, but said they gave no lift to anyone answering to the description of the wanted man.

The inquest on Miss Foster was opened by the Coroner, Mr. P. M. Dodds, on Thursday, January 8, at the Otterburn Memorial Hall.

Formal evidence of identification was given by the dead girl's father, and the inquest was adjourned until February 2. In the interval Professor Stuart Macdonald, a well-known pathologist of the College of Medicine at Newcastle, had been called in to consult with the doctor who made the post-mortem examination. It was not until February 5 that Professor Macdonald's evidence was given.

According to him, no external marks suggesting injury other than burning were found on any part of the body. He gave the cause of death as the result of shock caused by severe external burning.

He said that the distribution of the burned areas suggested that Miss Foster was sitting during some period of the burning, and he added that there was absolutely no trace or evidence of bruising of the face. There was also no evidence of outrage.

The next witness, Mr. W. Jennings, a motor engineer of Morpeth, said that it would have been very difficult for anybody to have driven the car from the position in which Miss Foster said that her assailant had driven it after taking the wheel from her, always supposing that she had offered any resistance.

And the Coroner put the whole problem flatly when he pointed out to the jury that the two main points before them were:

(a) Was the girl murdered?
(b) Did she set fire to the car, and in doing so obtain the burns accidentally?

If the latter, was her object to obtain money from the insurance on the car?

The jury, after a retirement of two hours, returned the verdict that Miss Foster had been murdered by some person or persons unknown.

Of course, the unfounded suggestion that Miss Foster had met her death by means self-inflicted in the course of carrying out a criminal fraud was hotly resented by her family, and Miss Foster's father wrote a letter on the subject to the Home Secretary.

"There was no title of evidence," he said, "to support such shameful theories," and he resented most strongly the fact that though the jury's verdict had vindicated his daughter's honour, the Chief Constable of Northumberland had stated in an interview with a newspaper reporter that the verdict was against the weight of evidence.

"The police," Mr. Foster continued, "were defending themselves in a case in which they had failed by attacking his dead daughter." And it transpired that, though there were two insurance policies – one for £450 and the other for £700 – in existence, Miss Foster left estate valued at £1400.

It must be remembered on behalf of the police that the description of Miss Foster's assailant was comparatively comprehensive; that he must almost certainly have had a good knowledge of the locality to have been able so effectively to disappear without leaving trace behind him; and yet that no one answering to his description was ever traced.

It is true that during the night of February 13, a seaman walked into the Newcastle police station and said that he wished to give himself up for the Otterburn murder. But after being interviewed, he was removed to hospital for observation and was presumably suffering from delusions, or an insane desire for notoriety.

The problem was infinitely complicated by Miss Foster's condition both of mind and body when she made her statement, combined with the very understandable confusion which seems to have emerged from some of the facts given by her mother.

The Coroner asked Dr. McEachran, of Bellingham, who was called in to Miss Foster when she was brought home injured, if he recollected the mother asking Miss Foster if she had been interfered with – using that or a similar expression. To which the doctor replied that there had been a question of that nature, and apparently the girl's reply was to the effect that she had been interfered with.

This fact seems to have been put in parallel with the medical report, which stated that there was no evidence of outrage.

And this, combined with the fact that no corroborative evidence could be found of the existence of the assailant, and no trace of anything inflammable except petrol had been found on the girl's clothes, led the Coroner to the summing-up which read distinctly adverse to the verdict as ultimately given by the jury.

What of the possibilities of accident? The car had left the road at not more than ten miles an hour. It had not overturned in crossing the embankment. It seems to have been definitely under control before it stopped. It had suffered no damage which could have caused it to ignite.

The valves, the ignition and carburettor were all in perfect order, and there was no trace of abnormal heat below the line of the float chamber. In the back of the car was a burned-out tin of petrol – but it was customary always to keep a full two-gallon tin in the car for emergencies. The cap of the petrol tin had been removed before the fire started.

It seems, therefore, quite definite that this tragedy cannot be put down to any misadventure, however singular. Nor, unless Miss Foster's is to be categorised as a most extraordinary case of mental instability, can the theory hold water – and it was only very tentatively put forward – that she might have been one of those persons obsessed with the idea of achieving notoriety.

We are left, therefore, with the alternatives of murder or suicide by mistake.

The Coroner himself, though evidently inclined to believe

the greater part of Miss Foster's statement to be unreliable owing to her condition at the time it was made, pointed out that the suggested motive of obtaining insurance money was inadequate. There remains that "Wilful Murder by a Person or Persons Unknown" which the jury gave finally as their considered opinion.

The murder has been described as motiveless. Miss Foster's money was in her bag and her personal ornaments were untouched. But, disagreeable though it may be to accept such a conclusion, the facts as they stand point, in my view, quite clearly in one direction.

There are three significant sentences in Miss Foster's statement which form strong links in this chain. First of all was her repetition of the phrase "that awful man," while she was being driven home by Mr. Johnson.

Next we find her first reply in answer to her mother's questioning as to what had happened to her: "It was a man. He hit me and burned me."

And thirdly her story that when the car stopped on the top of the hill by Wolf's Neck, the man offered her a cigarette, and when she refused it, made the remark: "Well, you are an independent young woman!"

Perhaps it should be added at this point that in reply to the Coroner's questions, Mrs. Foster insisted that her daughter's condition was perfectly lucid and sane while she was telling her story, and Dr. McEachran said he saw no reason to think that she had any idea that she was going to die.

It does not seem to me that this statement combined with the facts admits of more than one explanation. It remains, of course, questionable whether the assailant was a sexual maniac, who deliberately hailed Miss Foster because she was a girl driving alone, or whether his revolting purpose arose only with the incidence of opportunity.

It was, as a matter of fact, quite exceptional that Miss Foster should have been unaccompanied on such trips, and it had been suggested by her sister that she should take a man with her, but she had not done so.

But whatever his original motive, the lateness of the hour and the darkness of the moors provoked in the unknown an attitude to which Miss Foster objected, and in this connection his remark about the cigarette is by no means without significance.

Finding that his overtures were not welcomed – probably they were actively repulsed – the man must have lost both his head and his temper, with results catastrophic in an individual almost certainly pathologically abnormal. He then struck Miss Foster in the eye.

It seems likely that this first attack was comparatively slight, and that the girl was completely terrified, which in the circumstances is not an unlikely supposition. This would account for the absence of bruising on the face, which provoked the comment in the medical evidence.

He then bundled her into the back of the car, drove to the desolate neighbourhood of Wolf's Neck, and deliberately turned the car off the road. At that point, roused to frenzy by Miss Foster's continued resistance, he wrenched the cap off the spare tin of petrol, drenched her with it and, with a brutality almost unbelievable set her on fire.

That done, he disappeared over the moors into the darkness.

It is perhaps worth making a point in this connection that in pouring petrol from a petrol tin it flows in a stream and not with a splash, which would account for the comparatively localised nature of the burns. That the victim in this awful condition of physical and mental torment – that is to say, after the burning – should have believed that a casual car stopped on the road, and going on again, should have picked up her assailant, although, in fact, it had done nothing of the kind, is surely not stretching the issue to any great extent.

And it emerged that a motor salesman of Hawick, named Beatty, passed Wolf's Neck between half-past nine and ten that night, saw a blaze on the right-hand side of the road and put on his brakes. He saw that it was a car, but it appeared to him to be completely burned out and he saw no movement, so he imagined that it had been abandoned and drove on.

The only other clues that were discovered near the burned-out car were a single footprint, a glove and a cap. They were all systematically examined. They all led to nothing.

Mr. Foster was not alone in taking exception to the fact that the Northumberland police had shown the very minimum of inclination to call in the experience of Scotland Yard to help them towards the solution of one of the most remarkable unsolved crimes of modern days.

Val Gielgud

The Murder of Julia Wallace

The classic murder mystery of the 1930s was the Wallace case. In fact, as we shall see in the aftermath, the mystery is now almost certainly solved, due to the detective work of crime writer Jonathan Goodman and radio journalist Roger Wilkes. That is a recent development. But in the intervening years, there have been several full-length books about the case, and a dozen or so chapters devoted to it in books about famous murders.

The detective writer Dorothy L. Sayers wrote about it on two occasions, the longer of the two being "The Murder of Julia Wallace", in *The Anatomy of Murder*, (1936) an anthology of pieces by members of the Detection Club. Dorothy Leigh Sayers, born in Oxford in 1893, was primarily interested in religion, but began to write detective stories – about Lord Peter Wimsey – to support an illegitimate son she bore in 1924. As soon as she could afford to, she stopped writing detective fiction and returned to more serious interests, with a series of radio plays about Jesus, *The Man Born to be King*, and a translation of Dante. Her shorter account of the Wallace murder – from *Great Unsolved Crimes* – remains as excellent a presentation of the case as any in existence.

P erhaps the most remarkable thing about the murder of Julia Wallace is that from the beginning to end there was no important conflict of evidence. That is what makes it such a fascinating puzzle.

Except for the usual polite medical squabble over *rigor mortis* and a trifling uncertainty about the precise moment of a milkboy's visit, the essential facts were never in dispute. There they were, and you could make what you liked of them. The judge made one thing, the jury made another, the Court of Appeal decided that nothing could be made of them, and so set the prisoner free at the very gallows' foot.

The case has been compared to a detective story; but in fiction the author always supplies one key-incident which cannot possibly be interpreted in more than one way. In the Wallace case everything that the accused said or did might be construed as the behaviour either of an innocent man caught in a trap or of a guilty man pretending to be innocently caught in a trap. It is like a web of shot silk, looking red from one angle and green from another.

William Herbert Wallace was an agent employed to collect payments for the Prudential Assurance Company. He was fifty-two years old and of frail physique, had been married for eighteen years to a wife of about his own age.

For sixteen years they had lived together at 29 Wolverton Street, Liverpool, apparently in perfect harmony. Music, chess and science were the husband's inoffensive pursuits; Marcus Aurelius, the gentle stoic, his favourite philosopher.

The wife, delicate and retiring, played the piano, painted in water-colours, and listened with interest while he expounded as best he could, the new theory of atomic physics and the great riddles of the universe.

They took their few quiet outings together and enjoyed an ideal companionship. There was no other man; no other woman. No one ever heard a harsh word pass between this happily married, middle-aged couple.

At about 7.15 in the evening of Monday, January 19, 1931, Wallace left his house to play a competition game at a meeting of the chess club, held at the City Café, about half an hour away. About the same time a telephone call was put through to the café from a public kiosk just off Wolverton Street, and was answered by the club captain, Mr. Beattie.

The caller, who gave the unusual name of "Qualtrough," asked whether Wallace had arrived, said he was too busy to ring up again, and left a message asking Wallace to call on him next day at 7.30 p.m., at "25 Menlove Gardens East," about "something in the matter of his business."

At 7.45 Wallace reached the café and was given the message.

"Who's Qualtrough? I don't know the chap. Where is Menlove Gardens East? Is it Menlove Avenue?"

He entered the address in his note-book and went on to play and win his game of chess. Some time after ten he left the café with a friend, observing that he did not know whether he should keep this odd appointment or not.

On the Tuesday the Wallaces had an early supper at home, and between 6.30 and 6.45 Mrs. Wallace took in the milk from the milk-boy. *This was the last time she was seen alive.*

At 6.45, according to his own statement, Wallace set out to visit Qualtrough, and between 7.6 and 7.10 he was certainly boarding a tram about twenty minutes' ride from Wolverton Street. A few minutes later he changed trams again, making repeated and detailed inquiries of both conductors for "Menlove Gardens East."

He was put down at Menlove Gardens West and told that it would probably be somewhere in that direction. He replied: "Thank you; I am a complete stranger about here."

Now, in a sense, that was not quite true. Two years previously he had visited a Mr. Crewe, living in that neighbourhood, on five occasions. But since he had always gone there in the dark of the winter evenings it was scarcely surprising that he should not be familiar with all the adjacent streets.

After three and a half years' residence Mr. Crewe himself

had no idea whether there was or was not a Menlove Gardens East. Actually, having inquired at a house of a passer-by and of a police constable, Wallace was told by all three that, though there was a Menlove Gardens North, South and West, and also a Menlove Avenue (all of which he tried), Menlove Gardens East did not exist.

Unwilling, however, to lose the chance of a useful commission, he asked the constable where he could consult a directory, adding: "It is not eight o'clock." The constable agreed that it was only 7.45, and told him where to find a newsagent's shop still open. Here Wallace again searched, and asked for Menlove Gardens East, and was told for the fourth time that there was no such place.

It was now getting on for 8.20, and Wallace, remembering that there had been one or two burglaries of late in his own street, began, as he said, to feel uneasy. He took the next tram home.

A little before 8.45 Wallace's next-door neighbours, a Mr. and Mrs. Johnston, heard knocking at the back door of No. 29. The residents in Wolverton Street made frequent use of their back doors, which all led out into a long entry, running parallel to the street itself.

Going out themselves by the back at a quarter to nine they met Wallace coming down the entry towards his own back door. He greeted them with the rather surprising question: "Have you heard anything unusual to-night?" They said: "No; what has happened?"

He said: "I have tried the back door and gone round to the front, and they are both locked against me." Mr. Johnston suggested that he should try the back door again. He did so; called out: "It opens now," and went in.

The Johnstons, standing in the yard, saw him turn up the gas in the two upstairs back rooms and heard him calling as though to his wife. After about three minutes he came hurriedly out, saying: "Come and see; she has been killed."

Then they all went in, by way of the scullery and kitchen, and in the front sitting-room they saw Mrs. Wallace lying dead on the floor near the unlit gas-fire. Her head had been brutally battered in, and the wall and furniture was splashed with blood. In the kitchen a cabinet had been broken open and a cash-box emptied of its contents (about £4) and replaced on the shelf.

This box was where Wallace kept the insurance money each week, till Wednesday, when he paid it in. On most Tuesdays it would have amounted to £20 or £30, but that week he had paid out about £14 in benefits.

Wallace then ran upstairs to see if anything else had been stolen. He returned almost at once, saying: "There is £5 in a vase; they have not taken that." Mr. Johnston then went for the police.

Wallace and Mrs. Johnston returned to the sitting-room, where they looked round in vain for the weapon. They then noticed that a mackintosh, which Wallace at once identified as his own, was lying rolled up against the shoulder of the corpse, "as though," to quote a police witness, "the body was a living person and you were trying to make it comfortable."

They touched nothing, but went back to the kitchen, relit the fire, which was almost out, and waited. During this time Wallace, who till then had shown astonishing self-control, twice broke down and sobbed. When the police examined the mackintosh it was found to be heavily splashed and smeared with blood all over and also partially burnt. Mrs. Wallace's skirt was stained and burnt also. Upstairs, the bedclothes in the front room, which had not been used for a fortnight, were pushed off the bed and flung about the floor, though no cupboards or drawers seemed to have been disturbed or opened.

One clot of blood was found in the bathroom, but there were no damp towels. A small smear of blood was also found on one of the currency notes in the vase in the back bedroom. There were no finger-prints on the cash-box and no signs of forcible entry into the house. The locks on both doors, front and back, were discovered to be defective, so that they were rather awkward to open.

Wallace said he "thought" the front door had been bolted before he opened it to admit the police, but this point was never quite cleared up.

The police surgeon arrived at ten o'clock and asserted that Mrs. Wallace had by then been dead four hours. Actually, we know she was alive at least as late as 6.30; but *rigor mortis* is always a very uncertain indication, in spite of the dogmatic pronouncements of doctors in detective fiction. It seems unlikely, however, that she was alive much after seven.

Eleven ferocious blows had been struck, and it seemed clear that the murderer must have been heavily spattered with blood. Wallace, now once more "cool and collected," and smoking cigarettes, said he had no suspicion of anybody, and, after making a statement, was sent to sleep, if he could, at his brother's house.

Next day the charwoman who occasionally worked for the Wallaces, reported that two things were missing from the house since her last visit on January 7: a small kitchen poker and an iron bar used for cleaning under the gas-fire in the sitting-room.

A minute search of the drains and waste ground in the district failed to disclose these, or any other, weapons. On the 22nd Wallace furnished the police with a list of friends and acquaintances whom his wife might have admitted to the house during his absence.

He was also foolish enough to question Mr. Beattie closely about the exact time of "Qualtrough's" telephone call, remarking: "The police have cleared me." When asked why he had said this, he replied: "I had an idea; we all have ideas; it was indiscreet of me."

It was, indeed; and this explanation did not improve matters. On February 2, Wallace was arrested and charged with the murder of his wife.

The trial opened on April 22, and the prosecution put forward their reconstruction of the crime. Having (for no ascertainable reason) determined to murder his wife, Wallace had himself telephoned to the café in the name of Qualtrough, to prepare himself an alibi for the next day. The voice had been quite unlike his, but he could have disguised it.

On Tuesday evening he suggested a music practice, and asked his wife to light the gas-fire in the sitting-room, which was used only for music and receiving visitors.

Meanwhile, he went upstairs, took off all his clothes (to avoid bloodstains), put on his old mackintosh (to receive bloodstains), came down armed with the iron bar (or poker, or both), savagely killed the poor woman, made a futile attempt to burn the incriminating mackintosh, broke open the cabinet and cash-box to suggest burglary, went up and flung bedclothes about for the same purpose, washed his bloodstained hands and legs, dressed, and rushed away to catch his tram.

After drawing ostentatious attention to himself and his errand, by way of confirming the alibi, he returned, pretended to be unable to get in till he had secured the Johnstons as witnesses, and then "discovered" the body, preserving all the time a callous demeanour, except for a few crocodile tears in the kitchen.

Now, this story has a good many holes in it, the most obvious being the complete lack of motive. Mrs. Wallace was insured for £20 and had £90 in the Post Office; but her husband had his own bank-balance of over £150, and all his affairs were in perfect order.

There was no evidence of any quarrel. The police surgeon said that the number and violence of the blows pointed to homicidal frenzy. True, Wallace had always seemed eminently sane before and since the murder. "The mind," said the good doctor, "is very peculiar."

But a frenzy carefully prepared for by an alibi twenty-four hours in advance is almost too peculiar for belief.

Then the alibi itself fails in the very first duty of an alibi: it makes no pretence of covering the time of the murder. Wallace never attempted to suggest that he left the house before the milk-boy's visit, though nobody saw him go, and he might have said what he liked.

He made, in fact, no effort to fix the time till 7.45 – ludicrously too late to establish the alibi. Then, why his own mackintosh? Why not some garment of his wife's? Or a new mackintosh? Why any garment at all? And why the imbecile attempt to destroy the mackintosh on the sitting-room floor, when there was an open fire in the kitchen?

What did he do with the pokers? They were not thrown away anywhere along his route, and he had no time to carry them far. Why take them away at all? He had only to wipe off his finger-prints and leave them at home if he wanted to support the burglary theory.

As for his having washed himself in the bathroom, there is no real evidence that the murderer ever went upstairs at all, for it turned out that the blood-clot in the bathroom and the smear on the £1 note were quite likely carried there by one of the dozen or so policemen who hovered about the house all night, while the unconvincing disorder in the bedroom might well be explained otherwise.

But, indeed, every incident in the case might have two explanations, each as plausible as the other.

For example:

Question: How is it that "Qualtrough's" telephone-call was put in at a point about three minutes from Wallace's house about three minutes after Wallace left home? *Answer*: (*a*) Because Wallace put it in himself; (*b*) Because the murderer watched Wallace out of the house and then telephoned at once from the nearest point.

Question: Why did Wallace make so many inquiries for "Menlove Gardens East" after being told that it did not exist? *Answer*: (*a*) Because he wanted as many witnesses as possible to his alibi; (*b*) Because he was too careful a man to believe any statement he had not verified, and it was quite possible that Mr. Beattie had taken the address down wrong.

Question: Why did Wallace not display more emotion when the body was found? *Answer*: (*a*) Because he was a heartless brute; (*b*) Because, as a disciple of the Stoic philosopher he, in his own words, "tried to be as calm and as cool as possible."

And so on, at every point.

You pay your money you see, and take your choice. The judge summed up for an acquittal, calling the prisoner's account of the matter "wonderfully lucid and consistent," and warning the jury, "it is no use applying tests to evidence if none of them really excludes the possibility of the prisoner's innocence."

The jury, after an hour's retirement, found Wallace guilty. Two weeks later, the Appeal judges, "looking very grave," quashed the verdict, on the ground that the prosecution had not proved their case – a decision which made criminal history.

Who, then, murdered Julia Wallace? I think that if a detective novelist had to make a story to cover the facts it would run something like this:

There was a man – let us call him by his own assumed name of "Qualtrough" – who had got himself into financial difficulties through a dishonesty which, perhaps, Wallace had himself helped to expose. At any rate, he knew Wallace well – knew his habits with regard to the insurance money – knew that if the Wallaces went out together they took the money with them, but that if Wallace went out alone he left it at home in his wife's care.

He was also a frequenter of the City Café, and so could see by the list of club fixtures that always hung there which night Wallace was due to play chess. This man determined to rob Wallace's cash-box and throw the guilt on Wallace.

On the Monday night, Qualtrough hid at a point near the end of Wolverton Street which Wallace was bound to pass – by whichever door he went out – on the way to the café. As soon as he saw the little man go past he hurried to put in the bogus telephone-call before Wallace could be there to receive it and recognise his voice.

He may then have taken a taxi or motor-car to the café, arriving in time to hear whether Wallace got the message and meant to keep the appointment. In any case, he would again be in his hiding-place on the Tuesday night, and when he saw Wallace pass he would know that the bait had been taken. Even if Wallace went and returned immediately, Qualtrough had a good forty minutes in hand.

In the meantime, Mrs. Wallace, before sitting down to a quiet evening by the kitchen fire, bethought herself, like a careful housewife, that this would be a good moment to shake out the bedding in the disused front room, to prevent it from getting damp.

It was a January night, and she had a cold; so, on her way up, she took her husband's mackintosh from the hall-stand and slipped it on. While she is stripping the bed the bell rings. She runs down to answer it. The piled-up bedclothes topple over, as is their way, and fall on the floor.

There is a man on the doorstep. Perhaps he gives his own name. Perhaps, if she does not appear to recognise him, he says he is Qualtrough, detained by some accident, unable to get home in time for his appointment, hoping to catch Wallace before he starts. In any case, she asks him to come in and wait.

She takes him into the sitting-room, lights the gas-fire, strips off the mackintosh with an apology and lays it down. Now comes the crucial moment. Perhaps not intending murder (for in that case he would have brought his own weapon), Qualtrough snatches up the handy mackintosh and flings it over her head. But she resists – and in that moment recognises him – calls him by his own name.

That will never do. At all costs she must be silenced for ever! He catches up the iron bar from the fireplace and beats her down. In his terror and rage, he strikes her again and again.

She falls against the gas-fire, burning her skirt, and as he stoops over her the mackintosh swings out and catches fire also. Smoke – smell – fire – the neighbours alarmed – that must not happen! He turns out the gas-fire and stamps out the burning stuff on the hearthrug.

But the coat has been a good friend to him; it has taken nearly all the bloodstains, and now he uses it to wipe his boots and trouser-legs. Has he really killed her?

With a vague hope – a dim remorse – with God knows what confused idea in his mind, he rolls the mackintosh up and thrusts it under her shoulder. But she is dead; and now he must carry out his plan and get away. He goes into the kitchen and breaks open the cabinet with the kitchen poker.

Nothing there. Where, then –? Ah, the cash-box! That will be the thing! He opens it. Four pounds! Four pounds only as the price of murder! Automatically he takes the money out, automatically rubs his finger-prints from the box and replaces it on the shelf.

Finger-prints! How about the pokers? He forces himself to return to the horrible sitting-room, collects the iron bar, and then I think something – a passing footstep, a voice in the street – startles him. He extinguishes the light and creeps out the back way, taking the pokers with him.

The two pokers are a difficulty in any solution of the mystery. Somebody took them; and in Wallace to do so would have been madness. Qualtrough could remove them with less danger, especially if he had his own car waiting. Possibly they were taken purposely in order to incriminate their owner.

After the appeal Wallace returned to his employment with the insurance company, who believed wholeheartedly in his innocence. But in Liverpool he was a pariah. He removed to a little house in Cheshire and sought comfort in his garden, his scientific studies, and the fortifying counsels of Marcus Aurelius.

In a diary, which seems to be absolutely sincere, he has recorded his bitter and unceasing sorrow for the loss of his wife. "Julia, Julia, how can I do without you?" "I seem to miss her more and more."

Sept. 14, 1931. Just as I was going to dinner—

stopped me and said he wanted to talk to me . . .
He must realise I suspect him . . . I fear I put him
on his guard . . . I wonder if it is any good putting
a private detective on to his track?

Oct. 6, 1931. I am dreadfully nervous about
entering the house after dark.

In a newspaper article written in April, 1932:
I know the murderer. . . . He is capable of, and
has reason for, attempting to remove me before
I place him in the dock where I stood . . .

But "that fell sergeant Death is strict in his arrest"; and
before Wallace could accomplish this, the "only mission left
him in life," he was once more condemned to die, and by
this time by a court from whose sentence there is no appeal.
When Qualtrough learned of Wallace's death on February
26, 1933, he must have thought himself a lucky man.

And by the way, why "Qualtrough"? If we could know
what list, what book, what association of ideas suggested
that curious name, we might know to whose mind it was
suggested.

Dorothy L. Sayers

AFTERWORD

In 1960, I collaborated with Patricia Pitman on *An
Encyclopaedia of Murder*. Mrs. Pitman was convinced of
Wallace's guilt, I – in spite of misgivings about his character
– of his innocence. He simply had no reason to kill Julia.
Two or three years later, she surprised me by telling me that
she was now convinced of Wallace's innocence. It seemed
that she had been talking to one of Britain's leading crime
experts, J. H. H. Gaute, a director of Harraps publishers,
and he had told her the real identity of the murderer. I

hastened to contact Joe Gaute, with whom I had had much friendly correspondence about murder. It was from him that I first heard the name of the man he was certain was the killer of Julia Wallace: Gordon Parry. Wallace himself, it seemed, had believed that Parry murdered his wife, and after his retirement had made a public statement to the effect that he had had an alarm button installed inside his front door.

After the murder, Wallace had been asked by the police what callers might have been admitted to the house by his wife; he named fifteen people (including his sister-in-law Amy). Asked if he suspected any of them Wallace hesitated, then admitted that he was suspicious of a young man named Gordon Parry. This man had called at his house on business, and was trusted by Julia. But he had a criminal record. And he knew where Wallace kept his collection money. At the time of the murder, Parry was heavily in debt. Questioned by the police, Parry alleged that he had been with "friends" on the evening of the murder, and the friends corroborated this; however, two years later, Parry admitted that it had been "a mistake".

Crime writer Jonathan Goodman, who was writing a book on the Wallace case, decided to try to track down Gordon Parry. It was a long and complicated task, which began in Liverpool, but which eventually led him to an address in south London. Together with another crime writer, Richard Whittington-Egan, Goodman went to call on Parry.

Parry, a powerfully built little man with sleeked-back grey hair and a military moustache, received them with the "bogus bonhomie of a car salesman", and talked to them on his doorstep. They decided that "his manner masks . . . considerable firmness, even ruthlessness. He would be a nasty man to cross". Parry hinted that he could reveal much about Wallace, and described him as "a very strange man" and "sexually odd". He seemed to know what had become of everybody involved in the case, as if he had been carefully following its aftermath over the years. And when he finally dismissed Goodman and Whittington-Egan, they both had the feeling that he was thinking that he had fooled better people than they were . . . In his book *The Killing of Julia Wallace*, Goodman refers to Parry as "Mr. X", and it is fairly clear that he regards him as the chief suspect.

In 1980, a news editor in Liverpool's Radio City, Roger Wilkes, became interested in the Wallace case, and started researching it for a programme. He contacted Jonathan Goodman, who at first was understandably cagey about revealing Parry's identity, in case he found himself involved in a libel suit. But through Wallace's solicitor, Hector Munro, Wilkes tracked down Parry's record. At the time of the murder, Parry was twenty-two. The son of well-to-do parents, he had worked for the Prudential for a while, but had failed to pay in various premiums he had received – his parents had paid the money. Parry had been charged at various times with theft, embezzlement and indecent assault – at his trial a medical expert had described him as "a sexual pervert".

Wilkes persisted, but when he finally tracked down Parry to North Wales, he discovered that he had died a few weeks before, in April 1980. Nevertheless, he continued with his investigation. Who were the "friends" who had given Parry his alibi for the night of the murder? The answer that emerged was that it was not friends but *a* friend – a Miss Lily Lloyd, to whom Parry was engaged. And from Jonathan Goodman he learned that when Parry had jilted her two years later, Miss Lloyd had gone to Wallace's solicitor and offered to swear an *affidavit* saying that the alibi she had given Parry for the night of the crime was untrue. Wilkes then managed to track down Miss Lloyd, who had played a piano in a cinema in the 1930s. If the police had taken the trouble to check *her* alibi, they would have learned that she could not have been with Parry at the time of the murder – she was working in the cinema.

Finally, Wilkes uncovered the clinching piece of evidence. At the time of the murder, a young garage mechanic named John Parkes had been working near Parry's home. He knew

Parry as a "wide boy" – in fact, had been to school with him. On the night of the murder, Parry had called at the garage in an agitated state, and washed down his car with a high pressure hose. Parkes saw a glove in the car, and pulled it out to prevent it getting wet. It was soaked with wet blood.

Wilkes had finally tracked down the murderer of Julia Wallace, but half a century too late.

C.W.

The Vera Page Case

Like the Wallace case, the sex murder of 10-year-
old Vera Page in the Notting Hill area of London
is still officially unsolved. Ex-superintentendent
George Cornish, who wrote an account of the
case, had good legal reasons for not telling the
full story – as well, I think, as embarrassment at
the mistake that almost certainly prevented the
murderer being brought to justice. First, then,
Cornish's own account from Great Unsolved Mysteries.

The wanton murder of a child is always horrible, and
I think that the death of Vera Page was the most
terrible case which I had to deal with during my career as
a detective.

Late in the evening of Monday, December 14, 1931,
Mr. Charles Page, of Notting Hill Gate, went to the local
police station to report that his little daughter Vera was
missing.

She had, he told the police, returned home from school
as usual about half-past four that afternoon. Tea was at
half-past five, and the child had gone out again to visit her
aunt who lived a short distance away.

She reached her aunt's home safely and left again at a
quarter to five, carrying her school swimming certificates
with her. She never returned home, and although he made
inquiries from friends and relations to whom she might have
gone, no one had seen her.

The police made all the usual routine inquiries. The newspapers published her photograph and other details, and on Tuesday an SOS was broadcast. Still there was no news.

Early on Wednesday morning a milk roundsman discovered the body of a little girl lying in a patch of shrubbery in the front garden of a house in Addison Road, Notting Hill. Vera Page had been found.

When we arrived I suspected that we were confronted with one of the most difficult problems which a detective has to face, that unknown and variable quantity, the criminal maniac whose insanity is intermittent. Before I continue with the story of what followed it is important that something should be understood of the pathological side of this type of man.

In the first place, unless we could obtain definite evidence to the contrary, there was no real reason to suppose that he knew the dead child. He might very well be a stranger not only to her, but also to the neighbourhood.

Perhaps he was a Londoner, but he could equally well have come from some other place. He might have been staying in the neighbourhood, or merely passing through it. If he was suddenly seized with his mania he would probably accost the first woman or girl he came across.

Once the mania had passed, it was quite possible that he would have no recollection of what had occurred. It was not improbable that to his family, relations and friends he appeared a normal man.

It was very likely that somewhere, not necessarily in London at all, there was a man going about his usual everyday occupation with no knowledge that he had recently committed murder. He would read the details of the crime in the newspapers, but he would not know that they had anything to do with him, and therefore he would not do or say anything that might arouse suspicion in the minds of other people.

Our work was to try to find out whether this man had

been seen, where he had murdered the child, and whether he had left any clue which could assist us to discover his identity. From the evidence we obtained the following facts emerged.

Vera Page had last been seen alive between five and six o'clock on Monday evening. A school friend had spoken to her outside a chemist's shop not far from her home. The little girl wanted to buy some soap dominoes, which were being shown in the window, for a Christmas present, and she had probably gone to look at them.

We could discover no one who had seen her near, or with a man, but about that time some man must have spoken to her. The question at once arises as to whether she was in the habit of speaking to strangers.

We were told that she never talked to people she didn't know, but this would probably depend very much on how the strangers spoke to her. If, for instance, he had asked her where she was going, and she had told him "home," he might well have said that "Mummy had asked him to go with her," and she would have gone without hesitation.

Approximately forty hours had elapsed between the time when the child was last seen alive and the time when her body was found. Where had she been during that time?

Medical evidence gave us the information that she had been dead at least twenty-four hours, and probably longer. The body was not rigid; therefore she must have been in a fairly warm place, for it was cold December weather.

It had rained from 3 p.m. on Tuesday until 9 p.m. that evening and Wednesday morning was damp and misty. The child's clothes had absorbed very little moisture, and I formed the opinion that she could not have been lying in the garden for more than two hours before she was found.

This was confirmed by other evidence which showed that if the body had been there before eight o'clock, it would have been seen.

An examination of the clothes gave us little assistance except that there were traces of coal dust and one or two spots of candle grease. Her swimming certificates, which were printed on white paper, and the red beret which she was wearing on Monday evening had disappeared.

We must now set to work on this theory. Between, say, seven o'clock on Monday evening and about the same time on Wednesday morning the child had been somewhere dry and comparatively warm. It was possibly a coal shed or cellar which had been lit by a candle.

The beret and certificates might be there, or the murderer might have carried them away with him, or thrown them away. To find the place where the murder took place, even if it was in the immediate neighbourhood, was no easy task. But we set to work to make exhaustive inquiries, and hoped that some piece of useful information might come in as a result of the widespread public interest in the case.

We then had to try to solve another series of problems. How had the murderer brought the body to the garden from the place where it had been "hidden?" Had he carried it in his arms, brought it in a car, or perhaps on a coster's barrow or even in a perambulator? Had anyone seen him?

Although it was still dark, there were plenty of people about in the streets between seven and eight o'clock in the morning. Why had he chosen that particular place?

There was no attempt at concealment. The body had been laid gently down where the first person who walked along the path by the patch or shrubbery would see it.

To the first two questions we could obtain no answer. No one had seen or heard anything suspicious. To the third question the answer must lie in the psychology of the murderer. He had no reason for choosing that particular road or garden, he made no attempt at concealment either in bringing the body there or when he left it.

All he wanted was to put it away somewhere, and he put it gently down in the first place that seemed suitable. Probably the fact that he might be seen never occurred to him, nor that it would matter if he were.

As far as we could discover he was completely unobserved. But for this chance we might have discovered his identity.

On Thursday evening, December 17, a woman living in the Notting Hill Gate neighbourhood, not far from the garden in Addison Road, brought a red beret to us. This, she told us, she had found, soaking wet, in her area.

Near it were some torn pieces of paper and a bit of candle. The candle end she had used up, the bits of paper she had thrown away in her dustbin which since then had been cleared. It looked as though these might be Vera Page's beret and her swimming certificates.

Investigation showed that there was also an unlocked and empty coal shed in the area. Was this the scene of the murder? Had the child's body lain in this unlocked shed for forty hours, and had chance again stepped in and prevented anyone from opening the door?

Many of the children in the district were wearing red berets at that time and there was nothing to prove that the one found belonged to Vera Page. The candle end had gone beyond recovery, so had the pieces of paper. The most thorough and minute examination of the coal shed revealed nothing to show that anyone had entered it, or that a body had been left there.

We had one other clue. In the crook of the child's arm when she was found there was a finger bandage composed of boric lint and a piece of bandage. Without any doubt the murderer had had this on one of his fingers when he put the body down in the garden. But the most careful scientific examination of both bandage and lint did not help us, for they were of an ordinary type that could be bought anywhere for a few pence.

So ended this tragic case. No more information that could assist us was forthcoming. We could get no answer to our questions, nor could we answer another: Where had the murderer himself been during those forty hours?

Possibly he had stayed with the dead child. It is, however, more than possible that somewhere the murderer of Vera Page goes about his day's work without any knowledge that he is a murderer.

George Cornish

AFTERWORD

Discussing the case in *Written in Blood* nearly sixty years after it happened, I was able to supply the facts that Cornish was unable to reveal.

On the morning of 15 December 1931, a milkman entering a garden in Addison Road, Holland Park, saw the body of a child lying on the lawn. She was identified as 10-year-old Vera Page, who had been missing from her home at 22 Blenheim Crescent, in the Notting Hill area of London, since the previous evening. She had been raped and then manually strangled. When the body was moved, a finger-stall fell out from the crook of the arm.

A number of clues enabled the police to reconstruct roughly what had happened. Vera Page had last been seen alive at a quarter to seven on the previous evening; she had been on her way back from the house of an aunt, and had been seen looking in the windows of shops decorated for Christmas. Spilsbury's examination indicated that she had been raped and strangled not long after she was last seen, close to her home. Since she was a shy child, it seemed clear that she had been murdered by someone she knew and trusted. This man had probably taken her to a warm room – decomposition had already set in – and raped and killed her there. Then he had hidden the body in a coal cellar – this was indicated by coal dust on her clothes. The cellar had no electric light; this was suggested by spots of candle grease on the child's clothes. Some time around dawn, the murderer had retrieved the body and taken it to the garden in Addison Road, probably using a barrow. It had rained for much of the night, but the child's clothes were dry. As he removed his hands from under her arms, the bandage had slipped off his finger.

The murder caused intense public indignation, and the police mounted an enormous operation to track down the killer. Door-to-door enquiries were made over the whole area, and they quickly located a suspect. He was a 41-year-old labourer named Percy Orlando Rush, and he lived in a flat in Talbot Road, close to Vera Page. Moreover, his parents lived in the same house as Vera Page, so he often saw her. On the evening of the murder, his wife had been visiting her mother, and had not arrived home until later. So Rush could have murdered Vera Page, then taken her down to the coal cellar in the basement before his wife arrived home. Moreover, Rush had a wound on his left little finger, and had been wearing a finger-stall until recently.

The finger-stall was examined by Dr. Roche Lynch, the Home Office analyst. He found that it had covered a suppurating wound, and that the bandage had been soaked in ammonia. Percy Orlando Rush worked in Whiteley's Laundry, near Earls Court, and his job involved placing his hands in ammonia.

There was another damning piece of evidence against Rush. At dawn on 15 December, a man of his description had been seen pushing a wheelbarrow covered with a red cloth near the garden where the body had been found. When the police searched Rush's home, they found a red table-cloth.

From the point of view of forensic science, the most interesting clue was provided by the candle grease. In the previous year, an Austrian engineer had invented a new method of testing candle wax. It was melted, with careful temperature control, on a microscope slide, and allowed to cool. Examined thtough a microscope under polarized light, the wax would reveal its "fingerprinting", a characteristic crystalline structure. The wax on Vera Page's clothing was examined in this way, and compared with candles in her own home. They proved to be quite different. But it was identical with the wax of a candle found in Rush's home. So were certain spots of candle grease on Rush's overcoat.

But the crucial piece of evidence was the bandage. And here Superintendent George Cornish recognized that he may have made a mistake. He had let his suspect know about the finger-stall. And when he asked Rush for samples of bandage from his own house, Rush had handed them over with a faint smile that Cornish found disturbing. In fact, Roche Lynch's microscopic examination of the bandage established that it was not the same as that of the finger-stall.

Cornish's men scoured every chemist's shop in west London to try to find if anyone could recall selling bandages to Rush or his wife. If he could establish that Rush had bought some other type of bandage, and it proved identical with the finger-stall, then his case was complete.

Unfortunately, this attempt was a failure. The circumstantial evidence against Rush was overwhelming. But unless the bandage could be traced to him, the case had a fatal flaw. This became clear at the coroner's inquest, conducted by Dr. Ingleby Oddie, on 10 February 1932. Rush proved to be a short, thick-set man who wore horn-rimmed glasses and a black moustache. His evidence was punctuated by angry cries of "Liar!" from the spectators. But Rush stuck to his story that he had ceased to wear his finger-stall some days before the disappearance of Vera Page; he explained that he wanted to "harden" the wound. All the coroner's questions – and those of jurymen – make it clear that they were convinced of Rush's guilt. But no one had actually seen Rush with Vera Page, and after only five minutes, the jury decided there was insufficient evidence to charge him with her murder.

C. W.

Winnie Ruth Judd

When I was driving across America in 1967 – from
New York to Seattle – I called upon the poet and
novelist August Derleth at his home near Sauk
City, Wisconsin, and spent the day with him.
I was fascinated to observe on his bookshelf a
set of books about murders in famous American cities: *New York Murders*, *Chicago Murders*,
Denver Murders, and so on. As a historian of
crime, I looked at them with a certain predatory
envy. There were nine volumes, all dating from
immediately after the Second World War, and
now obviously out of print. But in the course of my
six-month stay in Seattle, I learned of a California
bookseller who specialised in locating second-
hand books, and in due course became possessor
of the set. They contain some marvellous items,
some by distinguished writers like Damon Runyon
(on Ruth Snyder) and Erle Stanley Gardner (on
the murder of William Desmond Taylor.)

The gruesomely fascinating case of Winnie Judd
is little known outside America – one very good
reason for including it here. Another is that this is
a first-hand account by a reporter who worked on
the case and who met the murderess. The decision
to include it was taken after some hesitation,
for it is, from the point of view of the present
anthology, rather too long. But after reading it
again, I decided that its air of immediacy is
irresistable.

Incidentally, the reference to the use of rattlesnakes as a murder weapon refers to the case

of Robert James, which will be found later in
this book.

The chamber of commerce doesn't mention it. But there is
something about Los Angeles that makes citizens knock
each other off in curious and fascinating ways. They use ice
picks, hammers, home-made bombs and rattlesnakes. They
bury their victims in cisterns, chicken yards and basements.
They even ship them about by rail. The most notorious
exponent of the latter method was a copper-haired lady
named Winnie Ruth Judd.

I have heard various explanations of this bloody phenomenon. One amateur criminologist blamed the weather, said
it had something to do with the seasons, or lack of them.
Another thought that the remarkable advertising campaigns
of funeral parlors were at fault. He said that when people
continually read billboards like "Bury Your Loved Ones in
High Dry Ground," and "Whatever You Do in Times Like
These Don't Ration Grief at the Grave," they begin to look
on death as something to be welcomed. Still another felt
that certain newspaper editors who tack fascinating labels
on every murder, no matter how cheap or grisly, should be
taken to task.

I am one who holds with this latter theory. In my time,
at the insistence of managing editors, I have taken some
run-of-the-mill killing worth no more than two paragraphs
and whooped it up into three columns. There was a poor old
witless janitor who could no longer stand his wife's tongue
lashings, hit her with an axe and then stuffed her in a trunk
in his garage. We made him an engineer. We made his wife
beautiful. And we called it the "Thin Man" murder. He
was thin. Then there was a Pasadena killing around the
corner from the Shrine temple. In front of the temple were
two stone sphinxes. It would have been necessary for the
sphinxes to walk a block to witness the crime. But that
didn't bother us. It became the Sphinx Murder. Only the

Sphinx, who saw this dark and gory crime, knew the secret of the riddle.

Such goings on in the press could arouse a competitive spirit in murderers, could set them to trying to outdo each other. Such a thought makes me uneasy, makes me thank God that I deserted a rewrite desk for one of my own – that I stopped writing about real killings and took up imaginary ones.

However, I was not the one who, back in 1931, called Winnie Ruth Judd the "Velvet Tigress" and the "Wolf Woman." Nor did Tom Treanor, who just missed capturing her single-handed; nor Lionel Moise, who took Tom's failure so much to heart.

Now, in 1947, Winnie Ruth is locked up in an asylum in Arizona. Moise is still making big reporters out of little ones in New York. And Tom Treanor sleeps in a French cemetery. When he was killed in 1944 during the invasion of France, no one mentioned his part in the Winnie Ruth Judd murder case. And no wonder, in the light of all the things he had done, all the great stories he had covered and written since he started as a cub on the old *Los Angeles Express*. I bring it up because it illustrates how wrong guys can be about other guys. In 1931 we thought Tom was in the wrong racket. We thought he should have taken his father's advice and gone into the cement business. Moise, city editor of that now forgotten paper, suggested it many, many times and in a loud voice.

Tom had just realized his ambition to become a reporter that day in '31 when the Winnie Ruth Judd case broke. He was a tall, merry, eager youth who resented the fact that he looked a lot like Charles Lindbergh. Tom had been writing a radio column for the paper when Moise became city editor. Hating radio, he turned his charm on Moise and that gentleman finally gave in and put him to covering Rotary luncheons and postoffice clerk's conventions at fifteen bucks a week.

We were in the middle of a fight with the police department

that bright October afternoon. Most of the staff was out digging up mean things to say about the cops. I was on rewrite putting the mean things together. Moise was on the desk making them even meaner. Tom was hanging around. The phone rang. Moise answered it, made a couple of notes and hung up. He beckoned to Tom.

"Go down to the SP station," he said. "Something is up. We do not know what because the coppers are not speaking to any gentlemen from the *Express*."

Something certainly was up, we discovered when Tom called back. A baggageman named Andrew V. Anderson had become curious about a couple of trunks in the baggageroom. The trunks had arrived a while before on the Golden State Limited. They had been shipped from Phoenix, Arizona and it was evident from the aroma rising from them that all was not well inside.

Mr. Anderson wasn't looking for murder evidence. He was looking for illegal shipments of venison into the state.

Blood dripped from the big black trunk onto the station platform. Mr. Anderson looked. Mr. Anderson sniffed. Mr. Anderson stuck around and waited.

Around noon a copper-haired young woman and a red-haired young man in a collegiate sweater and corduroys walked into the baggage room. The young woman handed two baggage checks to the man at the window.

"I want my trunks," she said coolly.

The man glanced at the stubs, nodded and disappeared, to come back a moment later with Mr. Anderson.

"Sorry," said Anderson. "You'll have to open the trunks."

The young woman hesitated. She tried to look hurt. Then she sighed and said, "My husband has the keys. I'll have to call him."

"We'll be right back," said the red-haired youth. He took her arm and off they went. Being a suspicious man, Mr. Anderson followed, got· the license number of the roadster the red-haired youth was driving, then went back to wait. He waited three hours. More blood ran out of the big trunk. The noxious fumes thickened. He decided it was time to call the cops, which he did.

Detectives Paul Stevens and Frank Ryan answered the call. They looked at the big black trunk and the smaller steamer trunk. They hefted them.

"Deer meat all right," said Mr. Ryan. "Get me a crowbar."

Crowbar in hand, Ryan set to work on the larger trunk. He pried off the lock and lifted the lid.

Tom wasn't on hand when the trunk was opened so I'll have to quote from a newspaper account what happened then. According to the newspaper version, Mr. Ryan said in a hoarse whisper, "That's not venison. It's a human body." If my memory of Mr. Ryan's speech is at all accurate, he said something much more pungent.

But undoubtedly his whisper was hoarse. Wedged in a crouching position and wrapped in a sheet was the body of a woman – a brunette about thirty years old. She was wearing orange silk pajamas.

"Taken aback momentarily," the newspaper account continues, "the officers stared at the grisly find. Then they set to work on the steamer trunk. By this time a small crowd had gathered. The lock gave way and the lid was raised. A man in striped overalls fainted. From the trunk protruded a human foot. Ryan took hold of it. A leg appeared – a leg severed at the knee."

The story I have at hand doesn't say how Mr. Ryan felt about it. I imagine he was more than taken aback, standing there holding a leg in his fist. Apparently he didn't faint. Because when Tom reached the station and joined the little group, Mr. Ryan was still on his feet directing activities. He had found another leg and the upper torso of a woman with head and arms attached. A few parts of the body, to wit, the upper legs from the knees to the hips, and the lower torso, were missing. He had also found evidence that the bodies were those of Agnes Ann LeRoi, thirty, twice-divorced nurse, and Hedvig Samuelson, twenty-three, a tubercular school teacher, both of 2929 North Second Street, Phoenix. The trunks were full of letters addressed to the dead women and snapshots of the pair.

Had Mrs. Judd disposed of the trunks, she might have got away with the murders. There was nothing in her history to indicate that she would start knocking off her friends. An ex-nurse, recovering from tuberculosis, she had lived a quiet life of respectability. Her husband was a Los Angeles physician. She had been a good wife, a model wife, and was only separated from him by her illness.

Into those trunks she had packed not only the bodies but letters revealing her close friendship with the dead women.

Police read the letters, looked at the photographs and the records revealing that Mrs. Judd had shipped the trunks to herself in Los Angeles. They were certain who the murderer was.

But there were mysterious aspects to the case.

Where was the rest of Miss Samuelson's body? (She occupied the steamer trunk.)

How could a woman as small and slight as Mrs. Judd was, have butchered that one body so neatly?

Did she have help?

Where in hell was she?

The first question was answered within a few hours. The woman who took care of the station restroom appeared carrying a suitcase. In it were the missing pieces of Miss Samuelson's body.

Whether Mrs. Judd had help or not is still a moot question. At first she said she didn't. Later on, at her sanity trial, she intimated she did. But she wasn't specific.

It wasn't long before the police were on Winnie Ruth's trail. Armed with a license number, they traced the roadster to one Burton J. McKinnell, twenty-six-year-old University of Southern California law student. Mr. McKinnell was Mrs. Judd's brother. He had an apartment in Beverly Glen, a very pleasant canyon north of Beverly Hills which was the scene, many years back, of two fine murders. When I was a novice reporter I accompanied an *Examiner* man named George Van Sands up the canyon on a hunt for a woman's body. Mr. Van Sands found her accidentally. It was a hot day and he bent down over a water tap and turned it on. He seldom touched water after that experience, for the woman, a Mrs. Young, was in the cistern. But that is another story.

Burton was not at home. The police searched the place, came up with the name and address of one Dr. William C. Judd, of 823 Seventeenth Street, Santa Monica. They hot-footed it to that address. At the curb stood Mr. McKinnell's roadster. Mr. McKinnell and Dr. Judd were waiting upstairs.

Both men, according to newspaper accounts, were quite calm. Dr. Judd admitted that Winnie Ruth was his wife, that the last time he saw her was in Phoenix, where she lived for her health.

Burton said she was his sister. "This morning," he continued, "as I left my classes at U.S.C., I found my sister waiting for me in front of the political science building.

"She had just arrived from Phoenix. We had not expected her. She was nervous and wrought up. About her left hand she wore a heavy bandage. When I inquired about it, reluctantly she told me she had been shot. Then she grabbed my shoulder and said, 'Burton, there are two trunks at the station. You must help me get them. We must take them to the beach and throw them in the ocean.'"

Mr. McKinnell admitted he was puzzled by his sister's behavior. His story continues:

"I was puzzled by the request and by the wound in my sister's hand but I accompanied her to the railroad station. When the baggageman refused to turn over the trunks without an inspection, I knew something was wrong.

"I asked Sis what it was she had in the trunks. She finally admitted there were bodies in them. I asked if they were men and women. She replied that the less I knew about it, the better. I drove her to Sixth and Broadway, gave her five dollars and that's the last I saw of her."

At the time there were men who felt that Burton McKinnell's attitude and actions were peculiar. They weren't, really. He was young and he was fond of his sister who was in a hell of a jam. What would you do if your sister asked you to help her get rid of a couple of bodies?

Dr. Judd was also a bewildered man. He hadn't heard from his wife. He hadn't the slightest notion why she was knocking off her friends and shipping their bodies around in trunks. To the day of his death, two years ago, I think he was still bewildered by it all.

There wasn't much the police could do about it but haul the two gentlemen in for further questioning and start looking for Winnie Ruth. They didn't find her for a while.

However, they did find another clue linking her to the murders. One of the toilets in the restroom of a department store wouldn't work. A plumber investigated. He found what was left of a long letter written by Mrs. Judd. I forget whom she wrote it to. And the boys in the newspaper morgues whose business it is to clip the papers seem to have mislaid all the stories pertaining to the letter. I remember it as a rambling, peculiar missive in which she admitted killing her friends during a quarrel. It isn't important because she showed up after a time to tell the story in her own inimitable way. I mention it only to show how inexperienced she was in the art of murder. You don't do things like that if you want to stay out of jail. You make it as tough for the masterminds as possible. Until she took it on the lam, Mrs. Judd left a trail my cocker spaniel, who has no sense of smell, could follow. Only when she started running did she use her wits. She might still be running if the bullet wound in her hand hadn't got infected.

According to the clippings I have at hand, the search for Winnie Ruth was the greatest, most exciting and most intense since the manhunt for William Edward Hickman a few years before. That is an exaggeration. There has never been anything like that hunt for Hickman – not in Los Angeles anyway. I remember a city in the grip of terror when Hickman was on the prowl – a city where it wasn't safe to venture forth at night because it was full of guys with guns who were ready to shoot on sight any young man with curly black hair.

It wasn't like that when they were looking for Winnie Ruth. The cops were excited, with the angry excitement of frustrated men, but the citizens bore up well. People phoned in now and then to say they had seen her in Mexico, or San Francisco, or Santa Barbara or at the corner of Hollywood and Vine, but people always do that. It makes them feel useful.

By the time the manhunt was well under way, we had the background of the crime from the boys in Phoenix. Mrs. Judd, it appeared, had been employed for a time in the same clinic where Mrs. LeRoi was a nurse. Off-duty, Mrs. LeRoi took care of Miss Samuelson, a former Alaskan school teacher who had come to Phoenix suffering from tuberculosis. For months the three women lived together in a bungalow on North Second Street. A few months before the murder, Mrs. Judd had moved to an apartment of her own at 1130 East Brill Street on the other side of town.

Even after Mrs. Judd moved, the three women were friendly. Every now and then they got together for a party. They had got together the night of October 16th, a Friday, at the Samuelson-LeRoi bungalow.

On Saturday, H. N. Grimm, a baggage-transfer man, was summoned to the North Second Street address. Mrs. Judd was there, apparently alone. She showed him a big trunk and said she wanted it taken to the station. Mr. Grimm hefted it. Too heavy, he said. Much too heavy to check on a ticket.

"What's in it?" he wanted to know.

"Books," said Mrs. Judd. "My husband's medical library."

Then she told him to take it to her Brill Street address. She said she'd put some of the books in another trunk. Mr. Grimm did what he was told.

Next day, Mr. Grimm got another call from Mrs. Judd. This time she had three pieces of luggage – the big trunk, a steamer trunk and a suitcase. He was not a curious man. To him baggage was baggage. It was his racket to move trunks. So he took them to the station, figuring that would be the end of it. Little did he wot what he was toting around. When he found out, he gulped and turned pale. You could have knocked him down with a feather, he admitted.

Mrs. Judd followed the trunks to the station. She bought a one-way ticket to Los Angeles. Fittingly, she rode in the first Pullman behind the baggage car in which were the trunks and their human cargo. When Tom Treanor learned about this he wanted to write a piece in rhyme. He pointed out that the song "The Baggage Car Ahead" was very well known and that if he didn't make use of it, someone else would. Moise was almost shocked into silence.

"Tommy," he said, "if you want to do something useful, go out and find Mrs. Judd."

Tom admitted that the idea appealed to him. But he pointed out that everybody and his brother was looking for her. Where should he look?

Moise checked the list of places where she might be. Before she went to Phoenix she had been a patient at La Vina Sanitarium in the hills back of Altadena. "Run out there and look around," suggested Moise.

I thought the idea was silly. I said the cops would have cased the joint by this time. Tom agreed with me. But Moise was insistent, so Tommy went.

Tom found the sanitarium easily enough. He drove in the gate and went straight to the superintendent's office.

"I asked if Mrs. Judd was hiding anywhere around the place," Tom told us when he returned. "He was very annoyed. I don't blame him, really."

"Did you look around?" Moise wanted to know.

"Of course not," said Tom. "The superintendent said she wasn't there. That's good enough for me."

It turned out that the superintendent had reason to be annoyed. The cops had asked him the same question several times. So had a couple of other newspapermen. He was a busy man with a hospital to run and he hadn't seen Mrs. Judd for a long time. How was he or anyone else to know she was hiding in an unused building up the hill back of the administration office?

You couldn't blame Tom for not finding Mrs. Judd. The police couldn't find her either. By Wednesday night they were convinced she had committed suicide and so stated publicly. As one police authority put it, "Undoubtedly she has thrown herself in the ocean where she intended to throw her victims. We will find her body on the beach in due time."

Dr. Judd disagreed. He was convinced his wife was alive, so he appealed through newspaper advertisements for Winnie Ruth to give herself up. He had employed two attorneys for her – Richard Cantillon and Louis P. Russill. He urged her to get in touch with them. He said every effort would be made to keep her off the Arizona gallows.

The following afternoon, while the coroner was conducting an inquest and a jury was blaming Mrs. Judd for the two murders, she called Mr. Cantillon.

"This is Mrs. Judd," she said. "Can you please put me in touch with my husband?"

Mr. Cantillon gave her the telephone number of Attorney Patrick Cooney. He said he and the doctor would wait in Cooney's office for another call. That was because Mr. Cantillon was very popular with the press and a number of reporters were in the outer office drinking his gin. I was one of them. Tom was another.

We tried to tail Mr. Cantillon but he gave us the slip. He and the doctor waited an hour. Then Mrs. Judd called again. For fifteen minutes the doctor argued with her and finally she said all right, she was fed up with hiding out and would meet him in the lobby of the Biltmore Theatre. That's where Judd met her. That wasn't where the cops and the reporters met her. Two hours later Mr. Cantillon, looking very smug, led us to the undertaking establishment of Alvarez and Moore at Court and Olive streets. We found Winnie Ruth lying in bed in an upstairs room looking pretty sick and bedraggled. Her wounded hand was infected and the wound had been freshly dressed. But she was quite calm.

Downstairs there were several bodies waiting for burial but that didn't worry her. It didn't worry us either. It gave us the opportunity for considerable fancy writing – such a fitting setting – such an eerie setting – candles and faded flowers and coffins and corpses – and upstairs a dame talking her head off to the cops. I give you her story in her own words:

"I met Mrs. LeRoi shortly after I arrived in Phoenix. We soon became fast friends. She told me about herself and I told her about my life.

"Anne invited me to her home. There I met her pal, Hedwig Samuelson, whom we all called Sammy.

"Sammy was ill. Anne took care of her. In return, Sammy helped Anne financially.

"Anne was a stunningly beautiful girl and loved all men. Not in an immoral way but as friends and companions. She loved a good time. Sammy, on the other hand, cared for no man. She was consumed by a very unusual love for Anne.

"I got to know both of the girls very well. Finally when Dr. Judd left Phoenix to come to Los Angeles I moved in with Anne and Sammy. We were very happy together.

"During my early months in Phoenix I had made the friendship of a millionaire lumberman. Jack was a splendid fellow, a good scout and a true friend to me.

"I introduced Jack to Anne. He seemed to like her. After I moved over with Anne and Sammy, Jack often came to the house in the evenings. We would have parties. He would bring his men friends.

"Jack, although he seemed to like Anne, was also kind to me. At first this was all right. Then Anne began to resent it. Finally I moved to my own apartment. Anne became very cool to me.

"There was another little nurse at the clinic and she was very cute. Her name was Lucille. Jack found out that Lucille was going on a hunting trip to the White Mountains. Jack planned a similar trip. He asked to meet Lucille, said they might make it a party. On Thursday evening, October 15th, I invited Lucille to my apartment for dinner. Then I asked Jack to come up. He brought two men friends. We had a happy evening. Anne learned about the party, for Jack had stopped by to see her on the way to my house. He had taken Anne and Sammy a radio.

"The next day, Friday, Anne went to lunch with me. She insisted that I come over to see her and Sammy that evening. I tried to renege but she insisted. I had special work to do at the clinic. I didn't get to the Second Street bungalow until after nine o'clock.

"Anne and Sammy were tired. They insisted I stay all night. I slept on the davenport. In the morning, Saturday morning, we were all three in the kitchen in our pajamas getting breakfast. Anne started to upbraid me for introducing other girls to Jack. She was angry because I had introduced him to Lucille. Sammy was furious because my action brought sorrow to her beloved Anne.

"Our words became heated. We were shouting at each other. Finally Anne screamed, 'Ruth, if that Lucille goes hunting with Jack I'll tell him things about other girls you have introduced him to.'

"The threat infuriated me. 'Anne,' I said, 'if you do a thing like that I will tell Jack about you.' At these words Sammy sprang to her feet, ran into the bedroom and came out with a little black-handled gun I had left behind with some other things when I moved to my own apartment.

"Sammy's face was drained of blood. Her eyes pierced me through. She pulled the trigger of the little gun. I threw up my arms. The bullet struck me in the hand. I threw my whole weight against Sammy and grabbed the gun. She fell behind the breakfast-nook table. I was over her. I shot twice.

"Anne screamed and ran at me with the ironing board. I pointed the gun at her and fired one shot."

That, according to Winnie Ruth, was it.

She had two bodies on her hands and she didn't quite

know what to do with them. While thinking it over, she went to work.

"I told the people at the clinic I was sick," she said. "I also told them Anne was sick. Then I went back to Anne's house."

Winnie Ruth was a busy girl that day. She packed both bodies in the one big trunk and had Mr. Grimm take them to her apartment. Then she cut Sammy up with a meat saw and a butcher knife and put most of her in the steamer trunk and the rest in the suitcase. Anne stayed in the big trunk.

After she left her brother in Los Angeles, Winnie Ruth started walking. She walked twenty miles to La Vina Sanitarium and hid in a vacant cottage. At night she crept to the kitchen to swipe food. Her hand began hurting, so she lit out, intending to give herself up, she said. En route she got hold of a newspaper, saw her husband's advertised appeal and called Mr. Cantillon.

Mrs. Judd stuck to that story all the time she stayed in the Los Angeles county jail. We liked it enough to try to buy an elaborated version of it. But the *Express* wasn't doing too well and another paper outbid us. However, the dickering gave me the chance to see a good deal of Winnie Ruth. I got the impression that she was a pretty cold-blooded article and so did the other guys who talked to her. We all figured she wasn't too sane, which, it turned out, she wasn't.

How true her story was, I can't say. Later on, at her trial, the Arizona authorities called her a liar. They said it wasn't self-defense but premeditated murder. They proved to the satisfaction of the jury that she went to see Anne and Sammy with a gun in her pocket on the night of October 16th, that she shot both women and then shot herself in the hand. Motive? Jealousy over the close friendship of her two victims, and jealousy over the attentions paid to them by some of Mrs. Judd's gentlemen friends.

The jury decided she should hang. She was in the death house waiting for the noose when the psychiatrists came to her rescue and called her insane.

Undoubtedly, the psychiatrists were right. All the evidence presented by the state pointed toward insanity. Premeditated or not, the murders were not committed by a normal woman, but by an insanely jealous one.

All of us who worked on the case wanted to keep Mrs. Judd in Los Angeles for trial. Things were dull around the courts at the time. But the boys in Arizona claimed priority and won.

It was Moise's idea that I join the caravan of officers and reporters on that trek to Phoenix. It was Tom Treanor's idea that he go along. He had a good car. I didn't. Moise gave in. Moise said maybe it would be good experience for Tommy. If Tom had stayed home you wouldn't find this squib in the files of one of the newspapers: "That night, in a surprise move, Sheriff McFadden started to Phoenix with her by motor. It was one of the most amazing treks in the annals of the west. Trailed by cars bearing newspapermen, the sheriff's automobile wended its way along shadowy, little-used roads throughout the night –" Why? Here's why.

Amazing is a mild word for that trip. There we were trailing the sheriff's car through the night when we found ourselves at Lake Elsinore.

If you ask any native how to get from Los Angeles to Phoenix he will certainly not mention Lake Elsinore. You just don't go that way. Yet here we were at Lake Elsinore. Someone had blundered.

"Now what do we do?" one of Mrs. Judd's escorts asked.

Mrs. Judd sat back calm and uninterested.

"We keep on this road to San Diego," a reporter suggested.

Tom stepped forward. "No, we don't. We take a short cut. I know a way that will save us hours of driving."

It was late and it was dark and everyone was cold and hungry and Tom sounded like a man who knew the country. They told Tom to lead on. He led.

The road got worse and worse. I was growing dubious. Tom assured me that all short cuts had shortcomings. Around two in the morning a settlement hove in sight. The sheriff honked at us and we stopped. The sheriff, too, was getting dubious. So was everyone else.

"Don't you worry," said Tom. "I know this country like a book. By the way, would you all like something to eat?"

Mrs. Judd said she could use some coffee. Tom disappeared behind one of the darkened buildings. Then things began to happen. Lights went on. Men came running. Stoves were lit. Food was produced. We were, it seemed, at Warner Hot Springs, and the management was more than glad to see us. I thought it odd but I said nothing. Tom kept out of my way.

The sheriff must have thought it odd too because I heard him asking the man who ran the place if we were on the right short cut. The man looked over at Tom and said yes, he guessed we were. If we kept going we'd hit the road to El Centro after a while.

"Isn't there a better way?" asked an officer.

"Not from here, there isn't," said the man.

"Maybe we should have gone to San Diego?"

"You're here," said the man. "So there's no use worrying."

When we got moving again I had it out with Tom. He confessed. This was a short cut of a sort, he said. It took a little longer in time, was all. "Anyway," he said brightly, "my father owns Warner Hot Springs. Think of the publicity we can give the resort in the *Express*."

We lost the caravan at dawn and we never caught up with it. We missed the triumphal return of Winnie Ruth Judd to the scene of the crime.

Just before we hit the El Centro road, a tire went flat. Les Wagner, of the United Press, paused to ask if we needed help. Tom waved him on. The other cars flashed by. Tom got out and opened the turtle back to get his tools. "How do you like that?" he said. "I haven't any jack."

79

That didn't daunt him. He was an inventive fellow and in two hours he rigged up a workable jack out of some rocks and a log and we got the tire changed. We stopped at the first gas station to phone the office. Tom stood at my elbow while I put the call in.

"Remember to mention Warner Hot Springs," he urged. "Tell Moise we went that way to escape the lynch mobs on the main highway."

What else could I do? And that's how the story came out, with a Warner Hot Springs dateline. Whether it brought the resort any extra business or not, I never found out.

Moise was satisfied. He liked the idea of the mobs waiting in the dark. He told us to hurry after Winnie Ruth to be on hand if any stray lynchers got her and we started hurrying. Out of El Centro we ran out of gas and had to push the car two miles. That was because Tom assured me his gas gauge didn't register accurately when it showed empty.

I didn't speak to him from El Centro to Phoenix. When we got there the tumult and the shouting had died. Tom wasn't at all upset. He said I had a good imagination. He said I could probably write a better piece than if I had been on hand. "You have all the expense money," he pointed out. "Let us take a few dollars and get a little whisky. There must be a bootlegger in town."

I refused. I said that any guy who forgot his jack and who let his gas tank run dry didn't deserve a drink. I said I was going to call Moise and suggest that Mr. Treanor be sent back to sacking cement. I called. I didn't get a chance to complain about Tom.

"By the way," said Moise. "Whose idea was that lynchmob story? We had it exclusive. It was a honey."

"Treanor's," I said. "And it was his idea to go around by Warner Hot Springs."

"I knew he'd come through," said Moise. "That boy has the makings of a great reporter. I need you here on rewrite. Give him the expense money and hop a train. He can handle the story from now on."

* * *

In due time, Winnie Ruth was tried, found guilty, then saved by the psychiatrists. They locked her up in the Arizona state hospital and that should have been the end of it. The tumult and the shouting died. Mrs. Judd was forgotten.

Apparently the peace and quiet of the hospital palled on Mrs. Judd. In October of 1939, she turned up missing. Six days later she was found hiding in an orange grove near Tempe.

In December of the same year, Mrs. Judd escaped again. For two weeks police in three states sought her. On the fifteenth of the month, a slim, bedraggled woman, shoeless and unkempt, walked into a drugstore in Yuma and asked for food. The drug clerk recognized her and called the cops and the saga of Mrs. Judd was ended.

"The door was open and I walked out," Mrs. Judd told police. "I kept on walking until I reached Yuma. Here I am."

That was Mrs. Judd's last escape. Since then she's been a model patient, quiet, tractable and good-natured. She seems perfectly satisfied to spend the rest of her life behind the hospital walls. Which is just as well – there's nothing else she can do.

Geoffrey Homes

How We Trapped Al Capone

Where law enforcement is concerned, the imprisonment of Al Capone on tax evasion charges was one of the most important events of the early 1930s. Capone, born in Brooklyn in 1899, had been summoned to Chicago by his boyhood hero Johnny Torrio, who was the chief lieutenant of mobster Big Jim Colosimo. In January 1920, America was turned into a gangsters' paradise by the passing of the Volstead Act, better known as Prohibition. Colosimo lost no time in extending his activities to bootlegging. But in May 1922, Colosimo was shot through the head by an unknown assailant – almost certainly hired by Torrio. It was widely believed that the killer was Al Capone. In November 1924, Torrio arranged the assassination of Irish mobster Dion O'Banion. O'Banion's remaining lieutenants swore vengeance, and in January 1925, Torrio narrowly survived an assassination attempt by Bugs Moran, and decided to return to Italy, leaving Capone in charge of his crime-empire. Capone's men succeeded in killing O'Banion's chief lieutenant, Hymie Weiss, in October 1926. And on February 13, 1929 – St. Valentine's Day – five Capone gangsters, two of them dressed as policemen, marched into Moran's garage and lined up seven men (including an innocent bystander) against the wall, then shot them down. Moran was not among them, but decided to retire. Which left Capone as the most powerful gangster in Chicago, with so many corrupt policemen in his pay that he

was apparently above the law.
Now read on . . .

When my wife and I left Baltimore for Chicago in 1928, all I said was, "Judith, I'm after a fellow named Curly Brown." If I'd told her that Curly Brown was an alias of Scarface Al Capone, she'd have turned the car around then and there and made me take up some respectable trade like piano tuning. My assignment was to find clear proof of income-tax evasion by Capone. In previous years he had filed no tax return or had reported insignificant income.

Art Madden, our Chicago agent-in-charge, told me that hanging an income-tax rap on Alphonse Capone would be as easy as hanging a foreclosure sign on the moon. The Grand Panjandrum of the checkered suits and diamond belts had Cook County in the palm of his hand. He did all his business anonymously, through front men. To discourage meddlers, his production department was turning out fifty corpses a year.

For a base of operations the government gave me and my three assistants an overgrown closet in the old Post Office Building, with a cracked glass at the door, no windows, a double flat-topped desk and peeling walls. I spent months in fruitless investigation through banks, credit agencies and newspaper files.

I prowled the crummy streets of Cicero but could get no clue to show that a dollar from the big gambling places, the horse parlors, the brothels or the bootleg joints ever reached Scarface Al Capone. Jake Lingle, a Chicago *Tribune* reporter, had been seen with Capone in Chicago and Miami and, from the tips I got, he wasn't just writing interviews. So I saw the *Tribune* boss, Robert R. McCormick, and told him Jake Lingle's help would be appreciated by the United States government. "I'll get word to Lingle to go all the way with you," said the colonel. Lingle was assassinated next day in a subway, right in the busiest part of the city.

I was stuck, bogged down. Sixteen frustrating months dragged by. Capone was all over the front pages every day. It was common talk that he got a cut on every case of whiskey brought into Cook County; that he ran a thousand speakeasies, a thousand bookie joints, fifteen gambling houses, a string of brothels; that he controlled half a dozen breweries. He had bought a Florida palace on Palm Island and was spending $1000 a week on banquets. He tore around in sixteen-cylinder limousines, slept in fifty-dollar pajamas and ordered fifteen suits at a time at $135 each. His personal armed forces numbered seven hundred, equipped with automatic weapons and armored automobiles. But evidence of lavish living wasn't enough. The courts had to see *income*.

One night, in a desperate mood, I decided to check over all the data which my three assistants and I had piled up. By one o'clock in the morning I was bleary-eyed, and while gathering up my papers I accidentally bumped into our filing cabinet. It clicked shut. I couldn't find the key anywhere. "Now, where'll I put this stuff?" I wondered. Just outside, in a neighboring storeroom, I found an old filing cabinet full of dusty envelopes. "I can lay this old junk on the table," I thought to myself. "I'll put my own stuff in overnight."

In the back of the cabinet was a heavy package tied in brown paper. Just out of curiosity I snipped the string and found three ledgers, one a "special column cashbook." My eye leaped over the column headings: "Bird cage," "21," "Craps," "Faro," "Roulette," "Horse bets." Here was the diary of a large operation, with a take of from $20,000 to $30,000 a day. Net profits for only eighteen months (the books were dated 1925–26) were over half a million dollars.

"Who could have run a mill that size?" I asked myself. The answer hit me like a baseball bat: only three people – Frankie Lake, Terry Druggan or Al Capone! But I had already cleaned up the Druggan-Lake case. Two from three leaves one.

The ledgers had been picked up in a raid after the murder of Assistant State's Attorney William McSwiggin in 1926. They came from one of the biggest gambling palaces in Cicero, The Ship, where diamond-studded crowds from Chicago laid down $30,000 a year in wagers. Here was a record of *income*. If I could hang it around the neck of Al Capone, we'd have a case at last.

Scarface must have found out that we were closing in. On the inside of the gang I had planted one of the best undercover men I have ever known, Eddie O'Hare. One afternoon word reached me that Eddie wanted to see me at once. When we met, he was red-faced and excited. "You've got to move out of your hotel, Frank. The big fellow has brought in four killers from New York to get you. They know where you keep your automobile and what time you come in and go out. You've got to get out this afternoon!"

"Thanks for tipping me off, Eddie," I replied. So I phoned Judith I had a surprise for her – we were moving to the Palmer House, where she had once said she'd like to live. I left word at my hotel we were going to Kansas and drove to the Union Station – but right on through and around to the Palmer. Judith was completely confused and I hoped Al's torpedoes were, too.

Later Eddie met me with another report: "The big fellow's offering $25,000 reward to anybody who bumps you off!" When the story broke in the papers that Capone had put a price on my head, Judith took it with amazing calm. She simply said, "We're going straight home to Baltimore!" I finally won her over by promising she could be with me as much as possible. Women always think they're bulletproof.

Meanwhile I was working on the handwriting in the ledgers of The Ship. I think we must have collected handwriting samples of every hoodlum in Chicago – from voting registers, savings accounts, police courts. The painful process of elimination finally left me with a character named Lou Shumway, whose writing on a bank deposit slip was a dead twin to that in the ledgers. I heard from a tipster that Shumway was in

Miami, probably working at Hialeah or the dog tracks. All I had to go on was a description: "Shumway is a perfect little gentleman, refined, slight, harmless – not a racetrack sport at all."

In February 1931, I stood by the rail at Hialeah looking at the man I had been stalking for nearly three years. Scarface Al Capone sat in a box with a jeweled moll on either side of him, smoking a long cigar, greeting a parade of fawning sycophants who came to shake his hand. I looked upon his pudgy olive face, his thick pursed lips, the rolls of fat descending from his chin – and the scar, like a heavy pencil line across his cheek. When a country constable wants a man, I thought, he just walks up and says, "You're pinched." Here I was, with the whole U.S. government behind me, as powerless as a canary.

Two nights later, I spotted the "perfect little gentleman" my tipster had described, working at a dog track. I tailed him home, and picked him up next morning as he was having breakfast with his wife. He turned pale green. When I got him to the Federal Building, I said cold-turkey: "I am investigating the income-tax liability of one Alphonse Capone."

Gentleman Lou turned greener yet, but he pulled himself together and said, "Oh, you're mistaken. I don't know Al Capone."

I put my hand on his shoulder. "Lou," I said, "you have only two choices: If you refuse to play ball with me, I will send a deputy marshal to look for you at the track, ask for you by name and serve a summons on you. You get the point, Lou. As soon as the gang knows the government has located you, they will probably decide to bump you off so you can't testify.

"If you don't like that idea, Lou, come clean. Tell the truth about these ledgers. You were bookkeeper at The Ship. You can identify every entry in these books – and you can tell who your boss was. I'll guarantee to keep it secret until the day of the trial that you are playing ball with me.

You will be guarded day and night, and I'll guarantee that Mrs. Shumway will not become a widow." Lou quivered like a harp string but finally gave in. I spirited him out of Miami and hid him in California.

But we still had to show that *income* actually reached the pockets of Al Capone. A painstaking checkup on all the recorded money transactions in Cicero finally showed that one "J. C. Dunbar" had brought gunnysacks full of cash to the Pinkert State Bank and bought $300,000 in cashier's checks.

Agent Nels Tessem and I caught up with "Dunbar," whose real name was Fred Ries, in St. Louis. We tailed a messenger boy with a special-delivery letter and slapped a subpoena in Ries's palm. He was annoyed, especially since the letter was from Capone's headquarters telling him to flee to Mexico. He wouldn't talk at first. But after a week in a special vermin-ridden cell in a jail we picked out for him – we knew he had a pathological fear of bugs – Ries cried uncle. We sneaked him before a Chicago grand jury in the middle of the night. His testimony put the profits of The Ship squarely in the pockets of Scarface Al! I packed my scowling little treasure off to South America with government agents to guard him until we should need him in court.

In the autumn of 1931, two weeks before the Capone trial, Eddie O'Hare reported to me: "Capone's boys have a complete list of the prospective jurors. They're fixing them one by one – passing out thousand-dollar bills, promising political jobs, giving donations to churches. They're using muscle, too, Frank." Eddie handed me a list of ten names and addresses. "They're right off the jury list – names 30 to 39!"

Next morning I went with U.S. Attorney George E. Q. Johnson to the chambers of Federal Judge James H. Wilkerson, who was to sit in the Capone trial. The judge was reassuring – somehow he seemed like a match for Scarface Al. Sure enough, the ten names Eddie had given me tallied with the judge's list. But the judge didn't seem ruffled. He said calmly, "Bring your case into court as planned, gentlemen. Leave the rest to me."

The day the trial started, I fought my way through reporters, photographers and sob sisters. Al Capone came into the courtroom in a mustard-colored suit and sat down at the counsel table just a few feet from me. Phil D'Andrea, Al's favorite bodyguard, sat beside him, sneering at the crowd. As Judge Wilkerson entered in his black robe, Capone, behind the mask of his moonface, seemed to be snickering over the jury of new-found friends and intimidees who would soon send him back to the overlordship of Chicago.

Judge Wilkerson called his bailiff to the bench. He said in crisp, low tones, "Judge Edwards has another trial commencing today. Go to his courtroom and bring me his entire panel of jurors. Take my entire panel to Judge Edwards." The switch was so smooth, so simple. Capone's face clouded with the black despair of a gambler who had made his final raise – and lost.

The trial marched on. My gems, Gentleman Lou Shumway and the bug-bedeviled Ries, stood their ground on the witness stand, though Capone and Phil D'Andrea were staring holes through them the entire time. I kept my eyes on D'Andrea. When he got up to stretch during a recess I could have sworn I saw a bulge in his right hip pocket. But no, I thought, there wasn't a crumb in the world who would dare to bring a gun into federal court. I saw him stretch again. I had the boys send in word that a reporter wanted to see him. I followed him out of the courtroom. Nels Tessem and Jay Sullivan, my colleagues, led him down the corridor. As we passed Judge Wilkerson's chambers I shoved him inside. "Give me that gun!" I snapped. D'Andrea handed it over. "Give me those bullets!" He ladled out a handful of ammunition.

Judge Wilkerson interrupted the trial to cite D'Andrea for contempt and send him away for six months. Capone growled, "I don't care what happens to D'Andrea. He's a damn fool. I don't care if he gets ten years." Al was cracking.

The trial wound up in mid-October. As the jury returned I felt sure we had won. "Gentlemen," intoned Judge Wilkerson, "what is your verdict?"

"Guilty!" The courtroom broke up like a circus after the last performance. Reporters ran out of court. Lawyers ran. Mobsters ran. Everybody seemed to be running but Scarface Al Capone. He slumped forward as if a blackjack had hit him.

When I got home, Judith cried, "You did it! I knew you were going to do it all the time!" Then she sighed. "Now can we go back to Baltimore?"

Frank J. Wilson

The Ma Barker Gang

In the mid-1950s, Kurt Singer, a distinguished bio-grapher of, among others, Goering and Hemingway, had the excellent idea of persuading leading police-men from all countries to write about "my greatest crime story". The volume of that title was so successful that he went on to compile a second volume, *My Strangest Case*. This contains some classic first-hand accounts of crimes, including the following chapter on the Ma Barker gang written by J. Edgar Hoover. During the 1930s and 40s, Hoover was probably the most famous policeman in the world. Born in 1895, John Edgar Hoover became a clerk in the Department of Justice, and was appointed head of the Enemy Aliens Regis-tration Department during World War One. After the war, his job was "Red hunting" – for the 1917 revolution in Russia had set off one of America's periodic outbursts of violent anti-communism. His success in arresting and deporting communists and anarchists led to his appointment, in August 1921, to the newly-formed Federal Bureau of Investi-gation. Hoover became head of the Bureau in 1924, at the age of 29. He soon organised the FBI into a formidable unit, and in the 1930s, used it with deadly effect against the new breed of bank robbers and gangsters – Ma Barker, Machine Gun Kelly, Pretty Boy Floyd, Baby Face Nelson, John Dillinger – who were spawned by the Great Depression that followed the Stock Market Crash of 1929. Hoover died in 1972.

This account of the end of the Barker gang forms

an interesting companion-piece to Frank Wilson's account of the downfall of Al Capone.

They never came any tougher than "Ma" Barker and her brood, and that goes, too, for the other half of the gang – the hoods led by Alvin Karpis. I should know, for I helped to hunt them and, finally, to eliminate them. Of all public enemies they were unquestionably the vilest – a throng of wanton killers, vicious, depraved and incredibly ruthless.

We know all about murder and its motives at the Federal Bureau of Investigation, and possess the records of many men and women who have killed often and inhumanly but yet had a side to their nature that was not wholly despicable.

It is something that cannot be said of "Ma" Barker, her four sons and Karpis, and the mobsters they commanded. Without a single exception they were monsters, and pity was a word of which they had never heard. They moved in a welter of blood; mail robberies, bank hold-ups, kidnapping and pitched machinegun battles; they loved nothing better than to kill a police officer, and if some innocent bystander fell to the same hail of bullets that did not matter either. They executed their own traitors, bought over unfaithful police officials, "fixed" paroles and prison breaks. Their anarchy fouled the very roots of law and order.

I remember their heyday and the various impressions I received from the tortuous investigation, the interrogation of witnesses, and the study of reports which came in from special agents all over the country. "Ma" Barker, for instance, renting an apartment from an unsuspecting landlord, knowing that if he looked into her hard eyes he would guess the truth; a drunken doctor shaving the fingertips of a crazed hoodlum no longer under an anaesthetic; Karpis, the slit-eyed killer, explaining how he was going to wipe out top F.B.I. agents in Los Angeles, Chicago, New York and myself in Washington by using automobiles and planes, and hating it like hell because somebody had called him a rat;

an afternoon search in St Paul when we were sure we had the gang dead to rights and a flood of sound unexpectedly broke out – church bells, kids yelling and a dog howling.

Yes, Alvin Karpis, otherwise Francis Albin Karpavicz, had dreams of gunning the F.B.I., and never more vivid than at the moment we grabbed him.

So intensely did the Barker-Karpis alliance live by the gun that it is impossible to give an orderly picture of their stained history. They intertwined murder with corruption, but it is probably right to ascribe to "Ma" Barker the gang's inspiration for organised crime. She was born Arizona Donnie Clark of very mixed blood – Scots, Irish and Indian. She grew up in the Ozarks, the wild, mountainous region of Missouri and among people who were as stark as the scenery. She is supposed to have coached her four sons, Herman, Lloyd, Fred and Arthur, on the principle of how to do business with bankers – with a tommy-gun. But in the beginning she herself had no criminal experience on which to draw. She indulged them, though, wilfully and wickedly, and it is beyond dispute that the four Barker boys owed their criminal careers to their mother. She was both resourceful and ruthless and they looked to her for inspiration and guidance, if those are terms which can be used in respect to a she-wolf and her vicious whelps.

A theme that repeats itself with great frequency in the Barker-Karpis combination is the strength it derived from friendships that took root in various penitentiaries and Federal prisons. For example, Fred Barker and Karpis learned to understand and admire each other while both were imprisoned in the Kansas State Penitentiary. Karpis, allegedly dubbed "Old Creepy" because of the feeling he inspired in other mobsters with his cold, fishy stare, was smart enough to take advantage of conditions in Kansas. Convicts assigned to the coal-mines there were rewarded for extra production by having days lopped off their time, but Karpis found that working alongside him were a number of lifers.

It did not take him long to figure that for these men there was no incentive. They could, however, be stimulated into more active mining with money and such small services as he was able to render, and soon Karpis was buying the extra coal output of a half-dozen lifers and thus appreciably shortening his own sentence.

It was the kind of trick that appealed to Fred Barker, and their jail friendship was translated into a partnership on their liberation, and they committed their first murder together. It was a cowardly affair. Two days before, they had used a De Soto to pull off a robbery, and when Sheriff C. R. Kelly, of West Plains, Missouri, saw the car in a garage he recognised it as suspect. He walked over to question the occupants and was cut down by a blast of gunfire before he could draw his own weapon.

Fred Barker, Karpis, "Ma" Barker and her paramour, Arthur V. Dunlop (alias George Anderson), occupied a cottage in Thayer, Missouri, but with the murder of the sheriff they fled to St Paul, leaving behind their latest haul. They took over a furnished house, and had not long settled in when they were joined by William Weaver, known variously as "Phoenix Donald" and "Lapland Willie." Weaver had been paroled from Oklahoma State Penitentiary, where he had been serving a life sentence for murder during a bank robbery, and where he had met "Doc" Barker and Volney Davis, jointly convicted for the slaying of a night watchman.

"Ma" Barker and Karpis were satisfied with Weaver's credentials, but although the gang lived quietly, and as inconspicuously as possible, it was noticed that whenever they left the house together one of them carried a violin case. All five knew how to play the instrument inside, but it didn't make them musicians!

It was uncanny the way the Barker-Karpis gang throughout its lifetime was able to smell danger before it was too late. When the St Paul police raided their hide-out early one morning it was to find an empty house. It had been a hasty departure, and for some reason we were never able to discover they decided that Arthur Dunlop was a squealer. The day after the gang left St Paul Dunlop's nude, bullet-riddled body was found on the shores of a lake near Webster, Wisconsin. Close by was a woman's blood-stained glove.

Kansas City was the next stop, and here the gang was reinforced by the addition of Thomas Holden and a fellow mobster, both of whom had escaped from Leavenworth; Harvey Bailey, a notorious bank robber; Larry DeVol and Bernard Phillips, a renegade policeman turned bank bandit. In June a bank at Fort Scott fell to the gang and some of the loot was used to stage an elaborate "Welcome Home" party for a classmate of Fred Barker at Kansas State Penitentiary.

The celebrations had not long been over when late in the afternoon of July 7th, 1932, F.B.I. special agents stepped out from some bushes surrounding the Old Mission Golf Course and put the bracelets on Holden, Bailey and another gangster. The other member of the foursome, Bernard Phillips, happened to be absent when these arrests took place and went streaking with the news to "Ma" Barker. The gang took off in such haste for St Paul that a raiding party found they had left their quarters just as dinner was about to be served!

St Paul once more – and another murder! It stemmed from the arrest of Harvey Bailey, who was tried for participation in the Fort Scott bank robbery. He was defended by J. Earl Smith, a criminal attorney of Tulsa, Oklahoma, but the evidence against him was too strong and he was convicted. Shortly afterwards a mysterious telephone call lured Attorney Smith to the vicinity of the lonely Indian Hills Country Club, fourteen miles north of Tulsa. The following morning Smith's body was found, full of bullet holes.

To offset casualties that occurred for one reason or another the gang was ever on the look-out for new recruits, but they had to measure up to tough requirements. During the next few weeks two newcomers were roped in, Earl Christman, confidence man wanted in several states, and Frank Nash, who had slipped out of Leavenworth. Christman brought his moll with him. They took part in an audacious daylight raid on the Cloud County Bank at Concordia, Kansas, that yielded over 240,000 dollars.

With all this coin to play with the Barker-Karpis organisation turned to the task of springing some of its old hands now tucked away. It was successful in getting "Doc" Barker paroled from the Oklahoma State Penitentiary and in securing from the same institution an incomprehensible "two years leave of absence" for Volney Davis. An attempt to secure the release of Lloyd Barker, another brother, doing twenty-five years in Leavenworth for mail robbery, failed.

Looking for Christmas money the gang descended on Minneapolis and murdered three in taking the Third North-Western Bank for a heavy score. Two policemen who got in their way were chopped down by machine-gun fire, and, as they were about to leave, one of the Barker-Karpis mob thought a civilian was trying to memorise the licence number of their automobile. He too died from a stream of hot lead.

It was in Reno, Nevada, that the gang holed up to enjoy the stolen money, and while there Volney Davis made a trip to Missouri to pick up his favourite moll, who had escaped from a Mid-Western penitentiary. She stayed with Davis when the mob shifted its headquarters first to St Paul and in April of the following year to Chicago, from which city they struck successfully at the Fairbury National Bank, Fairbury, Nebraska.

In this raid, however, Earl Christman was so badly wounded that he was rushed to the home of Verne Miller. He died despite medical care and one night was secretly buried. Christman's mother wanted to know where her son's body rested, but nobody would tell her.

It was about this time that Fred Barker began to yearn for a mate, and found one in the widow of a well-known bank robber killed while following his "profession." She had a history that satisfied even "Ma" Barker.

Either Christman's death or a belief that it had got into a rut persuaded the gang that new ideas were needed, and a fling was taken at kidnapping. The first victim was William A. Hamm, junior, of the Hamm Brewing Company, St Paul. The ransom collected was 100,000 dollars, and those who played the principal parts in the snatch were Fred and "Doc" Barker, Karpis, Charles J. Fitzgerald and a widely known underworld character – Fred Goetz, alias "Shotgun Zeigler," purportedly a former engineering student and football star at a Mid-Western university.

Wherever the gang moved it cast a shadow of murder, and two further slayings were added in quick succession to the lengthening list. In a stick-up of the Stockyards National Bank, South St Paul, a police officer was killed outright and another crippled for life; the loot was 30,000 dollars. In Chicago the mob pounced on two bank messengers, but again they got very little, and in fleeing became involved in a minor mishap with their car. Unaware of the robbery which had taken place only a few minutes earlier, Patrolman Miles A. Cunningham approached the bandit car at an intersection on Jackson Boulevard to inquire into the accident. Without warning he was blasted to death with a machine-gun.

By the end of the year the mob, now idling in Reno again, was more motley than ever. "Ma" Barker was there and so, too, was Fred, with the widow of the bank robber, who still stuck to him. A seasoned shoplifter had teamed up with William Weaver and Karpis, Volney Davis and Fred Goetz had their molls with them. Towards the end of the year all of them set out for St Paul. They had planned to rob the Commercial State Bank, but on the way they got another idea. Instead of a hold-up – the danger was great and the reward uncertain – why not snatch the bank president, Edward George Brenner? The task would be much easier and it would open the bank vaults for whatever sum they demanded.

On the night of January 13th the gang gathered at the apartment of William Weaver and his paramour for a final check-up. Everything had been worked out, and those who were to do the job were soon able to leave. But as they drew away from the kerb another car, containing several men, one of them in uniform, fell in behind them. One of the bandits yelled "It's the cops" and instantly guns began to blaze. The bandit car sped away at last, leaving behind two badly wounded employees of Northwest Airways – the "cops" the gang thought they had spotted.

This fiasco did not upset the original plan, it only delayed it, and four days later five members of the Barker-Karpis outfit "took" Brenner as he halted his car at a street signal after dropping his nine-year-old daughter at a private school. There followed almost a month of complicated negotiations, with the F.B.I. keeping close watch but deferring to the family wish to effect the bank president's release before taking action. The gang collected 200,000 dollars in five- and ten-dollar bills. Brenner was then released in the vicinity of Rochester, Minnesota.

It was at this juncture that things began to get complicated for the gang. Fred Goetz offended some of his gangland pals and was executed by two blasts from a shotgun which blew off his face. There is no evidence to show if it was the vengeance of the Barker-Karpis mob, but it was certainly effective! Soon the strain of associating with the mob – their unbridled violence and the frenzy of escaping from one hide-out to another to avoid the special agents they knew were hunting them – proved too much for Goetz's moll. She became deranged and was placed in an asylum.

Converting the hot Hamm and Brenner snatch money to clean bills was a problem far from easy to solve, and the tortuous negotiations and fixing that were required almost transcend belief.

First to offer assistance was a suspect Chicago politician and ward heeler known as "Boss" McLaughlin. He was not too bright, though, and our special agents picked him up in quick time. His wife telegraphed both the President of the United States and the Attorney-General protesting against his arrest. Nevertheless, McLaughlin stayed in jail.

Next to be recruited to handle the hot money was a certain Dr Joseph P. Moran, who had once served time for abortion and of late had looked after any hood who needed his services. In turn Dr Moran got his nephew to help him, and apparently the arrangement was that Dr Moran would get hold of enough of the ransom funds to put his nephew through medical school!

Yet a third character emerged in the negotiations. He was a fifty-year-old Chicago gambler with connections reaching all the way to Havana. He managed to exchange nearly 100,000 dollars of the tainted money for Cuban gold, which a well-known bank then converted into one-thousand-dollar American bills at a discount of a quarter of one per cent!

During this time Dr Moran (he was to disappear later, and according to reliable underworld reports his weighted body was dumped by his "pals" into Lake Erie) operated on Fred Barker and Alvin Karpis in an attempt to obliterate their fingerprints and change their looks. Both realised time was running out, but what they suffered on the operating table did no good. They could not hide their identity as public enemies; they nor other members of the gang for whom there was no escape from justice.

Volney Davis, "Doc" Barker and Harry Campbell also underwent the agonisingly painful Moran "refresher" treatment to no avail. The gang did not stay in one place long. They doubled back on their tracks, dodged to this city and that county, but they could not throw off the pursuit of F.B.I. agents and decided to split up into small units. They then scattered to locations as widely separated as Glasgow (Montana), Allandale (Florida), Las Vegas, Miami, Cleveland and Havana. It was the beginning of the end.

On the night of January 8th, 1935, special agents arrested "Doc" Barker in Chicago. He was traced through a woman with whom he had become infatuated. When the apartment of the couple was searched a sub-machine-gun was found which had been stolen from a guard at the time of the St Paul payroll robbery.

The same night special agents surrounded the apartment occupied by Russell Gibson and another mobster and their girl friends. Ordered to surrender, all but Gibson complied. Armed with a Browning and a Colt automatic he tried to get out through a rear door, but it was being watched. Gibson fired and missed, and that was the end of him. As his body was carted to the morgue the F.B.I. were collecting a small arsenal inside the apartment.

Oddly enough, it was an alligator which put the finger on "Ma" and Fred Barker! In "Doc" Barker's apartment agents found a map of Florida and a circle round Ocala and Lake Weir. Earlier they had been tipped off that mother and son were hiding out in some southern area that sheltered an ancient alligator known to the natives as "Old Joe." Now they knew for certain, and at five-thirty on a crisp January morning, with the mists hanging over Lake Weir, a picked group of special agents surrounded a cottage on the shore in which "Ma" Barker and her son were holed up.

"We are special agents of the Federal Bureau of Investigation," called out the leader. "I'm talking to you, Kate Barker, and you, Fred Barker. Come out one at a time and with your hands up!"

Further commands were issued, but in the cottage all was silent. The minutes ticked by, and once again the Barkers were ordered to come out singly, unless they wanted to be driven out by tear gas and any other means deemed necessary.

After fifteen minutes "Ma" Barker shouted: "All right, go ahead!" For a moment it looked as if mother and son had decided to throw in their hands, but then a machine-gun began to speak from the house and it swept the surrounding trees and tore into the undergrowth. It sparked off a battle that went on for hours. Tear-gas bombs were tossed into the cottage and a deadly fire from automatics was concentrated on the firing points within. It was a fight to a deadly finish, and when the F.B.I. were at last able to enter the cottage they found "Ma" Barker dead, still grasping a machine-gun in her left hand. Fred was doubled over in death, a .45 Colt automatic beside his stiffening body.

There was enough ironware in the cottage to keep a regiment at bay; two Thompson sub-machine-guns, Browning .12 gauge shotgun, Remington shotgun, two .45 automatics, two Winchester rifles and a .38 Colt automatic, along with machine-gun drums, automatic-pistol clips and ammunition for every weapon.

There was a letter, too, from "Doc" Barker, in which he wrote: "I took care of that business for you boys. It was done just as good as if you had did it yourself. I am just like Standard Oil – always at your service. Ha, ha!"

"That business" referred to by "Doc" was, as to be expected, a slight case of murder! The victim, if such a term can be used, was William J. Harrison, who had moved within the orbit of the Capone syndicate before he joined the Barker-Karpis mob. Later his reliability became suspect, and from his Florida hole Fred Barker had ordered Harrison's execution. "Doc" Barker had seen to it. They took Harrison to an abandoned barn near Ontarioville in Illinois on a wild, dark night and shot him. The body, and the barn itself, was then saturated with paraffin and a match was tossed in.

As the F.B.I. ring narrowed Alvin Karpis and Harry Campbell, with their women, scuttled from Miami to Atlantic City. There a gun battle with the police took place and Karpis and his crony came temporarily to rest in Toledo, Ohio. Meanwhile, Volney Davis was picked up by special agents in St Louis. He was found to be carrying a counterfeit hundred-dollar bill, and was quick to explain that he "wasn't shoving the queer." He carried the bill with him, he said, to offer as a bribe should he be arrested by law-enforcement officers!

One of the gang surrendered in Kansas after a gun fight,

and then William Weaver and his moll were cornered and captured in a house in Allandale, Florida. Although the Barker-Karpis organisation had not merely been split open but virtually destroyed, Karpis and Campbell still had some fight left in them, as can be seen from what followed. It was so fantastic that it is hardly believable.

Karpis picked up a few hoods, among them several ex-convicts, and a gambler who must have believed in his luck. On April 24th, 1935, three heavily armed raiders pounced on a mail truck at Warren, Ohio, and got away with 70,000 dollars and then pulled off a robbery worth 30,000 dollars against the Erie train – Detroit to Pittsburgh. Introduced was a new tactic in robbery – the thieves escaped by aeroplane.

These exploits were followed by an alliance that only a script writer could dream up. Karpis and his crony fled to Hot Springs, Arkansas, where they were afforded protection by the chief of police and the chief of detectives. While an F.B.I. "wanted" poster for leaders of the mob aged and yellowed in the very centre of the jail door at Hot Springs, Karpis and his pals roamed at will through the streets of the spa. Nor was that all, for Karpis bedded up with an adroit woman who not only kept him happy, but also one of the law-enforcement officers as well. She divided her time between the two and owed her vast experience to the fact that she had begun operating brothels at the age of seventeen.

Eventually Hot Springs became a little too warm for Karpis. He was well aware he was being hunted, and in the early part of 1936 he again got on the move. With him was a crony who brought his girl along – a twenty-one-year-old prostitute. This time Karpis's destination was New Orleans, and although he may have thought he had again slipped the net it was in that city he had a rendezvous with justice!

Evil and merciless, Karpis had dealt out so much death that he had every reason to declare, as he had often done, that he would never be taken alive. We knew he was a problem, and planned the raid carefully. It was approximately five-fifteen in the afternoon of May 1st, 1936. Four assistants and myself were to enter by the front door. Other squads were deployed at each side of the building and at the rear. We were about to move in when a man on a horse moved into the lane beside the through traffic.

We waited, anxious to avoid attention, until the horseman had passed down the street. Now was the time for action, but then two men stepped from the doorway and walked briskly down the steps. We recognised Alvin Karpis and his crony. As they made their way towards their car, a little boy on a bicycle scooted between the pair and our vantage-point. We did not want the child hurt, as he might be if shooting started at that moment, so we moved out and hurried forward, calling for the surrender of the fugitives as they were getting into the car.

Perhaps Karpis had come to believe in his own indestructibility. I am sure he had never expected to meet the top G-man and a squad of what he had been pleased to call "sissy" agents. His expression was divided between amazement and fright and his colour was ashen. Neither he nor his shaking companion raised as much as a finger. There was no gunplay, not the remotest chance of any. Like all their breed they derived their courage from getting the drop on their victims. When they were on the wrong end of a gun the fight went out of them – as it does with every hoodlum, who is a coward at heart. Karpis told me that he thought he would never be taken alive – but then Karpis did not know Karpis.

Six days after his arrest we picked up the rest of the gang in Toledo. It was the end of an era of violence.

J. Edgar Hoover

1932

Crime of the African Crater

It would be a pity to confine a book of this kind to famous crimes of Europe and America, as though other parts of the world did not exist. Benjamin Bennett's *Famous South African Murders* appeared in 1938, and contains some fascinating cases, including that of Detective Coetzee, who turned murderer when a girl with whom he had become involved tried to convince him that he was the father of her unborn child, and the account of the serial "killer of the White Mountain." Most of the cases in the book are too long to include here, but the rather odd "crime of the African crater" – presumably a sex crime – is an interesting example.

N akuru, a little town in Kenya, hard by the shores of a lake, surrounded by mountains, sloping pastures and extinct volcanoes, awoke on the morning of Saturday, October 8, 1932, with misgiving.

For thirty-six hours three of its young people had been missing. Unaccountably. They left Nakuru by car on Thursday evening, October 6, presumably to visit a cinema, and were seen driving along the Eldama Ravine Road.

Then they had vanished as though into thin air. When they failed to return the first night, it was believed they were staying with friends. But this was soon disproved. They were not in Nakuru.

The blue Chevrolet in which they set out had not been seen

on any of the roads in the neighbourhood, or even farther afield. The possibility of their organizing an impromptu hunting-trip to popular Lake Baringo was considered – and ruled out.

Driving the car was Charles William Ross, nineteen-year-old son of the late Major Ross, soldier and noted big-game hunter of British East Africa. Educated in his early years at a school in England, he had gone to live in Kenya in 1927, and was employed by the Kenya Farmers' Association, whose headquarters were at Nakuru.

Ross's companions were two young women, Margaret Keppie and Winifred Stevenson. Miss Keppie, a qualified chemist and druggist and member of the Pharmaceutical Society, had arrived in Kenya four months previously from Leeds, England, where she lived with her parents. She first joined the Nairobi firm of Messrs. Howse & McGeorge and was transferred to the Nakuru branch. A week before, her engagement to a fellow employee was announced.

"Winnie" Stevenson, twenty years of age, was the daughter of Mr Harry Stevenson, known in Nairobi, capital of Kenya, as Harry Venson, entertainer. A bright, vivacious girl and accomplished linguist, speaking the native languages of Swahili and Kikuyu fluently, she was generally understood to be Ross's sweetheart. He was known to be devoted to her.

Anxious consultations were held among the parents and friends of the missing trio as Friday passed without word or trace of them. Anxiety gave way to alarm when the strange tales of Ross's eccentricities and unusual behaviour were revived. Though mostly shy and reserved in the company of women, he was said to have exhibited vicious sexual tendencies which, apparently, were satisfied only by sadistic frenzies or indulgence in orgies of bloodshed.

A story was told of his stabbing of animals after he had shot them and then smearing himself with the blood.

He was accustomed, as well, to wander off by himself and mingle with the natives of the Colony, converse with them in their own dialects and participate in their quaint customs. The men of one tribe called him their young "White Chief".

The police were called in and interviewed Ross's stepfather, Major Matthew W. Whitridge, at his home, Maji Mazuri, some miles from Nakuru. He was unable to enlighten them. But he instructed Gordon, Charles Ross's twenty-one-year-old brother, to drive along the Eldama Ravine Road on his motor-cycle and keep a look-out for the blue Chevrolet.

About seven miles from Maji Mazuri he found his brother. Dressed in a navy blue suit and light blue shirt, he was grimy and dishevelled as though he had spent several days in the open. Ross did not seem at all surprised when his brother rode up and alighted.

He pointed to the car. It was ditched. "Can't get the bus out," he remarked casually, "and I have been pottering around here."

Not a word did he volunteer about his two companions. Together the brothers attempted to reverse the car out of the ditch on to the road. The engine roared and strained, but the wheels would not grip. They waited in vain for a passing motorist to come to their assistance. In desperation, Gordon Ross suggested that he ride into Nakuru and arrange for a car to haul the Chevrolet on to the road.

His brother point-blank refused. "What's the use of going down there?" he asked evasively. "Let's potter around here a bit longer."

He seemed strangely preoccupied and disinclined to leave the neighbourhood. Finally, however, he consented and agreed to be driven home on the motor-cycle. On the journey, Gordon Ross told his brother that Assistant Police Inspector May was making inquiries about the disappearance of Miss Keppie and Miss Stevenson. The news did not appear to disturb or interest him unduly.

"I didn't go out with them," he rejoined, "and I know

nothing about their disappearance. I was just coming back home from Nakuru."

The motor-cycle trip continued to within three miles of Maji Mazuri. The road was rough and both driver and passenger were severely jolted. Charles Ross asked to be allowed to walk the remainder of the distance. His brother pulled up for him to dismount, then pressed on alone to report to Major Whitridge. He returned to escort Ross home.

About half an hour later Major Whitridge, keeping observation on the road, saw the two approaching. He stood behind the door and waited. As Charles Ross entered he gripped his arm and demanded to know whether he was armed. For a moment the youth hesitated, then, shrugging his shoulders, replied, "Yes, I am."

"Disarm him, Gordon," said Major Whitridge, holding Charles Ross so that he was powerless to draw his revolver. Gordon ran his hands through his brother's pockets and found a revolver with six .32 cartridges in the chambers. Major Whitridge pocketed it.

"Now," he demanded, "what did you do with the two girls you took out on Thursday night?" The family had by then gathered in the dining-room. Mrs Whitridge, too, begged her son to tell where he had left the companions of his Thursday night drive.

He had not the remotest idea where they were, he replied, and had gone out shooting "for a party". "If Winnie Stevenson was with me she could have driven the car home herself," he added impatiently.

"You are responsible for the girls you took in the car," Major Whitridge rejoined, "and the police have been here making inquiries and looking for you. You will accompany me at once to Inspector May."

"But I tell you I can't remember taking the girls out at all," young Ross persisted. "And I'm not going to Inspector May either. If he wants to see me, he can come here."

After further argument and persuasion, Ross agreed to

accompany his stepfather and brother to the police camp at Eldama Ravine, near Nakuru. They reached the camp at 3.15 on the Saturday afternoon. Ross was handed over to Assistant Inspector A. Poskitt and detained.

News of young Ross's reappearance was communicated to the Nakuru police. A search-party scouring the country-side hastened to the spot where the Chevrolet was found ditched.

Among the searchers was Mr M. Ritchie, the Nakuru manager of Messrs. Howse & McGeorge. Working his way carefully to the bottom of a ravine below a forty-foot cliff, he came across the body of his employee, Margaret Keppie. She was shot through the head and had evidently been dead some time.

The body was removed to Nakuru. Fears for Winnie Stevenson grew apace. Every inch of ground at the foot of the cliff and in the vicinity of the ravine was combed. Yet not the slightest trace was found of the second girl when darkness fell on Saturday and ended the day's painstaking search.

On the Sunday nearly every man in Nakuru and many of the women and children banded themselves into search-parties. The authorities instructed members of the Nakuru section of the Kenya Defence Force to assist, and requested the trackers of a native tribe, who knew the countryside well, to organize a separate party.

The murder of Miss Keppie and the futile efforts to trace Miss Stevenson roused the whole of Kenya. An aeroplane left Nairobi to survey the Nakuru area from the air.

One of the search-parties in the bush stumbled across a camping-place that seemed to have a sinister link with the tragedy. There were the remains of a fire, a quantity of fresh provisions, a number of shawls, articles of women's clothing and toilet requisites. All appeared to be brand new and recently deposited. A revolver and two empty cartridge cases lay on the ground. From a nearby tree dangled a piece of rope.

Had Ross camped there? If so, at whom was the second shot fired? Could Winnie Stevenson have suffered the fate of her companion? The search went on, grimly, tirelessly.

Back at Nakuru on the Sunday afternoon the body of Margaret Keppie was borne to a little chapel covered with Golden Shower under the lea of the great hill where her life was taken. Rain fell as the coffin was lowered in a shower of beautiful flowers.

Darkness came on once more. Monday dawned. Nakuru was deserted. European business men, Indian bazaar merchants, clerks and official left shops, offices and desks to continue the search. Women carried on what work and business there was to be done.

Ross was charged before the Nakuru Resident Magistrate with the murder of Miss Keppie and kept under strict guard in goal. He refused to reveal where Miss Stevenson was, maintaining stubbornly and impatiently that he knew nothing of her movements.

The police, in a despairing effort to ascertain the prisoner's movements on the Thursday night, issued a notice:

"Will any person who saw an aluminium box body Chevrolet motor-car with a blue bonnet, number B 8633, between 8.45 p.m. on Thursday, October 6, and 11 a.m. on Saturday, October 8, communicate at once with the police at Nakuru or Nairobi.

"The car may have travelled on any road within a radius of 150 miles from Nakuru. It probably contained three passengers.

"Information is still urgently sought by the police as to the whereabouts of Miss Winnie Stevenson, missing from her home at Nakuru since the evening of Thursday, October 6."

As the days passed without the efforts of the searchers meeting the slightest success, the people of the town became incensed against the youth who maintained an obstinate silence and an air of unconcern when, it seemed certain, he alone could clear up the mystery and spare the parents of Miss Stevenson untold agony.

The rumblings of anger swelled. There was talk of "rushing" the gaol and of submitting Ross to a public third-degree grilling. To avoid the possibility of the townsfolk taking the law into their own hands, the police decided to remove their prisoner to Nairobi.

Before he left Nakuru, however, the authorities allowed Winnie Stevenson's mother to see Ross in his cell and plead with him to tell her the fate of her daughter. Her entreaties had no effect. He simply did not know, he declared, and that was the end of it.

After she had been led away, sobbing, Ross ate a hearty meal and that night slept peacefully as an innocent child, not like one loaded down with a ghastly secret he feared the world to know.

When the search-parties and pilots began to despair of ever solving the riddle of Miss Stevenson's disappearance, hopes were suddenly revived. A woman of the Kikuyu tribe, named Mukenye, who was credited with much success in her practice of witchcraft and divination, proclaimed that she had a clue for the white people. Two European women from Nakuru and then a reporter visited her to hear her claims.

Crooning weirdly, she poured oil and water into the palm of her hand. Thus aiding her divinations, she croaked out her discovery. Margaret Keppie, she said, had been shot on the Saturday morning, but her companion lay in the Menengai crater. She was alive – but completely hidden.

"None can save her," said Mukenye oracularly, "except one man."

The Menengai crater, close to Lake Nakuru, home of many flamingos, is almost nine miles in diameter, and commands from its rim a view of Rift Valley. The saucer-like walls contain great crevices, and thick jungle growth makes progress difficult. Though many scoffed at the native woman's psychic claims and directions, over a thousand people from Nakuru scoured the Menengai crater on Thursday, October 13, from dawn to dusk.

The great body of searchers split up into two sections one working round the crater lip to the south, and the other to the north. Not a thought was given to personal inconvenience and the peril from deadly snakes infesting the crater.

But reluctantly even the warmest supporters of Mukenye were forced to admit that she had put them on a false trail.

Eventually Ross, yielding to persuasion, and tired of putting off his questioners, agreed to show where his sweetheart was. Late on Friday night, October 14, he was taken from the Nairobi prison, handcuffed and, under armed guard, escorted back to Nakuru.

The following morning he directed Mr Neil Stewart, Superintendent of the C.I.D., and Mr S. L. Vincent, Assistant Superintendent of Police, Nakuru, to a secluded spot off the main road, just outside the Menengai crater. Beneath a coating of leaves and grass lay the decomposed body of Winnie Stevenson.

She had been shot to death within a mile of her home. Her family and friends passed near the spot daily.

Ross then asked to be allowed to dictate a statement. On the return of the party to Nakuru he appeared before the District Commissioner and admitted his crimes in these words:

"I promised to show the police where the body of the girl was on condition that I was shot immediately afterwards. I admit killing both Miss Keppie and Miss Stevenson for *nothing*.

"It happened at 9.30 on Thursday night. I shot Miss Keppie near the camp. She was sitting next to me at the time and grabbed at my revolver which I kept in my left-hand pocket.

"I ordered her out of the car and took her about thirty yards from the camp. She was a yard from me when I shot her. I threw her down a sort of square pit nearby.

"After that I returned for Winnie. She was sitting in the car. When I took Miss Keppie away, I had ordered her to get into the car. She had not moved when I got back. She was terrified. She wanted to go home. I told her I would lead the way and she could follow.

"When we were near her home she said she could not go any farther. She lay on the grass under a tree. She did not know what was going to happen to her. I shot her in the side of the head.

"I had no reason for shooting her either. I covered her up and returned to the car, where I remained until the Saturday morning. I ate some oranges and drank lemonade. Then I threw everything out of the car and made up my mind to go home.

"I reached the ditch and stuck. I reversed the car and backed out. Next, I rushed the ditch but the clutch burnt out and something broke . . ."

That was all. Not a twinge of pity did he show for what he had done, as he said, *"for nothing"*. Obviously he did not tell all he knew in his confession and some of his statements did not ring true.

Was it likely, for example, that Miss Stevenson would have sat paralysed with fear in the car – under instructions to wait – while Ross took Miss Keppie into the bush and shot her? Would she not have heard the shot and attempted to drive the car away? Or would she not have escaped into the night?

Then again, what was the truth behind the unworn women's apparel at the camp? Ross was believed to have been escorting the girls to a cinema, not to a camp to live in the open for several days. Could the strange collection of clothing have had some bearing on the youth's sexual peculiarities?

We can only guess at what occurred before the dastardly murder of the unfortunate girls. Perhaps it is better that the truth shall never be known . . .

On October 18, Ross, manacled to a warder, was charged

with a second murder. On November 4 he was committed for trial.

Ross stood his trial at Nairobi on November 28, 1932, before the then Chief Justice of Kenya, Sir Jacob Barth, and a jury. He was pale and haggard. His composure and self-assurance had gone.

The Attorney-General, Mr A. D. A. Macgregor, K. C., led Mr R. F. Branigan for the Crown. Ross's counsel were Mr Humphrey Slade and Mr M. J. Hogan.

The trial aroused great interest far beyond the borders of Kenya. A battle royal was waged between the law and science over the responsibility of the drawn youth in the dock, for his terrible deed. Both in England and South Africa the newspapers gave great prominence to the proceedings.

The task of the Attorney-General was not to pin the crime to the prisoner, but to destroy the only possible defence – that he was not in his sane senses when he committed the murders.

It was a painful story the witnesses for the defence told; as horrible, too, as anything Edgar Allan Poe imagined. They described Ross's desire to butcher animals for the mere sake and delight of killing.

At times he was stated to have slaughtered a number of animals and to have left the carcasses untouched. Again, he had been known to rush wildly up to the dead beasts, stab and slash at them in a frenzy – and then cover himself with the blood.

Other testimony concerned the behaviour of Ross's father, a psychopathic case from the description of those who knew him in his lifetime. Two men who served under him in the Boer War recalled his savagery and ungovernable temper.

He shot prisoners without mercy. Once when a native dared insist on payment for eggs supplied, Major Ross had drawn his revolver and emptied it into the man's head. So brutal was he to all who crossed his path and so ruthless with his men, that they were goaded to revolt.

Only then did they see something human in the pitiless soldier. He went to his tent and sobbed.

No woman could have faced a greater ordeal than Ross's mother when she entered the witness-box to reveal the intimacies and tortures of her life with her former husband, and to convince the jury that the son of such a father could not be normal.

Her life had been one of unending horror. Her husband thrashed her unmercifully. Frequently he threatened to shoot her. Once, in a towering rage, he seized her baby and attempted to put it on the fire. A moment later he dropped on his knees and begged forgiveness.

Her son, Charles Ross, was sensitive and during recent weeks a change had come over him. He was rude to her and his stepfather. He lost his good manners and charm.

"I have lost my boy in the last six months in every way," sobbed the grief-stricken mother.

The evidence of Mr E. R. Pratt, head master of the Nakuru school Ross attended after his arrival in the Colony from England, was that the lad was untruthful, often guilty of petty misdemeanours, and had a misdirected sense of adventure. This, of course, did not indicate abnormality; neither did the testimony that he was found with the servants in the kitchen of a man with whom he stayed for several months.

Other witnesses, however, described incidents suggesting that Ross had committed acts which were certainly not those of a normal person. He had been seen to kick a cat to death. When out fishing, he would squeeze his first catch and mumble senselessly to himself. One rainy night he went to the Menengai crater and killed a hyena. His hands and clothes were covered with blood and slush.

It was also proved that he suffered from a venereal disease in 1930 and again when he was taken into custody. The clothing he wore on the fatal car journey on the night of October 6 was examined at the Government laboratories and traces of semen were noticed on the waistcoat and trousers.

Dr R. F. G. Dickson, Medical Officer of Health to the Nairobi District Council, Doctor to H. M. Prisons and in charge of the Infectious Diseases Hospital, was prepared to state, from his observations of Ross, that he showed indications of insanity, and possibly did not know the difference between right and wrong when he committed his crimes.

"On what facts in the evidence," the Attorney-General questioned Dr Dickson, "do you base your theory of the prisoner's insanity?"

"I base it," replied Dr Dickson, "on his alternating moroseness and excitement; his solitariness and shyness; that he sat by himself for hours on a rock meditating; that he went hunting by himself; did not like the society of girls and left them. In addition to all that, there were his emotional outbursts and his quite unnecessary attacks with knives on dead animals."

The Attorney-General was not satisfied. "We have heard about the prisoner's moroseness," he said, "and of his slow, smouldering temper and sulking. But are those conditions symptomatic of insanity?"

"They may not be symptomatic of legal insanity," the doctor retorted, "but they are of insanity as I know it."

An X-ray photograph of Ross's head was used by Dr H. L. Gordon, mental specialist and leading witness for the defence, to illustrate the youth's abnormality. The smallness of one section of the brain, he pointed out to the Court, was associated with certain forms of mental deficiency. The pituitary gland, that part of the brain containing the essential to life, had reached its limit of growth.

Besides, there was a depression in the skull which somewhat cut the brain. The curious mottled appearance at the back of the skull, clearly shown in the X-ray photograph, Dr Gordon had not seen before, although it was not unknown in the skulls of South African natives.

Dr Gordon deduced, from the evidence of Major Ross's conduct, that he conformed to the type suffering from a constitutional psychopathic inferiority or pronounced mental instability. Had he attempted to put one of his children on a fire and his wife, then about to give birth to her son, Charles, had witnessed it, there was a scientific possibility that the child might be affected in later life.

From his examination and tests of Ross, Dr Gordon found his brain capacity equal to that of a lad of fourteen or fifteen years, and his intelligence quotient 65.7. A quotient below eighty was abnormal. He was, thus, midway between the feeble-minded and the moral-deficient.

"Do you think," Mr Humphrey Slade asked, "that mere overwork could have caused a temporary upset in a case such as the present?"

"Yes," Dr Gordon agreed, "but one has to qualify what one means by overwork. I think it would contribute. A strong sexual impulse might have that effect as well, particularly in the class of mental defectives to which I consider Ross belongs."

Mr Slade: Have you formed an opinion as to whether he has a strong or weak sex urge?

Dr Gordon: I have had evidence that he has a very strong sex urge. As a rule such an urge lasts until it is gratified. It might be momentary, or last a week or ten days.

"If," Mr Humphrey Slade suggested, "at some time between October 6 and October 8, he killed these two girls without apparent motive; and if, before or after the killing he underwent some sexual excitement, is there a possibility that, at the time of the murders, he was without the power of passing rational judgment on his action?"

"Provided he was suffering from what I have definite evidence he has got," replied Dr Gordon, "and that he had a strong sexual urge – of which he had no more understanding than he would have, say, of Relativity, he would be without control of his actions."

There was a sparkling duel between the mental specialist and the Attorney-General in cross-examination. The Attorney-General kept to the letter of the law; the legal interpretation of insanity, or uncontrollable impulse. The doctor answered pungently, with the conviction that the law had not kept pace with the advance of medical science and was still hedged about by the opinions and definitions of a half-century ago.

"I put it to you," the Attorney-General said, opening his cross-examination, "that there has been a good deal of hypothesis and speculation in your statement?"

"You disappoint me, Sir," Dr Gordon rejoined. "I thought the advantage I was placing before the Court was that I was facing it with concrete evidence as to mental deficiency."

"Quite, mental deficiency," commented the Attorney-General. "But as to legal insanity, hypothesis! There was the exception in the matter of the prisoner's very strong sex urge. On that you are emphatic?"

Dr Gordon: I am.

The Attorney-General: Assuming the continuousness of that urge at the time of this tragedy, are you equally emphatic that it deprived the prisoner temporarily of his control?

Dr Gordon: I am.

The Attorney-General: Your theory is that the murders were committed by him under an impulse caused by a sex urge he was unable to resist. I presume, Dr Gordon, you have studied the legal side of this problem, as well as the medical?

"I have tried to, Sir," Dr Gordon declared, "but it is very difficult to study the legal side."

"Are you aware," the Attorney-General went on, "of the attitude the courts have taken up towards the inability to control action? That the courts of justice of our country do not regard it as legal insanity?"

"That is not so," Dr Gordon contended. "The reverse is the case."

"You surprise me," was the Attorney-General's observation to this. But he was not to have the last say. Another question gave the doctor an opening to retaliate.

"What mental state was the prisoner in at the moment he killed Miss Keppie?" he asked.

"Oh, Sir!" Dr Gordon reproached. "How *can* I answer that? My opinion, from all the evidence before me, however, is that he was temporarily insane."

The Attorney-General impressed on the jury that Ross had not been proved *legally* irresponsible for his crimes in spite of the defence evidence adduced to portray his and his father's abnormalities.

The Crown was entitled to the verdict. Justice must be done, notwithstanding the contentions of medical science.

Mr Humphrey Slade argued that the crime was not a deliberate and calculated planned deed by Ross, but due to heredity and environment.

"You have been awkwardly placed in Court, gentlemen of the jury," he said. "You have not been able to see the prisoner well. I ask you to look at him now. You see a child, gentlemen, a child."

On December 1, 1932, the jury listened to the summing-up and exposition of the law concerning a defence of insanity, by the Chief Justice. For fifty-five minutes they were closeted, then returned with a verdict of "*Guilty*".

The announcement of the foreman in a hushed Court left Ross unmoved. He declined to add anything to counsel's plea for his life.

Sir Jacob Barth expressed agreement with the verdict and passed sentence of death.

For over a month Ross remained in the Nairobi prison calmly awaiting his end. He did not fear death. Most of his time was spent reading and marking passages in a prayer-book.

The date fixed for the execution was withheld from the public, and it was not until January 7, 1933, that the death warrant was signed.

At five o'clock on the morning of January 11, the gloomy condemned cell was converted into an impromptu chapel.

An altar was erected. Candles were lit. The Dean of Nairobi conducted Holy Communion.

Ross prayed fervently during the service. At its close he asked that the prayer-book, in which he found solace during his last days, be buried with him.

Ross met his end bravely and without complaint. He was laid to rest in a tiny cemetery just outside the prison walls, the victim of an abnormality whom Society could not allow to live.

Benjamin Bennett

Samuel Furnace: History's Greatest Manhunt

Like Rouse, Samuel Furnace decided that fire
would provide a convenient means of escaping
his debts – although these seem to have been
relatively small. The crime was clumsy, and Furnace's own death far more unpleasant than that
of his victim. The author of this account, Roland
Wild, produced two notable volumes, which can
still be found in second hand shops: *Crimes and
Cases of 1933* and *Crimes and Cases of 1934*. The
story of the Furnace manhunt is from the former.

On the second of January 1933 Samuel James Furnace,
a builder living in Chalk Farm, rose late, after a New
Year's Day party with his wife and three children, and went
to work. He had not far to go. From Crogsland Road he
walked to Hawley Crescent, Chalk Farm Road, and entered
his yard. There he set his employees to work, and after
attending to some details in the office walked to a café in
Camden Road to meet friends.

Among them was Walter Spatchett, a rate-collector and
former colleague of Furnace in the firm of Westacott & Sons,
of Camden Road. Eighteen months before, Furnace had left
the firm to work on his own, but the friendship continued,
and the two men often met in the café or played billiards
together in local saloons.

They drank coffee. They talked of the New Year fes-
tivities. They parted, Furnace to return home to lunch,

Walter Spatchett to continue his round of rent-collecting. He was in the local bank before closing time to deposit the £60 collected that morning. He made his usual call on a builder at five o'clock, where he made up his accounts. He counted £35.

"Have a cup of tea?" invited the builder.

"No, thank you," replied Spatchett. "I have one more call to make."

He went out, pocketing the £35, and walked to the shed which was Furnace's office.

The workmen had gone home. The yard was silent.

And some time during that period when Spatchett was in the office Furnace shot his friend in the back. Nobody heard the shot. Spatchett died instantly.

Furnace went out into the cool night air to reassure himself that nobody was about. Then he returned, bundled the still-warm body under the desk, and locked up the office.

He went home, saw his children to bed, listened to a broadcast of "Jane Eyre," and went to bed early.

He was up in good time. He made his wife a cup of tea, and hurried to the workshop. He sent the men away on various jobs. Then he sat down and reviewed the position.

Already the parents of Walter Spatchett were anxious at the non-arrival of their son. Old Mr. Spatchett, a chauffeur living in Dartmouth Park Road, was particularly worried, as his son regularly came home between six and six-fifteen. Furnace knew that the police would soon institute a search and inquire into the movements of the missing man.

Furnace also considered his own position. At forty, he was in somewhat grave circumstances. He had three children to provide for, an overdraft at the bank, and debts amounting to nearly £100. He employed four men and a boy, but work was scarce in spite of his energetic attempts to find commissions. He had always assured his wife of his progress, but secretly he was worried. He had already been pressed to pay various amounts.

Among his debts was one for a considerable sum to Spatchett.

Then, as he sifted the facts, he recalled the insurance policy taken out on his own life. The policy had been taken out with the Britannic Assurance Company for £1,000 at death and £100 a year for twenty years from the inception of the policy. He had paid the premium of £28 odd the month before.

There was a clause in the agreement that rendered the policy void if the assured person committed suicide within twelve months of its inception. That day, January 3rd, the policy was one year and three days old. And in addition Furnace had another policy for £100 with profits to be paid in twenty years or at death.

He walked home to lunch. Then he called on the firm of Westgate & Sons, and asked if there was any work for him to do. Then he went back to the shed.

That morning he had been lucky in concealing the body from the eyes of his workmen, who occasionally came into the office. The body was hidden with an overcoat, and unless someone was openly searching, it would remain undiscovered. But his thoughts ranged always over the insurance policy. With this in mind he drew towards him a piece of paper and a pencil and wrote: "Good-bye to all. No work, no money. Sam S. J. Furnace."

He walked out of the shed just before four o'clock and stood looking at it. A workman spoke to him.

"What are you doing, Mr. Furnace?"

"Just having a stroll round," he said.

He went back into the shed, pulled out the body, now rigid, and propped it into the straight-backed wooden chair. He pulled a bag of money out of the pockets of the dead man, took the silver from the trousers pockets and the gold watch from the wrist.

He took down the hanging lamp and poured the oil on to the body. He found tins of paint in a corner of the shed, and poured their contents on to the floor and on to the body. He found waste paper and shavings, dry and combustible.

These he stacked round the chair. Finally he pinned the note signed by his own hand on to a table in the outer office, and lit a candle. By seven o'clock he was ready. He lit the pile of shavings, locked the doors, inner and outer, and saw the flames licking up to the chair before he left the shed, taking a bag of tools with him.

But within a few minutes of his leaving the fire was discovered.

A small child, going into the yard where Furnace's shed was situated, saw the flames. By half-past seven the fire brigade had been called. Already civilians were doing their best to quell the flames, and had broken open the outer door.

Throwing water on the fire, they were able to force the inner door, which was held with an automatic lock. And shining an electric torch through the smoke, they were able to see the dim outline of a body in the chair against the desk. With the arrival of the brigade the fire was quenched sufficiently for the helpers to drag out the body. The features were indistinguishable, the clothes scorched and frail, and the flesh destroyed.

But while the police were taking the body to the mortuary a workman employed by Furnace made another discovery. Walking into the outer shed, he came upon the note written by Furnace.

That night the police, after an interview with Mrs. Furnace, informed her that the body was that of her husband. She related that her husband had that morning about £47 in his pocket, and was to pay the workmen that day before banking the remainder.

Meanwhile Furnace went to a lodging-house in Princes Road, merely a walk from the charred scene of the murder. He booked a room under the name of Roy Rogers. The next morning he slung the bag of tools on his back and took a train to Wembley, threw away the revolver into the canal at Camden Road, flung away the revolver holster at Dagenham, and returned again to the Princes Road apartment-house.

But during the day, unknown to him, there had begun the

greatest man-hunt that England has ever known, involving the watch of 20,000 men of the police force, every available detective from Scotland Yard and the big provincial cities, the B.B.C., the dock police, the shipping companies, and the newspapers. For the fire that Furnace had lit in the little office-shed had been put out a few minutes too soon for his purposes by the fire brigade, and the flames had failed to destroy vital evidence which Furnace had thought hidden for ever.

If the little girl who had warned her father of the fire had been ten minutes later in discovering the flames, Furnace would have been free to make his life anew. During the first few minutes of the doctor's examination it was proved beyond doubt that the body was not that of Furnace. By a simple process of elimination it was discovered to be that of Spatchett. There were laundry marks on the collar of the shirt. Fragments of the shirt itself were identified by Spatchett's parents. There were the remains of a pocket-wallet, and a portion of a girl's photograph, which Spatchett always carried with him. Although Mr. W. Abbott, who lived in the same house as Furnace, definitely identified the body as that of Furnace, conclusive evidence was given by a dentist, who was able to say that he recognised the teeth as those of his former patient Spatchett. But if the fire had continued for ten minutes longer, clothes, pocket-wallet, and all the other evidence would have disappeared, and the police would have been forced to base their conclusions on the farewell note signed by Samuel Furnace.

Now, with the case reversed so dramatically, that note was to bear a very different and ominous part in the situation. Furnace must have written it; it was in his handwriting. Furnace wished, then, to lead the police into believing that he was the victim of the fire.

Where was Furnace?

That whisper, spoken at the inquest at St. Pancras, among the grim relics of the fire, grew into an everswelling thunder of inquiry. It was asked in millions of homes over the radio, asked by hundreds of police-officers making systematic house-to-house searches at midnight in suspected areas. It was asked by cordons of police strung across the roads of England and checking the occupants of every car, examining the driver and the passengers. It was asked in the captain's cabins of little tramp steamers at the ports, in the stokeholds of cargo-boats which had signed on crews at Tilbury and Liverpool. The question was flashed across the ocean to ships labouring in the January storms. Where was Furnace?

Before considering the drama of the greatest manhunt in history it is as well to consider at this stage the possibility that Furnace was the innocent victim of circumstances. When, a fortnight later, he was to die without being proved guilty of the crime of murder, it was suggested that there was a faint possibility that he had run away from the consequences, not of his guilt, but of an accident.

His own statement to the police was to the effect that he and Spatchett were examining a service revolver in the shed when "the gun went off" He thereupon lost his head, according to his own version, and made a bid for escape.

Both these statements are upset by common-sense consideration. Furnace was not a nervous man or untutored with firearms. He had served through the whole of the War, and had later joined the "Black and Tans" in the Irish troubles. It was unlikely that he would at any time behave foolishly with a revolver. The experienced man never points a gun, even by accident. In a statement made to a friend on the day of his arrest he is reported to have said, "Spatchett was in the office – you know what a box of a place it was – and saw the revolver lying in a case at the side. He took it up, fiddled with the trigger, and tried the grip. That frightened me. 'Hold hard, boy,' I warned him. 'It's loaded.' With that he handed the gun to me, saying, 'You know more about it than I do.' He was ready to go home then. I had the gun in my left hand as he jerked the office door wide open. There was a shot then, and down he went in a heap. What happened was that the door hit my hand as he flung it open, and the revolver went off. I was staggered, dumbfounded, scared stiff . . ."

But the man who was "dumbfounded, scared stiff" was able to calm his fears sufficiently to bundle the body under the desk, sit quietly at home that evening, lie to his employees about the "bag of cement" under the desk the next morning, plan the fire, and cover his tracks sufficiently to outwit the police forces of the whole country for a fortnight afterwards.

Would he have stood a chance of safety if he had reported the "accident" to the police there and then?

It is true that he owed money to Spatchett. The shooting would have appeared an easy way out of debt. On the other hand, he could have enlisted many of his friends to speak well of him – as a good husband and father, as an honest and conscientious workman. He could have pointed to his foresight in paying the premium for his life insurance, in order to protect his wife and children in case of accident. He could have enlisted the support of Mr. MacDonald Smith, the Britannic Assurance manager, who said in court, even when Furnace was a sought-for murder-suspect, that "he was a man with a heart of gold – the kind of man who would help anyone who was down and out; anyone who asked for a pound got it."

Or Sydney Furnace, his brother, would have said that "he was devoted to his wife and three children; he had no vices, was a rigid teetotaller from birth, loved his home, spent his life between his work and his home. When he was at sea Sam saved all his wages and gave the money to his mother."

It is true that he was financially embarrassed. Who is not? Many small contractors are content to continue with more difficulties than faced Samuel Furnace. Most certainly he had a case to support his plea of innocence if he had at the time informed the police of the "accident."

There is a further suggestion that the murder and the burning were carefully planned days or weeks or months before the second day of January. That theory is also unsupported by evidence. Furnace is said to have been influenced, long before that fateful evening of January 2nd, by stories of Rouse and other burning crimes. It was suggested that he had planned to stage his fake suicide as soon as possible after the New Year, when the clause in his insurance policy regarding suicide became out of date. This theory is quite incredible. It is inconceivable that Furnace would delay twenty-four hours after the shooting before escaping. With Spatchett missing from home, and in all probability traced to his shed, Furnace could not have run the risk of being questioned about his friend's disappearance. As it happened, he was not questioned, but sooner or later the distracted parents of the missing young man, who knew his regular habits, would have come to Furnace for information. And there was always the risk of his own workmen blundering into the office and inquiring into the strange bundle under the desk.

One of them, indeed, did notice it, even when Furnace was sitting in front of the desk.

"What have you been buying?" he asked.

"Only some cement," replied Furnace.

It is only reasonable that if Furnace had shot Spatchett according to plan he would have found some other and safer hiding-place for the body.

Further, a man who is carefully planning a fake suicide does not take the first opportunity after the lapse of a prohibitive clause. He waits some time, weeks or months. Would Furnace have planned the crime for only two days after that clause had lapsed?

There is another point connected with the insurance policy. Furnace did not himself take steps to insure his own life. The insurance was the suggestion of Mr. Macdonald Smith. Furnace had been paying insurance premiums on property but had sold the property and had no more need of the policy. Mr. Smith then suggested that he should take out a policy on his life. This Furnace agreed to.

The Furnace we are asked to believe in now, if this

premeditation theory is correct, is a systematic and careful criminal. He would surely have taken every step necessary for his safety. If he had wanted a body to burn, and invest the charred remains with his own identity, would he have taken a neighbour and friend? It must be remembered that he would not have taken into great account the money he owed Spatchett – about £60. It may be said that he wanted to kill two birds with one stone, choosing Spatchett for the victim firstly for the insurance money on his own death, and secondly to get rid of his creditor. But that would have been arrant folly. The debt owed by Furnace could not have been levied on his wife, and with the thought of £1,000 coming to his wife he would surely have scorned to consider a matter of £60.

No, if Furnace had planned a fake suicide, and only murdered in order to get a body for the burning, he would not have chosen a friend and neighbour. There are other methods of obtaining unknown men to walk into the death-house, particularly in these days when the unemployed will walk twenty miles in a day for a chance of a job. A man in the position of Furnace could easily have manæuvred a strange man into his office, at whatever time and on whatever day he liked, on the promise of a job, and with quite a possibility of the man never being traced or reported missing. After the Rouse case there will remain always the sombre reminder that there are men in this small island unknown, unremembered, friendless, and unnoticed when they have disappeared for ever . . .

The conclusion must be that Furnace would have made some preparations if he had planned the shooting of Spatchett. When Spatchett came to the shed, therefore, Furnace had no intention of shooting him. What happened during that unknown period, before the shooting, that made him press the gun to the back of his friend and pull the trigger?

Anger? A sudden quarrel?

Spatchett might well have resolved, with the beginning of a New Year, that his friend had owed him money long enough. It must have taken some pluck for the young man to press the older and experienced man of 40 for the money. Perhaps he was tactless in his demands. Perhaps he provided, on that evening, the last irritation that was to make Furnace desperate. Nobody will ever know why and how Furness came to the last desperate resolve of the murderer.

He knew Spatchett had money on him. Perhaps he expected that it would be more. But he had money in his pocket; he usually had. The presence of money, however insignificant and disproportionate an amount, has before now pressed a desperate man to an act which in less impulsive moments he would never have considered.

Now, in considering the probability of a sudden impulse being the cause of Furnace's crime, the same arguments which dispose of the accident theory can be used in support. He was a man familiar with fire-arms. He had seen death and violence. If rage had driven him, he would not have been repelled at the last by the grim physical action of pointing the gun and pulling the trigger.

Impulse, then, is the only possible cause of the shooting. It is established that before Spatchett's visit to the shed Furnace did not contemplate murder, burning, disappearance, or the fake suicide. Some time after he had bundled the body under the desk, and had gone home to his wife for the night, the thought must have come to him of ensuring his safety by the fake suicide.

Remember, that only the month before he had been reminded of his life insurance. He had paid the £28 16s. 6d. annual premium during December. The payment must have been difficult, but with the foresight of a careful man he knew that regular payment was more personally important than the debts which he had contracted among his business acquaintances. He must have thought a great deal about that insurance. The payment extended his overdraft at the bank too far for him to pay and forget. And it is probable that during the last month, when paying the premium, he had looked at his policy and been reminded of the suicide clause which would become void during January.

There was another detail which may have shown him the way to what appeared to be safe disappearance. On the morning of Tuesday, after the murder, he woke early and hurried down to the shed to send his workmen away. He may, however, have chanced to look at the newspaper that morning. One of the most startling sensations of the morning's news was an account of a fire tragedy at Hordean, Hampshire. A bungalow had been burned, and two bodies were found in the charred wreckage. And it had been found impossible to identify either of the bodies . . .

There had, of course, been other cases. The Rouse case was not unique. Sidney Fox, who strangled his mother in a Margate hotel for the sake of the insurance money, set fire to the bedroom and was only accidentally discovered in his crime. Lindsay Marshall, a Bedfordshire farmer, tried by setting his car on fire to hide the evidence of the murder of his wife and his own suicide. And on that morning when Furnace decided on a fire at his office-shed, there was evidence before him in the day's newspaper of the obliterating efficiency of fire as an aid to crime.

Despair turned him, during the course of that day, from a home-loving and work-loving family man into a fugitive. He was willing to forget family love and fatherhood in his fear. Probably he now considered it too late to contemplate throwing himself on the charity of the law and chancing a protestation that this had been an accident. He was willing to pit his cleverness against the law.

In support of the theory that he had planned the whole crime months before it had been suggested that Furnace had for years led a double life. It was said that he had consorted with women in London, and had regarded his marriage and his home-ties as a burden. It was said that he spent considerable sums of money in West End restaurants, entertaining women, and that he owed his indebtedness to this extravagance. Indeed, a woman came forward during the search for Furnace and stated that the wanted man had been a frequent companion of hers for months past, and that she had known him under another name. It was also stated that Furnace had for months used the second name of "Roy Rogers" under which he engaged rooms after the crime.

Generally, however, little hard fact came to light supporting this reputation that had been given to Furnace. It was never proved that he had been regularly leading a double life. All his intimates described him as a faithful husband and father. The reputation of a gay adventurer and a spendthrift Casanova is easily fitted to notorieties. It is supposed to invest them with a greater public interest.

Furnace was also represented as a smart man-about-town, *habitué* of West End bars and restaurants. It was said that his clothes were expensive and his taste in women worthy of a rich idler. These improvisations provided human interest, but did not contribute to the truthful story of Furnace and his crime.

These suggestions can be discounted, and leave Furnace, on the day when he was faced with the necessity of disposing of the body of his friend, as a man resolved to sacrifice the happiness of his home and his obligations in a desperate bid for freedom. And with this thought in mind he bid good-bye to his wife and children with a nonchalance that he could not have felt.

Certainly, some support for the theory that Furnace had long ago contemplated a new life is given by the account of a former companion in arms during the Irish trouble. This man told how Furnace had, during the last weeks of 1932, questioned him closely as to the best way of getting to Ireland. He had asked what was the rate of pay in the Free State and Republican Armies, and seemed vitally interested in the question of whether he could enlist.

His friend laughed, but Furnace said, "Don't laugh; just look at this." And he showed him his old discharge, and, pointing to the name, explained how easily the initial "J" could be so changed so that his name appeared to be "Samuel O'Furnace."

"And there's another thing," Furnace said to his friend. "Supposing a man could get to Dublin, it would be easy to tramp to the west side and hide up in Mayo or Connemara. None of the natives have learned to read up there, and if anybody went after him from England they would hinder them rather than help. So that's where I might be going one day – to Mayo or Connemara."

And later he said, "Supposing a fellow couldn't get to Ireland, what about Canada or America? How would he manage that?"

At the end of the conversation Furnace wrote down in a note-book the address, given him by the friend, where the return halves of tickets to America could be bought cheaply.

There is no doubt that this evidence caused the police to concentrate a search on the ports, particularly at Liverpool; but the arguments against Furnace having contemplated a disappearance were strong enough to dismiss this conversation as a coincidence. Many are the men who "talk travel" in these days, particularly when they have at some time in their lives enjoyed a varied and thrilling existence. The context for such a conversation is not given. It may have been theoretical enough to reduce the whole incident to a mere love of conversation. In any case, the evidence to the contrary is strong enough to dispose of it as unimportant.

We have, therefore, Furnace in the position of a man deciding to fake his own suicide, with the possibility of his wife benefiting from the insurance money, himself financially secure, for the moment at any rate, and the body reduced to a heap of ashes which nobody could identify. He himself could vanish. Perhaps, even, it was fortunate that he had no contacts with boarding-house keepers or women under an assumed name. It should be easy for a man to disappear and lie low for a while . . .

The note, written as if by an intending suicide, was perhaps an unnecessary detail. He scorned to remove the wallet in the dead man's pocket, or any of the clothes. The fire would remove any trace of identity better than he could.

And now that man-hunt, started as a result of the inquest findings on the day after Furnace had walked away from the burning shed in full confidence, was driving him desperately.

At first the official information issued by the police was to the effect that Furnace was "wanted to be interviewed" by Scotland Yard regarding the fire in his office-shed. A description was given: "Height, five feet ten and a half inches; fair complexion; fair hair, thin in front; hazel eyes, full face, and a square jaw. One of Furnace's teeth is missing in the front of the upper jaw. He has marks of gunshot wounds on the left leg and both arms, and on the right bicep has a long scar showing the marks of thirteen stitches. When last seen he was wearing a navy blue suit; a new light blue shirt and collar to match, a lightish brown overcoat fully belted; a grey trilby hat with a black band and straight brim; light brown socks and black shoes.

"It is known," continued the statement, "that Furnace has been a ship's steward, and has served in the Rifle Brigade and the Black and Tans. He may endeavour to obtain employment in the decorating trade as a clerk or in the mercantile marine. He may also endeavour to leave the country."

Photographs of the missing man were issued to the newspapers. But it is not surprising that from this commonplace description the police for the next week were deluged with reports from all over the country to the effect that Furnace had been seen. When, also, Furnace was eventually captured, it was admitted by the detectives that the official photographs, of which many thousands were printed for distribution in country police offices, would not have led anybody to recognise the wanted man.

Superintendent Cornish and Chief Detective Inspector Yandell were put in charge of the case, and worked unceasingly for a week, when the former collapsed with influenza, then raging throughout England. They personally followed every clue which seemed at all hopeful, and daily widened the scope of the investigations being made all over the country.

It became known to the police, and through them to the public, that Furnace had been in London on Tuesday, January 5th, two days after the burning. An acquaintance saw him in Leicester Square, and informed the police. A squad of men converged on a café, but drew a blank. But that was only one of the disappointments that were to be the lot of the searchers.

On that day Furnace had made his way down to Southend, by a method not known. It is probable, however, that he walked all through the night, or at any rate slept on the way, for in the only account he gave of the period during which he was a fugitive he omitted to mention where he had spent the night. During the sixth day, however, the police received a report that a telegram had been received by the manageress of a Camden Town lodging-house. It was dated from Southend and signed "Rogers." This was enough to send flying-squad cars to Southend to organise a beat of the whole town, and a siege of the main roads leading out of the seaside town. The detectives drew blank. So far as is known, Furnace did not stay the night of the 5th at any lodging-house, and according to his own statement did not book rooms in Southend till the night of the 6th. And by that evening he would have found it very difficult to move about by ordinary methods in England.

Southend police were watching railway stations and motor-coach stations. Every Board of Trade official at the ports had been given a picture of the wanted man. Captains of every ship at sea which had sailed from an English port since the crime were asked to compare new members of their crews with the descriptions wirelessed to them. On the evening of the 7th Scotland Yard disclosed that every detective engaged on the search for Furnace had been armed "as a matter of precaution." Another important description of Furnace was

133

given. The police had traced every detail of the purchases made by him during his visit to London on the 5th. "He may now be wearing a brown check cap and carrying a dark brown leather kit-bag, with two handles, such as is used by bank messengers." Just before his arrest, Furnace told a friend that he was terrified reading the details of his "disguise" in the newspapers, and dare not enter a shop to buy a change of clothes.

On Sunday the 8th, and the fourth day of the search, the police took the unprecedented step of stopping every car on the main roads leading from the capital to the south coast. A special conference at Scotland Yard, presided over by Lord Trenchard, decided to mobilise every available wireless car in the Force for the search, to comb out every lodging-house in Camden Town, where Furnace was now believed to be, and to concentrate men in other centres where Furnace might be found. By that time 200 reports had been received from various parts of the country. Information came from almost every large city in England. One of the apparently hopeful reports was from a docker at Liverpool, who stated that he had seen a man attempting to board a ship. Police formed a cordon round the docks, but with no result.

All England was keyed up to the scent. There was not a newspaper reader in the country who was not in possession of a theory. The fact may be regrettable, but it remains true that a man-hunt, and all the grim details of an organised search for a criminal, holds a terrible fascination for the public. In view of this nation-wide interest in the hunt it is not surprising that the police were hindered on all sides by the reports of amateur detectives. A prominent Northampton business man, for instance, was stopped three times by the police while on a journey from his native city to Leicester and required to give proof of his identity. He had, it was said, a faint superficial resemblance to Furnace.

The climax of drama was to follow, for on the evening of Monday, January 9th, the B.B.C. announced that Furnace was "wanted for murder." It was the first time since the

Crippen case, in 1910, that the police had appealed for a murderer in this way, and it was the first time that a broadcast "S.O.S." had been issued for this purpose. A warning was also given to landladies.

"It is earnestly requested," ran the appeal, "that any one prepared to take male lodgers, particularly at quiet apartment-houses, will keep a look-out for this man, and, if he is seen, communicate immediately with the nearest police station. Furnace takes his room in a false name. He is believed to be in possession of a Service revolver, without the holster, and he may endeavour to board a ship."

During that Monday night a train travelling from Southend to London was held up and every passenger examined. During the night more than 2,000 police, beginning at eleven p.m., carried out a house-to-house search for Furnace on the Essex side of London. The majority of the small boarding-houses in an area housing 300,000 people were visited, the owners knocked up, and questioned about their visitors. Other inquiries were made at cafés and in Soho, Euston, and Paddington.

Meanwhile, how was Furnace managing to evade the watchful eyes of every police-officer and landlady, every shopkeeper and passer-by in the streets?

He stayed only two nights in the boarding-house of Mrs. Lilley, in Hartington Road, where he had first engaged a room. On the second morning the newspapers were full of his description. Paying his bill, he walked out of the house, and the police were only a few hours behind him. But he moved, perhaps with infinite cunning, only two streets away, into another boarding-house kept by Mrs. Shaw in Whitegate Road, near Southend station.

Furnace told Mrs. Shaw that he had 'flu, and went to bed in a back room on the first floor. After one night, he said he "wanted to know what was going on" and changed to a room on the ground floor, in the front of the house. Mrs. Shaw looked after him well, and he satisfied her inquiries as to why he did not go out by saying that he was feeling too unwell. The public imagined a haunted fugitive constantly changing his bolt-hole, sleeping in huts on waste ground, running the gauntlet of prying eyes day after day, or perhaps hanging round the docks on the chance of sneaking on board a ship. In actual fact, however, the wanted man was lying in bed all day, reading detective thrillers and the newspapers containing accounts of the search. He planned to stay in the room until a friend had brought him a change of clothes, in which he could venture out in a dash for permanent liberty in another country.

The search continued unabated. On the night of the 10th, the greatest comb-out in police history took place in London. Altogether an area of 800 square miles was covered. Late tram-cars and omnibuses were stopped and searched. Cinemas were watched. There was no result.

On the 11th, reports were received that Furnace had been seen, *inter alia*, at Kettering, Guildford, and Hastings. In Kettering he was supposed to have been seen in a cinema. Police locked the doors, turned on the lights, and scrutinised every patron. On the 12th, Canvey Island, offering shelter for a fugitive in various unoccupied bungalows, was searched. Reports still came in to Scotland Yard at the rate of eighty a day. On the 14th, Saturday, Scotland Yard admitted that they had no knowledge of the whereabouts of Furnace, and had not had a workable clue since the Southend landlady, Mrs. Lilley of Hartington Road, had reported his staying there on the nights of the 6th and 7th.

But on the same day, Saturday January 14th, a week after he had been seen for the last time, the police gained the information which led swiftly and easily to the arrest of Samuel Furnace.

A letter fell through the letter-box of Mr. Charles Tuckfield, a brother-in-law of Furnace, into the hall of his home at Harringay Park. It was stamped Southend, January 14th, and had evidently been posted late the night before and caught the early post to London. The letter was in pencil. It read:

"*Dear Charlie*,

"Just a line to you in hope that I shall be able to see a friend before I end it all.

"I am writing to you because I know they will watch May [Mrs. Furnace] for a long time.

"I am at Southend, quite near the station, making out I have been ill with the 'flu, so have been able to stay in all the week.

"I am far from well through want of sleep. I don't think I have slept one hour since the accident happened. I will tell you all about it when I see you.

"Now what I want you to do is not for me, but for May and the kiddies. My days are numbered. I want you to come down Sunday, on your own, please. Catch the 10.35 from Harringay Park; that gets you down in Southend at 12.8. Come out of the station, walk straight across the road, and down the opposite road; walk down on the left side.

"I will see you. I am not giving my address in case you are followed. Just walk slowly down.

"If you come will you bring me 15½ shirt and two collars – any colour will do. Also one pair of socks, dark ones, and one comb. I think that is all now. Don't let anyone know, only Nell [Mrs. Tuckfield]. If possible say you have to work or something.

"Best of luck. Mine is gone.

"*H. Farmer*."

It was from Furnace.

Charles Tuckfield took the letter to the police. They advised him to follow the instructions to the detail. The next day he went down to Southend, walked down the road indicated, and looked for a sign. Suddenly, at a ground-floor front window, he saw a piece of paper thrust to the glass. On it was printed in large letters: "S-A-M." The door opened as he came to it, and he walked into the

137

front room with Samuel Furnace, white-faced and twitching with fear.

The story of that talk, between the man for whom all England was looking and the brother-in-law who knew that the house in which they were sitting was surrounded by a force of police, appeared in the *News of the World* under the signature of Charles Tuckfield, and is the only indication of Furnace's thoughts and actions during the whole of the time during which he was a fugitive from the police. It is true that in a brief statement to the police after his arrest he stated that the shooting affair was an accident, but to Charles Tuckfield he related in dramatic fashion all the incidents of his hiding.

It has already been described how he explained the cause of the accident. Furnace also told his friend that he was going to give himself up to the police on several occasions after the murder and the fire. "But my nerve failed me," he said. "Now my number is up. It's only a matter of hours now. The 'tec's are round me like a swarm of bees. But if I could get in touch with someone who would bring me some different clothes I could get out of this fix."

Soon after lunch Charles Tuckfield left him. At the end of the road the detectives and uniformed police were waiting. Police constables had entered neighbouring houses and made their way to the back of Mrs. Shaw's boarding-house. The road was blocked both ends. There were police on the roof. A detective disguised as a street violinist was on duty near the house watching the front door. Then Superintendent Cornish walked into the room, followed by two other Scotland Yard men, rushed at an unresisting and calm Samuel Furnace, and held his hands.

The twelve-day search was over, and the greatest fugitive in English police history had betrayed himself by a letter to a relative.

He was taken to London in a police car within a few hours, after being searched and charged at Southend Police Station. He helped the police by pointing out to them the spot in the

Camden Road canal where he had thrown his revolver. He made a short statement, was searched again in his cell at Kentish Town, and locked up for the night. During the night he was under constant observation by police constables, who watched him through a wicket gate in the cell door.

At seven in the morning, after the prisoner had paced his cell ceaselessly all through the night, Constable Partridge looked through the wicket gate into No. 3 cell. He saw Furnace's hand come suddenly from behind his back with a medicine bottle. Before the constable, rushing in, could take it from his hand, he had swallowed some of the contents. Furnace collapsed, and in spite of constant care throughout the day and the following night at St. Pancras Hospital died at seven a.m. on the morning of January 17th. Morphia eased his pain, but the spirits of salts which he had swallowed from the bottle killed him after terrible agony in the usual period of twenty-four hours. His wife and brother kept watch at his bedside with the detectives, but the only words he was heard to mutter were, "My wife, my wife . . ."

Thus Furnace provided in death yet another thrill for the crowds of people who had waited in the pouring rain outside Marylebone Police Court to see the fugitive of the generation appear before the magistrates on a charge of murder. They were disappointed.

"Charge No. 22, your worship," said the court jailer. "Samuel James Furnace. Reported ill, sir."

Two poison specialists were even then in attendance on him. They could do no more than try to relieve the pain.

There remained only the inquests on the two bodies in this swiftly moving tragedy which had shown so many facets of the criminal mind.

On the next day Superintendent Cornish stated at the inquest on Furnace that the dead man's pockets and clothing were properly searched, but that there was afterwards found to be a slit in the bottom of the trench-coat which Furnace was still wearing in the cell. He took the four-ounce bottle from the lining in the few seconds' interval between the changing of the guard. The jury quickly returned a verdict of suicide. "The deceased had well prepared for suicide," said the foreman.

At the inquest on Spatchett the Coroner stated: "One would have thought that if the shooting had been an accident the incident would have upset Furnace considerably. Yet you find him perfectly rational telling an entirely fictitious story to a landlady an hour later." The jury returned a verdict of "Murder" against Furnace.

When the body of Samuel Furnace was taken to St. Pancreas Cemetery, East Finchley, excited women held up the cortège, a street musician played jazz music during the passing of the procession, and the police cordon was broken by hilarious onlookers. A short service was held in a Nonconformist chapel, and the voice of the chaplain at the graveside was drowned in the chatter of onlookers. A wreath in the form of a heart was dropped on the grave. It bore the words: "From his heart-broken wife and babies." Another bore the inscription: "To err is human, to forgive divine."

There were two later echoes of the case which during the first month of the year had filled the newspapers. One was the decision of the Britannic Assurance Company that the claim made upon them by Mrs. Furnace was untenable, since the coroner's verdict on Furnace was *felo de se*. The company, however, had decided to make a generous grant to Mrs. Furnace. "The law of the land being that no person can benefit himself or his estate by a felonious act, the policy is, therefore, void, and the company is in no way liable thereto."

Later, Scotland Yard pursued an inquiry into the circumstances in which Furnace was able to conceal in his coat a bottle of poison in spite of being searched on two occasions.

In all the concentrated and swiftly-marching thrills of the man-hunt and dramatic end of the principal character, the name of Spatchett was only in the background of the public memory.

Roland Wild

Georges Sarret: The Acid Bath Killer

For the modern reader, the acid bath murderer is John George Haigh, the swindler who, between 1944 and 1949, dissolved six victims in sulphuric acid in his rented factory at Crawley. But Haigh had a French predecessor, Maitre Georges Sarret, who was also, in his way, a criminal genius. This account of Sarret and his two mistresses is again taken from Roland Wild's Crimes and Cases of 1933.

A woman was walking alone in the squalid streets of Marseilles. Suddenly she was recognised by an old friend. That sudden recognition led to the revealing of a series of crimes, and the exposure of a monster comparable in infamy to the famous Landru.

The case which has become known as "The Acid Bath Murders" takes its place among the most gruesome trials of criminal history. The details which came to light during the proceedings at the little provincial town of Aix-en-Provence grew more forbidding as time went on, culminating in the most rigorous sentence being passed by the jury on the chief actor.

Georges Sarret, once a lawyer, and described during the proceedings as "The High Priest of Murder," was accused of systematic and diabolical murder in company with two Bavarian sisters, over whom he was said to have exercised a powerful and malignant influence.

Katherine Schmidt and Philomene Schmidt were also charged with murder and with extensive insurance frauds at the bidding of the master-mind Sarret.

The little town presented a strange appearance, accustomed as it had always been to the serenity and peace of provincial France. The indignation of the populace reached such limits, long before the first day of the trial, that it was thought wise to guard the court with troops, the road to the assize court being lined with gleaming bayonets. The whole of the *gendarmerie* of the district, and mobile guards from Marseilles, were also brought to form an avenue of steel, along which there marched the principal figures in this sensational and horrifying exposure of a clever man's greed and the cruelty of his two dupes.

Further interest was added for English observers by the fact that, during the proceedings, the name of a distinguished Englishwoman, Lady Arnould, the aged widow of Sir Joseph Arnould, Chief Justice of Bombay, cropped up from time to time.

The public indignation was evident by the crowds which clamoured for entry, so that even counsel had difficulty in gaining admittance to the court, and were seriously incommoded throughout the trial. The formidable indictment was read during the first day and the details of the crime alleged against the chief character caused universal horror. But there were others also accused, in company with Georges Sarret, of the extensive insurance frauds in which this Landru the Second seems to have specialised.

It was a fantastic story that the black-robed lawyer unfolded on that first chilly morning in October. The court was deathly silent. The peasants and shopkeepers, who had waited outside from an early hour, felt their eyes drawn towards the dock. In addition to Sarret and the two sisters, there stood a certain Doctor Maurice Guy, a former Deputy-Mayor of Marseilles; Andrée Sarret, daughter of the ex-lawyer; a frightened cook, Calixte Lufeaux; and two insurance agents, Antoine Siotis, and Marie Nicolas Brun.

At strategic points in the court stood armed *gendarmes* and soldiers. It was difficult to breathe, and the atmosphere seemed charged with tension. Into that tense assembly the Public Prosecutor, in a still, small voice, poured chapter by chapter a story of human cruelty and greed more sensational than any fiction.

The indictment covered ninety pages, and no more was heard in the court that day than the methodical and unemotional voice of the lawyer reading from its gruesome pages. Only once or twice did his voice reveal that he himself was conscious of the drama he unfolded. For the most part he spoke in a monotone. But the contents of the indictment were, to be sure, sensational enough to shock without the aid of human histrionics.

Georges Sarret had been born in Trieste, of Greek parents, in 1880. He looked, however, more than his fifty-three years, and though for many years he had lived in France and had become a naturalised Frenchman early in life, his cold composure and lack of emotion seemed to indicate that here was no Frenchman, but a creature of more Eastern phlegm.

Of his early life in France little is known, but the first relevant date on which the police had bent their attention was in 1924. It was then that he had met the two sisters, who had up till that date been teaching in France for a period of seven years, and had on many occasions taken position as governesses in some illustrious families. Lady Arnould, indeed, had lived with the two women in 1922, and it was while she was at their house that she died. This fact was only mentioned in passing, and although Georges Sarret, treacherous as a snake even to his friends, had accused the two sisters of being concerned in her death, the police had made investigations, and early in the proceedings directed that the death of Lady Arnould was quite irrelevant, and that the sisters were guiltless of any wrong-doing in that instance.

It seems that from the first meeting Sarret was able to

exercise his baneful influence over them. He dominated them and was the prime mover in the terrible list of crimes which now came to light. In 1924 Philomene married a man named Villette, and Sarret was best man at the wedding. Perhaps it was even while he was at the altar that the idea came to him of practising frauds on insurance companies by causing the death of a man who had been persuaded to marry his accomplice. Soon afterwards, at any rate, he persuaded the other sister, Katharine, to marry a man named Deltreuil. The most significant thing to be noticed about this union was that, whereas the woman under his control was comparatively young and beautiful, the husband was twenty-four years her senior and in failing health. It is perhaps not surprising to learn that the husband Deltreuil was forthwith insured in the sum of a hundred thousand francs.

The prosecutor was warming up, and when he proceeded to give further details of the daring and criminal scheme evolved by Sarret, he was rewarded with a ripple of excitement that ran round the court.

It had been obvious to Sarret that considerable difficulty would be encountered in insuring an invalid like Deltreuil. But this difficulty meant little to the man whose greed dictated his every move. He had already met an unfrocked priest, named Chambon, and had noted his strong appearance and the likelihood of impressing any insurance company. Without any hesitation, Sarret persuaded Chambon to impersonate the sick Deltreuil for the insurance examination, and when Deltreuil died some months afterwards, the company paid and Sarret pocketed the sum of a hundred thousand francs as first earnings in his new life of crime.

It seems that at that period Katharine Schmidt was not in the conspiracy, for she evidently protested to Sarret, asking him where he had gained his sudden riches. To this Sarret, never without an answer, said that a friend had left him a legacy.

Some time after that, however, the two women seemed to have become willing to co-operate with Sarret even in the most nefarious of his misdeeds. They made no objection when he informed them that he must get rid of Chambon, because, he said, Chambon was blackmailing him. Katharine and Philomene even helped him actively in the preparations for the deed. What he required was a secluded villa, and it was the women who made a thorough search through the lists of estate agents until they found, in the "Hermitage," near the town of Aix, what they required.

That villa was to become notorious in the history of crime, and is still regarded to-day as a place of evil omen, from which its walls and picturesque thatched roof will never be rid.

If Sarret only told the sisters that he had to get rid of Chambon, in the recesses of his evil mind he had a far more dastardly idea. For Chambon had a mistress named Ballandreaux, and it was with that thought at the back of his mind that he bade his helpers prepare the villa for habitation. His second order was far more significant. He told them to buy, as unobtrusively as possible, an old bath. When he himself went shopping it was to buy a hundred litres of sulphuric acid; soon the stage was set for the carrying out of his idea.

It was in the summer of 1925 that he contrived to meet Chambon, as if by chance, in the streets of Marseilles, and after a friendly conversation, he invited him to look over the villa. The prosecution's story had a weak link in the chain at this point, for, whereas some believed that Sarret brought his victim back to the villa, other opinions were that Katharine Schmidt, by now a fully-fledged member of the conspiracy, lured him in a taxi-cab to her home.

But the prosecution's story was decided at any rate in regard to the next act in the drama. As Chambon and Katharine walked upstairs to view the first floor, a single shot rang out, and Chambon fell dead.

Whether Katharine was surprised or not is not known,

but on turning round she saw emerge from behind a screen the bland and self-assured figure of Sarret.

Something of the coolness of his nature is revealed by his unemotional comment as he surveyed the body. He merely said: "I am going to Marseilles to arrange this thing." Two hours later he had gone, and that night returned to the villa with the mistress of the dead man.

The sisters were by now certainly in the plot. According to the prosecution's story, Katharine helped her lord and master in the performance of his second evil deed for the day. Acting on instructions, she went out into the yard and started the engine of a particularly noisy motor-cycle, which may or may not have been bought for the purpose. As the engine spurted into life it drowned the noise of another shot, and the woman Ballandreaux fell, shot in almost the exact spot as Chambon had been a few hours earlier.

It was then that the cunning and cleverness of Sarret was fully revealed. Perhaps up to that moment neither sister had realised the purpose of Sarret's strange purchases. They were soon to know. The next morning the sulphuric acid was poured into the bath until it was half full, and the bodies dragged into the cellar and flung into the acid.

His plan went off without a hitch. In a few days nothing recognisable remained of the two bodies, and he was able to distribute the remains over the garden without incurring suspicion. Sarret and the two women thereupon left the villa, and for some time after that lived in comparative luxury in Marseilles. It seems strange that not a breath of suspicion was directed to the owner of the villa owing to the disappearance of the unfrocked priest and his mistress, but perhaps a man of his history and circumstances might well have lived for years without inviting friendship. Nobody missed him, at any rate, and though Sarret undoubtedly passed through a few days of anxiety when he learnt that a villager had reported to the police the presence of acid in the villa garden, the subsequent investigations came to nothing, and for many years the crime was never brought home to this new Landru.

It was no doubt the ease with which Sarret had accomplished his crime that led him to contemplate further essays in the art of murder. He was living in luxury, and though, so far, he had had funds enough to keep him in comfortable style, he realised that his bank balance would need to be further augmented from one source or another.

Since murder was so easy, why not insurance? He must have devoted many hours of thought to the problem before he acted, and it was not, in fact, until 1931 that he perpetrated a fraud on the insurance companies with the aid of Katharine and Philomene. Even so, caution was necessary, and with real patience and forethought the two sisters prepared the ground before the coup. They became fervent "lovers of the poor" and charitable workers in the sordid slums of Marseilles, and in a few months were well known for their sweetness of character and their widespread benevolence. Particularly kind were they to women who were obviously destined to spend but a few more years in this world, and, if the truth were known, they kept a sharp look-out for those suffering in the advanced stages of consumption.

Not till the end of the year did they reveal their hands, and it may be presumed that not till then had they found the perfect subject for the furtherance of their criminal intention. It was Philomene who recognised in a woman named Lorenzi, then dying in hospital from tuberculosis, the perfect ally. Philomene gave her money lavishly, and together with many other promises, guaranteed to find her husband and help him. But she protested that she would be helpless unless Lorenzi supplied her with all the personal papers of identification with which the French people are always equipped.

It was not surprising that Mme Lorenzi handed over the papers to her benefactress, and Sarret soon had them in his hands, later handing them over, the prosecution alleged, to

Lufeaux, the strong and healthy cook. Lufeaux forthwith took out an insurance policy in the name of Lorenzi in the sum of two hundred thousand francs. The fact that Sarret was now aiming at double the reward was no doubt due to his having introduced other confederates to the plot. But after consideration he was not even content with the prospect of that large sum of money, and within a few months a man known to the insurance companies as Lorenzi was insured for the sum of no less than a million francs.

But a great disappointment was in store for Sarret. He had expected that the real Lorenzi would die within a year or two, and he was willing to wait for that event, armed as he was with his papers. Lorenzi however, died almost immediately, and when an insurance agent expressed surprise and seemed likely to institute uncomfortable inquiries, Sarret was suddenly panic-stricken. He knew that none of his dealings would bear investigation. He decided to cut his losses on the instant. "The widow renounces all her claims," he said briefly. It must have been a bitter blow, but he realised that accidents will happen even in the best regulated crimes.

A considerable sum of money had been put down in this attempt, and it was unlikely that Sarret would be long in re-entering the business which seemed so certain to bring in vast profits. His next exploit seemed more foolproof, and Sarret became even more ambitious with the expectation of netting nearly two million francs. The method was almost the same, and there was still the same risk of the insured person dying too early to avoid the inquisitiveness of the insurance companies. But that risk had to be run, and the prize was sufficiently tempting for a man of the character of Georges Sarret, by now completely in command of the morals of the Schmidt sisters, and himself unperturbed by conscience.

Katharine Schmidt was this time to fill the rôle for the benefit of the insurance company while Philomene was to find a young girl who might soon be expected to die. The girl was easily found by Philomene during her benevolent visits to the Marseilles hospitals. Magali Herbin, aged only twenty-four, but already in an advanced stage of consumption, seemed to be ideal for the purpose. As it happened, the choice was not a happy one from the point of view of the conspirators, but there was nothing to indicate then that she would not fall a victim to the disease in the space of a year at the most. And having obtained her papers of identity, Katharine Schmidt called on the insurance companies, showed the papers giving her age as twenty-four, and arranged for insurance for the sum of one million seven hundred thousand francs, this being, she explained for the benefit of her aged mother in Germany.

Magali Herbin was taken from the hospital by the kind sister who had so often befriended her, and told that she was now going to live in the country where she would be given treatment under the supervision of a qualified doctor . . .

All these incidents in the deliberate campaign were recounted by the Public Prosecutor on that first day of the trial in the packed and expectant court in Aix-en-Provence. Now, for a moment, the lawyer allowed himself to make a dramatic gesture. The whole assembly was waiting on his words. Describing the promises made to the sick girl and the assurance that she would be in charge of a doctor, he turned and waved an arm towards the dock.

"She had strange fare for a consumptive!" declared the prosecutor. "They took her out at night, gave her cocktails and ice-drinks, and generally treated her to a high life."

There was no doctor to look after her. The intention of the benevolent sisters was soon evident. Although she did not realise it herself, Magali Herbin had been taken under their care to hasten her death. But strange as it may seem she lived on, and becoming desperate with impatience, the monster Sarret had to make a chance in his plans. One night he brought home two bottles of champagne, for a continuance of that "high life" which had failed to end her life. But he brought home also a packet of phosphate of zinc.

Two days later the girl was dead.

The prosecution allegation was that Dr. Maurice Guy, who now stood in the dock, had given a burial certificate in the name of Katharine Schmidt. He was, however, acquitted of the charge. A certificate was obtained and presented to the insurance companies by Philomene, now posing as her own mother, and the huge sum of money was paid over without demur. Sarret had every cause to be well pleased with the success of his plan. There was now no hint of suspicion from the insurance company, so well had Katharine and Philomene performed their tasks. It seemed as if there would be no flaw in similar operations to be carried out whenever the sinister trio were short of money.

And it is undoubted that similar atrocities would have been attempted had it not been for the folly of Katharine Schmidt. After lying low for a time the lure of Marseilles was too much for her good sense, and she took to visiting her old haunts from time to time. Apparently she did not even trouble to move in new circles or find new friends. The inevitable happened. An old acquaintance, shocked at seeing one day the familiar face and figure of the Katharine Schmidt she had believed dead, mentioned her astonishment to a friend. Word got round that the reports of Katharine Schmidt's death were untrue. An insurance agent heard the whisper. Mere inquisitiveness led to serious inquiry. The police arrived suddenly at the Sarret *ménage* and arrested Katharine. She could not stand up to the fierce hail of questions put to her by the police, and confessed, not only to the impersonation of the sick girl but to her part in the whole of Sarret's series of intrigues. Her sister Philomene, terrified out of her wits, gave herself up to the police. Sarret's arrest followed immediately, and, according to the Prosecution's story, confessed himself a murderer . . .

The Public Prosecutor sat down. He left the stuffy court in a fervour of speculation as to when Sarret would give evidence. All eyes turned suddenly to the principal figure in the dock, the grey-haired and intelligent-looking man who was now given the opportunity of answering a few formal questions put to him by the judge. He admitted having been twice divorced, and the judge's comment was that he was known to possess a most immoral reputation.

That same day the judge also disposed of the suggestion, first made by Sarret, that Philomene Schmidt had poisoned Lady Arnould. Philomene broke down when told of Sarret's allegation, and declared that she had been most devoted to Lady Arnould during the latter's illness.

On that note the day's proceedings ended, and an indignant and horrified crowd of spectators left the court and walked through the lane of dark-skinned soldiers to their cottages in the little town which had become so suddenly notorious.

During the week-end further facts came to light of the lives of the three principals. Sarret, it seems, had started life in France as an hotel clerk, and was later a street-trader, becoming a lawyer after the War. The Schmidt sisters were daughters of a Bavarian police-officer, having had a good education and coming to Paris in 1912, where they entered the service of a count. They made such a good impression on their employer that he was able to keep them out of an internment camp during the War, though the police at one time suspected that they had been engaged in spying activities. It was further revealed that Lady Arnould had left them a legacy of several thousand pounds, and they were still in possession of some of their money when they first met Sarret. It was on Sarret's advice that they married Frenchmen in order to attain French nationality, though in the case of Katharine her husband was a consumptive sailor who performed the act of marrying her for a few pounds, and was then turned adrift. When they were arrested the body of Lady Arnould was exhumed, but Sarret's allegation that they had poisoned their benefactress was scotched by the analyst who examined the body for traces.

By Monday morning, when the trial was resumed, the

public indignation was at fever heat, and if those who crowded the court were looking for sensation, they were soon satisfied.

Sarret was not long to remain the calm personality which he had seemed on the opening day. There was a stir in court when it became known that the prosecution were going to cross-examine his daughter. Sarret lost his nerve, bowed his head, and sobbed brokenly. Questions were flung at Mademoiselle Andrée Sarret regarding the period when she had acted as secretary to her father in his capacity of lawyer.

"Did you know what business was being conducted in your father's office?" she was asked.

"If I had known," she replied, "I would not have remained an hour with him."

One after the other her answers piled up the weight of evidence against her father, until, with his face suddenly purple, he thumped his fist on the ledge of the dock and yelled: "Sarret! Sarret! You talk of nothing but Sarret! I am getting tired of all this!"

But at other times he was enigmatic. Right at the beginning of the proceedings a storm was caused by the judge saying to Sarret: "You have been a lawyer, and therefore you can present your case without being questioned."

Two barristers jumped up at once to protest, one of them shouting:

"That man has never worn our robes; he is not a member of the Bar!"

Sarret was therefore questioned, and put forward an entirely new and fantastic explanation. The gist of his defence was that he shot Chambon accidentally after he had been told that Chambon had killed Mme Ballandreaux.

The Public Prosecutor jumped up immediately. "I have never heard such impudence!" he shouted. "This is the first time that such a version of the crime has been given!"

Throughout the next few minutes there was a tumult of shouting in the court, the judge, the Public Prosecutor, the lawyers and the chief prisoner all contributing to the uproar. It was Sarret's voice which dominated, however. He went on imperturbably: "These women have been telling lies about me. It is time for me to defend myself. I upbraided Chambon for what he had done as he stood there with a revolver in his hand. I tried to disarm him, but the revolver went off and he fell dead."

Asked why he did not tell the police, he said that he was frightened of them, and in explanation of his purchase of sulphuric acid, he answered lamely that he thought he might need it some time.

Philomene Schmidt repeatedly interrupted the examination, shouting: "My sister and I were his slaves. He kept us prisoners and threatened us with arrest."

She shook her clenched fist at Sarret and exclaimed: "You are a monster, the worst monster the world has ever seen!"

Evidence was given regarding Philomene's inspired acting when she took the part of the mother of Magali Herbin. It was stated that she wept profusely in the insurance company's office when collecting the money, and enlisted the sympathies of the whole staff.

At other times Sarret was calm and impressive; his steady voice dominated the court, and with one hand smoothing his grey hair, he blandly offered an innocent version of the whole affair while the Schmidt sisters trembled in the dock with fury, Katharine tearing her handkerchief with her teeth. When he put forward his new explanation of Chambon's death, never heard previously since inquiries began two and a half years before, the court was dumbfounded, the Public Prosecutor himself exclaiming: "Ah!" as if his breath had been taken away.

Whereas, in sharp contrast to his calm demeanour, Philomene provided a series of outbursts, at one time shouting: "He lies, he lies; you must believe me! You can imprison me all my life, I have suffered less during two years in prison than when I was free under the domination of Sarret!"

All eyes turned on the Greek: he was the most composed man in the court. But he seemed as if he were paying no attention. Only after hours of damning evidence given against him did he once more show any emotion, and that was when Philomene entered the box and gave evidence about the death of Magali Herbin. Philomene seemed determined to take revenge on Sarret. Both she and her sister sobbed continuously and frequently referred to the time when they were prisoners in his house and under his control.

Katharine said that she had been "buried alive in Sarret's house in Nice," and said that for many months after the death of Magali Herbin she had been forbidden to leave the house owing to Sarret's fear that she would be recognised.

As Katharine made further incriminating statements she rubbed her hands together as if she was enjoying herself. Sarret was obviously fighting his own emotion, but eventually his patience wore out and the court was treated to the amazing spectacle of witness and prisoner shaking their fists at each other and engaging in a shouting match, each protesting the untruthfulness of the other.

There was a long duel between Sarret and the Public Prosecutor.

"I implore you to tell the truth," said the prosecutor. But when Sarret began speaking his counsel jumped up and shouted: "Stop speaking, Sarret!" Suddenly there was renewed turmoil. The prosecutor protested that this was contempt of court, to which Sarret's counsel replied: "This man is fighting for his head! He owes nobody respect!"

Before that day's hearing was concluded the principal actors in this strange drama had cast aside all pretence, and were displaying the most primitive emotions.

The whole country was by now following the "Acid Bath Trial" with intense interest. The Paris newspapers were devoting more columns a day to the description of every passage in court than they had to the famous Landru trial.

For here was every factor which makes a *cause célèbre*. There was the dominating personality of Sarret himself, a clever man who might have prospered in any occupation he had taken up. There were the full-blooded personalities of the two sisters who had come under his influence. There was excitement in plenty, and when Philomene or Katharine was giving evidence the court could always be certain of the spectacle of women under the guidance of strong emotion, of which vengeance seemed always to be in the ascendancy.

The next day even laughter was added to the other ingredients of the drama. A seventy-eight-year-old accountant, M. Caracal, an important witness, was giving evidence. Before, however, he consented to speak, he made a spirited protest to the judge. It will be recalled that at that time the French Government was undergoing one of its periods of re-shuffling. The day before, in fact, the Government had resigned. M. Caracal complained that he had been kept waiting four days to give evidence.

"If I have to wait any longer," he declared, "I shall lose my job. In that case I shall sue the Government."

"Which Government?" asked the Judge blandly; "we have not got one."

The whole court exploded with laughter, Sarret himself joining in.

But if for a moment or two the atmosphere had changed from grave to gay, later on the court was to be reminded that this was a serious occasion. The prosecutor began fiercely to attack Sarret's version of the death of Chambon.

He said that Sarret, giving his version of the Chambon affair, had made statements which in every case were impossible to confirm, since the people he spoke of were dead.

"Sarret," he said, "you are surrounded by corpses! All your clients of yesterday are dead to-day! A curious coincidence!"

The opposing counsel were frequently unable to control their anger, and on many occasions abuse was thrown about the court. When, for instance, the prosecutor objected to an argument made by Sarret's lawyer, he sprang to his feet, saying: "It is a pity that you are to-day at the Bar!"

Immediately there was pandemonium. Every lawyer in court was on his feet in a second. "Leave the court" they shouted, and the public joined in the demonstration. On one occasion the court was suspended for half an hour to allow tempers to cool down, and, in fact, the judge adjourned the court early in the afternoon in the hope that a night's sleep might tend to obliterate memories of bitter scenes.

With truly Gallic resignation, however, the lawyers later shook hands and recriminations were forgotten.

The bad atmosphere, however, was not helped by a letter produced in court which a witness stated had been forged by a lawyer in order to removed from Sarret's shoulders the responsibility of having purchased the fateful bath. Allegations were freely made that a lawyer had arranged for a false witness to appear in court, and for a large part of the day the squabbles of the legal luminaries completely obscured the main issue. Meanwhile Georges Sarret looked down sardonically on the protagonists.

He smiled when Maître Roche, defending Sarret, admitted that he had given his client a certain document. Maître Moro-Giafferi, "the Marshall-Hall of France," who was appearing for Katharine Schmidt, protested against the insult to the Bar and, followed by all the other lawyers, gathered up his cloak and swept out of the room with great dignity. Nor was farce absent from these buffooneries. Sarret, smiling once more, rose in the dock and making a movement as if to leave said: "I am clearing out too." The court rocked with laughter.

During that day too a change of heart was apparent in Katharine Schmidt. She seemed now to be making desperate efforts to shield Sarret, who, it was proved, had undoubtedly been her lover. She was unmoved when Maître Moro-Giafferi implored her to remember her own dangerous position.

"I appeal to you, Katharine!" he cried, wringing his hands. "Now is the time to tell the truth!"

But Katharine would not budge from her quixotic position. She shook her head emphatically, repeating her previous statement, while her lawyer hung his head and swung his arms in the air, so that the voluminous sleeves of his black robe gave him the appearance of a huge bat, and once more he turned to his client with a hopeless gesture of despair. But she was still defiant, refusing to save herself if it meant incriminating the man, who it seemed, still exerted over her the old power and the old influence.

Sarret was now definitely at bay. It was considered inevitable that his version of the shooting had been privately ridiculed by the jury. The excited mobs which besieged the court every day, as this week of sensations grew to an end, were often violent and demonstrative when Sarret was driven to the court. The Senegalese troops sometimes had considerable difficulty in keeping them in order, and day by day there was additional trouble in keeping the fortunate ones who had gained admittance in proper order.

But although ridiculed at one stage, Sarret now produced an even more daring defence. Briefly, he challenged the court to continue with the prosecution of Katharine Schmidt, as, he explained, she was legally dead, for the consumptive Magali Herbin had been insured and buried in Katharine's name.

Though sometimes both sisters united in defending Sarret, at others they were most helpful to the prosecution. It seemed as if the sisters did not know their own minds themselves. Often enough they refused to compromise Sarret, but during his own evidence they frequently sprang to their feet, abusing and reviling him.

Sarret was next confronted by two of his former wives. The first of these collapsed in the witnessbox and could not give evidence, but the second wife, Mlle Airaud, disclosed that Sarret married her after he and his first wife had been divorced.

"But I was never considered a legitimate wife," she stated.

"His first wife was the only one who counted, and after a time he became completely reconciled to her."

She also revealed a curious side to the man's heartless nature. She had been pleased, she said, to find he was so lavish with presents for the home – furniture, ornaments, and even bed-linen. It was only later that she discovered the origin of these gifts. They had been the property of Chambon and his mistress . . .

Another defence attempt was the theory that Sarret intended to open a chemical business with the sisters Schmidt, thus accounting for the last purchase of sulphuric acid. In the ensuing tumult, when lawyers were on their feet shouting abuse at each other, while the judge was vainly appealing for order in this most extraordinary court, Sarret's voice could be heard above the others, his livid face turned towards the sisters, angry words on his lips.

"It is you who have brought us here, you two idiots of women!" he shouted, "and yet I am glad to be here instead of still living that disgusting life!"

The vitriolic abuse in reply from the sisters brought the court to its senses, and order was once more restored.

The hospital matron who had entrusted the consumptive girl to the care of Sarret was an interesting witness.

"Katharine came to me with the story that a fond relative had asked her to make pleasant the last years of a dying girl," she recounted. "Then Philomene told how Magali Herbin had died in Nice with a nun by her bedside. She had actually died in Marseilles."

"You see how you lied!" remarked the judge.

"We had to lie!" shouted the sisters; "we had to lie at his orders!" And both pointed at Sarret.

Another witness was the undertaker who buried Magali Herbin.

"Sarret," he said, "was the only mourner, and seemed desolated as he rode in the funeral procession." Sarret had told him that he wanted the funeral carried out as quickly as possible, and the driver of the hearse proceeded at a trot. "It was a modest funeral," concluded the undertaker sorrowfully.

"Yes," the judge commented dryly, "it was a modest funeral; but it brought him over one million francs."

The next day new evidence was forthcoming. This was in support of Sarrat's oft-repeated statement that it was Chambon who bought the sulphuric acid. He had frequently declared that it was Chambon who killed his mistress, Mme Ballandreaux, and now put into court two documents which seemed to show, to the great excitement of the court, that Chambon had certainly had a hand in these damning purchases.

The prosecution openly called these documents forgeries, and intimated that they would be subjected to the examination of Dr. Beraud, the famous handwriting expert, who thereupon set to work and promised to report on them by the next day. The defence lawyer naturally exhibited these documents with a flourish and was not at all perturbed when the judge turned to Sarret and asked why he had not produced these documents before. But before he could reply his counsel shouted that Sarret had nothing to do with the direction of the defence.

Thus one more line of defence was revealed at the eleventh hour. Sarret, after at first being defiant, had produced several theories to account for his actions, none of which could be substantiated. The latest attempt had at any rate the virtue of novelty, and when the court adjourned that day the town was in a fervour of excitement to know the fate of this last argument on behalf of a man who might already be feeling the steel of "Madame Guillotine" on his neck.

That day's sensation, however, and the results which the two documents might be expected to bring, were eclipsed the next day when the Public Prosecutor rose to outline the case against Sarret, and to demand the supreme penalty. The two documents were never heard of again, a fate perhaps which they deserved. At any rate, the speeches for the prosecution, and later for the defence, seldom had any relation to facts, and in the main were composed of high flights of rhetoric, and sometimes abuse.

The prosecutor spoke for four hours, his magnificent voice emphasising every outstanding point, continuing sometimes in a low key and sometimes dying out altogether while he permitted a lengthy silence to make his artistic performance more impressive. He had a good case and he enjoyed it. For a time he contented himself with a recital of the curious circumstances of Sarret's life, later he turned to the chief occupant of the dock, and reviled him with sonorous phrases, spitting out epithets and insults.

He told a story of the crime in eight episodes. The court followed him intently as he described Sarret persuading Chambon and his mistress to stay in the villa; Sarret and Katharine arranging the bath; the careful search for a suitable villa; the ruse of the motor-cycle to cover the sound of the shot; the absurdity of a bath in a house where there was insufficient water; Sarret obtaining a shooting permit when he was no sportsman; Sarret ordering the sulphuric acid; and lastly, Sarret hiding behind the screen and shooting his victims.

He concluded on a high note: "This monster," he said, "deserves no pity. I demand the supreme penalty. You had ordered sulphuric acid previously in 1923! That proves, Sarret, that you have other corpses on your conscience! You are an indescribable criminal and the whole world turns from you in disgust!"

No fewer than 197 questions were presented to the jury by the defence. These singled out the discrepancies in the prosecution's story, and made much of the best side of Sarret's character. In his own family, apparently, he had been well loved, and it was recalled that the only time he had manifested any emotion during the trial was when his daughter had given evidence against him. One of his sisters had stuck to him gallantly during the two and a half years of the police investigation, and if she ever suspected the truth of the allegations, she had never shown it. One of the minor tragedies of this amazing trial was that the agony of suspense killed her just before Sarret's first appearance in the dock.

When the time came for the defence of the sisters to be opened there was a pathetic incident. Just as Maître Moro-Giafferi was about to begin his speech on behalf of Katharine Schmidt, the woman who had struck every one in court by her beauty, bent down, took hold of his hand and kissed it. Both lawyers defending the sisters placed the entire blame for their crimes on Sarret. It was stated that they were completely under his power, and that they had paid bribes to the police totalling over £600 in a vain attempt to call off the hunt.

It was revealed at this stage that Sarret's legal knowledge had enabled him to delay the trial for two years, on the strength of his argument that Katharine Schmidt was legally dead, and that no action could lie against her.

The judge was exhausted when making his final speech to the jury, and had to pause in the middle of reading the long list of questions. By the evening, however, of a day entirely given up to counsel's speeches, he had finished. Nobody doubted that Sarret would receive the death penalty, and the public paid greater attention to the question of the sentences to be meted out to the two sisters.

In expectation of the increased public excitement still more troops were drafted into the town, and all preparations were made for an organised defence of the prisoners if the crowd became out of hand. Such was the public indignation, indeed, that the fear of a lynching of Sarret was well justified. The crowd outside the court had become ominously larger day by day, and it was observed that their temper was at a dangerous heat. It was decided to conclude the whole case that evening if possible. The jury retired to consider the verdict, and without being absent from court very long gave the expected reply.

Sarret was found guilty of murder of Chambon, Mme

Ballandreaux, and the consumptive girl Magali Herbin. He was sentenced to death.

Every eye in the court was turned upon him, and it was astonishing to observe that over his lips there played a charming smile. Perhaps it was no shock to him, since after the collapse of his various defences he could have expected no other penalty. But there was another reason for the smile. Coupled with the jury's supreme penalty was the recommendation that he should be fined. And the sum which he was thought to owe to the police authorities was sixteen shillings.

Soon after the case was over it was announced that his execution would take place in public. This was due to his having been convicted of murder without any extenuating circumstances, and this detail also precluded him from the privilege of appeal. Nominally, of course, all executions in France are held in public according to the Napoleonic code, but during the past sixty years the custom has been to exclude the public except those officials provided with special official passports. It was announced, however, that in the case of Sarret there would be no bar to the public approaching as near as they wished to the actual scaffold.

The two sisters received sentences of ten years solitary confinement and ten years banishment from the locality. It was a revelation of human character to observe their passive lack of interest on receiving their sentences, for, whereas they faced bravely enough their judges, Sarret himself, who was said to have been the dominating personality, was a pitiful wreck of humanity.

But the reserve of the sisters gave way when the tension broke and the jailers came to remove them to the cells. Katharine swayed, and with her platinum-blonde hair falling in disarray over her beautiful ashen face, was carried in a fainting condition below. For one moment Sarret looked up, and his old self-confidence was seen in a cynical smile.

Thus ended one of the most terrible criminal stories ever revealed in a French court of law. No adjectives or epithets were too strong to be used against the principal character. Press and public combined in reviling him and in suggesting that here was a monster in human form.

Some of the secrets of his astonishing life of crime were revealed after his conviction. It was fully expected that he would confess in the condemned cell, and indeed it was said that before he was taken from the dock he leant over to his counsel and whispered in a matter-of-fact tone of voice: "I have something to say to you. Come and see me some time."

But there were others who said that he would follow the example of that other monster to whom he had been so often compared. Landru never confessed, although for years after his death there were rumours that a written explanation of his crimes was in existence.

The character of Sarret was such that he might quite feasibly have boasted about his many crimes and might have made some reference to other feats of corruption and violence. The cryptic words of the Public Prosecutor were not forgotten. The world wanted to know what lay beyond that official's belief, impossible to prove, that Sarret had in the past caused many people to disappear for his own convenience. Though known at home as an honest, mild-tempered, and kindly man, he had revealed himself as callous and heartless where money was at stake, and it was not unlikely that such a man would revel in his ability to shock the world. One curious side-line of his personal character was his mania for tidiness. Every man has his own weakness. Sarret could not bear to see a paper or a book out of place, and it was said that he could never refrain from brushing away a speck of dust from the coat of a visitor.

The two sisters, who had been acquitted of murder, and were sentenced only for their part in the insurance swindles, were driven away from Aix separately from Georges Sarret, a last glimpse of whom they had obtained in the dock. The crowds gathered outside were ignorant of their departure, but a mistake led to Sarret's carriage being recognised, and the ranks of black troops had a considerable task in keeping the crowds in check. "To death! To death!" shouted the populace, and for a time it seemed as if human desire for vengeance would cheat the guillotine of its victim.

Roland Wild

The Cleveland Torso Killer

The Cleveland Torso killer has some claim to
be regarded as the American equivalent of Jack
the Ripper. The crimes are, in some ways, more
horrific than those of the Whitechapel murderer.
The author of this present account is my son
Damon, who wrote it for our second *Encyclopedia of Unsolved Mysteries*, although the present
version is, in fact, a longer account that he wrote
for magazine publication.

On a warm September afternoon in 1935, two boys on
their way home from school walked along a dusty,
sooty gulley called Kingsbury Run, in the heart of Cleveland,
Ohio. On a weed-covered slope known as Jackass Hill, one
challenged the other to a race, and they hurtled sixty feet
down the slope to the bottom. Sixteen year old James
Wagner was the winner, and as he halted, panting, he
noticed something white in the bushes a few yards away.
A closer look revealed that it was a naked body, and that
it was headless.

The two police patrolmen who arrived minutes later found
the body of a young white male clad only in black socks;
the genitals had been removed. It lay on its back, with
the legs stretched out and the arms neatly by the sides,
as if laid out for a funeral. Thirty feet away, also hidden
among the weeds, the policemen found another body, lying
in the same position; it was of an older man, and had also
been decapitated and emasculated. The decomposition of

the second body made it clear that it had been there some time longer than the first.

When Assistant Police Chief Emmet J. Potts arrived at the scene, he found it swarming with policemen, and the heights above crowded with spectators. The desolate gulley known as Kingsbury Run was used by the locals as a rubbish dump; railway tracks ran along its floor to join the industrial valley known as the Flats, with its factories and warehouses. In the remote past, a stream had flowed through Kingsbury Run to join the Cuyahoga River which had created the flats. After dark, the whole area was crowded with hobos amd vagrants – for this was the height of the American Depression – and Potts made a shrewd guess that the two corpses belonged to this fraternity of transients.

The first thing that struck Potts, as he viewed the remains, was the absence of bloodstains, either on the ground or on the bodies themselves. The obvious conclusion was that they had been killed and decapitated elsewhere, allowed to drain of blood, and then washed before being taken to Kingsbury Run.

By that time, the missing heads had also been found; hair sticking out of the ground had revealed one of them buried a few yards away; the second proved to be buried nearby. Moreover, both sets of genitals were also found lying nearby, as if casually discarded by the killer. Potts ordered the removal of the bodies to the police morgue.

That evening, Coroner Arthur Pearse performed the autopsies. The younger corpse was that of a good-looking young man, and he had been dead for two or three days. The rope marks on the wrists, and the torn skin, made it clear that he had struggled violently. But for Dr. Pearse, the most chilling observation was that the muscles of the neck were retracted. That could mean only one thing: that the man had been beheaded while he was alive and conscious. The decapitation had been done smoothly and cleanly with a few strokes of a very sharp knife.

The second body was more puzzling. Although decomposition had destroyed the fingerprints, the skin itself was of a curious red tinge, and had the texture of leather. Pearse was inclined to speculate that some unknown chemical preservative had been used on it. The man's age was about 45, and he had been dead for about two weeks. Decomposition made it impossible to tell whether he had also been decapitated while still alive.

The investigators felt more cheerful when the first of the two bodies was identified by the fingerprints. He was 28 year old Edward Andrassy, and he had a minor police record for carrying a concealed weapon. Andrassy had lived quietly at home with respectable parents. But he apparently lived a double life. At night he liked to frequent the sleazy brothel quarter that adjoined Kingsbury Run; rumour had it that he was a pimp. It seemed that he had recently stabbed an Italian in a fight, and that the man's friends were looking for him. Mafia killings often involved mutilation of the genitals. And when a witness claimed to have seen two Italians in Kingsbury Run shortly before the bodies were found, it began to look as if the case was nearing a solution.

Newspaper reports of the finds made many Clevelanders feel queasy at breakfast time the next day. But Cleveland's new Public Safety Director, Eliot Ness, had a stronger stomach. At the age of thirty two, Ness had an enviable record as a crime fighter. In Chicago, as a Prohibition agent, he had been largely responsible for the downfall of Al Capone. After this he had moved to another "city of sin", Cincinatti, Ohio, to clean up its bootlegging rackets. And when, in 1934, the Cleveland authorities decided that their city had become a cesspool of racketeering and gambling, Ness was invited to come and clean up its "mobs." His main problem here, as in Chicago, was that there was so much corruption in the police department and the D.A's office that he had to operate with a very small group of people he could trust absolutely – his "Untouchables", who were forced to remain strictly anonymous. With corrupt lawmen to worry about, not to mention the Mayfield Road Mob and the Lonardo Gang, Ness had little time or inclination to brood on the psychopath who had killed two vagrants.

That attitude seemed to be justified as the rest of 1935 passed without incident. Admittedly, the Italian mobster theory of the double murders led nowhere. But when the investigators learned that Andrassy had been bisexual, they switched their attention to the possibility of a love triangle, in which both men had been murdered by a jealous third party.

On January 26, the homosexual theory was dramatically challenged. That snowy Sunday morning, the howling of dog finally drove a black resident of East Twentieth Street – on the edge of the Flats – to go and investigate. She found the dog straining at its leash to get at a basket that had been left against a factory wall. A glance under the burlap bag that covered it convinced her that it was full of raw butcher's meat. As she walked away, she told a neighbouring butcher that the basket contained hams. Wondering if they might have been stolen from his own shop, he lifted the burlap and removed one of the "hams." It proved to be a severed human arm. The police who rushed to the scene found that the basket contained the dismembered remains of a woman. One of the thighs was wrapped in a newspaper dating from the previous day. Some parts of the body were still missing – including the head.

Fingerprints identified her as a 41 year old prostitute named Florence Polillo, a dumpy little woman who had a police record for soliciting and bar-room brawling. She had last been seen alive two days before her body was found. The police were inclined to dismiss the notion that she might have been the victim of Edward Andrassy's killer. But one ominous detail seemed to contradict them. The muscles of the neck were still retracted, as if she had been alive when decapitated.

More pieces of Flo Polillo were found in the backyard of an empty house, although these did not include the head.

(It was never recovered.) The most promising lead was the description of an Italian with whom she had been seen recently; he sounded like one of the Italians the police wanted to interview about Andrassy's murder. But he was never traced.

This latest murder presented Sergeant James T. Hogan., the new head of Homicide, with a troublesome question. If she *was* another victim of the "Head Hunter of Kingsbury Run" (as some journalist had christened the killer), then the theory of a homicidal triangle would have to be discounted. This man was not a jealous lover, but a perverted psychopath with an obsession about decapitation and dismemberment. And that in turn raised another disturbing question. Eighteen months ago, on September 5, 1934, the lower half of a female torso had been found on Cleveland's Euclid Beach; it had been severed at the waist and at the knees. The upper part was found some miles away – minus the head and arms. Coroner Pearse estimated the age of the woman as in her mid to late thirties. The curious feature of the case was the leathery texture of the skin. At first Pearse speculated that there had been an attempt to destroy the body by burning – then concluded that it had been preserved in chloride of lime. The head was never found and the woman – who became known as "the Lady of the Lake" – remained identified.

No one had thought to connect this victim with the "Head Hunter", even though the body of Andrassy's unknown companion had also been "preserved" in some chemical. Now the Polillo case suggested that the police should be looking for a psychopathic killer who had already claimed four victims, and who might now be looking for more.

Cleveland's Public Safety Director was still more concerned with police corruption than with the "Head Hunter." In May 1936 Ness brought a police captain to trial on bribery charges and had the satisfaction of seeing him convicted. A month later, he was chiefly concerned with organising safety precautions at the forthcoming Republican Convention, which was to be held in Cleveland.

Three days before the Convention was due to open, the Head Hunter reminded the police that he was still at large. On June 5, two black children walking through Kingsbury Run found a severed head wrapped in a pair of trousers. The following day the rest of the corpse was found a quarter of a mile away. The body proved to be that of a tall, good-looking young man in his mid-twenties, with a number of tattoos. Retracted neck muscles again indicated that he had been beheaded while alive, although it was not clear how the killer had restrained him, since there were no rope marks on the wrists. The coroner theorised that the killer had cut his throat with a single sweep while the victim was asleep, then allowed him to bleed to death before continuing the decapitation. He had been dead about forty eight hours.

It looked as if he was a vagrant, or a man looking for work, who had been killed as he slept in Kingsbury Run. Yet the most careful search of the area failed to reveal the kind of bloodstains that would indicate the spot. And the absence of blood on the body suggested an alternative theory – that he had been killed indoors and carefully washed before he was disposed of.

The body was still unidentified when, on July 22, 1936, a 17 year old female hiker in woods to the south of the city saw a naked and headless body lying in a gully. It was badly decomposed, and it became clear that the victim had been killed before the tattooed young man who had been found in June. Blood that had soaked into the ground indicated that he had been killed where he lay. No identification was possible. The cheap clothing found near the body suggested that he was a vagrant, and the presence of a disused hobo camp nearby supported that theory. Again, it looked as if the head hunter had found his victim lying asleep, and had killed him with one stroke of a large and very sharp knife.

Fortunately, Clevelanders had other things to think about. A Great Lakes Exposition was packing in the visitors, with everything from an exhibition of scientific wonders to Hollywood film stars. With his natural flair for publicity, Ness had organised an exhibition on the history of criminology. This included a· plaster cast of the head of Victim No. 4 – the tattooed man – with a note asking for information about his identity. But no one came forward.

The head hunter returned to Kingsbury Run to dispose of his next victim. On September 10, 1936, a hobo about to jump on to a slow moving goods train tripped over a headless and armless torso. He raised the alarm, and the police soon discovered the lower part of the body – minus the legs – nearby. Both parts had been washed from a nearby sewer which flowed into a foul-looking pool. Fragments of flesh on the side of the pool indicated that the rest of the body might be in its depths. Using grappling hooks, the police succeeded in recovering the legs.

The coroner determined that the latest victim was a young man in his mid-twenties. Since the head and the arms were missing, identification was impossible. But a hat found near the body – together with some bloodtained clothing – led the police to a hat shop in nearby Bellevue, and eventually to a housewife who had given the hat to a young tramp two weeks earlier.

Ness decided that one way to thwart the killer was to deprive him of potential victims; he sent police officers in to Kingsbury Run with instructions to order the vagrants to move on. He also had railway police search trains entering Cleveland; one of these contained no less than two hundred tramps. A hobo ejected from Kingsbury Run had an interesting story to tell. As he was sitting in the darkness on the edge of the hobo camp, a man dressed in black had approached him; when he saw a big carving knife in the man's hand, the tramp had not stayed to find out what he wanted . . .

It was clear to Ness that he had to direct some of his attention to catching this psychopath before bad publicity about the murders swamped the increasing amount of good publicity about his war against organised crime. A meeting held on the evening of Monday September 14 included pathologists and police chiefs. The conclusions they reached were that the head hunter possessed a certain anatomical knowledge, that he was big and strong enough to carry corpses around, that, like London's Jack the Ripper, he preyed on "down and outs", and that he probably possessed a "laboratory" somewhere near Kingsbury Run where he could murdered and dismember his victims without fear of interruption. It also seemed to be a reasonable assumption that he owned a car.

A "hot line" was set up at City Hall, and two detectives, Peter Merylo and Martin Zalewski, assigned to full time work on the case. One interesting lead was about a man known in brothels as "the Chicken Freak", a powerfully-built man who entered brothels with a chicken under each arm. Naked prostitutes had to behead the chickens with a butcher's knife while the man looked on; if this failed to bring about the desired result, a prostitute had to rub the bloody knife against his throat until he climaxed. After a search that lasted weeks, Merylo and Zalewski arrested a truck driver who admitted to satisfying his sadistic impulses on chickens. But when shown photographs of the head hunter's victims he was so obviously nauseated that the police let him go.

The unknown tramp was the last victim of 1936. And as the months went by without further gruesome discoveries, Clevelanders began to hope they had heard the last of the Head Hunter – or the "Mad Butcher", as other newspapers preferred to call him. That hope was dashed on February 23, 1937, when another female torso was cast up from Lake Erie close to the spot where the "Lady of the Lake" had been found nearly three years earlier. The head and arms had been removed with the same ferocious skill as in the other cases. The only major difference was that this woman had been dead before her head was removed. She was apparently in her mid-twenties and had borne children. But an extensive search failed to reveal any other parts of the body, and the victim remained unidentified.

Ness begged his friends in the press to tone down their coverage of the case – the headlines about head-hunting maniacs were beginning to cause panic. Merylo and Zalewski redoubled their efforts, and tracked down half a dozen possible suspects – alcoholics with a penchant for carrying concealed knives or razors. All were released after questioning.

The Cuyahoga River, not far from Kingsbury Run, was the site of the next discovery. A teenager discovered a skull under the Lorain-Carnegie Bridge on June 6, 1937; nearby, police found fragments of a female skeleton inside the remains of a burlap bag. A piece of newspaper in the sack dated from June of the previous year confirmed the coroner's view that this unknown victim had been killed before the tattooed man. Black hair found on the skull enabled him to say that the victim had been a black woman of about thirty five. It seemed that the possibility of identifying her was remote. But since the pathologist had the skull to work on, dentists were circulated with a description of the teeth. This long-shot paid off; a dentist was able to identify work he had done on a woman called Rose Wallace, a prostitute who had vanished in the previous August. She had last been seen in a car with three white men, on her way to a party. Moreover, she had lived close to Flo Pollilo – in fact, they had even shared a lover. But the trail ended there.

But since this victim belonged to the previous year, the police had every reason to expect another victim around the time Rose Wallace was identified. The Mad Butcher seemed to kill about once every four months. And on July 3, when Ness's attention was taken up with a strike in the Flats – which often led to violent encounters between strikers and strike-breakers – a factory guard saw a white object floating in the Cuyahoga River below West Third Street bridge, and recognised it as a legless lower torso. The upper half was found floating in a burlap bag – minus, inevitably, the head. The legs, also separated into halves, were found nearby; so eventually, were the arms and feet. Only the head was never found. This victim, number 9, had been a man in his thirties, and death was again due to decapitation. And, more ominously, he had also been disembowelled, and the heart removed. The compulsions of the Mad Butcher were becoming increasingly sadistic.

That same afternoon, a drunken man who was heard boasting that he "knew all about the torso murders" was swiftly arrested, but proved to be an ambulance driver who was able to prove his innocence.

A few months later, Merylo and Zalewski became convinced that they had caught the Head Hunter. Examining the effects of one of the first victims, Edward Andrassy, they found some undeveloped photographs showing Andrassy in a bedroom with flowered wallpaper. This, they speculated, might be the "laboratory" in which the killer dismembered the bodies. The picture was published in newspapers and recognised; in fact, to Merylo's embarrassment, it turned out to be a bedroom he had entered at one point in the investigation. It was the room of a middle aged homosexual, who proved to possess a trunk containing a butcher's knife and bloodstained clothing. The man was jailed on a sodomy charge, and Merylo and Zalewski prayed fervently that they had heard the last of the torso killer . . .

They were disappointed. On April 8, 1938, the lower part of a leg was discovered caught in a tree root on the Cuyahoga River. The new County Coroner, Samuel Gerber, pronounced it to be that of a woman in her late twenties or early thirties. Four weeks later, on May 2, two burlap bags were pulled out of the river, and proved to contain more parts of the same body – minus the head. No identification was possible.

The new coroner was convinced that the Head Hunter was a man who had had medical training, and that he probably drugged his victims before killing them. Traces of drugs in the latest victim seemed to confirm his theory.

And when Ness heard about an ex-hobo in Chicago who claimed to have seen the killer, he had him brought to Cleveland. The man had a strange story to tell – of how he had been invited to the office of a man who claimed to be a doctor – he described him as short, with ginger hair. There, as he ate a meal, he felt he was losing his senses, and realised he had been drugged; he lurched to his feet and managed to escape. But this had been before the first two victims had been found in Kingsbury Run, three years ago. The "doctor's" office had been in East Fifty Fifth Street, near Kingsbury Run. But the police were too late; only a local bartender seemed to recall the short doctor, and he had not seen him for two years. One detective pointed out that the doctor's description matched that of Victim No. 9, which suggested he was victim rather than killer.

Press criticism of Ness was mounting. Why was he not personally engaged in the hunt? There were two answers: first, that Ness had no idea of what to do, and second, that he felt he had more important things to do anyway. In his own eyes, one of his most successful schemes was to organise youth recreation programmes in slum areas with a high rate of teenage crime; the result was a remarkable fall in juvenile delinquency. But Clevelanders were not interested in this type of achievement; they wanted to see the Head Hunter behind bars.

Criticism reached a climax when two more bodies were found on the same day. A group of blacks scouring a rubbish dump near the City Hall found a female torso wrapped in an old quilt. Nearby, police found the head wrapped in brown paper, and the arms and legs in a cardboard box. Not far away, human bones were found half-buried. A tin box proved to contain a man's head.

The woman had been in her mid-thirties, and the hardening of the flesh suggested that she had been kept in a refrigerator. But although the whole body had been recovered, identification proved impossible. The set of bones proved even less revealing. A reconstruction of the face indicated that he had a broken nose. A detective recalled that Victim No. 1, Edward Andrassy, had been seen around with a man named Eddie, who had a broken nose, and who seemed to be about the same build as the skeleton. But all attempts to trace "Eddie" were a failure.

Although these latest remains clearly pre-dated those of the woman found in the Cuyahoga River, Ness felt that it was time he took swift and drastic action. There were still no clues to the identity of the killer. But there could be no possible doubt that most – if not all – of the victims were down-and outs. If they could not catch the killer, at least they could deprive him of victims. The cardboard box containing "Eddie's" skull had been traced back to the Central Market, in the Flats. This area housed the largest of the hobo "shantytowns", thirty home-made shacks.

On the day after the discovery of the two bodies, Ness co-ordinated his plans. Shortly after midnight, police and fire engines surrounded the shantytown. Floodlights were switched on and the raid commenced. Sleepy tramps were dragged out into the warm August night and taken to the Central Police Station. Another camp near the Lorain-Carnegie Bridge was the next target; ten more tramps were detained for questioning. Finally, the police poured into the camp in Kingsbury Run, and arrested fifteen men. Back at the station, these were made to identify themselves. Eleven out of sixty three hobos had criminal records and were kept in custody. The others were sent to the workhouse. The following day, all three shantytowns were burned to the ground.

Ness received harsher criticism than usual for his summary treatment of the vagrants. But his method worked. Deprived of victims, the Head Hunter went out of business. He had killed twelve people in three years – thirteen if the Lady in the Lake was counted. And at the end of that time, the police still lacked the slightest clue to his identity.

But although the Torso murders were over, no one yet realised it, and police activity was more frantic than ever.

The crimes had reached foreign newspapers. In Germany, Dr. Goebbels himself had unfavourable things to say about America's decadent civilisation, and Mussolini's newspapers were equally scathing. But as no more dismembered corpses were found, the fever slowly abated.

By the following spring, Merylo was one of the few policemen still working full-time on the case. The sheriff's department had also hired a private detective named Lawrence J. Lyons, known as Pat. And it was Pat Lyons who unearthed what seemed the most significant clue so far. He learned that three of the victims – Edward Andrassy, Flo Polillo and Rose Wallace – had frequented the same tavern on East Twentieth Street and Central Avenue. There Lyons heard tales of a man called Frank, who boasted that he was an expert with knives. When he learned that Flo Polillo had lived with Frank at one point, Lyons felt he had a prime suspect for the murders.

"Frank" proved to be a squat, middle aged immigrant bricklayer named Frank Dolezal. Further investigation revealed that he had been seen with Rose Wallace, and a man who resembled Andrassy. Moreover, Dolezal was bisexual, and had often been seen accosting strangers near the Central Market shantytown.

Detectives gained entrance to Dolezal's four room apartment on Central Avenue. On the bathroom floor they found ominous stains. Scrapings were taken and sent for analysis to Lyons' brother, who was a chemist; he declared them to be blood.

The sheriff's office was excited by the breakthrough; it would be a triumph if they could solve the case that had baffled Ness and the Police Department. But when he heard that Merylo was asking questions about Dolezal, Sheriff O'Donnell decided it was time to arrest their suspect. On July 5, 1939, Dolezal was picked up and taken in for questioning.

Two days later, O'Donnell called in the newspapermen. "Boys, Frank Dolezal has confessed to the Polillo murder."

Dolezal had signed a confession describing how he had quarrelled with Flo Polillo two days before her remains were found, and had killed her accidentally by knocking her against the bath tub. Then he had dismembered her and disposed of part of the body, throwing some – including the head – into Lake Erie.

It certainly looked like the solution. Ness was generous in his congratulations. Yet when the "bloodstains" in the bathroom were re-examined by a pathologist, he declared positively that they were *not* blood. Discrepancies were also noted in Dolezal's statement. He claimed to have thrown the arms and legs into Lake Erie, yet they had been discovered with the body in the basket. When Dolezal was finally accused of manslaughter, interest in him waned.

On August 24, 1939, four weeks after his arrest, Frank Dolezal was found hanging from a hook in the ceiling of his cell. An autopsy performed by Coroner Gerber revealed that six of his ribs were cracked, and that this injury dated back to soon after his arrest – supporting Dolezal's complaint that his confession had been obtained by force.

Nevertheless, as far as Clevelanders were concerned, Dolezal's death was the end of the story of the Head Hunter of Kingsbury Run. Cleveland's Safety Director held other views – which, for the moment, he kept to himself.

Sadly, the last decade of Elliot Ness's life – he died in 1957, at the age of 54 – was full of poverty and disappointment. He resigned as Cleveland's Safety Director in April 1941, after a scandal involving a hit-and-run accident. In 1947 he was heavily defeated when he ran for the post of mayor of Cleveland. A year later he was even turned down for a sixty dollar a week job. "He simply ran out of gas," said one friend. In 1953, after five years of obscurity and poverty, he became involved with a paper-making company which tottered on the verge of bankruptcy. But it was through a friend in the company that Ness met a journalist called Oscar Fraley, and began telling him the story of his anti-bootlegging days. And in the course of their conversations, Ness told Fraley that he was reasonably certain that he knew the identity of the Torso killer, and that he had driven him out of Cleveland.

What Ness told Fraley was as follows. He had reasoned that the killer was a man who had a house of his own in which to dismember the bodies, and a car in which to transport them. The skill of the mutilations suggested medical training, or at least a certain medical knowledge. The fact that some of the victims had been strong men suggested that the Butcher had to be big and powerful – a conclusion supported by a size 12 footprint near one of the bodies.

Ness set three of his top agents, Virginia Allen, Barney Davis and Jim Manski, to make enquiries among the upper levels of Cleveland society. Virginia was a sophisticated girl with contacts among Cleveland socialites. And it was she who learned about a man who sounded like the ideal suspect. Ness was to call him "Gaylord Sundheim" – a big man from a well-to-do family, who had a history of psychiatric problems. He had also studied medicine. When the three "Untouchables" called on him, he leered sarcastically at Virginia and closed the door in their faces. Ness invited him – pressingly – to lunch, and he came under protest. Sundheim refused to either admit or deny the murders. Ness persuaded him to take a Lie Detector test, and Sundheim's answers to questions about the murders were registered by the stylus as lies. When Ness finally told him he believed he was the Torso killer – hoping that shock tactics might trigger a confession – Sundheim sneered: "Prove it."

Soon after this, Sundheim had himself committed to a mental institution. Ness knew *he* was now "untouchable", for even if Ness could prove his guilt, he could plead insanity.

During the next two years Ness received a series of jeering postcards, some signed "Your paranoid nemesis." They ceased abruptly when "Sundheim" died in the mental institution.

Ness went on to collaborate with Fraley on a book called *The Untouchables*. It came out in 1957, and was an immense success, becoming a bestseller and leading to a famous TV series. But Ness never knew about its success; he had died of a heart attack on May 16, 1957, six months before *The Untouchables* was published.

Damon Wilson

The Rattlesnake Murder

The Rattlesnake Murder case was partly responsible for my decision to produce an encyclopedia of murder in 1959. I was introduced to Sunday Express journalist Robert Pitman by the novelist John Braine, and was delighted to discover that his wife Pat shared my interest in murder. We began to discuss cases that fascinated us – Jack the Ripper, Sylvestre Matuska, ("the man who wrecked trains"), and Kreuger and von Arbin, who disposed of an unwanted business partner by placing a bomb in his taxi. And, inevitably, the name of Robert James was mentioned. It was Pat who wrote up the case in *An Encyclopedia of Murder*, indulging her macabre sense of humour: "The obliging Hope (he said afterwards that James had 'hypnotized' him) went the round of local snake vendors, but his purchases were puny specimens; James, getting progressively more furious, would test their lethal efficiency on hordes of rabbits and chickens, who seemed to thrive on snake bites."

Pat's article is too short to include here, but the account by lawyer Eugene D. Williams (in *Los Angeles Murders*) is a minor classic in its own right.

You ask if I remember the rattlesnake murder case – that fantastic, almost unbelievable nightmare of torture and death. I remember it. The word "rattlesnake" brings a kaleidoscope of memories. The picture of the D.A., a small crew of detectives and myself deciding to "go to work" on the death of Mary James – the days and nights at the dictagraph, listening to James' southern drawl, his love making – the arrest – Hope's bizarre confession – in the morgue looking at the body of Mary James, taken from the grave – days and nights of work, work, work. Then the trial, Judge Charles W. Fricke, calm and competent – the jury, intent and interested – "Wild Bill" Clark, Russ Parsons and Sam Silverman, ably and forcefully fighting for their client – the crowded court room – the press row – special writers – Gene Markey, Carey Wilson, Bradley King, Bartlett Cormack, Tod Browning, Florabel Muir, Walter Winchell who dropped by to listen for a half-day session, Peter Lorre, the character actor studying abnormal psychology at first hand.

I remember the murderer's impassive face and beady eyes as he watched the witnesses and later on the witness stand as he lied and lied, and finally lied himself into a noose. I remember the "experts," herpetologists who told us about the Crotalus Atrox and a dozen other varieties of rattlesnakes and about snake venom and its effect – the rattlesnakes brought into the court room – the long days and weeks of trial – the tension, the snap decisions as to whether to ask or not to ask a certain question, to call or not to call a certain witness, always with John Barnes at my side bearing his share in the smooth team work which we had learned by experience and by which we fitted piece by piece the jigsaw puzzle which showed "beyond a reasonable doubt and to a moral certainty" the guilt of the defendant.

I remember the arguments – Johnnie Barnes, cool and logical, putting the case together bit by bit – Bill Clark and Russ Parsons, dramatic, forceful, emotional – and dangerous. And then my job of pulling all the loose ends together, pulling the jury up to the task of doing its hard and solemn duty, asking the death penalty, in a packed court room still as death itself – the judge's instructions. The jury goes out – God, how tired I am – weighted with the responsibility, wondering whether some mistake, some error of judgment, some lack of tact, on my part, might let a guilty man loose again to prey on defenseless women. The jury comes back quietly. The stir in the court room is hushed.

"Mr. Clerk, read the verdict."

"We, the jury . . . guilty of murder . . . first degree."

Silence. No recommendation for life imprisonment. That means death.

The stir – movement – excitement – relief – congratulations! – pats on the back – headlines – but God, am I tired!

The long drawn-out appeals – the Supreme Court of California: "Judgment affirmed." Then the arguments before the Supreme Court of the United States – the kind but stern white-bearded Chief Justice – the keen and searching questions by the Associate Justices: "Affirmed."

I remember the weighted rope hanging all alone in the little room adjoining the death cell at San Quentin. The guard said:

"Did you ever hear of the rattlesnake murder?" I had. "We're saving this one for him – he's the last one – we're going to gas 'em after this."

I remember when they hanged him. I wasn't there, I'm no ghoul, but I remember –

Robert S. James was born on a little cotton patch in Alabama. He wasn't christened "Robert S. James." His folks gave him the colorful name of "Major Raymond Lisenba." When and why he abandoned his true name and adopted "Robert S. James" is unknown, but at a certain time "Lisenba" disappeared and "James" sprang into existence.

He had a hard youth. At eight he was working in the cotton mills. He got very little schooling, perhaps three or four years. One of his older sisters married a kind, upstanding man who was a master barber. He took James into Birmingham, sent him to barber school and gave him a job. James became a good barber – but he got into trouble (with a girl, rumor has it) and left Birmingham between suns.

Years of adventure followed – hazy years, but always there was a woman. Marriage, affairs, another marriage, one half-told tale of a wife who returned with him from a rowboat ride on the lake one night dripping with water, fearful, who left him then and there. Apparently he was a good barber, but always women were his first and foremost interest.

He was always after a new woman. He liked to spend money, be a "big shot" for their benefit. Men didn't care much for him, nor he for them – but certain types of women did! He had a sallow complexion, wavy red hair carefully oiled, a suave, pleading "Southern" voice – and a way with women. One woman, after enjoying his masculine charms, effusively confided to him that he was the "most nutritious man I ever knew."

Being a good barber, working in high-class shops, he learned about good clothes from observing his customers. He was doing all right for himself – but it takes a lot of money to impress a lot of women.

His mother died. She had been carrying a small insurance policy payable to him. This opened his eyes. Then a nephew was killed in an automobile accident. He had an insurance policy and James was the beneficiary. Twice death paid benefits to James. That set him thinking.

In 1932 in Los Angeles, he met and married Winona Wallace. She had had for a long time a thousand-dollar insurance policy payable to her sister. James got her to make him the beneficiary. He also induced her to take out other policies payable to him, each paying double in case of accidental death. In case of her accidental death he would receive about $14,000. The first quarterly premiums on these policies safely paid, but with little money in his pockets, he took his bride on a honeymoon trip.

Late one night he appeared at the office of the toll-road

company at Glen Cove, near Pike's Peak, Colorado, and told the superintendent and others that his wife had been driving their car, had lost control and gone over the edge of the road. He had jumped. She was undoubtedly dead. The superintendent looked at him. "You jumped?"

"Yes."

"How far down?"

"About fifty feet."

The superintendent eyed James' natty, well-creased blue suit. "You must have made a perfect landing," he muttered. He was suspicious and he observed everything carefully.

They went to the site of the wreck. Luck had been against James. About one hundred fifty feet down the hill a big boulder set solidly in the ground had stopped the car. Except for this boulder it would have ended in a twisted mass of wreckage hundreds of feet below. Winona was lying on the ground at the right side of the car, unconscious but not dead.

In the hospital at Colorado Springs skilful surgeons saved her life. She had no memory of what had happened. Soon James took her from the hospital and went to a lonely cabin in a summer resort at Manitou, which at that fall period of the year was practically unoccupied. Their cabin was remote and they were to all practical purposes alone.

James was in bad shape financially. He had had to borrow some money from Winona's father, who had come to see her in the hospital, and then he had to borrow some money on Winona's old thousand-dollar life insurance policy. His first effort to collect death benefits on the insurance had failed and he needed money badly. Winona was getting well. In a short time they would have to move on. James, watching Winona with his beady eyes, gave thought to the subject. That thought resulted in action.

One day he took the stage to Colorado Springs. He dropped in to see his acquaintances, the hotel proprietor and others. At each place in response to questions about Winona's condition he said he was worried about her; that her head was still bad; that she kept insisting on washing her hair, although the doctor told her she shouldn't. He said she was having dizzy spells. This seed implanted in fertile soil, James returned to the cabin.

Shortly thereafter he appeared at the store at Manitou, said he was just back from Colorado Springs and that he was tired, and asked that the delivery boy take him and some groceries he bought up to his cabin. This was the first time that any such arrangement had been made, but the boy went with him. James asked him to carry the groceries into the house. As the boy was putting the groceries on the sinkboard, James came into the kitchen, having been around in the bedroom part of the house, walked from the kitchen into the bathroom, and then called the boy and showed him Winona's nude body lying on its back in a tub of warm, soapy water. She was dead from drowning. The tub was small and Winona's position, lying with her feet over the end of the tub and on her back, was such that it appeared almost impossible for her to have gotten into that position or to have drowned without "help." However, no one seemed interested, so no official investigation of Winona's death was made at that time.

James collected for accidental death by drowning, complicated by injuries received in the automobile accident, a sum of over $14,000. And then he went to town! He bought himself a new Pierce Arrow convertible coupe. He bought a lot of clothes and expensive luggage. He took a trip back to Birmingham, Alabama, and visited his relatives. He splurged all over town, bought himself some fighting game cocks and entered into the life of the sporting fraternity in Birmingham. He bought presents for his sisters and other relatives.

There he met for the first time his pretty little eighteen-year-old niece, Lois, daughter of the master barber who had befriended him. The details of her seduction are unpleasant and not necessary to this story. It is sufficient to say that when he left Birmingham, she left with him, traveling toward California as "man and wife."

After arriving at Los Angeles, James purchased a barber shop in a good downtown location. He had several barbers and a manicurist working for him. He sent his niece to beauty school and had her learn the manicuring trade. At times she worked in his barber shop as a manicurist.

By the time he was well settled in Los Angeles, although he was making good money as a barber, he began to feel the need of more money. He was carrying on affairs with various women. On one drunken spree he married one of them who later sought to have the marriage annulled. Before the annulment was effected, however, he met Mary Busch. She went to work for him as a manicurist. He talked her into marriage, and at the same time made all of the preliminary arrangements and got her to take out $10,000 worth of life insurance payable to him with double indemnity in case of accidental death. He was still a married man, as his annulment had not been completed. But Mary was insistent, and he was described as her husband in the policies which were about to be issued.

Under the circumstances, he hired a friend to act as minister and had a mock marriage ceremony performed. Of course, Mary thought it was legitimate. They then went to live in a small bungalow which James had rented in a section of Southern California lying at the foot of the Sierra Madre mountains known as La Canada.

This place was well adapted for James' purposes. The house was set amid a grove of trees, well concealed from the road and from the neighbors by luxuriant shrubbery, and was sufficiently distant from all other houses so that very little noise, if any, could be heard by the neighbors. On one side of the house, entirely surrounded by a thicket of shrubs and bamboo, was a fish pond.

Well settled in this "love nest," James started his plans.

On Monday, August 5, 1935, James made arrangements by telephone to take two friends of Mary's out to his house for dinner. He explained to them that Mary would prepare the vegetables but that he would buy the meat and they would have steaks. They arrived at the house about dark. There were no lights, no sign of Mary. James procured flashlights. He started one way, one of the friends started another way around the grounds looking for Mary.

The friend found her body in the fish pond. James came, very agitated, helped get her body out of the pond, and wept over his dead wife. The police were called. James played the bereaved husband to perfection.

The coroner pronounced it death by accident. Notwithstanding the suspicion which arose from the fact that Mary was heavily insured (far beyond the normal insurance for a person of her means), and that James had had the fortunate coincidence of having another heavily insured wife die by accident, the investigation was dropped.

In the meantime, however, James, not content, spent an evening with a woman acquaintance of his. He made love to her, talked of marriage, and then told her that the police were trying to frame him for the death of his wife, which he said was a "lot of bunk." But he said, "You know I worked at my shop all day Monday, and if you would testify that you drove by my house about ten o'clock Monday morning and saw Mary sitting on the porch, I could call you as a surprise witness. That would knock out any effort to frame me. If you'll do this, I'll pay you two thousand dollars." The woman half-heartedly agreed.

No further action was taken by the authorities. James proceeded to try to collect the insurance. One of the insurance companies asserted some defects in the policy and succeeded in settling with him for $3500 on its $10,000 liability. The other company refused to pay. The case was brought to court and tried, and judgment rendered in favor of the insurance company and against James on the ground of a defect in the application for insurance.

James now purchased a small bungalow in the southwest part of Los Angeles and moved in with his young niece, Lois. The furor about Mary's death had been forgotten, all was quiet, and he was proceeding on the even tenor of his ways. He hadn't done so well, but he felt safe. He had his niece and other women. He was again seriously considering marriage – and insurance. Then all hell broke loose.

In March, 1936, some seven months after Mary's death, a crew of detectives of the D.A.'s office, working under my direction, had just completed an extensive murder investigation which resulted in the conviction of a woman for having killed her husband eight years before. We were temporarily free, and we felt that the James case deserved investigation. We knew that James had insured his wife, Winona, and later, Mary, for sums greatly in excess of what would normally be carried by wives in their station of life, that Winona had died as a result of what appeared to be an accident and that he had collected her insurance, that Mary was dead, apparently by accident, and efforts had been made to collect her insurance. We felt it was unlikely that within three years after one such fortunate accident for James, a similar accident, equally fortunate for him, should happen to another wife, likewise heavily insured.

It was known that in the celebrated bathtub murder case in England, the defendant, George Joseph Smith, had had three wives die from drowning in bathtubs, and in each case had collected substantial sums from their estates and insurance. We were aware of the fact that in that case the eminent British jurist who presided had advised the jury:

> "If you think that the prisoner has a system of obtaining money from women by going through the form of marriage with them and then getting the money either by robbery or murder, you may use the evidence of the other deaths for that purpose.
> "Now, I want to give you one or two illustrations of that sort of thing, in order that you may exactly understand for what purpose you may use

these other deaths. Let us get away from crime for a moment. You are playing cards for money with three men; suddenly in the pocket of one of them is found a card of the pack you are playing with. Possibly your first view could be – it would depend a good deal on what sort of a card it was; if it was a 'two' of one of the suits that was not trumps you would not think very much of it. Cards do sometimes tumble into odd places. If it happened to be the ace of trumps in the game you were playing at that time you might regard the matter with more suspicion, and, perhaps, in view of the fact that cards do tumble about, you might say that in that one case only, you could not form any opinion about it. But supposing on your mentioning it to someone else it turned out that on five previous occasions of playing for money the gentleman had had the fortunate accident of finding the ace of trumps in his coat pocket, what would you think then?

"What the law says you may think is that that series of fortunate accidents does not usually happen to the same person so many times, and that you may draw from that series of fortunate accidents the inference that it was not an accident at all, but that it was designed. That illustrates the way in which you may use, in dealing with a criminal case, the occurrence, the repeated occurrence, of the same accident to a person who benefits by the accident each time."

With this in mind, we investigated the circumstances of the insurance of both Winona and Mary, getting all the details. We learned that James, in both cases, had initiated the applications for insurance, had secured the cheapest insurance which would pay double for accidental death, had paid but one quarter's premium. We located a witness who testified that as early as January, 1935, James had stated that he expected a large sum of money from an estate. Investigation disclosed that he had no relatives who had any large estates, so we connected that in our thought with his subsequent effort to collect the large sum of insurance on Mary.

We then rented a furnished house next door to where James was living with his young niece. We installed microphones connected with a dictagraph, and set a twenty-four hour watch on James. We heard and recorded everything that was done and said in that house. We were there for almost a month.

To our disappointment there was not one word said about the death of Mary James. Our suspicion that perhaps the niece had been party to the murder found no support in anything we heard. But we did learn that James was having sexual relations with this niece (as well as with a number of other women). These relations with the niece constituted the crime of incest, a felony under the laws of California, so at a certain time in the course of the investigation, having become convinced that nothing further could be learned by means of the dictagraph, I instructed the investigators to go into James' house the next time he committed an act of incest with his niece, and arrest him in the act.

Locks on certain windows were "jimmied," screens loosened and the men waited for the right time. That time came on April 19, 1936, and James was placed under arrest. After questioning, it was determined that he would admit nothing in reference to the crime of murder. He tried to laugh off the crime of incest by asserting there wasn't any such crime. However, he was booked in the county jail. The newspapers played up the arrest. The story of the untimely deaths of his wives was again revived, and the thing happened which very frequently happens in the investigation of crime: somebody started to talk.

It is a sad commentary on human nature but nevertheless true, that men (and women, too) like to kick people when they are down. It happens very frequently when a criminal is under arrest, definitely in trouble, that people who know things about his crimes will start to talk. That is well known to experienced prosecutors and investigators. As anticipated, it happened in this case.

The owner of a liquor store spoke to a lawyer friend. He said that he knew something about this fellow James, and he didn't think that a fellow who would treat his little niece the way James had was entitled to any protection. The lawyer agreed. The liquor man said he didn't want to get mixed up with the police or D.A. in any way or come to the fore in the matter, but if the lawyer thought it was all right and could keep his name out of it, he could give some interesting information. The lawyer assured him he thought it was all right and suggested that a friend of his, "Pat" Foley, a reporter for the *Los Angeles Herald-Express*, could carry the information to the D.A.'s office. They arranged to meet.

The liquor man's "information" was that he knew a fellow named Hope. That on a certain day in August of the previous year, Hope had appeared at his liquor store in an obviously nervous, jittery condition. He babbled about going around the country buying rattlesnakes, about a woman having been bitten by a rattlesnake, about a murder and a woman's body in a pool. The liquor man had thought that Hope was on the verge of d.t.'s and ordered him out of the store and had given him a bottle of wine to "sober up" on. He had regarded the fantastic story as a "wino's dream." But the next day he had read in the newspaper of Mary James' body having been found in a fish pond. Upon reflection he had come to the conclusion that Hope perhaps really knew something of that murder.

Pat Foley conveyed this information to me. There was one added item: Hope owned a certain make of automobile. Within hours our investigators had got the name and address of every person named Hope in the State of California who owned an automobile, and had ascertained that the only one of that make had been registered to Charles Hope, Los

Angeles. They also learned that he had disposed of that car and had purchased another. From the latter license they got an address. They located Mrs. Hope. She told them that "Chuck" was working as a cook in a hamburger stand at Hermosa Beach.

Within an hour Hope was under arrest. In another hour he was in the D.A.'s office. Two hours later he had told me of the drowning of Mary James. He had said nothing about rattlesnakes. I wasn't satisfied. I ordered him placed in jail over night.

Before he left I said, "Chuck, you've told us part of this story; you haven't told it all yet. You are trying to protect yourself. There's something about rattlesnakes. As long as you're going to confess, I think you should tell the whole truth. Go to bed, have a good rest and tomorrow morning we'll talk it over some more."

The next morning Hope was taken to the scene of the crime. In the bathroom of the cottage he turned white and shaky – and told the whole gruesome story.

About June of 1935, Hope had dropped into James' barber shop. He was broke and he asked James for some barber work on credit. James agreed, and while he was barbering Hope he asked him if he knew anything about rattlesnakes. Hope said he didn't. James said, "Well, there's a chance for you to make a hundred bucks. I have a friend whose wife has been bothering him and he wants a couple of snakes to use to bite her."

Hope thought that James was kidding, but James said he really wanted the snakes, and Hope undertook to buy them. He finally located and purchased some snakes from a man running a little side show on the Pike at Long Beach. The snakes cost but a few dollars. James told Hope to have some boxes made in which to put the snakes, which Hope in due time delivered to James at his home in La Canada. The hundred dollars was paid. James experimented with the snakes by putting some chickens in the boxes with them.

The snakes didn't kill the chickens. James then complained to Hope that the snakes were no good and urged him to buy others.

James had heard that there was an exhibit of rattlesnakes in a side show at Ocean Park. He and Hope, after having a few drinks, drove down to Ocean Park and visited the side show. They were both drunk and a little noisy and attracted some attention by arguing with the proprietor as to whether the snakes were "hot." The proprietor offered to bet money that they were. After leaving the side show James arranged for Hope to go back alone and buy one of the snakes. This was done. The snake was put in a box with a rabbit. The next morning the rabbit was still hopping about, but the snake was dead.

Again James put it up to Hope to get a "hot" snake, and Hope made some investigation which finally resulted in his purchasing from "Snake Joe" Houtenbrink, a snake dealer, for the sum of six dollars, two guaranteed "hot" Crotalus Atrox rattlesnakes gathered in the Colorado desert. These snakes, upon being tested with live chickens, killed the chickens promptly. Thereafter, they were kept in boxes in James' garage for future use.

In the meantime, James was somewhat worried as to the legality of his marriage to Mary. He was fearful that upon investigation it would be found to be no marriage, and that his status as a beneficiary of the policies of insurance would be weak. Soon, however, his annulment decree was entered and he took Mary on a little trip down into one of the adjoining counties and there they were legally married. He made sure, by questioning one of the insurance agents, that the fact that he was legally married after and not before the policies had been issued would not invalidate the insurance. He was then prepared for the final steps in the drama to be enacted.

Mary was pregnant. She was very anxious to have a baby. James tried to persuade her to have an abortion performed. After weeks of persuasion she agreed. James told her that

Hope, whom she had met, was a doctor or medical student competent to perform an abortion, and that he would do the job. Mary agreed to this. James then explained to her that it would be necessary to strap her on the kitchen table, blindfold her and seal her lips with adhesive tape because, as he explained, there must be no noise, and Hope insisted that she not see him so that she would never be able to testify against him.

On Sunday morning, August 4, 1935, Hope met James in the garage of James' home. James then told Hope that he intended to use the rattlesnakes to kill his wife, Mary. He offered to split the insurance money with Hope. He said, "You're in this as deep as I am. You've been going all over Southern California buying rattlesnakes. It's too late for you to back out now. Bring one of the snakes and come into the house."

Hope seized a box with a sliding glass cover, containing one of the proven rattlesnakes, and followed James into the house through the back door. Mary, scantily dressed, lay strapped to the table in the kitchen. Her mouth had been taped shut and her eyes were covered with adhesive. James ordered Hope to place the box near Mary's foot. The lid was slipped back. James seized Mary's leg and thrust it into the box with the rattling, vibrant snake. It struck. Hope pulled the box away, the cover slid back, and James motioned him to take it out of the house. Later that day Hope, using James' car, took the two snakes back to "Snake Joe" and sold them back at half price. He then threw the boxes into a field as he was passing, and returned to James' home.

All that happened in the James house that day is not known. But it is known that Mary must have suffered the tortures of the damned. Her leg was swollen to almost double its normal size and was black and blue. Her suffering must have been excruciating. Much whisky must have been fed her.

Whether from drunkenness or pain or threats, or a combination of all, she was induced to write a letter in an almost illegible scrawl (although she usually wrote very well), in which she told that she was "pretty sick," that "my leg is all swollen, something bit me – I cut my toe," and how much she loved and relied upon her "daddy" – "He takes good care of me." This letter, addressed to her sister, was found in the James' home after Mary's death. It was an important bit of evidence in James' plan to lead the authorities to believe that Mary had met her death by accident.

Notwithstanding that the snake's venom was gradually working up Mary's leg, thigh and hip, and toward her vital organs, notwithstanding the disintegration of the cells that was taking place and the horrible pain, Mary continued to live. Hope stayed out in the garage. Late that Sunday night he and James were out there drinking. James was worried – Mary wasn't dying fast enough. He said, "Hell, she's not going to die; the damned snake didn't work." Hope suggested, "Let's call a doctor."

James replied, "Hell, no. They'd string us higher than a kite. She'd squeal."

They had another drink. Silence. James was thinking. Perhaps a vision of Winona, dead in the bathtub at Manitou, came to him. Finally he arose. "I'm going in and drown her." And into the house he went. He was gone for a long time, while Hope sat in the garage and drank more whisky.

Finally James returned. He looked at Hope. "That's that," he said. He went into the house again. About six-thirty in the morning he came back. He said, "She's been dead since four o'clock. I've got everything cleaned up. You come in and help me carry her out."

They went into the house. In the hallway just outside the bathroom lay the dead body of Mary. She was dressed in fresh lounging pajamas. Except for some moisture in her hair, she appeared to be dry.

On direction from James, Hope took Mary's feet. James took her shoulders and they carried her out through the kitchen into the back yard, around to the side of the house by the fish pond. At this point Hope refused to go farther. The body was placed at the side of the fish pond. James then dragged it so that it lay with the head and shoulders in the fish pond, face down, in such position as to indicate that Mary had fallen from the path headfirst into the pond. They then gathered the wet towels, clothing, blankets, the pieces of adhesive tape and rope with which Mary had been tied. By that time it was daylight on Monday morning.

James drove Hope to his home in Los Angeles. Hope took the towels, clothes and blankets, bits of rope and tape, to dispose of them. James then went for a ride out Wilshire Boulevard, so timing himself that he came back to his barber shop in time to open it. Hope disposed of the towels, clothing, rope and tape by burning them in an incinerator. The blankets he kept and took to the cleaner.

James stayed in jail for eleven days and then one morning he was taken into the chaplain's room, where he was confronted by his accomplice, Hope. The story of the murder was recited to him. He was asked what statement, if any, he had to make. He said, "Nothing." Then he was taken out to the murder house. He saw the officers in company with Hope. He saw pictures taken. He saw the investigative process at work. He was taken back to the D.A.'s office. He was again questioned about his participation in the death of Mary James. He was asked about the death of Winona up in Colorado. He refused to make any statement or any admission.

Finally, as he sat there, he saw that the authorities believed Hope's story. He thought that Hope might get out and put it all on him. A dull but deadly anger stirred him. He called one of the officers to his side. He said, "Let's go out and get something to eat. I'll tell you the story."

James, accompanied by three officers and a young lady (fiancée of one of the officers) went to a cafe, had a steak dinner, accepted a cigar, lighted it and sat back. One of the officers said, "Do you want to tell the story now or shall we go back to the D.A.'s office?" He said, "We might as well do it here." And then, in that public place, he recited his version of what had happened.

He admitted he had insured Mary. He admitted he had agreed with Hope to murder Mary and divide the insurance money, but he claimed that Hope had devised the idea of the rattlesnakes, had urged the unwilling James to agree to the murder. He asserted that he, James, had backed out at the last minute ("I couldn't kill her; she'd been too good to me") and that Hope, under a pretext of committing an abortion on Mary, had probably killed her. He denied any knowledge of the exact details of the killing. While inadvertently and unknowingly admitting sufficient participation in the crime to render himself guilty as a principal in the murder, he viciously tried to throw the greater burden and onus of the conception and carrying out of the murder upon Hope's shoulders.

Detectives were sent out and in a short time the various persons from whom rattlesnakes had been purchased, the individual who had built the boxes for the snakes, and all of the other witnesses were brought in. Mary's body was exhumed. The mark of the snake bite, the swollen and discolored limb, testified all too clearly to the truth of Hope's confession.

Hope was taken up into the chaplain's room of the jail and there confronted James with his story of the murder. James failed to deny the accusation. Then another "break" came. The woman who had been asked by James to testify falsely to having seen Mary alive on the Monday following her death approached her lawyer and she came to the D.A.'s office and told her story. The tentacles of the law were wrapping themselves around James.

In the midst of all of the flurry of local investigation, it was decided that at this time it would be well to inquire further into Winona's death. Jack Southard, ace investigator, was sent to Colorado. He interviewed the superintendent of the Pike's Peak Toll Road Company, who told him what he had observed about James and about his examination of the footprints at the scene of the "accident," the blood-smeared hammer, the blood on the upholstery of the coupe back of the right seat. The surgeon who had treated Winona testified as to the character and type of the injuries to her head. The boy who had helped discover her body and other witnesses were interviewed, pictures and diagrams obtained, and in five days Southard returned with proof that Winona had been murdered.

Hope pleaded guilty to first-degree murder and received a life sentence. He prepared to testify against James. A mass of detailed corroborative evidence was gathered. We had, as you know, James' admission of participation in the murder of Mary. The investigation was completed. We were ready for trial.

Under the law, as indicated by the reference which I have already made to the famous English case of Rex v. George Joseph Smith, it is permissible upon a prosecution for murder to establish the facts relating to prior similar death for the purpose of showing intent, design, identity of the murderer and the fact that the death was intended and not accidental. Under that rule, evidence of the murder of Winona was admissible in our California prosecution for the murder of Mary.

The sum total of our evidence demonstrated that James had engaged upon a career of marrying, insuring and murdering women. At the very time of our investigation we learned over the microphone that he had become engaged to still another woman, was intending to marry her and was talking to her about the advisability of insuring their mutual future by carrying insurance for each other's benefit.

I have not the slightest doubt that if we had not solved the prior murders and convicted James when we did, there would have been a third and perhaps a fourth to add to his list. After his success in collecting the insurance on Winona, he became convinced that he was smarter than the insurance companies and smarter than the "law." This egotism carried him on to further efforts. He had absolutely no compunction, no thought of the suffering of his victims, no emotion other than an egotistical desire to satisfy his own perverted tastes. Even at the time we were questioning him about the murder of Mary, he said, "I don't see why you are so worried about her. Why all this investigation? She was nothing but a damned whore when I married her."

A few months later James was on trial. Five weeks later he was convicted of murder in the first degree with the death penalty. After long-drawn-out appeals, he was finally "hanged by the neck until dead" in San Quentin penitentiary, the last person to die by the rope in the state of California.

Eugene D. Williams

Jerome Braun von Selz: The Laughing Killer

Herewith another strange and little-known murder case, this time from the San Francisco area – it concludes the volume *San Francisco Murders*, edited by Joseph H. Jackson and published in 1947. It is an odd little affair, involving a man abundantly endowed with charm combined with a dangerous criminal streak. It is difficult to know whether the "Laughing Killer" was insane or feeble minded, or whether he killed one or three people. The key to von Selz seems to be an over-developed craving for "fame", which led to his arrest.

In *The Encyclopedia of World Crime*, Jay Robert Nash concludes his short entry on von Selz by recording that in 1962, he again escaped, this time from the San Luis Obispo prison, but was recaptured within three days. Finally released in 1966, he was back again within a year on charges of welfare fraud. Nothing is known about his subsequent career. I find myself regretting that no one took sufficient interest in this oddly puzzling killer to write a book about him. I am sure he would have collaborated enthusiastically.

The poker murder of Mrs Ada French-Mengler-Rice was a suburban affair, and, as is well known to all connoisseurs and chroniclers of violence, not many metropolitan murders can approach the suburban slaying when it comes to stark and grisly appointments. In the city, a corpus delicti is ordinarily quick of establishment. A homicide there too often assumes the coziness of parlor, bedroom and bath, and if you must dig, it is usually in the cellar. For contrast, I recommend the setting of the Woodside Glens, where at night the hills lie dark and brooding, and wraiths of fog ride down on the lonesome wind from San Francisco's Skyline Boulevard.

Those were the hills that rang with the mirth of the mercurial young man who killed Mrs Rice. His confession was not easily obtained, but once started it was gleefully given. "Ha ha!" he roared when they showed him the long-buried body. "Hell of a looking thing, isn't it? Teeth? No – ha ha! – they don't look like her teeth. But, hell" – and another burst of laughter – "it must be her. I killed her and put her there!"

I met this young man before he killed. Later, I became involved, in the remote fashion of a news editor, in assembling and presenting the story of his crime, and his dubious and equally mirthful confession of having done away with a doubly dubious Bulgarian cavalry officer. And as I look back on the singularly fey characters then peopling the city room of the *San Francisco Chronicle*, I know this:

That pixilated place, and no other, was proper setting for an introduction to Slipton J. (for Just) Fell. Under its soundproofed ceiling, his hearty, booming laughter had no hollow echo, as it must have in San Quentin. And where else would he have gone to seek a couple of fellow adventurers named Upton Rose and Faran Wide?

Slipton Fell must have sensed these things when he wandered into the city room one afternoon early in the spring of 1935. To me, those were lighthearted days in which newspaper work was a delightful form of peonage; no uninformed visitor could have guessed that many of us were engaged in any serious enterprise. As I remember it, Mr Fell entered just as a hundred-pound Jap *yawara* instructor was paving the way for some publicity by throwing a two-hundred-pound reporter flat on his back before anybody could hiss "Excuse please." A copy boy was running hot dog and coffee errands in white tie and tails: he belonged to one of the Peninsula's most prominent families, and was going to a formal dinner when he got off work. The copy desk used to sing at its labors, and there was an ancient retainer in the Sunday department who emitted a series of nine tremendous sneezes – never any more, never any less – every hour and a half. A legend had sprung up around him – if he ever sneezed a tenth time, he would die.

In addition to these, we were currently busied in freeing a brilliant but erratic member of the staff, who loved to ensconce himself in a cab, bottle in hand, wave airily at the driver, and say, "Drive elsewhere, my man!" He usually ran up a bill of twenty or thirty dollars, was unable to pay, and landed in city prison. To complicate matters, he was extremely coy about giving his right name. I remember that on this occasion the day police reporter had to pick him out of the collection in the drunk tank, and convince authorities that he was not really "J. Hannegan, cook."

The personable young man calling himself Slipton J. Fell had no difficulty in attracting attention, despite these rival sideshows. He wanted a story in the paper. He was lately returned, he said, from Latin-American vagabondings, and somehow had become separated from Upton Rose and Faran Wide. He wanted to apprise them of his whereabouts.

There was about him the air of a soldier of fortune who had plotted a revolt that failed, and had just managed to conceal himself aboard the lugger in time to escape alive. He laughed, and his mirth was infectious. Anybody, we said, who would adopt the name of Slipton Fell was worth a story . . . and never mind his real name.

He got a story, with a picture. He went happily on his way, and when he had gone the city room seemed a quiet and sober place, and the managing editor decreed a more conservative make-up for the first street edition . . .

A short time later, the personnel department of a large oil company was pleased to note frequent letters commending the courtesy and efficiency of one of their employees, currently filling gas tanks and wiping windshields in a station at Woodside. This paragon of industry was Jerome Braun von Selz, twenty-six, born Ralph Jerome Selz in San Francisco (alias Ralph Sells, alias Charles Oliver, alias Slipton J. Fell). What the company did not know was that Selz had worked for them previously, in Oakland, and had been discharged there. Nor was it discovered until later that his adroit pen had produced the letters of recommendation which reinstated him in the company's employ at Woodside – as well as the letters from sundry customers, praising his work.

At the *Chronicle*, we were ignorant of a few facts, ourselves. We did not know that when Slipton J. Fell visited us, any Latin American adventurings he might have had were in the past, and that his last voyage was only from Alcatraz to the Army pier. He had been in the disciplinary barracks of more than one post, and had come to Alcatraz as an Army deserter.

He was six feet at this time, weighing two hundred and thirty pounds. He had slate-gray eyes, light brown hair, and a ruddy complexion; he talked volubly, and in a positive manner. He spoke Spanish, French and German, and was – as described years later in a statewide police bulletin – "restlessly active."

On April 6th, when everybody had forgotten Slipton Fell, the *Chronicle* city room was occupied in toning down a particularly gory bit of business for its breakfast-table audience. A girl variously described as Betty Coffman and Lena Coffin was found dead in her bed at the Bay Hotel on that date, with one of her breasts sliced off. There was no special class to the story; it had its day on the lips of newsboys, and died . . .

Somewhere around this time, Mrs Ada French-Mengler-Rice returned to her home in the Woodside Glens from Seattle, where her last marriage had gone on the rocks. Not too much is known about her, now, and some of the alleged facts brought to light in a later investigation, when she was no longer around, appear contradictory. She had neighbors, but was not friendly with them; they knew nothing of her movements. She had been a newspaper woman and a writer, and was traveled. August Mengler married her in 1930. In 1932, she became president of the Redwood City unit of the W.C.T.U. A newspaper clipping observed later that she was not remembered as a very good leader, although she had reportedly caused the home of a neighbor to be raided on suspicion that a still was being operated there.

In 1933, Mr Mengler sued for divorce, charging that his wife had become obsessed with social welfare work. Two days later, he dropped dead in a San Francisco hotel lobby.

The then Mrs Mengler later married Charles Freeman Rice, who was seventy-two, a Seattle contractor, and known as a former mayor of Nome. Newspaper files show that Mr Rice obtained his divorce on February 2, 1936. This also was at a time when Mrs Rice was no longer around, or interested, as will be presently revealed . . .

Mrs Rice had been in Seattle a considerable period, and her sedan was standing in her Woodside Glens garage, blocks under the wheels. She went to a service station and asked that a man be sent out to pump up her tires and remove the blocks. The manager told her that one of his very best employees lived only a short distance from her home.

She went by the address given her, awoke Selz, took him

to her house, and gave him a glass of lemonade. Then, according to his story and that of officers – who obviously could have heard it only from Selz – she proposed that he move into her house.

This may be one of the contradictory elements. Mrs Rice was fifty-eight, and a former leader, remember, of the W.C.T.U. She lived alone in a square sort of house with a penthouse sunroom, where workmen remembered seeing her sunbathing.

But remember, too, the infectious, booming laugh of that personable young man. Whatever the arrangement, he moved in with his matchless mirth. And somewhere around the early part of June – the date has been fixed as June 13th – Mrs. Rice vanished.

Apparently she was not missed for several months. She had been in the habit of coming and going; the neighbors paid no attention. Meanwhile, however, Mr Rice went to the courts to seek his freedom, and the sheriff's office of San Mateo County began hunting her to serve the papers.

"Mrs Rice?" the neighbors said. "Oh, she went to Greece, or the Balkans, or somewhere over there. Took a job as a foreign correspondent for some paper . . ."

The thin shade of one Baronovich – Michael Baronovich of the Bulgarian cavalry – was beginning to stir vaguely in the wings, off stage.

Jerome Braun von Selz loved publicity; there is no telling how many clippings he had of that *Chronicle* story. His next appearance in the public prints, however, was, in a way, involuntary. It occurred in February of the following year – 1936 – when he reported that the service station where he now worked had been held up and robbed.

Von Selz was attending San Mateo Junior College, now. In describing the gunman, he exhibited a form of egoism that bordered on the psychopathic – he furnished police with a perfect description of himself.

The result was his arrest, a few days later, on a charge of having made a false robbery report, and his subsequent confession and restitution to the till of some twenty-eight dollars. He was sentenced to thirty days in jail.

That was the end of freedom, except for a stolen period years later, for Selz. Slipton Fell had done just that. He had been tripped by a misdemeanor, by, perhaps, his restless activity and his equally restless imagination. The oil company must have been shocked – it was still getting those neatly forged letters, all in varying chirography, telling what super service he gave . . .

On Leap Year Day, February 29th, 1936, Inspector George O'Leary of the San Francisco police department's auto detail, and M. L. "Jimmy" Britt of the National Auto Theft Bureau, went to the Redwood City jail to interview Selz on another matter. He had reported an auto stolen. The insurance had been paid. A finance company held title to the car; Selz had received eighteen dollars for his equity.

Deputy Sheriff Thomas F. Maloney, who probably deserves the major credit for solving the mystery of Mrs Rice's slaying, sat in on the questioning. Selz laughed, but after two and a half hours and a promise of no prosecution, he led the officers to a private garage in Burlingame, where the car was stored. It now bore stolen license plates, and Maloney and the others searched it.

They found a passport, bearing the name and photograph of Mrs Rice when she was Mrs Ada French. They found rope, adhesive tape, cotton, ammonia, and a blanket.

Jerome Braun von Selz – they were calling him Jerry, now – laughed jovially. Sure, he had been keeping those things in the car. He was looking for a couple of fellows who had done him harm.

Tom Maloney jumped out to the Woodside Glens.

"Who told you," he asked the neighbors, "that Mrs Rice went to the Balkans as a correspondent?"

"Why, the young man who lives in her place. He said she went away with a Bulgarian officer – what was his name? Something ending in 'itch.'"

That night, Maloney and the others searched the house. They found checks bearing Mrs Rice's signature, but written after she had disappeared. Maloney went to the bank in Palo Alto the next day, and saw a letter allegedly written by Mrs Rice from Coxsackie, N. Y. – but posted, it was revealed later, in Redwood City. The letter asked the bank to transfer a hundred and thirty-five dollars from her savings account to her checking account.

Further investigation revealed almost everything but the all-important body. Mrs Rice had deeded Selz her property in the Woodside Glens; he, in turn, had transferred to her certain mining property in Sierra County. It is interesting to note that the latter not only wàs found to be worthless, but that Selz owned only a part interest in it – and even that under another name.

Maloney and Britt began work in earnest. Selz laughed and laughed. They saw that they were dealing with a very strange young man, whose mental processes were best described by one of his own statements when he basked, later, in the light of notoriety.

"No one knows," he boasted then, "what is in my mind!"

Tom Maloney and Jimmy Britt didn't know, but they were finding out a few interesting things. That Selz hadn't been sleeping at the Woodside Glens place – not unless somebody else was there, too. He snatched sleep a couple of hours at a time, in the car he had reported stolen. He drove a lot at night. He was filled with a great and fearful respect for the Secret Service and the F.B.I.

He had tried to get men with whom he worked to move in with him. They refused. He picked up an itinerant marathon dancer on the highway – there was always some sort of curious attraction for the grotesque – and took her to live with him. She was there when he was arrested for making the false report. He had been going to see a girl in Oakland,

and when she went out with another man, he threatened her with a gun. She complained to police, but did not want to prosecute him, and the Oakland authorities merely warned him to stay away from that city.

He had been trying to trade the Woodside Glens property for a large and powerful cabin cruiser, and was going to take this girl on a tropical cruise. And just before his arrest, he had asked the Redwood City public library for a manual of toxicology. He simply had to have the book, he said, before March 25th.

Nobody knows what laughter might have been planned for March 25th. Fortunately, the book had to be requested from the state library, and before Selz could call for it, he was in jail . . .

Maloney and Britt began a campaign to win his confidence. They waged this mainly through the medium of food – steaks and chicken – because Selz, a big man, was a tremendous eater. They never put handcuffs on him; they laughed with him, and called him Jerry. Maloney drove the car, Britt asked the questions, Maloney listened and studied their man. He discovered that Selz' mind was very receptive: if an idea were planted in it, he adopted it as his own, and almost always brought out some version of it later.

Tom Maloney may be no student of psychology, but he has learned a lot of it in his years as a law enforcement officer. They could find no body – they knew there was one, somewhere. They could not break down the laugher – they knew he had a story to tell. It occurred to Maloney that if he were to plant the idea of accidental death, this might cause Selz to tell that story, and that it might be the stepping stone to the truth.

They took Selz to the Woodside Glens house. The ceiling was covered with blow flies, and he was afraid of them. Tom Maloney searched the attic for a body, and found none; he does not really know to this day why the flies were there. They drove the lonely roads that lead to Skyline Boulevard, and Maloney called attention to a shallow depression covered with the same sort of flies.

"This looks like a grave," he remarked. "And that canyon would be a fine place to throw a body – nobody would ever find it."

"Say," Jerry asked in jail the next day, "do you get premonitions?"

"No," Maloney said casually. "Why?"

Selz guffawed. "Well," he said, "yesterday up on the Skyline, you made a couple of remarks too close to suit me!"

Tom Maloney knew, then, that Mrs Rice was buried somewhere by Skyline Boulevard. But that is a long road, and lonely; the redwood canyons drop away from it by the hundreds, and restless fogs come in from the sea to enshroud it. On Skyline, but where?

They had photostatic copies made of the forged checks and the letter. They called Captain Thomas Foster of the U.S. Secret Service, and had him come from San Francisco to question Selz about misuse of the mails, about the fraudulent removal of funds from a national bank.

For the first time, Selz' laughter wavered and turned weak. Fear of the federal officer made him crack – just a little way, at first. He agreed to tell his story.

But the first account had nothing to do with the body. Britt said, "Jerry, we know there is a body up there, somewhere. If it were your sister or your mother, you'd want it brought in for a decent burial. If you – "

Selz had never lost his temper, but now he leaped to his feet. "I'll be God-damned if I'll confess to something I didn't do!" he screamed.

Tom Maloney sighed, and started all over again. He made Selz a friendly little speech, pointing out to him that events since June 13th of the previous year had encircled him like a boa constrictor. He reminded Selz that he couldn't sleep at the house when alone, that he was afraid to stay there, that he was haunted.

"You cry out in your sleep here in jail!" he said. "Why? Because there's something on your mind. You know Mrs Rice was killed. Maybe she fell and hit her head – perhaps it was an accident. But I figure it this way: she tried to burn the deed to the property, and there was a fight. She was killed in that fight."

Selz was silent for a space, and his chin sank to his chest. "There was a hell of a fight, all right," he said finally. "Give me time to think . . ."

The story broke in the newspapers. Selz responded to the rays of the spotlight: he roared with laughter again, and jested with reporters and cameramen. A lie detector test showed him guilty, and he ate another big steak, and autographed the white starched collar of the waitress who couldn't believe such a personable young man could possibly be suspected of murder. By this time, the newspapers had unofficially linked his name to the mutilation slaying of Betty Coffman.

They took him to the Woodside Glens house again, spiriting him there in a mad night dash to elude the reporters. Selz bathed and changed clothes and shaved.

Then he told his story.

It was an accident. He had come into the house at night. No lights were on, but he immediately sensed the presence of two other persons, who began fighting. In the darkness, he grabbed something – the fireplace poker, he thought – and swung. Somebody fell, and the other person rushed out the door. There was moonlight outside, and it glinted on a saber in the fugitive's hands.

That man, he said dramatically, was none other than the Bulgarian cavalry officer – Baronovich. Michael Baronovich. He had had a lot of trouble with Baronovich.

He left Mrs Rice's body in the living room all that next day. With nightfall, he put it in the sedan, drove down the Skyline, turned four miles on the road to Big Basin, and dumped the body in a canyon. He had stolen two sacks of lime from a warehouse. He went back the next night on a motorcycle, carrying a shovel. He dug what amounted to a foxhole, broke the shovel handle doing it, and couldn't make the grave very deep.

He buried Mrs Rice there, jackknife fashion, head down, hands behind her back, and poured the lime over her.

"What about Baronovich?"

Von Selz roared with laughter. Oh, he had killed the Bulgarian, too, some time later. A big man, Baronovich was, with husky hair. It was, Selz said, the survival of the fittest: Baronovich had attacked him. He had killed the Bulgarian, tied a large collection of iron plates to the body, and heaved it from the San Mateo Bay bridge . . .

He finally led them to the spot where he had buried Mrs Rice, and he made the canyons echo his mirth there while they dug her up. A couple of the newspapermen became ill, but Selz laughed all the harder. He posed and tapdanced. He enlarged upon his story of killing Baronovich – in self defense, of course – and shouted with mirth as he offered to toss Fred Glover, a newsman, into the Bay to show how it was done.

About this time, one Otto von Feldman came forward in Southern California, to say he had been the night porter at the hotel where Betty Coffman was killed, and to identify Selz as the man who had registered with her. Now the papers called Selz "triple murder suspect." They also called him "burly Lothario," "soldier of fortune," and "the Laughing Killer of the Woodside Glens."

He did not confess to the Coffman killing. He was having too much fun with Baronovich. They dragged the Bay at the spot he indicated, and brought up wire, and – once – something that might have been flesh.

But Selz was a mercurial sort, and when reporters asked him questions about his family, the publicity suddenly began to pall. He begged Tom Maloney to shield him from the newspapermen. He didn't want his family, or his lodge –

Maloney had found a lodge uniform in the house – brought into it.

Maloney hid the uniform, but a reporter found part of it, and reached a rather whimsical conclusion after they had dug up Mrs Rice's body, and were looking for that of Baronovich.

The reporter spread the word that Selz had the uniform of a grave digger from Holy Cross cemetery . . .

S elz agreed to plead guilty to murder in the first degree, after a dentist had identified Mrs Rice's remains, and after he had chortled at the sight. The trial set a record for brevity in San Mateo County murder cases, and one seldom equaled anywhere. It lasted fifty-five minutes, and on that same afternoon Jerome Braun von Selz became a number in San Quentin prison, serving a life sentence. That was on March 12, 1936.

He made a little speech to the reporters who followed him to the prison gates – a speech in which Tom Maloney had carefully rehearsed him. He stopped laughing, and said: "I'm going in to make good," after the fashion of a football player about to do or die for dear old alma mater.

And did he? Well, San Quentin heard his incredible laughter, and he made friends there, and became the strong man of the prison's tumbling team, as well as its champion weight lifter. He may have been responsible for the plea – quickly denied – that inmates be allowed to take up pole vaulting. He tried to enlist in the Army during the war, but was rejected by a psychiatrist as a "constitutional psychopathic inferior."

He laughed, and acquitted himself so well (although his plea for parole had been denied) that he was transferred to the California Institution for Men, at Chino, on May 23, 1944.

This is something of an honor institution, and Selz virtually advertised his intention to flee from it. He obtained and studied maps of Mexico. He shipped out his favorite possession – a mandolin. On the evening of May 3, 1945, he simply walked away.

But he didn't go to Mexico. He went to Minnesota, instead, and somehow managed to register there with a draft board – which fingerprinted him.

The master file of the F.B.I. did the rest. It took a little while, and by the time they caught up with him, Selz was in the Canadian Army – a corporal, known as Ralph Jerome "Tiny" Morgan, teaching physical education. He roared with laughter, and told how he had written back to San Francisco for his birth certificate.

They brought him back with extradition papers later that month, and his mirth is heard at San Quentin again, and may be for a long time to come. The confession of a merchant seaman cleared him, in 1940, of the "unofficial" charge of Betty Coffman's mutilation murder. Nobody has ever cleared him of his own charge that he disposed so gleefully of one Michael Baronovich . . .

But I think I know who Michael Baronovich was, and who Upton Rose and Faran Wide were, too. I think all three of them were none other than Slipton J. Fell.

Allan R. Bosworth

214

An Axe for Frau Marek

The story of Martha Loewenstein seems to have
been designed as a moral fable. It is the kind of
tale that has fascinated our ancestors down the
centuries. It is difficult to understand how an
exceptionally beautiful girl turned into a multiple
poisoner; most murderesses have been plain or
downright ugly. Beauty, after all, gives a girl
confidence, and confident girls usually develop
a certain ability to cope with life. Even when
things go wrong, they seldom resort to murder.
I am inclined to believe that Martha's original
"protector", Moritz Schmidt, whose mistress she
became while still little more than a schoolgirl,
was to blame. He accustomed her to luxury,
and the idea of a return to poverty became
intolerable. It seems appropriate that her lover
probably became her first victim.

"An Axe for Frau Marek", by ex-Police Com-
missar Ignatz Peters, is again taken from Kurt
Singer's remarkable collection *My Strangest Case*.

Luck, I am convinced, often can be misfortune in disguise,
and if this were not true I should not now be telling you
the story of Martha Löwenstein. She, of all people, had
good reason to curse the day she thought she was lucky.

Many will remember her as a very beautiful girl, always
stylishly dressed every day she took the electric car for
Kirtnerstrasse, where she worked in a dress shop, from
Ottakring, one of the shabbiest places in Vienna. It was

a district of down-at-heel houses and depressed people, and Martha was one of the rare flowers that grew there. Men would put down their newspapers as soon as they saw her and always she had a bright smile for her fellow passengers.

She was well worth looking at, blonde, slim and with a fine complexion that certainly did not come from a box. Every day she wore something different and her elegance piqued the women to whom she was known by sight. They whispered that no girl from a poor neighbourhood could dress so expensively unless . . . well, that was what they said, but it was untrue. Martha was virtuous, and there was a simple explanation for everything.

She confided the truth to Moritz Fritsch, the owner of a large department store in Vienna and a wealthy and cultured man. He was in his sixties, but looked very much younger. He found an opportunity to speak to Martha one evening as she was on her way home. He told her that he had often seen and admired her and he complimented her on the way she dressed. Martha said she came from a very poor home and worked in a dress shop. Her employer had always been exceedingly kind, and treated her almost as a daughter.

"She likes to see me in good clothes," Martha said, "and says I am a splendid advertisement for her shop. But for her I should look as poor as do many girls who have to work for a living."

Herr Fritsch promptly offered to find her a well-paid job in his store, but the young girl would not hear of it. She was devoted to her employer and on no account would she leave her.

"I must say I admire your loyalty," said Fritsch. "But you will, of course, allow me to take you home?"

Martha stepped into the chauffeur-driven limousine, and on the way to Ottakring explained that she and her mother lived alone. Her father had emigrated to America many years before and they had not heard of him since.

Back at his villa at Mödling that evening, Moritz Fritsch

could not get the girl out of his mind. Her home was deplorable, and so, too, was her mother, a hulk of a woman, vulgar and tactless. She had told him all there was to know about the family, and it had turned out that Martha was, in fact, a love-child and her daughter by adoption only.

Fritsch was divorced and his two children were married. Except for his servants he lived alone, and that night he felt how empty his home had become. He was very rich and very lonely.

Shortly afterwards he took Martha out to dinner, and not only showed her a glimpse of luxury but suggested that she should become his ward. It would give her, he said, the right to everything her beauty deserved – clothes and jewels, education and travel and the company of intelligent people.

Martha did not need to be persuaded, and the fashionable villa in the suburbs became her home. Fritsch kept his word. He sent her to a school for young ladies and, for holidays, to France and England. At eighteen Martha was more lovely than ever and she had acquired poise and social polish.

When she returned to live at the villa her benefactor introduced her to his friends at parties and dinners. He never refused her anything and soon she possessed more jewels and clothes than she could ever have dreamed of. However, when the gilt had worn off a little Martha began to suffer from the moods that harry all unfulfilled young women. Whenever she was in a tantrum Fritsch would buy her some new piece of jewellery and he seems to have understood just why his fascinating ward behaved as she did.

Fritsch's devotion to the girl had, of course, long been the subject of gossip, particularly among the servants. A maid said she had seen him embracing his ward in the garden and in a manner that was hardly fatherly. On another occasion they were together in Martha's bedroom, both rather carefree and lively from the champagne they had drunk.

Three years went by, and towards the end began a period during which Martha could not be roused from her black moods, despite all the presents Fritsch gave her. The old man felt, as he told his friends, that he was, perhaps, demanding too much from her and was certain that she feared the day when he would no longer be alive to protect her.

Fritsch was probably right, for when he told Martha that he had made a new will in which she had not been forgotten, she cried a little and put her arms round the old man. It was the end of her unhappiness. Fritsch by law was bound to leave a third of his estate to his ex-wife and he had settled money, too, on his children. Martha was to have what was left, including the house.

A year after this arrangement was made Fritsch died at the age of seventy-four. Present at the bedside were Martha, the old man's family and Dr Pollack, his physician.

When the will was read Betty Fritsch was furious. "I do not understand it," she protested. "At the time of our divorce Moritz solemnly promised that the estate would be left to the family."

"I drew up the will according to Herr Fritsch's wishes," said the lawyer sharply.

But Betty was not to be persuaded. "My husband was old, but his health was good. I think this girl knows something about his death. There is only one way to find out. The body must be exhumed."

Everybody was horrified by the suggestion, particularly Fritsch's son and daughter. "Mother was always terribly jealous of Father's ward," said young Fritsch. "Under no circumstances must Father's body be disturbed."

There was no inquiry and Martha received her inheritance in due course, but got far less money than she had anticipated. Although she was not seen about much a handsome young man began to visit her at the villa, and three months after Fritsch's death it became known that she had married him. His name was Emil Marek and he was studying engineering. Martha had been meeting him secretly for over a year.

It was not until some time afterwards that I heard the name of Martha Löwenstein Marek for the first time, and it happened in this way. One day I got a telephone call from Herr Möller, the vice-president of an insurance company. He said he was at the Billroth Hospital and asked me if I would go at once to meet him there. Möller was waiting for me and we went into one of the smaller rooms of the hospital, where a man's leg, severed just below the knee, lay on a table. The shoe and sock had not even been removed.

Möller explained why he had called me at the *Polizei Dezernat*.

"The leg belongs, or rather belonged, to a young man named Emil Marek. He lives in a villa in the suburbs with his wife, and the maid telephoned me to say that he had injured himself badly while cutting down a tree in the garden. He was brought here and the surgeon who completed the amputation tells me the leg was hanging only by a sinew."

"Why were you telephoned about the accident, Herr Möller?"

"Because Marek is insured with us for a considerable sum of money."

Möller gave me the details. About a week before Marek had called on him to take out a policy by which he would be covered for £10,000 in the event of any serious accident. Marek told him he was studying engineering at the Vienna Technical Institute and not long ago had married a young woman who had money. The Government was interested in an electrification scheme for Burgenland which he had prepared, and he felt that it was only fair to his wife that he should be adequately insured against the possibility

219

of an accident. He did not want to become a burden to her.

"I was dubious about the proposal," said Möller, "and refused to entertain it. All the same I was impressed by Marek. He seemed a very decent young man, honest and very intelligent. Later I wondered if I had done the right thing and made some inquiries. I found that he has a good name at the institute and I was able to confirm that he had told me the truth about the scheme he has put up to the Government. In fact, I became convinced that he was a good risk and made arrangements to issue the policy. He came back, signed the papers, and paid the premium."

We were still talking when Dr Rudolf Küster came into the room, and Möller introduced him to me. "Marek has had a very narrow squeak," said the surgeon, "and if his wife had not used several tourniquets he would have bled to death before anything could have been done for him. He is very shocked and has lost a lot of blood, but he is young and healthy and should get over it."

I asked the surgeon the angle of the wound and he looked at me curiously.

"It is rather puzzling," he said. "The cut is almost straight, and it is difficult to say exactly how it happened, but an accident can often show a freakish result."

"If it was an accident," said Möller.

It was asking a lot to believe that a person would hack off his leg to collect insurance, but then one can never tell. Marek was far too ill to be questioned, but Martha, too, was detained at the hospital, for she had collapsed as soon as her husband had been taken into the operating theatre.

She had been given a sedative, but was conscious and able to talk. She cried as she told us that her husband had been cutting down a tree when the axe slipped. She had heard his cries and so had the neighbours. They had found him in a great pool of blood, and everybody had helped with the tourniquets while awaiting the ambulance which had been telephoned for.

Despite her pallor and distress she looked very elfin and lovely as she lay in the hospital bed. She murmured that she would always love her husband, and soon she was sleeping like a tired child.

In the meantime I sent Detective Carl Huber to the villa to have a look around, and he came back with some surprising news. In the garden was a half-felled tree, a great patch of blood and a razor-sharp axe. "Somebody had wiped the axe clean," said Huber. "There was not a spot of blood on it, nor a fingerprint."

It was possible of course that the axe had been wiped innocently by a maid or someone, but it was not possible to explain away the expert evidence Möller and I heard the following morning at the Vienna Medical Institute, to which the leg had been sent for examination.

Removing his pince-nez, which he wore attached to a silk cord, Professor Meixner pointed to Exhibit A and said: "Gentlemen, there can be no question but that these wounds were inflicted deliberately. The partial amputation required three separate strokes of the axe, and the marks on the limb are plainly discernible, each going deeper than the previous one."

Quite involuntarily I exclaimed, "But that is incredible!" and then remembered that it is the incredible that gives the police their employment.

"What is credible," remarked Möller sagely, "is that Marek had help in mutilating himself."

"You mean his wife, I suppose?"

"Yes; I believe she can tell us what really happened."

There were many inquiries to be made before the Mareks could be arrested on a charge of attempted fraud, and, in any case, Emil Marek could not be moved from hospital for some time. I learned a lot about Martha and how she had become an old man's darling. The case was so unusual that it became the talk of Vienna, and Martha herself was astute enough to take part in the controversy.

Shortly after being released on bail she invited me to call

on her at the villa. A smart little maid opened the door and showed me into the drawing-room, where I found her lying – Recamier-like – on a chaise-longue surrounded by an audience. The room, beautifully furnished, and with many rare pieces, was full of reporters, and Martha offered me her hand to kiss as if I were a courtier instead of a police officer.

"You must pardon me for not rising, but I am still very weak. I have invited the reporters here in order to tell them that my husband and I are being prosecuted at the instigation of an insurance company which hopes to evade paying the money it owes us."

She paused and gave me a cool stare, and I could see that she had won the sympathy of everybody present. "You see," she went on, "I have received certain information of which I am sure the police cannot be aware. It was given to me by a person who works at the hospital and he tells me that he had seen Herr Möller talking very confidentially with one of the surgeons. Later, and I am assured of the truth of this, this witness saw this selfsame surgeon extending the area of the wound on poor Emil's amputated leg."

This was sensational "copy" for the newspapers, and one of the reporters asked: "Can you tell us the name and occupation of your witness?"

Martha smiled a little sadly. "No, I am not able to say who he is, for reasons I am sure you will understand. He was kind enough to volunteer this information, and that is all I can tell you for the time being."

I stayed behind, and it took me a long time to secure from Martha the name of the person who was supposed to have witnessed an act of collusion between Möller and a surgeon. It was a very ugly allegation and not for one moment did I think it was true.

The person in question was a hospital orderly named Karl Mraz. He was a frail creature and not very intelligent. He bore out Martha's story when first questioned, but he did not stand up to the interrogation and finally admitted that

Frau Marek had offered him 10,000 schillings if he would repeat the story she had concocted.

A further charge of attempting to obstruct the course of justice was added to the indictment when the two prisoners were tried, but they were not seriously inconvenienced.

Crime has an ugly face and nobody looked less like criminals than Emil Marek, a most handsome cripple, and Martha, his enchanting wife. They had the newspapers on their side too, and the charge of attempted fraud was dismissed for lack of sufficient evidence. On the second count they were found guilty and sentenced to four months' imprisonment, but it was ruled that since they had already spent a similar period in custody while awaiting trial the sentence had already been served.

Over coffee with Möller I could see he was very worried at the prospect of his company having to meet the Mareks' claim. Had I not been convinced that it was fraudulent I would not have offered him certain advice. I knew the history of Martha, and of the doubt in Betty Fritsch's mind that her husband had died a natural death, and advised him that Martha, quite literally, might not care to have her past dug up. I offered him this advice as a friend, and not as a police officer, and said that no doubt a little heart-to-heart talk with her might persuade her to accept a more modest settlement.

Möller dropped in at a party the Mareks gave to celebrate their freedom and he said enough to convince Martha that in the circumstances it would be wiser to settle for £3,000, which she did. After all the costs of the defence had been met Emil's amputated leg did not return much of a profit.

They had been very lucky to escape a long term of imprisonment, and it was because I felt so certain of their guilt that I kept an eye on them. The scandal of the trial ruined all prospects of Emil's electrification project, for the Government promptly withdrew its support and he could find nobody as a private backer. He tried to make money with a fleet of taxis he bought, but the venture was a costly failure and ended in the villa having to be mortgaged to meet his debts.

The Mareks disappeared for some time, and one of my detectives discovered they had gone to Algiers to manufacture radio sets for foreign markets. Labour was cheaper there and no doubt the couple regarded this move as a fresh start.

The next time I saw Martha I could hardly believe it was her. She was selling vegetables from a barrow on a street in one of the poorest sections of Vienna. She had not lost her looks entirely, but her face was drawn and angry. I stopped my car to speak to her.

"Yes," she said bitterly, "we're as poor as I look. Nothing has gone right for us. Emil's business failed in Algiers, and that meant the end of the villa, which was already mortgaged. This is what I have been reduced to. I escaped once from the filth and ugliness of poverty, but now I am a prisoner again."

Martha was wearing a soiled cotton dress and shoes that appeared too big for her. Her appearance would have horrified Moritz Fritsch. I realised how much she disliked me, but at least I was someone she could talk to. "We are really up against it. I have to do this to keep a bit of bread in our mouths. My husband is no longer able to work and we have a young daughter and a baby boy."

The Mareks had been knocked about pretty badly, but Martha was so viperish that it was difficult to feel any sympathy for her. I did not see her again for some time, but in July 1932 I read of Emil Marek's death in one of the newspapers. I got thinking about it and made some inquiries among neighbours. Emil, they said, had been ill for some time. There seemed to have been some paralysis, loss of vision and other painful symptoms. Martha, I was told, nursed him and did everything that was possible until neighbours made a collection among themselves and paid for an opinion by a specialist. Emil's illness was diagnosed as advanced tuberculosis and he was admitted to the charity ward of the Calvary Hospital, where he died soon afterwards.

These facts I was able to confirm, but I might not have been so convinced that Marek's death arose from natural causes had I known that a little over a month afterwards the death also occurred of his daughter, Ingeborg. In the rush of police work the event escaped my notice.

It was 1933 and Hitler already was in power and Europe's long night had begun. Five years of darkness and change went by, and in March 1938 the Nazis marched into my country, and nobody, not even those who welcomed the *anschluss*, could foretell what awaited them tomorrow. The past seemed completely wiped out and with it the record of one's own life and work. Perhaps that explains my feeling of astonishment when I again heard the name of Frau Marek.

She had, according to a report placed on my desk, been the victim of the theft of a number of valuable tapestries and paintings. She was living in Kuppelweisergasse, one of the better parts of the city, which was certainly an improvement on selling carrots, onions and potatoes to the under-privileged, as she had been doing when last I saw her.

I thought it would be interesting to call on her, and, at first, Martha did not recognise me. With a graceful gesture she indicated the bare walls of her large and handsome apartment. "They were stolen during the night," she said tersely. She looked at me a second time and with recognition. "Well, *how* very nice to see you again," she said, as if she actually meant it.

"You've had a change of luck," I said.

"Yes, indeed. This house was left to me by Mrs Löwenstein, a relative of my father. Please do your best to recover the stolen articles."

Martha had plenty of nerve, I had to admit to myself. I said to her: "I suppose you had the valuables insured?"

"Naturally. Herr Neumann, who incidentally is a tenant here, issued the policy."

It was my turn to be surprised, and I wondered if she had been up to her old tricks again. Surely, I thought, she must have learned her lesson, but frauds invariably repeat their offences, and I decided it would be worth my while to make a few calls. If the robbery had been faked, then Frau Marek must have had the tapestries and paintings removed, and eventually I found the removal firm who had done the job. Martha had arranged for the collection to be made at night-time and her valuables were in safe storage at the Omega repository in Ottakring.

For the second time I arrested Martha on a charge of attempted fraud. The newspapers had not forgotten her trial eleven years before, and, since she began once more to dominate the front pages, things began to happen. While the fraud case against her was pending a young man named Herbert Kittenberger called on me and told me he was convinced that Frau Marek had poisoned his mother. He wanted her body exhumed.

From what he told me, his mother, Felicitas Kittenberger, had rented a room in Martha's apartment house and had died there after a brief illness. Her son had not been told of her death until after the funeral.

"Why not?" I asked.

Herbert Kittenberger said he had not even known of his mother's illness. He admitted that he was often away looking for work, but asserted that Frau Marek could have got in touch with him had she wanted to. "I tried to get an explanation from her and she said she had tried to find me, but I am certain she was lying."

Although Frau Kittenberger's doctor maintained that his patient had died from natural causes I thought it advisable to apply for an order to exhume her body. During the last few years death, it seemed, had followed Martha around, and I sensed there was much to be explained. It meant a lot of work and a lot of back-tracking, but I found out that shortly after the death of her husband Martha had moved into the home in Kuppelweisergasse of her aged relative, Frau Susanne Löwenstein. In the neighbourhood there were still those who remembered the old woman's pretty companion. Martha had visited Frau Löwenstein to begin with, and had then persuaded her that she needed someone to look after her.

Once again Martha was able to escape from poverty. She was still young, just over thirty, and the old woman must have bought her some clothes, for she dressed well and had apparently saved a few of the jewels that Fritsch had bought her years before.

She did the cooking for Frau Löwenstein, read to her, and, according to a witness, when the old woman told her she intended leaving her all she possessed Martha had replied: "Everything I do for you is a labour of love. I do not do it for money."

Frau Löwenstein did not long survive, and in her final illness the symptoms were similar to those reported of Martha's late husband – numbness in her legs, dim vision and a difficulty in swallowing. When she died she left Martha the house and a substantial parcel of money.

One of the persons I talked to about Martha was Herr Neumann, her insurance agent, and the occupant of a couple of rooms at her house. He was garrulous but co-operative.

"I first met Frau Marek in 1935," he said. "One could not but be impressed by her – she was very good-looking and had superb manners. We saw a great deal of each other and she used to confide in me. She had been extravagant and had run through the money Frau Löwenstein had left her. The house in Kuppelweisergasse was expensive to keep up and she asked my advice.

"I suggested that she rent me a couple of rooms to help her out, and later Frau Kittenberger joined our little family. Frau Marek became very fond of her."

"Really?"

"Oh, yes. They were the best of friends. You can't believe a word that Herbert, Frau Kittenberger's son, says. He was a great trouble to her. I can assure you of that. He could not keep a job and money ran through his hands.

"Frau Kittenberger told Martha that the little money she had would go in no time if Herbert got hold of it, and there would certainly not be enough left to bury her. Martha consulted me about the problem and I worked out an insurance policy for Frau Kittenberger. The money was to go to Martha, and it was just as well the arrangement was made, for she was decently buried when her time came."

"What was the amount of the policy?" I inquired.

"It was very little, about three hundred pounds."

It appeared logical to assume that if Martha had indeed murdered Frau Kittenberger it was not the first occasion she had killed, and it became necessary therefore to open the graves of Emil Marek, Ingeborg, her daughter, and Frau Löwenstein.

While awaiting the medical findings of each of the four autopsies a question that had irked my subconscious mind for some time was suddenly liberated. What had happened to the other Marek child – the little boy? On their return from Algiers Marek and his wife had lived in Hitzing, and it was in this district of Vienna that detectives traced the child, Alfons, who was boarded out with neighbours. He was reported to be very ill.

The woman who looked after him told me that she feared little Alfons was suffering from tuberculosis, which she believed he had contracted from his father. The symptoms were greatly similar. Frau Marek, she said, was a constant visitor and often arrived in time to give him his evening meal. Frequently she brought him something special to eat.

"Frau Marek is a very brave woman," said my informant with tears in her eyes. "I heard her telling the little boy he would soon be with his father, and she herself looked just like an angel."

"Don't you ever read the papers?" I asked her.

"*Nein*, Herr Peters. We are very poor."

We got the little boy into hospital, and during the

trial of his mother doctors had to fight hard to save his life.

Martha was charged with the multiple murders of her husband and daughter and of those of Frau Löwenstein and Frau Kittenberger. All of them had died from one of the poisonous compounds of thallium, and a pharmacist in Florisdorf produced records of sale of the poison to Martha on a date prior to the death of each victim. There was other evidence that dovetailed and proved the guilt of the accused beyond all possible doubt.

White and tense, Martha heard the public prosecutor brand her as a creature more vile than Lucrezia Borgia herself. With the advent of Hitlerism the death penalty had been restored in Austria and Martha was sentenced to be beheaded.

On December 6th, 1938, she was taken from her cell to the execution block. Her hands tied behind her, she knelt down to receive the death-blow and her head was severed from her body in a single and fearful swing of the axe.

I am not able to say what were her thoughts during the short time she awaited the carrying out of the sentence. She may, of course, as she had every reason to, have thought of the days when her beauty attracted Moritz Fritsch and how lucky she had imagined herself to be for the golden chance of turning her back on poverty. Ultimately, though, it had brought her face to face with murder.

Perhaps even as a young girl she had possessed the instincts of a killer, but it is just possible that had she remained poor she might well have stayed alive.

Who can say?

A Mixed Bag

There are certain cases whose omission from a book on crimes of the 1930s would be absurd. The Lindbergh kidnapping is in many ways *the* crime of the 1930s, as the Jack the Ripper murders were of the 1880s. The story of Sylvestre Matuska is so bizarre that it surely ranks among the strangest cases of all time. The Jeannie Donald case deserves to be remembered for its brilliant forensic detection. The murder of Mona Tinsley is equally remarkable for its well-authenticated piece of "psychic detection". Finally, the Ruxton case shares with the Wallace mystery the distinction of being *the* British murder of the decade. I might have chosen longer accounts of each one of these, but space was running out. So the "mixed bag" of cases that concludes this book is selected from my own *Written in Blood*, with the exception of the Mona Tinsley case, which is from *The Psychic Detectives*.

THE MAN WHO LOVED TRAINS

The most extraordinary sexual criminal of the post-war years was undoubtedly the Hungarian sadist Sylvestre Matuska, the "man who played with trains".

On 8 August 1931, a bomb had exploded on the Basel-to-Berlin express near Jüterbog (not far from Potsdam) injuring 100 passengers, some of them seriously. On 30 January of that year, there had been an unsuccessful attempt to derail a train near Anspach, in Lower Austria, and it seemed likely that both crimes had been committed by the same man – perhaps for political motives. On a telegraph pole there was a notice with swastikas and "Attack! Victory!"

Only a month after the Jüterbog attack, on 12 September 1931, a tremendous explosion shook the Budapest-Vienna express as it crossed a viaduct near the station of Torbagy, hurling five coaches into the depths below. Twenty-two people were killed, and many more injured. A 20-year-old reporter on the *Vienna Morning Post* named Hans Habe was asked to rush to the scene of the disaster. He found dozens of ambulances, stretchers taking away the injured, and wooden coffins beside the track. Some victims had been blown into pieces, and he saw two heads in one coffin and three legs in another. While Habe was talking to Superintendent Schweinitzer, who was in charge of the investigation, a short, well-built man with a military haircut came up to them. He introduced himself as Sylvestre Matuska, a Hungarian businessman who had been in one of the coaches. He seemed a lively, friendly man, and had apparently had a miraculous escape from one of the wrecked carriages that lay below the viaduct. Habe agreed to give him a lift back to Vienna. The next day, Habe met him by appointment in a café and found him describing the accident – complete with sketches – to a crowd of fascinated onlookers. "I saw one woman with her arm torn off . . ." Habe quoted him at length in his story, which brought the young journalist much favourable notice from colleagues.

But Superintendent Schweinitzer was suspicious. Matuska looked healthy and unshaken – quite unlike a man who had just survived a train wreck. He questioned all the surviving passengers on the train; none could recall seeing Matuska. Forensic examination had established that the train had been blown up by an "infernal machine" in a brown fibre suitcase – virtually a mine which had exploded by the weight of the train. A great deal of explosive must have been used, and explosive was not easy to come by. A few days after the explosion, a taxi-driver came to the Vienna police and told them that he had been hired by a short-haired man to take him on a long journey to two munitions factories, where he had bought sticks of dynamite. This raised the question of how the man had managed to obtain an explosives permit. The answer came a week later when a society woman name Anna Forgo-Hung went to the police with another piece of the jigsaw puzzle. Sylvestre Matuska had approached her about leasing some of her property, but had finally rented only a quarry, explaining that he wanted to do some blasting. This is how he had obtained his permit to buy explosives.

Matuska was arrested and charged with blowing up the Torbagy express. When Habe heard the news, he hastened to see Matuska's wife, a pretty blonde with an obviously gentle nature. Frau Matuska told him that her husband was undoubtedly innocent; he was travelling on the train himself, and she had seen his ticket. Yet her attitude convinced Habe that she herself had her suspicions; a wife who believes her husband incapable of a crime says so plainly, and does not talk about tickets and other "proofs" of his innocence.

In fact, Matuska soon confessed. He *had* been on the train from Budapest; but he had got off at the next station, hired a car, and drove to Torbagy in time for the explosion. Forensic examination of the trousers he was wearing at the time showed semen stains, and psychiatrists who examined Matuska verified that he was a sadist. He was also, like Bela Kiss, a man of insatiable sexual appetite, who slept with a different prostitute each night when he was away from home on business trips. Yet his gestures in courts – his trial began in Vienna on 15 June 1932 – were oddly effeminate. From the beginning, Matuska set out to give the impression that he was insane, declaring that he had been persuaded to wreck the train by a right-wing guru called Bergmann, who had tried to persuade Matuska to have intercourse with his incredibly beautiful wife – Matuska rolled the word "intercourse" round his tongue – and then

persuaded him to help him found a religious sect. Matuska
spoke of spiritualist seances, and claimed that he had been
under the telepathic influence of an occultist called Leo
since he was 14. But perhaps the most interesting piece of
evidence was that he had bought his son an electric train
set, then spent all his time playing with it.

The jury was unconvinced by all this talk of mysticism
and occultism, and sentenced Matuska to life imprisonment
– there was no capital punishment in Austria. He was retried
in Budapest, and this time sentenced to death; but since the
Viennese court had sentenced him to life imprisonment, the
sentence was not carried out.

At the end of the Second World War, a reporter asked
the Hungarian authorities what had become of Matuska,
and learned – after many evasions – that the train-wrecker
had been released.

In 1953, towards the end of the Korean War, an American patrol near Hong-Song captured some North Korean
commandos who were about to blow up a bridge; they
were led by a white man who seemed to be about 60.
After long interrogation, during which he apparently failed
to answer the questions, the man announced: "I am Sylvestre
Matuska". His interrogator was obviously unimpressed, at
which point the man explained with pride: "I am Matuska,
the train-wrecker of Bia-Torbagy. You have made the most
valuable capture of the war."

An American report of the incident stated that Matuska
had been freed from his Hungarian prison by the Russians,
and told them that he had wrecked the Jüterbog train on the
orders of a Communist cell of which he was a member; this is
how he came to be accepted as a volunteer on the side of the
North Koreans. As a saboteur trained to blow up bridges,
he must have felt as contented as a necrophile placed in
charge of a morgue. Habe is of the opinion that Matuska
betrayed Communist military secrets to the Americans, and
was then released. What became of him after the Korean
War is unknown.

THE LINDBERGH KIDNAPPING

March 1, 1932, was a rainy and windy day in Hopewell, New Jersey, and the family of the famous aviator Charles Lindbergh were all suffering from colds – which is why they had decided to delay their departure to the home of their in-laws by 24 hours. At 10 o'clock that evening, the nurse Betty Gow asked Ann Lindbergh if she had taken the baby from his cot. She said no, and they went to ask her husband if he had the baby. Then all three rushed up to the room where 19-month-old Charles jun. should have been asleep. On the windowsill was a note demanding $50,000 for the child's return.

There were few clues. Under the window the police found some smudged footprints; nearby there was a ladder in three sections and a chisel. The ladder, a crude home-made one, was broken where the top section joined the middle one. There were no fingerprints in the child's room.

The kidnapping caused a nation-wide sensation, and soon Hopewell was swarming with journalists – to Lindbergh's anger and embarrassment: he knew that the furore would make it more difficult for the kidnappers to make contact. Crooks all over the country had reason to curse the kidnappers as the police applied pressure. Meanwhile, the kidnappers were silent.

The note offered few clues. It had various spelling mistakes, like "anyding" for "anything", and a handwriting expert said that it had probably been written by a German with low educational qualifications. It was signed by two interlocking circles, one red, one blue.

A week after the kidnapping, a well-wisher named Dr. John F. Condon sent a letter to his local newspaper in the Bronx offering $1,000 of his own money for the return of his child. The result was a letter addressed to Condon signed

234

with two circles – a detail that had not been released to the public. It asked him to act as a go-between, and to place an advertisement reading "Mony is Redy" when he was ready to hand it over.

Lindbergh was convinced by the evidence of the two circles; he instructed Condon to go ahead and place the advertisement. That evening, a man's deep voice spoke to Condon on the telephone – Condon could hear someone else speaking Italian in the background – and told him the gang would soon be in touch. A rendezvous was made at a cemetery; at the gates, a young man with a handkerchief over his face asked if Condon had brought the money; Condon said it was not yet ready. The man took fright and ran away; Condon caught up with him and assured him he could trust him. The man identified himself as "John", and suddenly asked a strange question: "Would I burn if the baby is dead?" Appalled, Condon asked: "Is the baby dead?" The man assured him that the baby was alive, and said that he was now on a "boad" (boat). As a token of good faith, he would send Condon the baby's sleeping suit. In fact, it arrived the following day, and the Lindberghs identified it as that of their son.

On 2 April 1932, Lindbergh himself accompanied Condon when he went to hand over the ransom money; he clearly heard the kidnapper's voice calling "Hey, doctor!" But the baby was not returned. Lindbergh flew to look for a boat near Elizabeth Island, but failed to find it. And on 12 May, the decomposing body of a baby was found in a shallow grave in the woods near the Lindbergh home; he had been killed by a blow on the head – apparently on the night of the kidnapping.

The police investigation made no headway. The maid Betty Gow was widely suspected by the police of being an accomplice, but the Lindberghs had no doubt of her innocence. Suspicion transferred to another maid, Violet Sharpe, when she committed suicide with poison, but again there was no evidence.

Meanwhile, a wood technologist named Arthur Koehler was continuing his investigations into the ladder. He had written to Lindbergh offering to trace its wood, using the laboratory of the Forest Service in Wisconsin. Slivers of wood from the ladder had been sent to him for identification soon after the kidnapping. Now he spent four days studying the ladder microscopically, labelling every separate part. Three rails were of North Carolina yellow pine, four of Douglas fir, and ten of Ponderosa pine. The yellow pine rails contained nail holes, indicating that these pieces had been taken from elsewhere, and "rail 16" had square nail holes, and differed from all the others in that it had obviously been planed down from something wider. The whole ladder was "of poor workmanship", showing poor selection of wood and little skill in the use of tools. The microscope showed that the yellow pine rails had tiny grooves, which indicated that the lumber mill that had processed them had a defective knife in the planer. Koehler was aware that this was virtually a fingerprint; if he could find that planing machine, he would stand a good chance of finding what happened to this shipment of wood.

The investigation that followed has been called (in *The Trial of Richard Hauptmann*) "one of the greatest feats of scientific detection of all time". Koehler discovered that there were 1,598 lumber mills that handled yellow pine, and sent duplicated letters of enquiry to each of them. It took several months, but eventually he identified the mill as the Dorn Lumber Company in South Carolina. Between September 1929 and March 1932, they had shipped 47 carloads of yellow pine to East Coast lumber yards; Koehler and Detective Lewis Bornmann spent 18 months visiting yard after yard, and finally had to admit defeat; most of them had long ago sold their consignments of yellow pine, and had no record of the customers. Yet for some reason, they decided to revisit the National Lumber and Millwork Company in the Bronx, and there found a wooden bin which had been constructed of some of the pine they were looking for, with its distinctive planing. Of course, that was no proof that the wood of the ladder had come from that particular lumber yard; it could have come from 29 others. But it was certainly a triumph of sheer persistence . . .

The ransom bills – which included "gold certificates" which could be exchanged for gold – had all been marked (without Lindbergh's knowledge). Now banks were asked to look out for any of the bills, and in 1933 they began to turn up, mostly in New York, although some as far away as Chicago. This seemed to indicate that the kidnappers lived in New York or thereabouts. In early September 1934, $10 gold certificates began to appear in northern New York and the Bronx. In May of that year, Roosevelt had abandoned the gold standard, and called in all gold certificates; but they continued to be accepted by banks – and, of course, shops.

On 15 September 1934, a dark-blue Dodge sedan drove into a garage in upper Manhattan, and the driver, who spoke with a German accent, paid for his fuel with a $10 gold certificate. Because these had ceased to be legal tender, the pump attendant noted the car's number on the back of the certificate. Four days later, a bank teller noticed that the certificate was part of the Lindbergh ransom money, and saw that it had a registration number on the back: 4U-13-41-NY. The police were informed. They quickly discovered that the vehicle was a dark-blue Dodge sedan belonging to Richard Bruno Hauptmann, a carpenter of 1279 East 222nd Street, the Bronx. It proved to be a small frame house, and that night, police surrounded it. The next morning, when a man stepped out of the door and drove off, police followed him and forced his car over to the kerb. Hauptmann, a lean, good-looking German in his mid-30s, made no resistance and was found to be unarmed. In his wallet, police found a $20 bill which proved to be from the ransom money. Concealed in his garage, they found a further hoard of Lindbergh money. Later, a further $860 of ransom money and a gun were found concealed in a plank in the garage.

The evidence seemed overwhelming – particularly when police discovered that Hauptmann bought his timber at the National Lumber Company in the Bronx located by Koehler and Bornmann. But Hauptmann protested his total innocence. The money, he explained, had been left in his care by a friend, Isidor Fisch, who had returned to Germany in December 1933, owing Hauptmann over $7,000, on a joint business deal. When Fisch had died of tuberculosis in March 1934, his friends in America – including Hauptmann – began looking into his business affairs, and realized that he had been a confidence trickster who had simply pocketed investments. Hauptmann and Fisch had been involved in a $20,000 deal in furs; now Hauptmann discovered that the warehouse did not even exist. In August 1934, said Hauptmann, he had noticed a shoe box which Fisch had given him for safe keeping before he left. It had been soaked by a leak, but proved to contain $14,600 in money and gold certificates. Feeling that at least half of it was his by right, Hauptmann dried it out and proceeded to spend it.

That was Hauptmann's story. It sounded too convenient to be true. And when Hauptmann's trial opened in Flemington, New Jersey, on 2 January 1935, it was clear that no one believed it. But the most important piece of evidence was the ladder. Not only was there a clear possibility that some of its timber had been purchased at the Bronx yard where Hauptmann bought his timber, but one of the rungs (16) had been traced to Hauptmann's own attic: Detective Bornmann had noticed a missing board, and found what remained of it, with the "rung" sawed out of it. The evidence could hardly have been more conclusive. Moreover, Condon's telephone number had been found pencilled on the back of a closet door in Hauptmann's house, together with the numbers of some bills.

It was true that there was nothing conclusive to connect Hauptmann with the kidnap itself. The footmarks found outside the child's bedroom window were not Hauptmann's size; none of Hauptmann's fingerprints were found on the ladder. But a man called Millard Whited, who lived near Lindbergh, identified Hauptmann as a man he had seen hanging around the Lindbergh home on two occasions. And Lindbergh himself declared in court that Hauptmann was the "John" whose voice he had heard at the cemetery. All this, together with the ladder evidence, left the jury in no doubt whatsoever that Hauptmann was the kidnapper, and on 13 February 1935, he was sentenced to death. By October, the Court of Appeals had denied his appeal. But when the prison governor, Harold Hoffmann, interviewed Hauptmann in his cell in December, he emerged a puzzled man, feeling that Hauptmann's pleas of innocence rang true, and that the case deserved further investigation. The truth was that Hauptmann could easily have been "framed". Soon after her husband's arrest, Anna Hauptmann had made the supreme mistake of moving out of the house, leaving it empty for police and reporters to examine. It was after this that Bornmann had discovered the missing board in the attic. But was it likely that a carpenter, with plenty of wood at his disposal, would prise up a board in his attic and plane it down to size? Even the ladder itself gave rise to suspicion; as Koehler pointed out, it was crudely made, and showed poor judgement. But Hauptmann was a skilled carpenter . . .

For Lindbergh, Governor Hoffmann's attempts to prove Hauptmann innocent were the last straw. He was totally convinced that Hauptmann was guilty, and he felt that Hoffmann was seeking publicity. He and his wife sailed for England, and did not return for many years. He went to Germany, was impressed by Hitler's revolution, and became a frequent guest of the Nazis; later he tried hard to prevent America entering the war on the side of the British.

But Hoffmann's efforts were of no avail, and on 3 April 1936, Richard Hauptmann was finally electrocuted, still protesting his innocence.

Is it conceivable that Hauptmann was innocent? According to one investigator, Ludovic Kennedy, it is almost a certainty. In the early 1980s, Kennedy took the trouble to interview all witnesses who were still available, and to look closely into the evidence – that which was presented in court and that which was not. His book *The Airman and the Carpenter* (1985) makes one thing very clear; that if all this evidence *had* been presented in court, Hauptmann would have been acquitted. Hauptmann came to America as a stowaway in 1924; he had a minor police record for burglary during the black days of inflation. But in America he prospered; he and his wife worked hard, and by 1926 he was in a position to lend money and to buy a lunchroom; the day after the Wall Street crash he withdrew $2,800 from his account and began buying stocks and shares at rock bottom prices. Hauptmann had no need to kidnap the Lindbergh baby; by modern standards, he was very comfortably off in 1932.

Kennedy's investigations revealed that Hauptmann's story about his friend Isidor Fisch was true. Fisch *was* a confidence swindler; he and Hauptmann were in the fur business together, and Fisch *did* owe Hauptmann over $7,000. His swindles were uncovered only after his death in Leipzig in 1934.

Then how did Hauptmann – or Fisch – come to be in possession of so much ransom money? The probable answer, Kennedy discovered, is that the Lindbergh ransom money was selling at a discount in New York's underworld – one convict bought some at 40 cents in the dollar. Nothing is more likely than that Fisch, with his underworld connections, bought a large quantity, and left it with Hauptmann when he sailed for Germany. Forensic examination of the money showed that it *had* been soaked and dried out, confirming Hauptmann's story that he had left it on a top shelf in a closet and forgotten about it.

But Kennedy's major discovery was that so much of the evidence against Hauptmann was fabricated. When arrested, he was asked to write out various sentences; the court was later told that Hauptmann's misspelling of various words had been exactly as in the ransom note. This was untrue; he had spelled correctly the first time, then been *told* to misspell various words – "singature" for signature, "were" for where, "gut" for good. The court was also assured that handwriting experts had identified Hauptmann's writing as that of the ransom notes; Kennedy submitted the samples to two modern experts, who both said they were *not* written by the same man. Kennedy's investigation revealed that Millard Whited, the farmhand who identified Hauptmann as a man he had seen hanging around the Lindbergh property, had earlier flatly denied seeing anyone suspicious; he was later offered generous "expenses", and changed his story. As to Lindbergh himself, he had been invited to sit quietly in a corner of the room in disguise when Hauptmann was brought in for questioning; he therefore knew him well when he identified him in court as "John". As to the writing in the closet, Kennedy established that it was made by a reporter, Tom Cassidy, who did it as a "joke". Hauptmann had no reason to write Condon's telephone number on the back of a door; he had no telephone, and in any case, the number was listed in the directory. The numbers of bills written on the door were not, in fact, those of Lindbergh ransom bills.

The most serious piece of evidence against Hauptmann was, of course, the ladder. This constituted the "greatest feat of scientific detection of all time". Examined closely, it is seen to be highly questionable. Koehler's efforts established that some of the yellow pine was sent to the Bronx timber yard, and it may have been from this consignment that the rungs of the ladder were made. But this was only one of thirty timber yards to which the same wood was sent; the man who made the ladder could have bought the wood at any of them. Hauptmann rightly pointed out in court that he was a skilled carpenter, and that the ladder was made by an amateur. If the jury registered this point, they may have felt that he had deliberately botched it to mislead investigators – for, after all, was there not the conclusive evidence of the sixteenth rung, whose wood was found in Hauptmann's attic? But, as Kennedy points out, this plank was "found" when Mrs. Hauptmann had abandoned the house to the investigators. Was it likely that Hauptmann would go to the trouble of tearing up his attic floor, sawing out a piece of wood from the plank, then planing it down to size, when it would have been simpler to get another piece of wood? He was, after all, a professional carpenter. Kennedy quite clearly believes that rung 16 was concocted by Detective Bornmann or one of the other investigators – he refers to the whole story as "Bornmann-in-Wonderland".

So in retrospect, it seems clear that the "greatest feat of scientific detection of all time" was based on false or suppressed evidence. The police firmly believed that Hauptmann was guilty, and they strengthened their case where necessary. Hauptmann may well have been guilty; but all the latest evidence points clearly to his innocence.

THE CASE OF JEANNIE DONALD

The murder trial of Jeannie Donald was rendered memorable by the brilliant forensic detective work that convicted her. The murder, of an eight-year-old girl named Helen Priestly, took place in a working class tenement in Aberdeen. On 20 April 1934, Helen failed to return from an errand; her body was found a few hours later in a sack under the stairs. The missing knickers and blood trickling from the vagina suggested a sex crime. But forensic examination revealed no traces of semen, and suggested that the injuries had been inflicted with some instrument like the handle of a pudding spoon. The body had been found close to the flat of a woman called Jeannie Donald, who was known to have a violent temper and to dislike Helen Priestly – the child liked to chant the nickname "Coconut" in her hearing. Jeannie Donald seemed to have a perfect alibi – she said she had been out shopping at the time of the murder – but when she named the prices she had paid for various items, it was noted that they were the prices charged the *previous* Friday.

Sydney Smith, Professor of Forensic Medicine at Edinburgh, was called in to see what he could make of the clues. A magnifying glass showed human and animal hairs in the sack in which the body had been found, and some washed cinders. Many people in the block re-used partly burnt cinders, but Jeannie Donald was the only one who washed them first to remove the ash. The human hair proved to be virtually identical to Jeannie Donald's, and the potato sack resembled others found in her flat (her brother was a farm worker who supplied the Donalds with vegetables). Blood spots found on a newspaper in Jeannie Donald's flat were type "O", the same as Helen Priestly's. But they could, of course, have been Jeannie Donald's. She refused to have a blood sample taken, but Smith was able to obtain one of her used sanitary towels from the prison; it proved to be of a different blood type. Finally, bloodstains found on a floorcloth in the flat were found to contain a rare type of bacterium, which was also found in Helen Priestly's intestines. It became clear that Helen had run past the Donald's flat chanting "Coconut", and that Jeannie Donald had grabbed her on the way back and dragged her inside. Her intention was probably to shake her violently by the throat, but Helen may have fainted. Then, assuming she had killed her, Jeannie Donald attempted to make it look like a sex crime, and placed the body in a sack.

The defence underestimated the strength of the scientific evidence, and decided to plead "Not Guilty". But Smith's performance in the witness box convinced the jury, who took only eighteen minutes to find Jeannie Donald guilty of murder She was sentenced to death, but it was later commuted to life imprisonment, of which she served ten years.

THE RUXTON CASE

September 29, 1935, was a cool autumn day; a young lady had paused in her afternoon walk to lean on the parapet of a bridge across a pretty stream called the Gardenholme Linn. As she stared at the narrow, rocky stream, she noticed some kind of bundle that had jammed against a boulder. Something that looked unpleasantly like a human arm was sticking out of it.

The police were on the scene by mid-afternoon, and had soon discovered two human heads on the bank of the Linn, as well as four bundles, each containing human remains – thigh bones, legs, pieces of flesh, and an armless torso. One piece of newspaper wrapped round two upper arms proved to be the *Sunday Graphic* for 15 September 1935.

When, the following day, Professor John Glaister – author of a classic *Medical Jurisprudence and Toxicology* – arrived with his colleague Dr. Gilbert Millar, he quickly realized that this killing was not the work of some terrified amateur; he had taken care to cover his tracks. He had not only dismembered the bodies, but removed the skin from the heads, to make the faces unrecognizable, and cut off the fingertips to make fingerprint identification impossible. He had made only one mistake: instead of tossing the remains into the River Annan, a few hundred yards downstream, he had tossed them into its tributary, the Linn, which had been swollen with heavy rains at the time. If the rain had continued, the parcels would have ended up in the Solway Firth. But there were a few days of fine weather; the stream dwindled to its usual trickle, and the parcels caught in the rocks.

The remains were sent to the Anatomy Department of the University of Edinburgh, and there treated with ether to prevent further decomposition and destroy maggots; then they were "pickled" in a formalin solution. Glaister and Millar found themselves confronted with a human jigsaw puzzle of 70 pieces.

The first task was to sort the pieces into two separate bodies, and this was made easier by the fact that one was six inches shorter than the other. And when it was finally done, Glaister and his team found that they had one almost complete body, the taller one, and one body minus a trunk. There was also an item that caused much bafflement – an enormous single eye, which certainly did not belong to either of the bodies; by some odd chance, this eye, probably from an animal, had also found its way into the Linn.

What could be deduced about the murderer? First, that he was almost certainly a medical man. He had used a knife, not a saw, to dismember the body, and a human body is almost impossible to dismember with a knife without detailed knowledge of the joints. He had also removed the teeth, recognizing that they could lead to identification by a dentist.

Fortunately, the murderer had either lost his nerve or been interrupted, for he had left some of the hair on the smaller body – which, at first, Glaister thought to be that of a man. And when more parcels were found in the river, Glaister found that he had a pair of hands that still had fingertips. After soaking them in hot water, he was able to get an excellent set of fingerprints. And the discovery that the assorted pieces of flesh included three breasts also made it clear that both bodies were of women.

The next problem was the age of the bodies. Glaister determined this by means of the skull sutures. Sutures are "joining lines" in the skull, and they seal themselves over the years; they are usually closed completely by the age of 40. In one of the two skulls, the smaller of the two, the sutures were unclosed; in the other, they were almost closed. This indicated that one body was that of a woman of about 40; the other was certainly under 30. X-rays of the jaw-bone of the younger woman showed that the wisdom teeth had still not pushed through, which meant she was probably in her early 20s. The cartilage, the soft material of which bones are originally made, gradually changes into "caps", called "epiphyses", and the age can also be estimated from how far this change has taken place. The epiphyses of the smaller body confirmed that this was a girl of 20 or so; the other was of a woman approaching middle age.

As to the cause of death, this was fairly clear: The taller woman had five stab wounds in the chest, several broken bones, and many bruises. The hyoid bone in the neck was broken, indicating strangulation before the other injuries had been inflicted. The swollen and bruised tongue confirmed this inference. Glaister reasoned that a murderer who strangled and beat his victim before stabbing her would probably be in the grip of jealous rage. As to the other body, the signs were that she had been battered with some blunt instrument. It hardly needed a Sherlock Holmes to infer that she had been killed as an afterthought, probably to keep her silent. The fact that the murderer had taken less trouble to conceal her identity pointed to the same conclusion.

Meanwhile, the police were working on their own clues. The *Sunday Graphic* was a special local edition, printed for the Morecambe and Lancaster area. And the clothes in which some of the remains had been wrapped were also distinctive: the head of the younger woman had been wrapped in a pair of child's rompers, and another bundle had been wrapped in a blouse with a patch under the arm . . .

And in Lancaster, a Persian doctor named Buck Ruxton had already attracted the suspicions of the local police. Five days before the remains were found in the Linn, Ruxton – a small, rather good-looking man with a wildly excitable manner – had called on the police and mentioned that his wife had deserted him. The police were investigating the murder of a lady called Mrs. Smalley, whose body had been found a year earlier, and in the course of routine investigations, had questioned a domestic in Ruxton's household; he wanted to protest about this harassment. And when he spoke of his wife's disappearance, they were not in the least surprised; they knew that the relations between the two were stormy. Two years before, Mrs. Isabella Ruxton had come to the police station to protest that her husband was beating her, and Ruxton had made wild accusations of infidelity against her; however, he had calmed down, and 24 hours later the two were apparently again on the best of terms.

The parents of Mrs. Ruxton's maid, Mary Rogerson, were not only surprised but incredulous when Ruxton came and told them that their daughter had got herself pregnant by the laundry boy, and that his wife had taken her away for an abortion. Nothing was less likely; Mary was a plain girl, with a cast in one eye, who loved her home and her parents, and spent all her spare time with them; she was as unlikely to get herself pregnant as to rob a bank. In spite of Ruxton's feverish protests, they reported it to the police. On the evening of 9 October 1935, 10 days after the remains had been found in the Linn, Ruxton came to the police and burst into tears. People were saying that he had murdered his wife and thrown her into the Linn; they must help him find her. They soothed him and sent him away. But, in fact, Ruxton had been the chief suspect since earlier that day. The Scottish police had been to see the Rogersons, and had shown them the patched blouse. As soon as they saw it, they knew their daughter was dead; Mary had bought it at a jumble sale and patched it under the arm. They were unable to identify the rompers, but suggested that the police should try a Mrs. Holme, with whom Mary and the three Ruxton children had spent a holiday earlier that year. And Mrs. Holme recognized the rompers as a pair she had given to Mary for the children.

The police spoke to the Ruxtons' charlady, Mrs. Oxley. She told them that on the day Mrs. Ruxton and Mary

Rogerson had disappeared, Sunday 15 September 1935, Ruxton had arrived early at her house and explained that it was unnecessary for her to come to work that day – he was taking the children to Morecambe, and his wife had gone to Edinburgh. The following morning, she found the Ruxtons' house – at 2 Dalton Square – in a state of chaos, with carpets removed, the bath full of yellow stains, and a pile of burnt material in the yard. A neighbour told the police that Ruxton had persuaded her to come and clean up his house to prepare it for the decorators, claiming that he had cut his hand badly on a tin of peaches. She and her husband had obligingly scrubbed out the house. And Ruxton had given them some bloodstained carpets and a blue suit that was also stained with blood.

On 12 October, the police questioned Ruxton all night, and at 7.20 the next morning he was charged with the murder of Mary Rogerson.

In spite of Ruxton's attempts to cover his tracks, and to persuade various witnesses to offer him false alibis, the truth about the murders soon became plain. Ruxton was pathologically jealous, although there was no evidence that his "wife" – they were in fact unmarried – had ever been unfaithful. A week before the murder, Mrs. Ruxton had gone to Edinburgh, where she had a sister, with a family named Edmondson, who were close friends of the Ruxtons. The Edmondsons and Mrs. Ruxton had all booked into separate rooms; nevertheless, Ruxton was convinced that she had spent the night in the bed of Robert Edmondson, an assistant solicitor in the Town Hall. Ruxton had driven to Edinburgh to spy on them. The following Saturday, Isabella Ruxton had gone to spend the afternoon and evening with two of her sisters in Blackpool. Convinced that she was in a hotel room with a man, Ruxton had worked himself into a jealous frenzy, and when she came back far later than expected, he began to beat her – probably in an attempt to make

her confess her infidelities – then throttled her unconscious and stabbed her. Mary Rogerson had probably
heard the screams and come in to see what was happening; Ruxton believed she was his wife's confidante in
her infidelities, and killed her too. He had spent the next
day dismembering the bodies and packing them in straw;
that night, he made his first trip north to dispose of the
bodies . . .

Ruxton's counsel, Norman Birkett, must have known that
his client did not stand a ghost of a chance. His line of
defence was that the bodies found in the Linn were not
those of Isabella Ruxton and Mary Rogerson, but of some
other persons. But when the medical experts – Glaister,
Millar, and Professor Sydney Smith – gave their evidence,
it was obvious that the identity of the bodies had been
established beyond all possible doubt. One photograph,
which has subsequently been used in every account of
the case, superimposed the larger of the two skulls on a
photograph of Mrs. Ruxton. She had a rather long, horsy
face, and it was obvious that the two fitted together with
gruesome exactitude. Ruxton seemed determined to trap
himself in a web of lies and evasions. The result was a
unanimous verdict of guilty, arrived at in only one hour.
He was hanged at Strangeways jail, Manchester, on 12
May 1936.

Yet examination of the evidence – and of Glaister's
famous book *Medico-legal Aspects of the Ruxton Case*
(1937) – makes it clear that Ruxton came very close indeed
to getting away with murder. If he had taken the trouble
to remove Mary Rogerson's fingertips, and destroyed the
telltale breast tissue as well as the trunk (which was never
found), the evidence against him would have remained
purely circumstantial; and since British juries are unwilling
to convict on circumstantial evidence, he might well have
been given the benefit of the doubt. Glaister's forensic
skill and Ruxton's failure of nerve played an equal part
in bringing him to the gallows.

The Nancy Titterton Case

The case had all the makings of a classic murder mystery.

The body of Nancy Titterton was found by two furniture removal men; she was lying face downward in an empty bath, naked except for a pair of silk stockings, and for the pyjama jacket knotted round her throat. Torn underclothes on the bedroom floor indicated that the motive had been a sexual attack. When the two men had arrived at four o'clock on that Good Friday afternoon – returning a love seat that had been under repair – they found the front door of the apartment standing open. The elder of the two, Theodore Kruger, had called Mrs. Titterton's name, and then, hearing the sound of a shower, glanced in through the open bathroom door; moments later, his young assistant, Johnny Fiorenza, was telephoning the police.

Beekman Place, where the Tittertons lived, was traditionally the home of New York artists and intellectuals. Lewis Titterton was an executive at the National Broadcasting Company, and his 33-year-old wife was a writer of exceptional promise. They had been married for seven years, and were known to be devoted to each other. Most of their small circle of friends were, like themselves, interested in the arts and literature. Neither of them was fond of socializing – Nancy Titterton was shy and introverted. Yet she had opened her door to her killer and let him into the apartment, which argued that she knew him.

It was the kind of case that would have driven a nineteenth-century detective to despair; a preliminary search of the apartment revealed no clues. But this was 1936, and the New York police had an impressive armoury of scientific and forensic aids. At the beginning of the twentieth century, the great criminologist Edmond Locard had formulated the basic principle of scientific crime detection: "Every contact leaves a trace." The criminal *must*, of necessity, leave behind something at the scene of the crime, and take something away with him. A single fibre from his clothing could be identified under the microscope; so could dust or mud from his shoes. A new process involving silver nitrate could raise fingerprints on fabric. Even the rapist's blood grouping could be determined from his seminal stains. This is why, as he surveyed the Titterton's flat, Assistant Chief Inspector John A. Lyons was not unduly discouraged.

In fact, a clue came to light as soon as the body was lifted from the bath: a 13-inch length of cord, which had been severed by a sharp knife. Marks on Nancy Titterton's wrists indicated that the killer had bound them before he raped her. He had cut them free when she lay, face downward, in the bath, and taken the cord with him; but in his haste he had overlooked the short piece that slipped under the body. This suggested that he knew the cord could provide a clue to his identity. Lyons ordered his men to check with every manufacturer in the New York area, to try to trace its source.

The mud samples on the carpet were disappointing. Microscopic examination revealed minute traces of lint, such as is found in upholstery establishments; that meant it had been brought into the apartment on the shoes of the two men who delivered the love seat.

A minute smear of green paint on the counterpane suggested another lead. The building was in the process of being painted in that precise shade of green. It looked as if the killer had brushed against the wet paint and left some on the bed. It also suggested that he might be one of the four painters. But a check revealed that only one of them had been working there on the day of the murder, and the other tenants were able to confirm that he had been working on another floor between 11 o'clock and midday – estimated by the medical examiner as the time Nancy Titterton had been killed.

A maid in the apartment below offered an interesting

piece of information; she had been preparing lunch when she heard a woman's voice call: "Dudley, oh Dudley!" The name of the janitor was Dudley Mings, and he was unable to offer a verifiable alibi. His story was that he had been working alone in his basement throughout the morning. But a search of his apartment revealed nothing to connect him with the murder, and he seemed to be a man of good character. On the whole, it was probable that his alibi was true.

The search for the origin of the cord seemed hopeless. It was of the kind used on venetian blinds, and was therefore commonplace. And the sharp kitchen knife that had probably been used to cut it from her wrists contained no fingerprints.

Now the general picture of the crime was beginning to emerge. The killer had entered 22 Beekman Place through the front door, either ringing the bell to request the tenant to release the catch, or by manipulating its defective lock. Again, this argued that he was known to the victim. Once inside, he had clamped a hand over her mouth to prevent her from screaming, then stuffed a piece of cloth between her teeth. He had tied her hands behind her with the cord he had brought with him, then carried or dragged her (she weighed only 100 lb) into the bedroom. He had removed her blouse and skirt, then thrown her on to one of the two single beds and torn off her brassière and panties – both were torn. After raping her, he had knotted a pyjama jacket round her throat, as well as a red blouse. He had carried her into the bathroom and cut the cord from her wrist, after which he had turned on the shower. Then he had hurried out of the apartment, leaving the door open behind him.

All this suggested a crime that was deliberately planned, not one committed on the spur of the moment. He had brought the cord with him and taken it away again; he had wiped his fingerprints off the knife he had used to cut it. Yet he had also placed her in the shower – presumably in an attempt to revive her. That suggested a man who was emotionally involved with her – perhaps a rejected lover – rather than some casual rapist. But as Lyons interviewed every known friend of the couple, he became increasingly convinced that Nancy Titterton had not been the type to engage in a secret love affair.

The break came, as Lyons had hoped, from the crime laboratory. Dr. Alexander O. Gettler, the city toxicologist, discovered a puzzling clue when he was examining the bedclothes in his laboratory at the Bellevue Hospital. Studying the candlewick counterpane under a magnifying glass, he found a piece of white hair, less than half an inch long. It was stiffer than human hair, and the microscope revealed it to be horsehair, of the type used for stuffing furniture. In fact, it was of the same type used to stuff the love seat that had been returned on the day of the murder. Since it was too heavy in texture to have been blown into the bedroom on a gust of air, it must have been carried there on someone's clothing. That someone, Lyons reasoned, could only have been one of the two furniture men. Yet both claimed that they had not entered the bedroom. And since they had been together in the apartment until the police arrived, the only alternative was that one of them had come to the apartment earlier in the day.

Kruger's upholstery shop was on Second Avenue; Lyons found the proprietor there alone. Asked where he had been on the morning of Good Friday, Theodore Kruger replied that he had spent the morning working in the shop.

"And your assistant?"

"Johnny was out until after lunch – he had to report to the parole officer in the morning."

"He has a criminal record?"

"Only for taking a car. Now he's turned over a new leaf – he's a good boy."

Outside, Lyons told his assistant: "Johnny Fiorenza claims he went to see his probation officer on Friday morning. But the office is closed on Good Friday. Keep a tail on him until further notice."

Back at headquarters, Lyons checked on Johnny Fiorenza's record; he had been arrested four times for theft, and spent two years in Elmira for car stealing. A psychiatrist who had examined him at the time of his first arrest had reported that he was a highly emotional individual. Fiorenza had been up to the Tittertons' apartment on two previous occasions, each time with his employer, so Nancy Titterton would know and trust him.

Then came the evidence Lyons needed. The piece of venetian blind cord had been manufactured by the Hanover Cordage Company of York, Pennsylvania, and a New York wholesaler had sold a roll of it to Theodore Kruger's upholstery shop.

Lyons ordered Johnny Fiorenza to be brought in to the office. For four and a half hours, the suspect was questioned, and continued to insist that he had not been near the Tittertons' apartment on the morning of Good Friday. Then the detective took out the length of venetian blind cord and dangled it in front of his eyes. "This is what convinced us you were in the apartment on Friday morning. We've traced it back to the furniture shop."

Fiorenza began to sweat; then he allowed his head to slump into his hands. "All right. I guess I may as well tell you about it." His story bore out what Lyons had already guessed. When Fiorenza first called at the apartment, two months before, he had become instantly infatuated with the attractive authoress; with her charm and social poise, she seemed to be everything he had always wanted – and could never hope to attain. And when he and Kruger called to collect the love seat, on the day before Good Friday, he had decided that he had to possess her at all costs. The next morning, he had telephoned his employer to say that he had to see his probation officer. Instead he had gone to Beekman Place. When Nancy Titterton called "Who is it?" he answered: "The man about the love seat", and she let him in. As he had grabbed her, she shouted: "Dudley, oh Dudley!", but only the maid in the downstairs apartment heard her. Fiorenza had rammed a handkerchief into her mouth, tied her hands with cord, and pushed her into the bedroom . . .

The jury took very little time to arrive at a guilty verdict; a few weeks later, Johnny Fiorenza went to the electric chair in Sing Sing.

One mystery remains: why did he carry her into the shower? His story was that he was shocked to find that she had died of suffocation, and tried to revive her. But in that case, she would have identified him as the rapist, and he would have been sentenced to a long term in prison. It seems unlikely that he was prepared to allow this to happen, and the only alternative is that he went to the apartment with every intention of killing Nancy Titterton. Then why place her in the bath? There can be only one explanation: it was intended as an insurance policy against getting caught. It would support his story that her death was an accident, and help to convince a jury that he was guilty of manslaughter rather than murder. Johnny Fiorenza was clearly an exceptionally cunning and far-sighted criminal, and there seems no doubt that if he had not been betrayed by a horsehair, he would certainly, as Sherlock Holmes might have said, have gone far in his chosen profession.

The Mona Tinsley Case

On 5 January 1937 a ten-year-old girl named Mona Tinsley failed to return home from her school in Newark, Nottinghamshire. A neighbour of the Tinsley family reported seeing the ex-lodger, a man called Frederick Nodder, loitering near the school. Two other people said they had seen Mona with a middle-aged man near the bus station. Nodder, who was living in the village of Hayton, some twenty miles from Newark, denied all knowledge of the child, but he was taken into custody on a bastardy warrant. Nodder had, in fact, been introduced to the Tinsleys by Mrs. Tinsley's sister, with whom he was having an affair. A few days after his arrest, Nodder changed his story, and admitted that he had met Mona in Newark and taken her home with him. But he insisted that he had put her on a bus to Sheffield, where his mistress lived. Nodder was charged with abducting Mona Tinsley – in the absence of a body he could not be charged with murder – and sentenced to seven years in gaol.

A few days after Mona's disappearance, Estelle Roberts, one of the most celebrated mediums in England, offered to help the police. Mona's parents agreed, and the police sent her a pink silk dress that had belonged to Mona. In her autobiography,* Estelle Roberts writes: "As . . . I held the soft material in my hands, I knew that Mona was dead."

But having obtained this information through psychometry, the medium then – according to her own account – addressed Mona Tinsley directly, through the agency of her "control", a Red Indian called Red Cloud. The child told her that she had been taken to a house and strangled, and Estelle Roberts "saw" a small house, with a water-filled ditch on one side, a field behind, a graveyard nearby, and an inn not far away. She seemed to travel across fields to a river.

When she described the house to the Newark police, they were so impressed by her accuracy that they invited her to go there, and sent a police car to fetch her from the railway station. The house looked exactly as she had "seen" it. She was allowed to wander around inside, and in the back bedroom, sensed the child's presence, particularly near a water tank. She was able to tell the police that Mona had slept in the back bedroom, and learned that they had found a child's handkerchief in the water tank. Mona was strangled in the back bedroom. She had spent much of her time in the downstairs front room, copying something out of a book. The police had found scraps of paper with the child's writing on it. She added that after killing her, Nodder

* Fifty Years a Medium.

256

had left the house with the body by the side door. The police asked "Why not the front door?", and she admitted she had no idea. They told her that the front door had been permanently closed with screws.

She then led the police past the graveyard she had "seen", over a bridge and across the fields. She told them: "Beyond these fields there is a river. You will find the child's body there."

The police had already dragged the river without success. But they now had good reason for supposing that the body would be found in the river. In her introduction to the *Trial of Frederick Nodder*, Winifred Duke states: "A clairvoyant insisted that Mona Tinsley was dead and had appeared to her. The child declared that she had been strangled, her body placed in a sack, and then conveyed on wheels to the water and thrown in." Another medium told Mr. Tinsley that Mona would be found in the River Idle. The medium had tasted mud in her mouth. A third woman informed the Newark police that Mona's body would be recovered in water at a place thirty miles in a north-westerly direction from Newark, "close to an open meadow or pasture land, with tall trees lining the bank". It is not clear which of these three references is to Estelle Roberts.

In June 1937, a boating party on the River Idle noticed an object in the water, close to the bank; it proved to be Mona Tinsley's body, the head jammed in a drain below water level; the place corresponded closely to the medium's description. A sack with an odour of decaying flesh was found nearby. Nodder was tried a second time, and although he still strenuously denied killing Mona, he was sentenced to death.

Nodder's wife had left him because of his numerous infidelities. He was a heavy drinker, who had lost jobs through drunkenness. It seems probable that, while he had been a lodger in the Tinsleys' house (he had to leave after three weeks for non-payment of rent) he had developed a sexual obsession with Mona – there is some evidence that he was a paedophile. He may have been drinking heavily at the time he impulsively decided to meet her out of school and abduct her. What happened after that is uncertain; but at midday on the following day, a child was seen standing in the back doorway of Nodder's house. By the time it was dark, Mona was dead, and Nodder hurried across the fields towards the river, which was swollen with heavy rains. By nine o'clock he was in the local pub, drinking heavily. He returned home to find the police waiting.

C.W

Part 2

Murder in the 1940s

Contents

Acknowledgements

The publishers would like to extend their grateful thanks to the following, authors, publishers and others for kindly granting them permission to reproduce the copyrighted material included in this book. Every effort has been made to secure and clear copyrights and the publishers trust that their apologies will be accepted for any errors or omissions.

"The Blackout Ripper" is an extract from *Cherrill of the Yard* by Fred Cherrill, Harrap, 1954. Copyright © 1954 Fred Cherrill. Reprinted by permission of the Harrap Publishing Group Ltd.

"The Blackburn Child Murder" is an extract from *Memories of Murder* by Tony Fletcher, Weidenfeld & Nicholson, 1986. Copyright © 1986 Tony Fletcher. Reprinted by permission of Weidenfeld & Nicholson Ltd.

"The Porthole Murder" is an extract from *Bodies and Crimes* by Denis Hocking, The Book Guild Ltd, 1992. Copyright © 1992 Denis Hocking. Reprinted by permission of the author and publishers.

"The Body in the Sack" is an extract from *Cavalcade of Murder* by T.C.H. Jacobs, Stanley Paul, 1955. Copyright © 1955 T.C.H. Jacobs. Reprinted by permission of Century Hutchinson Ltd, a division of Random Century.

"I Always Wanted to Torture a Girl" by George Vedder Jones. Originally published in *Master Detective*. Copyright © 1986 *Master Detective* magazine and George Vedder Jones. Reprinted by permission.

"Murder for Profit" is an extract from *Murder in France* by Alister Kershaw, Constable, 1955. Copyright © 1955 Alister Kershaw. Reprinted by permission of the publishers.

"The Wigwam Murder" is an extract from *Evidence for the Crown* by Molly Lefebure, William Heinemann Ltd, 1955. Copyright © 1955 Molly Lefebure. Reprinted by permission of the publishers.

Introduction

Criminologists of the future will see the 1940s as the first clear evidence that the "age of sex crime" had arrived.

It is natural for us to assume that there has been "sex crime" throughout the ages. This is untrue. The kind of rape that occurred in the past was essentially "opportunist"; invading armies regarded women as the spoils of war; so did the bands of robbers who attacked remote farmhouses. But the notion of a rapist deliberately *making* his opportunities – pursuing women as a hunter pursues game – was completely foreign to our ancestors. Of course, kings and emperors frequently used their position to treat their subjects as a kind of harem; but that applied to "good" rulers like Augustus and Peter the Great as much as to paranoiacs like Tiberius and Ivan the Terrible.

Sex crime – as I have pointed out elsewhere[1] – was a development of the pornography industry of the early 19th century. I say a development rather than a consequence, because it was not a case of cause and effect. Both were the effects of some deeper cause, connected with the frustrations of the Industrial Revolution. In other words, sex crime was one of the most unpleasant consequences of modern civilisation. Zoologists have made the same observation about apes; that in zoos sex is a non-stop preoccupation, while in the wild it is a mere "sideshow." When thousands of human being were cooped up in industrial slums, sex was only one of the natural instincts that reached bursting point.

The first sex crimes – in our modern sense of the word – occurred in the late 19th century: in England, the murders of Jack the Ripper, in France, those of Joseph Vacher the "disemboweller", while in America, a sinister crook who called himself H.H. Holmes built himself a "castle"

---

1 See "A Short History of Sex Crime" in *The Serial Killers*.

in which he could commit rape and murder like some mediaeval despot – his victims are believed to number at least twenty-seven.

In the 20th century, however, the Age of Sex Crime got off to a slow start. Between 1912 and 1914, a Hungarian Lothario named Bela Kiss murdered a dozen or so women and stored some of their bodies in oil drums; but although Kiss (who was never caught) was undoubtedly sex-mad, the motive of the murders was their savings. A Berlin pedlar named Georg Grossmann killed girls during the First World War and sold their carcases for meat. In Hanover soon after the war, a butcher named Fritz Haarmann – a homosexual – did the same to young men. Meanwhile, in America, a curious pervert named Albert Fish had already embarked on a career of child murder that would end in the electric chair in 1936. And during 1926 and 1927, a travelling rapist named Earle Nelson killed twenty-two women in America and Canada. These men were all sex criminals; and yet there is a sense in which every one of them was an "exception". Kiss, Grossmann and Haarmann were all partly motivated by greed; Fish "heard voices" and was undoubtedly insane. Earle Nelson had been subnormal since childhood, when he was knocked down by a street car and suffered a hole in the skull that rendered him unconscious for six days. Only the sadist Peter Kurten, who kept Dusseldorf in a state of terror in 1929 with his murderous attacks, can be truly classified as a sex killer. (Kurten was obsessed with blood, and said that his dearest wish was to hear his own blood flowing into the basket when he was beheaded.)

Oddly enough, the 1930s can offer no examples of sex crime that compare with those of Jack the Ripper or Peter Kurten. Perhaps the political violence of the time offered an outlet for the kind of pent-up emotions that lead to "lust murder". Whatever the reason, sexual violence marked time during the 1930s. By 1940, a historian with a taste for criminology might have concluded that the Age of Sex Crime had run its course.

The following decade was to show that it was only just beginning. Before I began selecting cases for this book, I made a "preliminary list" of killers, taken mostly from my

Encyclopedia of Murder (1961). Out of thirty-four cases, twelve were sex murders – more than a third. In other words, the whole of this book could, in theory, be devoted to sex crime – Cummins, Heath, Camb, Heys, Griffiths, Ludke, Ogorzov, Fearn and Heirens, to name only the best known (although, as we shall see, there are some interesting doubts in the case of Heirens). Even Christie, who will be represented in the volume covering the 1950s, committed his first rape murder as early as 1943, when he lured a colleague from work, Muriel Eadie, to his home during his wife's absence, persuaded her to bury her nose in a jar of Friar's Balsam – a catarrh remedy – then allowed coal gas to bubble into the jar until she lost consciousness.

Such a collection would be not only unrepresentative but absurd – who would want a volume on murder in the 1940s that excluded all mention of Haigh, Petiot, Fernandez and Beck (the "Lonely Hearts" killers) and the assassination of Leon Trotsky, not to mention such minor classics of detection as the cases of Harry Dobkin, August Sangret and Bertie Manton, or such strange unsolved mysteries as the Black Dahlia and the Texarcana Moonlight Murderer? Somehow a collection like this must strive to maintain an adequate balance, even if it means leaving out some of my own favourite examples of crime detection.

Now before we proceed, it is worth asking: why should there have been an outbreak of sex crime during the Second World War? The answer, though obvious enough, has some extremely disturbing implications. In a stable society, sex crime tends to be restricted to the mentally disturbed. But when society experiences a violent upheaval, normal human inhibitions are also undermined. Social instability has the same effect as alcohol, and a man who would usually feel "I couldn't possibly do that" suddenly asks himself: "Why not?"

This is clearly what happened in the case of the man who became known as "the S-Bahn rapist" of Berlin in 1940. The first victim, a gym teacher named Frieda Lausche was travelling on the S-Bahn (short for Schnell–Bahn, or fast railway) on the evening of September 20, 1940, when the man sitting opposite her in the dimly-lit carriage suddenly flung open the door and hurled her out. Because she was supple and in good training, she succeeded in falling safely, and hurried to the police. They were frankly incredulous. Why should a man simply fling a woman from a moving train, with no attempt either at assault or robbery? And why was she not scratched and bruised? They agreed to look into the case, then quietly shelved it.

Three weeks later they had to revise their opinion. On October 11, 1940, a secretary named Ingeborg Goetz was travelling on the elevated railway between Rummelsberg and Karlshorst around midnight when a man in the carriage struck her on the head with some sort of club, then slashed her stomach with a knife. After this he opened the door and threw her out. She recovered in hospital, but was unable to describe her attacker, except to say he wore a peaked cap and some kind of uniform with brass buttons.

Now the police were inclined to wonder if the attacker might have been responsible for a murder that had happened a week before the attack on Ingeborg Goetz; a war widow named Gerda Dietrich had been found stabbed to death in her cottage near the S-Bahn, in the suburb of Sommerland. It had been assumed she was the victim of a burglar, but wounds in the stomach – similar to those of Frau Goetz – suggested the madman who hurled women from trains.

Three weeks later, on December 3, the corpse of a girl was found near the S-Bahn station at Rummelberg; she was identified as 22-year-old Matilda Hollesch, and she had been clubbed to death with a blow on the back of the head, and then raped. A few hours after this attack, another woman was found by the S-Bahn track nearby; she had been struck violently on the head and hurled from the train. This victim, twenty-year-old postal clerk Irmgard Frank, had not been raped.

The following day, a passenger found the murder weapon down the back of a seat: a two foot piece of lead-covered cable, stained with blood and human hairs. Forensic tests established that it had been used to kill both women.

Nearly three weeks later, at 7 o'clock in the morning on December 22, the killer bludgeoned and hurled from the train a housewife named Maria Bahr, again killing her.

Now Detective Wilhelm Ludtke, one of Berlin's leading investigators, decided to try placing decoys on the trains – armed policewomen or volunteers. He also decided that "official guides" would escort young women who had to travel home late at night. But only two weeks later, on January 3, 1941, a man who had claimed to be an official guide pushed a cinema usher out of the train; fortunately, she was only scratched and bruised. But forty-eight hours later, a twenty-three-year-old telephone operator named Sonia Marke died when she was hurled from a train.

The skill shown by the S-Bahn rapist in avoiding traps suggested either a policeman or a railway employee: the description of survivors suggested the latter. But soon after the last murder one of the women "decoys" almost succeeded in arresting the killer. Alone in a carriage with an S-Bahn employee, she became suspicious of his sudden movements and his evident desire to make her nervous, and announced that she was a policewoman and that he was under arrest. The man leapt from the train as it pulled into a platform and disappeared.

On February 11, another woman, Martha Zernowski, was killed as she was clubbed and hurled from a train. On February 20, Lisa Novak, a thirty-year-old factory worker was raped, clubbed and hurled to her death from the train.

This time an arrest was made – a known sex offender named Richard Bauer, whose footprint was found in the girl's blood. He insisted that he had merely stumbled over her in the dark, but was kept in custody as a suspect.

Another possible suspect – among many – was a 28-year-old railway worker named Paul Ogorzov, a married man with two children. The Rummelsberg station master admitted that he was friendly with Ogorzov, and often told him what measures the police were planning. But Ogorzov was at work at the time of many of the murders, and workmates vouched for him; he was also dropped as suspect.

The attacks now ceased until July 3, 1941, when a woman named Olga Opell was found dead beside the tracks. Since Bauer was in prison, he was automatically exonerated and released.

But investigators now learned that Paul Ogorzov had slipped away from his job as a telegraph operator at about the time of the murder of Olga Opell – he had been seen climbing over a fence. Under interrogation, Ogorzov admitted this, and explained that he had a girlfriend who lived nearby. This proved to be true; moreover, the girl declared that Ogorzov had been with her at the time Olga Opell was attacked. But when traces of blood were found on Ogorzov's tunic, the questioning was renewed. He explained that one of his children had cut his finger. But Ludtke now took a long look at the map showing where attacks had taken place, and observed that most of them were along the route between the Rummelbberg station and Ogorzov's home. This seemed too much of a coincidence, so he began pressing Ogorzov about reports from women that a man had shone his torch in their eyes. Ogorzov finally admitted that he had done this on two occasions. Pressed to name precisely where this had happened, Ogorzov became confused, then mentioned a location where, in fact, a rape had occurred.

The victims who had escaped were brought in to confront Ogorzov; one positively identified him, and mentioned that he had worn a coat with a very wide collar; when police found such a coat in Ogorzov's home, he admitted to attempted assault on four women. Asked to pinpoint the places, he mentioned Sommerland, where Gerda Dietrich had been stabbed to death in her cottage. His state of confusion was now so great that he admitted that Gerda Dietrich had been one of the women he had beaten with his fists. This left Ludtke in no doubt that there had been so many victims that he was mixing them up.

Finally, shock tactics worked where long questioning had failed; when Ludtke showed him the smashed skulls of several victims, the harassed Ogorzov suddenly broke down, and admitted that he was the S-Bahn killer. He also admitted that he had also been guilty of a number of sexual attacks on women since 1939, mostly in the course of attempts to pick them up.

The incident that had turned him into a killer had occurred a few weeks before he threw the first victim – the gym teacher – from the moving train. He had accosted a woman near the

Rummelberg station, and she had screamed, bringing her menfolk from a nearby house. They beat up Ogorzov so badly that he had to spend a week in bed. He emerged vengeful and ruthless. Women would pay for this affront to his dignity . . .

And so the first two victims were hurled from the train, an act that he confessed gave him sadistic pleasure – his voice became hoarse as he described the sensation of opening the door and throwing them out into the darkness. But he quickly progressed to rape and murder, killing most victims with a tremendous blow from the lead-covered cable.

Perhaps because Ogorzov was a member of the Nazi Party, and the authorities wished to avoid embarrassment, his trial (on July 21, 1941) was rushed through in one day, and he was beheaded the following day.

I have described the Ogorzov case at length because it is virtually unknown outside Germany, and because Ogorzov is typical of the sex-killer of the 1940s. In effect, he was an opportunist predator, like a fox who has found a hole in the fence of a poultry farm. The same is true of many sex killers in this book – Cummins, Heath, Heys, Floyd, Cook, and the unknown Texarcana murderer. What is so disturbing is that the return of peace in 1945 did nothing to bring this era of sex crime to an end. On the contrary, the number of sex attacks on women has continued to rise steadily ever since, until in the 1990s, rape has become one of the commonest crimes.

This may be seen as a highly dangerous sign for our civilisation. In *Civilisation and Its Discontents*, Freud argued that man is basically a predator who is held in check by the artificial bonds of society. At the time he wrote it (1931), this seemed unnecessarily pessimistic. But the rise of the Nazis, and the increase in sex crime during the Second World War, suggested that he was basically correct. Zoologically speaking, the dominant male is intended to impregnate as many females as possible – in other words, man is born promiscuous. In nature, this natural promiscuity is kept in check by the fact that females are interesting only when on heat. Man has by-passed this limitation and is always ready for sex. For many centuries, society imposed its own natural restraints – in fact, most religion had always demanded fidelity from husband and wife. In the 19th century the social restraints began to dissolve, as increasing wealth and leisure allowed an increasing number of males to turn their attention to full-time seduction and adultery. The developent of human imagination – accelerated by the universal popularity of the novel – made women seem more desirable than ever before. In the 18th century, most rapes had involved some drunken workman and a bedraggled street girl; by the late 19th century, "gentlemen" like "Walter", the anonymous author of *My Secret Life*, prowled the streets in search of the "forbidden". Every woman had become an object of feverish desire, and the hero of Barbusse's novel *Hell* declares: "It is not a woman I want; it is *all* women." It was literally as if a monster had been unchained. Bela Kiss, the Hungarian Lothario, was a "satyr" who had to possess women after woman, and who was capable of sex with several women a day.

Sixty years later, Georges Simenon, the creator of Inspector Maigret, claimed that he had slept with ten thousand women (mostly prostitutes) and admitted that the first thing he did in a strange city was to make his way to the nearest brothel. The confession aroused some outrage; yet it was clear that Simenon felt that he was merely confessing to being a normal male. He possessed the money – and the time – to spend his life in pursuit of sex; most dominant males would probably be happy to do the same. And the last quarter of the 20th century has seen the rise of the serial killer who treats his "objects of desire" (whether male or female) as mere throwaways to be raped and killed, and whose victims often far outnumber those of Ogorzov, Kurten and Christie. It is difficult to see the end of this process; for although new techniques of criminal investigation and forensic detection have shortened the odds against the sex killer[1], the basic *conditions* that produce sex murder are likely to remain with us into the foreseeable future.

1 See *The Serial Killer* by Colin Wilson and Donald Seaman

INTRODUCTION

This, then, seems to me the major significance of the 1940s as a decade of murder. It is an ominous reflection, but one it would be pointless – and possibly dangerous – to ignore.

Colin Wilson

By the Light of the Moon

Although psychologists do not know the answer, police will tell you that whenever there is a full moon, there is a sharp increase in police activity. Neighbors suddenly quarrel, cranks keep stationhouse telephone wires busy with complaints, and certain criminals are galvanized into action.

To police, such people are known as "mooners", those who react to the influence of a full moon. The ancient Romans, who observed this phenomenon, coined the word "lunatic" to indicate their belief that the moon had something to do with people going insane. Some psychiatrists scoff at the theory, but police psychiatrists who have to handle mooners are prone to wonder.

There was a full moon on the night of February 24th, when a drama class at the Los Angeles City College was getting ready to stage a public performance in the school auditorium. Most of the young hopefuls were chattering nervously backstage as curtain time neared when the director noticed that one member of the cast, Anya Sosoyeva, an attractive, slender blonde, was not among them. He asked Wally Myar, another cast member, to look for her.

Myar stepped out to the back, expecting to find Anya nervously pacing the walk and puffing furiously on a cigaret, a habit she had before show time, but the pretty Russian-born girl was not in sight. Although there was a full moon, the gravel walks were mainly in shadows cast by the stately trees on the campus.

As Myar moved along a path he heard a stumbling sound in front of him and hurried forward. He finally saw the girl walking with a lurching gait. "Anya, what is it?" he called out as he ran to her side.

He found the girl bleeding from the head, her sweater torn, her clothes dirt-stained. Her eyes were closed, her fingernails torn, and she was groping for bushes lining the path.

"He hit me," she said, and then collapsed. Myar picked up the injured girl and carried her to a dressing room. By the time a physician arrived, the girl was in a coma from which she never recovered. The other young players went on with their roles, keeping the news of the tragedy from the audience.

The police investigation was headed by Captain Dalton R. Patton of the Homicide Squad. Officers found the murder scene only a few yards from the backstage entrance. The ground was badly churned up showing that she had put up a desperate fight. A blood-stained short length of a 2×4 was found in a nearby bush along with a man's blood-stained gray coat and a pair of gray gloves. From scuff marks in the gravel, detectives were able to follow the trail of the girl after the attack. She had staggered to a bench where she sat down and then had continued on her way only a short distance when Myar found her.

The victim's purse was missing. An examination of the gloves showed lipstick smudges, indicating that the killer had clapped his hand over her mouth in a surprise attack from behind.

One of the early officials to arrive was Dr J. Paul de River, police psychiatrist, who frequently was able to give investigators much helpful information about a killer just by studying the scene.

Dr de River cocked his head up toward the full moon overhead. "He may be a mooner," he informed Captain Patton, "one of those men who commit crimes, particularly attacks on women, during the time of the full moon. These attacks will continue until he is caught."

A thorough search was made of the campus without turning up any suspect.

Meanwhile, the routine mechanics of a police investigation went on. Members of the cast were interviewed after the show. Officials wanted to know if the murdered girl had any enemies, the names of her boy friends, and any information about the background of the victim that might give them a lead.

Ruth Alderman, a pretty drama student, reported that the previous October she had been crossing the campus when a man leaped at her from behind some bushes. She said she screamed and fought him off and he became frightened and ran away. She could only offer a vague description of the man and said she had not informed police at the time partly because she feared the man might come back and seek her out.

Investigators learned that Anya, who had played several bit roles in motion pictures, had been a stage dancer originally, working to earn money to further her ambition to become a dramatic actress.

Some years earlier she had been married to a young radio writer and lived with him in San Francisco. After several years she left him because she had learned that he was carrying on with other women and she returned to the stage, going to New York. Her husband then started living with a divorcee. One night police were summoned to his apartment and found his mistress dead on the living room couch. The man first told police that she had committed suicide, but when detectives pointed out that the direction of the shot made it impossible, he then said he had shot her accidentally while playing with a gun. Anya returned from New York to be with him during the trial. When two juries failed to reach a verdict, he was discharged and Anya again left him. Detectives hurriedly checked into his whereabouts and learned he'd died of natural causes.

Los Angeles is overrun with bizarre groups and cults and police learned that Anya had been a member of a campus society known as the "Purple Cult" or Thelemites. The members called themselves votaries of the "purple passion of exotic prayer." Most of the members were graduate students and their high priestess was a woman instructor at the college. Meetings were held in a candlelighted room known as the Temple of Thelema.

Wondering if the murder could have stemmed from the "purple passion of exotic prayer," authorities conducted a thorough investigation of the organization but finally decided the mystic rites and mumbo-jumbo that went on during the ceremonies were considered by most members as good-natured fun rather than anything serious.

One month later, on March 28th, Dr de River's prediction came true. Delia Bogard, a pretty 17-year-old actress, who had been a child star in the movies, was walking on North Wilton Street, hurrying home from a late movie on Sunset Boulevard, when a man suddenly sprang at her in front of a darkened house.

He placed a gloved hand over her mouth and began beating her with a stick. The young actress fought back vigorously, lashing out with her high heels, while he continued to rain blows down on her head. She managed to break loose and began to scream, before he seized her again.

Mrs Laura Lee, in front of whose home the attack was taking place, heard the screams. She seized one of her husband's golf clubs and dashed out. By this time the attacker had knocked down the girl and was bending over her. Running up silently on the lawn, Mrs Lee struck the man with the golf club. He turned with the stick in his hand and Mrs Lee brought it down again. By this time other neighbors had come out of their homes and were running toward them. The man tossed away his weapon, vaulted a high bush and disappeared in the darkness.

Miss Bogard was rushed to the hospital in a critical condition with severe skull injuries. Once again a short length of lumber had been used, and once again the victim's purse was missing.

Police were further disturbed by the third similarity, that Miss Bogard also was an actress and they wondered whether there wasn't some connection between the two crimes. Dr de River suggested that they would be wasting time pursuing that tangent. He pointed out that Los Angeles was filled with young actresses, so more than likely it was just a coincidence. What did alarm the psychiatrist was the fact that the same moonlight conditions existed at the time of both attacks.

"There's no doubt about it now that the man is a mooner,"

Dr de River said. "Unless we get him and get him fast, these attacks will continue every month."

The psychiatrist told the officers to concentrate their search on a young and agile man who derived a sadistic pleasure out of his attacks on helpless women, and to whom the thefts were not as important as the thrill of committing them. Such a person might not even bother to dispose of his loot.

"We're going to have more," was his gloomy prophecy.

Detectives found one possible clue at the scene, a foot print of a rubber-soled shoe that was in the soft earth behind the bush the man had leaped over.

Alarmed by the psychiatrist's warning, police began a roundup of all known perverts and sex deviates in Los Angeles, a task that required many days, but all were released after checking their alibis.

Miss Bogard recovered sufficiently from her injuries to be questioned. She described her attacker as a tall, slender man and said he was unshaven. She was certain that she had never seen him before the attack.

In late June, police thought the man had killed again when Mrs Margaret Campbell, a noted character actress in the silent screen days, was found battered to death in the room she shared with her son. She had been killed with a hammer and her nude body was streaked with blood. Adding an eerie touch to the death scene was a whistle, a book, and a candle, the tip daubed with red lipstick, arranged in a symbolic pattern near the body.

Several days later detectives located Campbell McDonald, the victim's son, and he confessed that he had murdered his mother because she wanted to place him in an institution.

"I put those objects beside her body because the dead should be buried with bell, book and candle," he explained. "I used a whistle instead of a bell." He was committed to an institution.

Meanwhile, although the attacks on women had ceased, police now were being confronted with a series of unsolved burglaries. After studying the records, Dr de River pointed out that these were occurring on fully moonlit nights and he

5

said the killer probably had switched his activity because of the intense search for him.

On August 23rd, the attacker struck again, this time entering a house and beating a young maid who had been baby-sitting. She was found unconscious on the floor, her clothes torn from her. Nearby was a bloody piece of wood.

The following night, all police leaves were canceled and hundreds of extra patrolmen were placed on the streets, while radio-equipped cruiser cars were stationed at strategic spots throughout the city so that they could close in and seal off any district.

Shortly before midnight, a couple was returning to their home on Oakwood Avenue when they spotted a man in the backyard. The husband quietly put in a call to police headquarters and within a minute several cars rolled up the street and officers surrounded the house. Several of them, with guns drawn, dashed into the back yard. They caught a glimpse of a man racing for the fence and fired several warning shots in the air.

The figure stopped and put up his hands. The prisoner was a tall, slender youth dressed in dungarees and sneakers. At headquarters he gave his name as DeWitt Clinton Cook, 20 years old, but refused to answer any questions.

Detectives went to his home and found a pair of shoes, the soles of which matched the footprint left by the attacker of Miss Bogard. They also found a large cache of loot hidden in his home. When they learned that he had a car, they cruised the neighborhood where he had been picked up and located the machine. On the front seat was a short length of 2×4.

Confronted by evidence found in his home, the prisoner admitted to some 300 burglaries, but he vehemently denied being the moonlight assaulter.

After examining the suspect, Dr de River, who had a flair for well-rounded phrases, told the officers. "This fellow's mind is like a house with the shutters drawn, concealing in its shadows the mystery of what goes on behind the curtain. Wiry, catlike, he is of sadistic tendencies, but legally sane and knows right from wrong. He is the lone-wolf type – a nocturnal prowler who likes to wander in lonely places at night."

In more prosaic language he added that he was certain that the prisoner was the moon man. Guided by this opinion, police resumed their questioning of Cook and he finally admitted the attacks.

"I didn't start out to hurt anybody," he said. "I always started after the girls to snatch their purses, but then impulse would get me and I beat them."

He said he had been lurking on the campus for some time and although several girls had passed, he had not molested anybody until the shapely Anya Sosoyeva went by. "I thought I saw a pretty good customer," he remarked.

He had seen Delia Bogard at the movie and had followed her. His attack on the maid occurred just after he had burglarized a home further down the street.

"I saw the maid sitting near a window, doing some embroidery. I don't know what came over me. I saw a hunk of wood in a woodpile near the back of the house, and I picked it up and climbed in through the window. The girl's back was toward me. I swung the club and she started to get up. So I hit her twice more. She sort of collapsed slowly. As the girl lay there I took off her clothes."

The following day Cook re-enacted the murder of Anya Sosoyeva in front of a movie camera.

When Cook was placed on trial in October, the film was shown to the jury. Dr de River testified that the prisoner was sane. Cook was convicted of first degree murder.

On January 31, 1941, the moonlight murderer was put to death in San Quentin Prison.

Edward Radin

Gordon Cummins: The Blackout Ripper

Inevitably, the pattern of murder in the first half of the 1940s is dominated by the war. And wars, as pointed out in the Introduction, seem to incubate sex crimes. So it seems appropriate to continue with the curious case of Gordon Cummins. Unfortunately, we know very little about the psychology of the "blackout ripper". In the account that follows – by Chief Superintendent Fred Cherrill, one of Scotland Yard's best fingerprint experts – we learn that he was born of "respectable parents", had an upper class accent, and liked to pose as "the Hon. Gordon Cummins". Yet Cherrill also mentions that he lost a succession of jobs, and finally joined the RAF in peace time; this seems to suggest a working class background. He always killed for money – sometimes fairly small sums. But he was also "a sexual maniac" (the description of Sir Bernard Spilsbury's biographers Browne and Tullett) who mutilated his victims, in one case tearing open the lower half of the body with a tin opener. His crime rampage during the blackout lasted only a few days; it if had stretched over months, like the career of Jack the Ripper, or years, like that of the Yorkshire Ripper, he would have caused widespread panic and been extensively chronicled. In fact, he was caught by his own carelessness – the same carelessness he displayed in leaving bloody fingerprints on the mirror of one of his victims – and promptly executed. It seems logical to infer that he was a sadist, like Neville

Heath (who will be found later in this volume), with that touch of the confidence trickster that is often found in multiple killers. But his execution – at the age of 28 – means we shall never know.

Spilsbury, who performed a post mortem on the second victim, also performed one on Gordon Cummins.

This account is taken from Fred Cherrill's autobiography *Cherrill of the Yard.*

In the pitch-like darkness of the blackout which enveloped London in February 1942 terror stalked through the blitz-shattered streets of our city. It was not just the terror that rained from the sky as Hitler's Luftwaffe flew overhead to wreak his mission of hate upon Britain. It was the terror created by a ghoulish slayer, who within four days strangled and mutilated four hapless women and attempted to murder two others.

Not since those panic-ridden days in 1888, when Jack the Ripper was abroad in the East End, had London known such a reign of terror as that which existed in this war-time February, when, night after night, death – fiendish, revolting, and gruesome – came to four unsuspecting women in the heart of the Metropolis.

There was no inkling of the orgy of murder which was to follow when, in the early hours of February 9, 1942, the body of Miss Evelyn Hamilton, a woman of irreproachable character, was found strangled in an air-raid shelter in Montagu Place, Marylebone. It was one of those ordinary surface shelters which lined the streets in those days, brick-built, with a seat along one side.

The dead woman was a chemist's assistant who had not long before resigned her post as manageress of a shop at Hornchurch, Essex, and had come to live in the Marylebone area of London.

When I arrived at Montagu Place it looked to me as though the body had been hurriedly pushed through the narrow door of the shelter after strangulation. It lay upon the floor against the seat, face upward. Round the mouth and nose the murderer had wound tightly the woman's own silk scarf as a gag. Her clothes were disarranged, and a hat lay near by. At her side were a matchbox and a powder-compact, which had been turned out of her handbag. A foot or two away was an electric torch, which she doubtless carried to light her on her way through the blackout.

What interested me most, however, were marks on the victim's throat. In the dim light of the shelter they appeared to have been made by the fingers of the murderer. From their position I rapidly made another deduction, and said to myself, "*This seems to have been a left-handed job.*"

Under a powerful light and with the aid of my hand-lens I made a close and minute examination of the marks in the hope that the murderer might have left some trace of his fingers – no matter how small – that would assist in deciding whose hands had choked the life out of this poor victim.

Luck was against me in this respect, for the marks were only bruises. But they enabled me to confirm my first impression that they had been made by the left hand of the strangler, whoever he might be. I was no more fortunate with the handbag and its contents, for the only finger-marks upon them were those of the dead woman.

I had only just reached my office at the Yard the next morning, February 10, when a message came over the 'phone asking me to go at once to a flat in Wardour Street, where a Mrs Evelyn Oatley (also known at Nita Ward) had been found murdered.

On my arrival I entered the bedroom. Lying across a bed, consisting of nothing but a flock mattress, with not even a sheet as covering, was the almost nude body of a woman. She was a ghastly sight. She had been the victim of a sadistic attack of the most horrible and revolting nature.

There were scarcely any signs of disorder in the room itself, articles on a table beside the bed being undisturbed. Some stockings hung upon a rail at the head of the bed, and, but for the still, dead figure of the murdered woman, there was little to show that anything untoward had taken place in that room.

It was only when one turned one's eyes to the bed that one realized the enormity of the crime which had been committed. Near the body of the dead woman lay a pair of curling-tongs and a blood-stained tin-opener. The latter was evidently the weapon with which the murderer had so wantonly mutilated his victim. At one side of the room was a couch, on which I found a woman's handbag. It was open, as if the contents had fallen out, but inside was a piece of mirror.

After a minute examination of the room and its contents I took possession of the tin-opener and the piece of mirror. To me these were very interesting exhibits, for upon that bit of looking-glass, into which the dead woman had doubtless looked a hundred times in the process of beautifying herself, I detected what I knew to be a thumbprint. I soon ascertained that it had not been made by the dead woman, and I assumed that it had been made by the murderer when he was turning out the handbag.

On the handle of the tin-opener I also discovered faint impressions of fingers.

They had been made by a left hand, and were not in such a position that they could have come there by the innocent use of this utensil. Indeed, they were so arranged that I decided this improvised weapon had been grasped in the *left* hand of the murderer during his attack on the woman. Moreover, certain aspects of the print on the mirror indicated to me that it had been made by a left thumb.

Were there any records in our files of corresponding prints? If so, it need be a matter only of minutes, perhaps, before a nation-wide search for the man who had made it could be set in motion. Alas, once more the fates were against us. The killer of Mrs Oatley had no criminal record. He had never been in the hands of the police.

Two days went by – two days during which Yard men followed up every slender clue in their possession in an effort to find the strangler of Evelyn Hamilton and the sadistic "ripper" who had murdered Mrs Oatley.

The husband of the latter was traced to Blackpool, and was able to prove that he and his wife had separated by mutual agreement some time before, and were living apart. A woman in the next room to Mrs Oatley described how she saw the latter enter the house with a man about 11.15 p.m., and heard voices and the wireless.

Evelyn Oatley had once been a promising young actress on the London stage, but, with the outbreak of war, engagements became few, and she drifted into the life which was destined to end in tragedy.

Already the reports of these two crimes, coming so quickly one upon the other, had aroused a feeling of alarm among the people of London. As women passed through the lightless streets at nights on the way to their regular air-raid shelters they looked apprehensively around them, wondering whether the silent and elusive murderer might be lurking in some door or alleyway ready to pounce upon another victim.

Nor was this alarm lessened when the evening papers of February 13 came out with the startling news that another woman had been found strangled and mutilated in a flat at Gosfield Street, just off the Tottenham Court Road.

The discovery was made by a neighbour of the dead woman. The victim was Mrs Margaret Lowe, a handsome and finely built woman who was known locally as "Pearl." The neighbour noticed that a parcel lying outside the door of the flat had not been taken in, and therefore notified the police. The door of the flat was forced, and the tragedy revealed in all its stark and vivid horror.

In a scantily furnished room, almost bare except for a single bed set lengthwise against a wall, an occasional table, a small carpet, a rug, and a chair or two, death had come to Margaret Lowe.

At first sight on entering the room there was no sign of the gruesome work which had been carried out by the sex-mad murderer. On the black eiderdown near the foot of the bed lay a woman's coat, skirt, and jumper, where they had been hurriedly flung down by their owner. Lying on the floor was a gay little hat with a feather, while on the mantelpiece stood a glass candlestick and a tumbler containing a liquid which looked like beer.

A sinister hump in the eiderdown gave an inkling of what lay beneath. There was an unnatural stillness about it. When the bedclothes were pulled back the nude dead body of Margaret Lowe was revealed. Round her neck was tightly knotted a much-darned silk stocking.

But it was not these things which attracted my eye so much as the vicious mutilations which had been wreaked upon the dead woman, and which were even more shocking than those inflicted upon Mrs Oatley. This, and the small armoury of weapons with which the mutilations had been inflicted.

A rapid survey of the room showed me that a candle had been wrenched from the glass candlestick on the mantelpiece. This candle appeared incongruous against the collection of sinister-looking implements surrounding the body. Yet that innocent-looking object was destined to lead to the identification of the murderer of Mrs Lowe, for it directed my attention to the candlestick from which it had been torn.

There were finger-impressions upon the base of it.

After examining the room where the body lay I went to the kitchen at the rear of the premises, where I found a bottle of stout. Some of the contents had been drunk. There were fingermarks on the bottle, and I came to the conclusion that the beer in the glass on the bedroom mantelpiece had been poured from this bottle.

I took possession of the glass candlestick, together with the tumbler and bottle. The marks on the candlestick were of particular interest to me, as they were prints of the fingers of a *right* hand. By means of a rapidly conducted experiment, placing myself in the position of the murderer, I was satisfied that a *right*-handed person, in snatching the candle from the candlestick, would naturally place his *left* hand on the base, using his right hand to grasp the candle. The process would be reversed in the case of a *left*-handed person, so that once more it appeared that a left-handed person had been at work.

If this deduction proved correct, in view of the similarity in the mode of killing and the nature of the injuries inflicted, it appeared likely – in fact, almost certain – that the two murders, those of Mrs Oatley and Mrs Lowe, were the work of one and the same left-handed man. It also struck me at this time that the same person might have strangled Miss Evelyn Hamilton, the victim of the air-raid shelter crime, on whose throat I had detected the finger-marks of a left hand.

In view of these premises, it may appear something of a paradox that I should make another check-up on the newly discovered prints, for were not the impressions found in the flat of Mrs Oatley available for comparison with those which I had now obtained from articles in Mrs Lowe's flat? Would not such a comparison either confirm or disprove my suspicions? They might do, but, on the other hand, they might not. A comparison of the prints in both places would not settle the matter one way or the other, for the simple reason that although they might well be the prints of the same man, they might be the marks of *different fingers*.

That is why I carried out a further search in our records for any prints corresponding to those found in Mrs Lowe's flat, only to come up against the same apparently impenetrable barrier. The search proved negative.

It now seemed pretty certain that a killer was abroad who murdered not only for gain – in each case the handbags of the murdered women had been rifled – but in order to indulge a wicked and insensate lust to perpetrate the most diabolical injuries upon the women he killed.

It was at 6.30 on the evening of February 13 that I went to Mrs Lowe's flat in Gosfield Street, the murder having actually taken place on the 12th. Having completed my fingerprint investigations there, I returned to the Yard. The time was then about 10.30 p.m., and I was just preparing to go home when the telephone-bell in my office rang again.

I lifted the receiver. "Fingerprint Office," I said, in what sounded to me a rather tired voice. And then came this: "Will you go at once to Sussex Gardens, Paddington? Another woman has been found murdered."

It only needs a message like this to snap one out of all sense of weariness. In a matter of minutes I was on my way to carry out a second murder investigation, within a few hours of the other, and both on the same day.

The victim was a Mrs Doris Jouannet. She was the wife of a London hotel manager, and he usually slept at the hotel, but saw his wife daily at their flat in Sussex Gardens. On the night of the tragedy he had supper with his wife, and she accompanied him to Paddington Station. But let Mr Jouannet tell his own story.

"She wished me good-night very sweetly, and her last words to me were, 'Don't be late to-morrow, darling,'" he said.

"I returned to the flat at seven o'clock on Friday night, and was surprised to see that the milk had not been taken in. When I got into the flat I shouted out 'Doris,' but there was no reply. On going into the sitting-room I found that the supper-things from the night before were still on the table, and the curtains had not been drawn. I was worried, and when I found the bedroom door locked I knew something was amiss. I could not get any reply, so I went to the housekeeper, and we sent for the police."

Mr Jouannet described how the police burst open the door, and how a kindly constable held him back from entering the room of death with a gentle, "Don't go in, sir," and then broke the news that his wife was dead.

Thus it was only an hour or two after the body of Doris Jouannet was discovered that I was in the flat where she lay.

One glance was sufficient to tell me that the strangling "ripper" had struck again. There was no doubt about it. He had left his signature to the atrocities as surely as if he had written his name.

Around the neck of the woman was a tightly knotted scarf. Her body, clad only in a dressing-gown, which had been dragged open in the frenzied lust of the murderer, was lying across a bed, the clothes of which had been flung back in haste by the killer after he had completed his crime. The body had been savagely slashed.

There had been no struggle. The murderer had worked swiftly and surely. The woman's clothes lay in a heap on a chair at the foot of the bed. A clock standing on a bedside table had stopped. It registered the time – 4.45.

I made an intensive search for fingerprints. On the door of a cupboard close to the bed I found several. I detected others on a hand-mirror lying on the dressing-table. From the dust on the latter I could see that some articles had recently been removed from it. On the door of the bedroom itself I found other impressions.

I took possession of the mirror, and had the cupboard and bedroom doors removed and brought to the Yard for a more detailed and exhaustive examination of the articles. This time, however, the murderer had left behind no fingerprints of any value. All those which were identifiable belonged to the dead woman.

Such was the position on February 14, when the whole resources of Scotland Yard were mobilized to run this wholesale murderer to earth. At that time we were not absolutely certain that Evelyn Hamilton had met her death at the hands of the same person, although, as you will remember, I was convinced that her strangler was left-handed.

Women police in ordinary clothes – always under the alert and watchful eyes of Yard men – strolled about the streets of the West End in the hope of being accosted by the unknown killer. So great was the terror which swept like a wave over the square mile in which these crimes had been committed that the regular street-walkers who haunted the area were too scared to venture out. Small wonder, for nobody knew when or where the killer would strike next. That he *would* strike again seemed certain, for the lust of killing appeared to have seized him in a merciless grip. And he *did* strike again! Though not with such fatal results.

On the night of February 12 – within a few hours of the murders of Mrs Lowe and Mrs Jouannet – a young woman, Mrs H——, was having a quiet drink in a public-house near Piccadilly when an Air Force cadet entered. He got into conversation with her, flourishing a wad of Treasury notes. He made a certain suggestion, which she rejected.

When she left he followed her into the darkened street, and, having caught up with her, pushed her into a doorway. "You must let me kiss you good-night," he said.

He placed his gas-respirator on the ground, and made as though to put his arm round her. Instead he seized her by the throat, maintaining his grip until she lost consciousness. One can only imagine what might then have happened but for the approach of a passer-by, who heard scuffling and saw a man disappear into the shadows. He then noticed

Mrs H—— lying on the ground. She was just regaining her senses. The stranger helped her to her feet, and when she had gasped out the story of the attack upon her he escorted her to the police-station.

At once police officers went to the scene of the attack. There they found the woman's handbag rifled of its contents, while in the doorway lay the respirator belonging to her assailant, which he had left behind in his haste to get away.

Meanwhile the young airman had happened on another woman, Mrs M——. The lust for blood must still have been upon him, for he persuaded her to enter a taxi-cab with him, and together they drove to her flat in Southwick Street, Paddington, less than a stone's throw from Sussex Gardens, where lay the undiscovered body of Doris Jouannet, for it was not till the following day, February 13, that her husband returned to the flat to find her dead.

While the airman was in the room with Mrs M—— the electric light failed, and it was at this propitious moment that her companion seized her by the throat and tried to strangle her.

The frightened woman fought and kicked with such violence, however, that she managed to free herself from the hand that was choking her, and gave vent to piercing screams, which aroused the household. Her would-be murderer fled the scene, but in his anxiety to get away left behind the belt belonging to his uniform.

So well within the space of forty-eight hours the mysterious murderer had slain and mutilated two women and had attempted to murder another two. He had gone straight from one crime to another almost without pause. I still felt that he was the man who had also killed Miss Hamilton.

But now he was no longer a mystery man. There was a definite clue to his identity – the respirator which he had left in the doorway when interrupted in his attack upon Mrs H——.

On this respirator was his Air Force number, 525987, and to trace its owner was just a matter of routine inquiry. A scrutiny of R.A.F. records was sufficient to establish that the owner of the gas-mask found in the doorway in Haymarket, and also of the belt left behind in the flat of Mrs M——, was a twenty-eight-year-old R.A.F. cadet, one Gordon Frederick Cummins. He was soon tracked down at his billet in North London, and put up for identification by the two women whom he had tried to strangle.

Mrs H—— had no difficulty in picking him out as the man who had attacked her. Mrs M—— could only say that his eyes were the same as those of her assailant, who was in R.A.F. uniform.

Cummins was charged with the murders of Mrs Oatley, Mrs Lowe, and Mrs Jouannet, and with the attempted murder of Mrs H—— and Mrs M——.

At that time there was not sufficient evidence on which to charge him with the murder of Miss Hamilton, although there was now little doubt that the accused was responsible for her death.

On his arrest he made a statement. In it he described how, on the night of February 9 – the night of the Hamilton murder – he and another cadet named Johnson spent the evening in the West End visiting various bars. About 11 p.m. they met two women and separated, arranging to meet later. Cummins insisted that they *did* meet, and that they were so drunk when they reached their billet that other airmen had to put them to bed.

When Johnson was interviewed he stated that after waiting for some time at the appointed rendezvous, and Cummins not putting in an appearance, he (Johnson) went off with another woman, and did not return to the billet until 6 a.m., when he found Cummins in bed. So the latter's story of his movements on that fatal night was obviously false.

When Cummins was brought up at Bow Street Police Court and formally charged I took his fingerprints. As is usual on these occasions, he was asked to sign the fingerprint form. He made no demur, and – *signed with his left hand*.

Meanwhile his respirator had been minutely examined. Adhering to the fabric were found particles of dust. On comparison with dust taken from the air-raid shelter where Miss Hamilton's body was found, these particles were found to be identical in colour and in form with mortar-dust taken from the shelter. Thus was forged the first direct link in the chain connecting Cummins with the murder of Evelyn Hamilton.

There was another link, for when his billet was searched a fountain-pen which had belonged to the dead woman was discovered among his possessions, together with a cigarette-case which was subsequently identified as the property of Mrs Lowe.

The strands of evidence connecting Cummins with the crimes which had created a reign of terror throughout the West End of London were gradually being woven into a noose. But still the final strand had yet to be included which would place that noose around the neck of this multi-murderer.

I was not idle after taking the accused man's fingerprints at Bow Street Police Court. On comparing these prints with those on the tin-opener found on the bed where lay the body of Mrs Oatley I was able to establish that the clearest mark was made by the left little finger of the accused, while the print on the mirror taken from the handbag of the dead woman was that of his left thumb. So much for Mrs Oatley.

The finger-marks on the base of the candlestick taken from the flat of Mrs Lowe were made by the fingers of the right hand of Cummins. Those on the tumbler and beer-bottle found in the flat of Mrs Lowe were also made by the same hand. The accused had been in that flat, and had undoubtedly joined his victim in her last drink on earth before killing and mutilating her.

As I have already stated, there were no prints of any value in connexion with the murder of Mrs Jouannet, and, apart from the left-hand marks on the throat of Evelyn Hamilton, none that helped in the inquiries into the deaths of these two women.

Cummins was brought to trial at the Old Bailey in April 1942. And it was there, while I was in the witness-box giving fingerprint evidence, that I was instrumental in stopping a trial for murder – a dramatic and almost unheard-of thing.

I should explain that Cummins was tried on *one* charge of murder only – that of Mrs Evelyn Oatley. This is the usual practice when a person has been committed for trial on more than one murder charge, and is an example of the scrupulous fairness with which justice is administered in our criminal courts.

It is necessary that you should know this in order to understand how I came to stop the trial of Cummins.

During my evidence I had just reached the point where I was about to describe to the jury how I had come to my conclusions regarding the print on the tin-opener and the mark on the bit of mirror when the fingerprint exhibits were put in. These were photographic enlargements of the marks on the articles side by side with the corresponding prints taken by me from Cummins, and copies were handed to the jury, so that they could follow what I was about to say. Mr G. B. McClure, counsel for the Crown, was just about to ask me to describe the similarities when, out of the corner of my eye, I observed that the jury had been handed copies of the fingerprints in *another* case on which Cummins had been indicted, but was not being tried.

Even from that distance, between witness-box and the box where the jury sat, just to my right, I could detect the difference in the prints before me and those they were gazing at. I stood for a moment, not a little perplexed. I realized that somehow a mistake had been made, and I had to think quickly. There was only one course to take. I turned to Mr Justice Asquith, the presiding judge.

"I think the jury has been handed a wrong exhibit," I said quietly.

Puzzled looks appeared on the faces of the jurors, and the copies with which they had been provided were hastily recovered. But the damage had been done, and the whole essence of that justice to which I have referred would have been vitiated if those same jurors had been allowed to continue the hearing of the case.

They were asked to retire while the legal position was discussed. On their return Mr Justice Asquith discharged them, explaining that "It is possible, and very probable, that from the exhibit before you you might have drawn certain inferences which would have made it impossible for you to try this action properly. I know I can rely on you not to mention anything that has come to your knowledge from this exhibit."

The judge also appealed to the Press to "treat this with every discretion," adding, "The full truth will be published later, but not until this trial is over."

It was the first time in the history of the Old Bailey that a trial had ever been stopped for such a reason.

On the following Monday the trial was reopened with another jury. I gave evidence, and was rigorously cross-examined by Mr John Flowers, K.C., counsel for the defence. How rigorously will be seen later. Cummins was found guilty and sentenced to death.

You may wonder what manner of man was this who, night after night, set out to murder and mutilate women with such wanton savagery.

Born of highly respectable parents, he was given every chance as regards education, but his school record was described as "poor". He fared no better when he took up work in the leather-tanning industry, being dismissed from one job after another as being "unsatisfactory", "irresponsible", and fond of the company of women.

In 1935 he joined the R.A.F. as a flight-rigger, and continued in the Service until his arrest. In 1936 he married, his wife continuing work as secretary to a theatrical producer.

Possessed of a vain streak, Cummins loved to pose as the son of a nobleman, and because of his cultured speech and polished manner became known as "The Count" or "The Duke" among his comrades. He was boastful of his conquests with women, and was doubtless helped in his amorous escapades by his masquerade as "the Hon. Gordon Cummins".

There are many such men, I am afraid, who love to swagger about assuming titles to which they have no right, and imposing on credulous women. But there are not many who resort to the murder of those who fall victims to their plausible tongues. One is left perplexed and horrified at the vicious cruelty which animated Cummins in his lust to kill.

Cummins appealed, and while seated between two warders in the dock at the Court of Criminal Appeal he listened to Mr D. N. Pritt, K.C., urging his case before the Lord Chief Justice, Mr Justice Humphreys, and Mr Justice Tucker. He laughed and appeared to be joking with his guardians. Now and again he looked across the court and smiled at his wife.

It was Mr Justice Humphreys who delivered judgment. In dealing with the ground that the "verdict was against the weight of evidence" he was at great pains to emphasize the fingerprint evidence which I had given in the court below.

"There was no scamping the evidence in this case," he said. "Superintendent Cherrill was examined fairly fully in chief; he was cross-examined most properly in the most minute detail by the learned counsel who appeared for the accused, and in order to make his points quite clear to the jury, counsel obtained permission from the learned judge to leave his place and go close to the jury-box, in order that he might point with a pencil to his copy of the photograph, so that the jury might see what it was that he was referring to . . . Superintendent Cherrill was cross-examined as to dissimilarities. He said, 'I quite agree that there are some dissimilarities which you have discovered and put to me,' and he added, 'I can show you some more if you want them which I have discovered and you have not. But as to those dissimilarities, the same observation is to be made with regard to all of them, and that is this. They are dissimilarities which may well be caused either by the shape or the movement of the article at the time the fingerprint was made upon it, inasmuch as there was no movement of the paper upon which the fingerprints of the accused were taken for the purpose of this case.'"

Mr Justice Humphreys concluded his reference to the fingerprint evidence by pointing out that no witness had been called to combat my evidence, which he described as being "this peculiar but singularly conclusive form of evidence, because it was claimed nearly 600,000 persons have been identified without any error being known to have been made, and in no case have two people been found to have fingers or thumbs which make identical marks."

The appeal was dismissed, and on the morning of June 25, 1942, Cummins went to his death at the hands of the hangman.

Fred Cherrill

The Man Who Wanted Voices

Two months after the killing rampage of Gordon Cummins, another serviceman went on a murder spree, this time on the other side of the world. Inevitably, newspapers compared him to Jack the Ripper. The truth seems to be that the "brown-out killer" of Melbourne was an emotionally unstable mother's boy, whose attitude to his adored mother was ambiguous enough to make him kill middle-aged women who reminded him of her, then rip off their lower garments without actually committing rape. John Godwin's account, from *Killers in Paradise* (1962), gives some insight into Leonski's peculiar psychology.

F ive months after the attack on Pearl Harbour the Australian city of Melbourne was hourly expecting the first Japanese bombs to scream down on her own roofs. And in those five months of waiting the face, character and outlook of the Victorian capital had changed more radically than in the fifteen years that preceded them.

Melbourne had been nothing if not a conservative town. Her police were unarmed, high-buttoned and helmeted on the traditional English pattern; her one-and-a-quarter million people dressed drably, went to bed early, and took their schools almost as seriously as their cricket; her broad, well-swept main streets were laid out in rigidly planned chessboard fashion and through them the traffic flowed at a remarkably slow and disciplined pace. Book and film censorship was the strictest in Australia, there was no night life to speak of, and a "temporary Emergency Regulation" of the first World War that ordered public houses to shut at 6 p.m. was conveniently still in force at the outbreak of the second.

The fighting in Europe and Africa did not affect Melbourne, except that fewer young men were seen in the streets. But on December 7, 1941, Japan struck, and suddenly the war had reached Australia's doorstep.

The city was "browned-out", meaning that enough lights were turned off to make driving as well as walking hazardous occupations. The beautifully kept public parks developed rashes of slit trenches, housewives spent hours pasting strips of paper over window panes, while their menfolk dug family air raid shelters in the back garden. Searchlights swept the night sky, wardens practised sprinkling sand on incendiaries, and every afternoon the harbour batteries filled the air with white shrapnel puffs. The only thing that was missing was the bombs.

Few Melburnians doubted that they would come. Malaya, Singapore and the East Indies fell, the Japanese tide was licking across the hump-backed razor mountains of New Guinea, in the far north of Australia Port Darwin was virtually flattened. It was just a matter of days . . .

With the exception of air raids came a curious feeling of helpless rage and frustration. Everyone knew that over New Guinea the tiny Royal Australian Air Force was trying to fight Japanese Zeros with converted training planes. The country's trained manpower lay dead in the Libyan desert or rotted in Jap prison camps. At home the Government was scraping up a new conscript army, half-trained and a quarter armed. The country lay wide open and exposed, and the people knew it.

Into dimmed-out Melbourne, almost denuded of able-bodied males, poured a flood of foreign servicemen. Dutch and Indonesian troops, evacuated from the East Indies, Free Norwegians and Fighting French, British Navy personnel, Malays, Filipinos, and – above all – Americans. Tens of thousands of G.I.s used the city as a supply and assembly base before being shunted to the fighting zones in the North, meanwhile filling it with alien-sounding English, the smell of Lucky Strikes and the clink

24

of immense pay packets, itching to be spent before their owners were killed.

With the civilian population in the grip of nervous apprehension, with the police force at rock-bottom strength through enlistments, with half the local wives minus husbands, and with an army camp on every sports ground, Melbourne's staunch moral fibre disintegrated and the town went – temporarily – haywire. Motivated by patriotism, profits, loneliness, unaccustomed freedom or long dormant erotic urges, respectable suburbanites held night-long bottle parties, hitherto scrupulous businessmen peddled black-market tyres and cigarettes, schoolgirls and middle-aged matrons smiled at anything resembling a uniform, and land-ladies and cinema usherettes closed both eyes at love scenes that would have sent them into screaming hysterics a year earlier.

This was the background against which three Melbourne women were murdered in identical circumstances and within less than three weeks.

Early factory workers of the inner seaside suburb of Albert Park found the first body, sprawling in a doorway on the chilly morning of May 3, 1942. It was a plump, middle-aged woman, her clothes hanging in shreds from her belted waist, her mouth gaping open as if frozen in a silent scream.

From the identity card in the dead woman's handbag police established that her name was Ivy Violet McLeod, that she was 40 years old, a "lady's domestic helper", and lived three miles from the spot where she was found. She had been lying on her back in the doorway, her eyes, knees and hands heavily bruised, her left temple fractured and her throat swollen. The police pathologist diagnosed that she had died of suffocation and a fractured skull. The doorway bore signs of a struggle, indicating that she had been murdered right there. Whoever did the killing had obviously first choked her into unconsciousness, then dropped her heavily on the ground, cracking her skull.

But whoever had killed her had also torn her clothes with maniacal force and with no apparent purpose. The woman had been neither robbed nor sexually assaulted, nor beaten up in the normal sense. Time of death was assumed to have been the late hours of the previous night, but even then the browned-out street was a fairly well frequented place. Had the victim screamed someone would have been bound to have heard her . . . but no one had. The attack, therefore, must have come as a complete surprise. Her throat must have been gripped so suddenly and powerfully that she couldn't utter a sound before blacking out. But since it had been gripped from the front the woman must have stood close to her assailant in the first place – probably in the doorway.

There was nothing in Mrs McLeod's character to indicate a semi-public cuddling session. She was a plain, motherly woman who would have looked most in place over a kitchen stove. Only these days nobody knew what sort of women were liable to get up to what escapades . . .

Melbourne's Criminal Investigation Branch were still probing into Mrs McLeod's past when – six days later – they were faced with another victim.

At four a.m. on Saturday morning a city night watchman found a lady's handbag on his beat. He delivered it to the nearest police station, and had barely returned to his rounds when he also found its owner. The second body lay on the steps of one of the hideously ornate lodging houses in Spring Street that Melbourne owes to her Victorian past. This time the woman was brunette, slender and pretty, but she had died in the same fashion as Mrs McLeod. Her neck showed bluish-red strangulation marks, her smart clothes were ripped to tatters, and the back of her head was fractured by a heavy fall.

The city police had no trouble identifying the dead woman as the owner of the bag – she was the wife of one of their colleagues.

She had been living on the fourth floor of the curli-cued apartment house on whose doorstep she was found. There she called herself Miss O'Brien. In reality she was Mrs Pauline Buchan Thompson, and her husband did duty as a police constable in the country town of Bendigo. Hazel-eyed and soft-voiced, Mrs Thompson had stage leanings not usually associated with policemen's wives. During the five years she lived with her husband in Bendigo she had become something of a local celebrity. She sang at troop concerts and charity shows, worked as announcer at the town's broadcasting station, and conducted a weekly women's session on the air. The Thompsons had two children; a four-year-old daughter and an adopted son aged seven.

But in February, 1942, acting on an impulse Mrs Thompson left her husband in Bendigo and moved to Melbourne. First she worked for a machinery firm, then she got a telephonist's job with another radio station. At the same time she moved to her city address and – for reasons of her own – began calling herself Miss O'Brien.

Dr C. H. Mollison, who conducted her post-mortem examination, reported that death was due "to pressure on each side of the neck. Considerable force had been used, causing nervous paralysis rather than suffocation or strangulation".

Three homicide officers, Detective-Inspector Gray and Detective-Sergeants McGuffie and Lyon, gathered what clues there were. Mrs Thompson's pearl necklace had been broken and the pearls scattered over the steps. One of her shoes had slipped off and was found two steps below the body.

These signs made it obvious that – like Mrs McLeod – Pauline Thompson had died where she was found. Her handbag, however, was picked up several streets away. As it was most unlikely that she had dropped it herself, it must have been taken and later thrown away by her murderer. But why?

This last Why was only one of many the detectives were asking themselves. The two killings were so similar that there was little doubt of their having been the work of the same murderer. Both women had been strangled by hand, both had been half-stripped, both were attacked in semi-public places and neither had been sexually interfered with. What sort of freakish satisfaction had they afforded their killer? And how did he, on each occasion, prevent them from uttering even a single cry?

For Mrs Thompson had died as swiftly and silently as her predecessor. The proprietor of the lodging house and his wife were sleeping in a basement bedroom a few yards from the steps where the murder took place. They hadn't heard a sound; neither had the half-dozen tenants who were at home at the time. Spring Street was no suburban lane but a city thoroughfare that is never completely deserted. Yet no late pedestrian could be found who could recall hearing the slightest suspicious noise.

Had the killer been lurking on the steps? Most improbable. If attacked by a stranger in the darkness Mrs Thompson would have had time for at least one scream. It was much more likely that she had known her murderer, stood close to him before the sudden assault – exactly like Mrs McLeod.

Somehow the killer in both cases had managed to get at least on speaking terms with his victims; a fairly easy task for virtually any male in wartime Melbourne. But then the chances were good that someone had spotted him with them. The problem: find that someone.

The C.I.B. investigators had no trouble tracing Mrs Thompson's movements up to about six hours before her death. Her constable husband had come on escort duty to Melbourne on the same day, bringing their adopted son with him. Mrs Thompson had spent most of the afternoon with them and saw them off by the 5.40 p.m. train to Bendigo. Before parting she had told her husband that she was going to the Theatre Lovers' Club that Friday night. From then on her movements became shadowy with only one certain point – she had not gone to the Club she mentioned nor, apparently, had she ever intended to.

This the police discovered very quickly. Melbourne's main railway station – Flinders Street – has a row of train departure clocks above the entrance. Apart from informing people how fast they have to run for their trains the clocks also mark the city's most famous rendezvous position. "Meet you under the clocks at Flinders Street," is a time-honoured Melburnian phrase, indicating a dating spot no one can possibly miss. And beneath those clocks Mrs Thompson had waited for about half-an-hour; waited for someone who evidently didn't turn up. Witnesses had seen her waiting and finally walking off with every sign of disgust. This was at around seven o'clock – but where had she gone from there?

"Where do you go around seven in the evening when you

28

don't have a kitchen of your own?" reasoned Detective-Sergeant McGuffie. "You go and have a meal. Chances are that somebody's seen her eating in a city restaurant. Let's find him."

At Russell Street, Melbourne's police headquarters, laboratory men got busy with a window dummy. They dressed the figure in the dead woman's clothes, superimposed a photograph of her face on the dummy's head and distributed the finished picture to every newspaper and cinema in the town. The portrait with the blazing caption "*Have you seen this woman*?" reached an estimated million people within 48 hours.

Several of them stepped forward at once. The first was the man who had stood Mrs Thompson up under the Flinders Street clocks. He turned out to be a young American soldier who had dated her in haste, then found something better to do and didn't bother to inform her of his changed plans. He may not have been everyone's idea of a gallant escort, but he certainly had nothing to do with her murder. His alibi for the evening was water-tight.

But to the detective who interrogated him the broken date provided a clue that turned out to be vital: Mrs Thompson had liked "the Yanks".

Next in line were three people who had noticed the constable's wife later that night. She had been drinking in a hotel in Collins Place – and with her was another young G.I.

According to the strange ritual imposed by Melbourne's licensing laws the two had to use the hotel's dining-room to drink; the bar was shut. Different witnesses noticed them between eight o'clock and midnight, when they left. They were sitting close together and occasionally the woman had stroked the soldier's hair.

Mrs Thompson was murdered some time between midnight and two a.m., which made it more than likely that the young man with her was her killer . . . *the* killer.

"What did he look like? Try and remember some feature about him – anything!" McGuffie prodded the witnesses. Their replies were discouragingly vague. He was tall – he was young – he was fair. No, he had no outstanding features. Was he an officer? No . . . but he could have been an N.C.O.

No one appeared to have seen the couple after they left the hotel. Which left the C.I.B. with a physical description that amounted to virtually nothing. Tall . . . young . . . fair, a private or N.C.O. – all this could apply to something like 20,000 Americans stationed in or around Melbourne.

A week had passed since the murder, Russell Street was getting restless – and so was Melbourne's population. The story of the two killings, their striking similarity and utter senselessness, had leaped at newspapers readers from among the welter of war news that seemed to be getting worse every day. Never mind about the yellow tide in the North . . . there was a maniac loose right here in town!

A maniac; certainly, but obsessed by what sort of mania? The man did not rape, bite or mutilate, which ruled out the more common variety of sex pervert. He did not inflict injuries that caused blood or suffering, which eliminated the most widespread forms of sadism. He invariably ripped his victims' clothing, a feature that indicated a fetishist; but fetishists are usually non-violent, preferring to steal the garments they desire to gloat over them in solitude.

Then, if the killer really was a U.S. serviceman, his particular psychosis would have to lie deep below the surface of his personality. In 1942 America was not yet scraping the bottom of her manpower barrel, this was before the time when medical examiners were ordered "Don't check their eyes – count 'em".

The C.I.B. consulted Melbourne's leading psychiatrists and received in reply a series of shoulder-shrugs couched in exquisite medical terminology. The man may be planning his murders weeks ahead, or he may be acting on the impulse of the moment – he may be handsome and popular or a repressed introvert – he may suffer from psychotic amnesia, in which case he wouldn't even remember the deed an hour later. Only one of the mind specialists offered an observation that turned out to be uncannily relevant: "The witnesses described this fellow as a *young* man. Well, the women he picks on aren't so very young – maybe he has some sort of mother complex?"

Retrospective analysis is as cheap in criminology as elsewhere, but in few cases could it ever have been so infuriating for the harassed investigators. For while the undermanned, overworked C.I.B. spent days listing the names of 1,000 known Australian sex offenders and shadowing the movements of some 80 "possibilities", the man they were seeking had already half-confessed the murders to a friend. While they were still trying to establish some sort of motive he had already demanded to be locked up "because I'm too dangerous to run around loose". While they were trying to guess his nationality he was weeping into his pillow at night, beating the mattress with his fists and screaming in a voice that sent shivers down the spines of the listeners: "I killed! – I killed! – I killed! . . ."

But all this the Homicide Squad officers had no way of knowing. No one stepped forward to tell them because of the curious unwillingness of the human mind to accept that someone you know and like can be a monster. It is a failing by no means confined to laymen. The highly skilled police of the German city of Hanover, for instance, kept on employing the services of their favourite stool-pigeon, Fritz Haarmann, long after they realised there was something "dangerously peculiar" about him. Herr Haarmann, who was eventually convicted of 24 murders, turned out to be a cannibal as well as a mass-slayer and a homosexual. None of his colleagues informed on Dr Palmer of Rugeley, even after it became a standing joke around town that the good doctor was poisoning his patients wholesale.

The hunt for new witnesses, fresh leads, dragged on, with 50 detectives of Victoria's meagre force detailed for this chase alone. They had made no visible progress at all on the morning of May 19, when a pale-faced gardener raced out of Royal Park screaming on top of his voice: "Police! Call the police, somebody . . . there's been another murder!"

The third victim turned out to be a tiny, thin spinster, whose neck was so hideously bruised that she looked like a corpse taken from the gallows. She was lying face down in the yellow sticky mud that had been excavated from a freshly-dug air raid trench in the park, her clothes clawed in strips from her child-like body. The soft mud around her was like a swamp; detectives waded up to their ankles as they pieced together the evidence embedded in it.

Scattered in a radius of 20 feet were the dead woman's gloves, shoes and handbag. Her umbrella – still open and wet from last night's rain – rested on a grass walk near by. The oozing clay told its own story. It clearly marked the spot where the little woman had been dragged into the park, limp and unresisting after having been strangled somewhere out in the street. The contents of her bag described her as Miss Gladys Lillian Hosking, 41 years old, private secretary to a professor of chemistry at Melbourne University. Miss Hosking had lived in a boarding house only a few hundred feet from the spot where she was found. In private life she was an enthusiastic amateur theatrical and member of an organisation rather painfully entitled "The Merrymakers' Concert Party".

The headlines that stared at Melbourne's newspaper readers that evening were the most frightening since the fall of Singapore. The maniac had struck for the third time, and now it was certain that the city's dimmed, wintry streets were haunted by something far worse than the fear of air raids. Women were bluntly warned not to go out unescorted after dark – an almost impossible advice for thousands of wartime night-shift workers. The war, clothing coupons and petrol rations were forgotten; the sole conversation topic was the monster prowling somewhere in the darkness out there, choosing his next victim.

There was now no doubt in anyone's mind that the strangler would leave his trail of corpses until he was caught: "How many did Jack the Ripper kill? – Was it six . . . or a dozen?" Tell-tale signs of panic flickered in every part of the city. Women breathlessly phoned police stations, reporting that they were being "followed by someone", that their lodger was "acting strange", that they "felt" they were being watched. Pure fantasies in most cases; but ominous symptoms of mass hysteria to those whose business it was to keep a finger on the national pulse.

Hysteria was precisely what a hard-pressed wartime administration could least afford. From "higher up" – from State Government and City Hall – came urgent, tensely-nervous nudges to the police force: "Why don't you fellows get a move on? We can't have another killing . . . not at this time . . ."

All police leave in the Melbourne area was cancelled, the C.I.B. worked double shifts, every man who could possibly be spared from other duties was put on the case. Within the next 48 hours the district of Royal Park was flooded with police – uniformed constables, plain-clothes officers, military provosts – knocking on every door up and down four miles of streets, questioning 650 men, women and children who might have noticed something – anything – that would offer one more clue.

The police didn't need goading from the press, reminders from the Government, or jitters from the public to realise they were racing against time. Every night that fell increased the chances of yet another body being found somewhere. Six nights between the first murder and the second; nine between the second and the third . . . the hunters didn't have much time.

Throughout Melbourne casual pick-ups virtually ceased, the hip-swinging ladies who used to patrol St Kilda Road vanished as if by magic, wives stayed home alone by the fireside, and young soldiers out for a spree found themselves forced to spree with other young soldiers. As one member of the U.S. Marine Corps, shortly due to leave for the Solomons, put it: "Why the hell don't they catch that bastard so we can all get back to having a good time before we croak?"

Within two days of the murder the C.I.B. was no longer thrashing around in the dark. They were following a definite line, based on the topography of the scene of the crime. In due course the line was bound to lead them to the killer. The question was only whether it would lead them there quick enough to prevent him from striking again.

Miss Hosking had been murdered in Gatehouse Street, a residential thoroughfare adjoining Royal Park. Since the beginning of the emergency the actual parkland, criss-crossed by air raid trenches, had been divided into two separate portions. The one nearest to Gatehouse Street was known as Camp Pell and housed an American army establishment. The other was an Australian camp site. The entire area was guarded and the chances were that one of the sentries had spotted the murderer returning to one of the two camps. Long, painstaking questioning revealed that no Australian had entered his camp from the direction of Gatehouse Street. This left an American. An American who was tall, fair, and had exceptionally large and powerful hands. This description was still too general to be of much use; but there was another point – a point connected with the spot where the body had been dumped.

It was an Australian soldier on picket duty that night who spoke the words that electrified the plain-clothes men: "I called out to a Yank who was plastered all over in yellow mud."

Yellow mud! In the whole of Royal Park there was only one freshly-dug trench – only one spot where a man could get covered in the moist clay: the place where the body was found.

"What did he look like?"

"Big bloke," said the sentry. "He was a bit full, too. I yelled out to him: 'Where the hell have you been?' And he said something about falling over a pool of mud while he was going through the park. And then he said – I remember this – he said: 'Boy, you should have seen the girl I was with. I thought I could drink, but she drank me right under the table.'"

The detectives looked at each other. Barring a truly fantastic coincidence they had located the strangler.

The following morning homicide officers F. Adam and W. Mooney entered Camp Pell and slowly walked down the long rows of tents. They stopped before each one, running expert eyes over the canvas, passing on to the next. At the 29th tent they paused for good. Near the entrance opening was an unmistakable patch of dried yellow mud. The detectives entered the tent, scrutinising the two iron bedsteads. On the frame of one were several yellow smears. The first officer scraped them off with his pocket knife and carefully placed the sample in an envelope.

Mooney turned to the American officer who had accompanied them. "Whose bed is that?"

34

The officer consulted his list. "Private first-class Edward Joseph Leonski."

Adam and Mooney took their samples to police analyst Charles Taylor; probably the most dreaded "lab man" in the Southern Hemisphere. Taylor's findings left little doubt – the dried mud was identical with the clay from the Royal Park air raid trench. The traces on the bed had been left by someone clutching the iron frame with mud-smeared hands.

The detectives hurried back to Camp Pell. There a surprise was waiting for them. Leonski's tent-mate and closest "buddy" in the camp had talked to his company commander. He felt he couldn't keep quiet any longer. He had, in fact, kept quiet at least a fortnight too long. But who could possibly blame him? Leonski, when drunk, was noted for his irrational behaviour.

Leonski, he said, had twice returned to the tent blubbering incoherently before sinking into twitching, tossing sleep from which he awoke at intervals, screaming. He had also pored for hours over the newspaper reports of the stranglings, mumbling things like "doorstep, doorstep" until his friend told him to "pipe down".

One day he had asked his tent-mate whether he believed that a werewolf could only be killed with silver bullets.

"What the hell do I know about werewolves," was the reply.

"Well, do you know Mr Hyde and Dr Jekyll?" Leonski had asked in an urgent whisper. "That's what I'm like – one guy, two personalities." Later he added: "All you guys are wondering about these murders. Only I don't – I know!"

It was then that the G.I. for the first time began to wonder seriously about Leonski and the murders.

"You see," he explained, "I've never known anyone to change so much when he's drunk as this Leonski guy. He might just have been blowing off steam – he always does when he's had a few. Half the time he doesn't know what he's talking about then."

He had challenged Leonski on his suspicions and Leonski had grasped him by the shoulder, tears in his eyes. "You're generous," he said, "you're the most generous man I've ever met. I'm depending on your generosity."

The detectives listened, their jaws clenched bitterly. "All right," they said finally, "let's have a line-up."

The Australian sentry was brought to the camp and shown the rows of assembled Americans. Then he was told to pick out the man he had challenged on the night of the 19th. The sentry stopped in front of a broad-shouldered, snub-nosed youngster with wavy fair hair and candid blue eyes.

"That's him," he said. "That's the man!"

It was Edward Leonski.

The American was taken to the guard house for questioning, but a real interrogation turned out to be unnecessary. He confessed all three murders, there and then, with an eager haste that sounded almost like relief. Drawing at a cigarette he murmured contentedly: "I knew all along this was the end of the trail."

In the latter part of the 19th century the Italian mind-specialist Cesare Lombroso expounded a theory according to which criminals are born, not made. The professor maintained, among other things, that all criminals are branded with certain physical characteristics and that these would show what sort of delinquent a person was going to be – even if he hadn't yet committed any crime. Lombroso maintained that criminals are degenerate types of a special, recognisable kind and that an expert – like himself – could spot them by appearance alone.

Among the characteristics discovered by the professor were: receding forehead, huge jaws and frontal sinuses, jutting chin, large quantities of body hair, and outstanding ears. "A type," Lombroso announced, "sometimes resembling the negro, sometimes the gipsy, sometimes the Mongolian. We note the large pale face, the prominent eyebrows, the wild eye – which alone is often enough to betray a criminal nature".

Luckily for the underworld and unfortunately for a great many innocent people the learned professor wielded considerable influence over the police theories of his time. He died in Italy in 1909, and was thus deprived of ever meeting Edward Leonski face to face. If he had he might have eaten his text books.

For the soldier who had reached "the end of the trail"

at the early age of 24 was a living refutation of everything Lombroso and his followers had dreamt up.

Tall, fair, magnificently proportioned, with a round baby face, button nose, and an engaging grin, he could have stepped straight from the campus poster of an American college. Eddie Leonski's outstanding characteristics were his gentleness, his almost permanent good nature, and his tearful nostalgia for "Mom back home".

Home was New York City and Mom – by all accounts – a formidable personality. Born in Poland, she had been a professional weightlifter before migrating to the U.S. Eddie had inherited his physique from her and she taught him how to lift weights at a very early age. His strength became immense. While working as a grocery clerk he used to entertain customers by lifting 100 lb. sugar bags above his head with one hand. Nor was Eddie merely a hunk of handsome brawn. To his mother's delight he played the piano, drew passable sketches, sang in the local church choir, and finished high school as an honours student.

But if ever a human being had been cursed by heredity it was Leonski. His father – a Russian – drank himself to death. His mother married again but the marriage was not a success. Embittered by two unhappy marriages Mrs Leonski clung fiercely to her favourite son; and he to her. Eddie had no girl friends, a harsh word from his mother could make him cry, and as long as she was near his behaviour was, if anything, too genteel.

Came the war and a call-up notice for Eddie. He seems to have spent the early part of his army career in tears – he cried when he was sent to a Texas training camp, cried when he received the first letter from his mother, cried when writing his answer, and cried the day he was shipped overseas. But between bouts of weeping another, hitherto submerged, facet of his character began to show through.

Cut off from his mother, Leonski started drinking. His army buddies, noting his crying jags, his sexual timidity and effeminate giggles, had put him down as "queer". He undoubtedly was that – but not in the way they imagined. For under alcoholic stimulus a completely different Leonski appeared; a swaggering show-off who would do anything to attract attention, fight at the drop of a hat, and wander off into the night on weird adventures of his own.

"The first thing that always changed was his voice," one of his fellow doughboys testified. "It became kinda soft and purry, like a girl's. Then he'd start telling you all kinds of creepy stuff – about werewolves and split personalities and jazz like that. After that he'd either want to hug you or fight you – you never knew which. And he was a pretty hard man to handle in a brawl."

It was at the Texan base of San Antonio that Leonski first fell foul of the law. A local girl charged him with rape and he had to answer to an army enquiry. It was a strange accusation for the girl-shy mother's boy. Eddie was acquitted. He definitely had not raped the girl, but had given her a terrible and quite inexplicable beating.

Shortly afterwards a bitterly crying Leonski was shipped to Australia in a signals battalion. From that day on his army record rapidly went downhill. His leaves became uninterrupted drinking sessions during which he dumbfounded Melbourne hotel patrons by mixing beer, whisky, gin, ice cream, mustard and ketchup in one glass and swallowing the concoction in one gulp. He also walked up and down bar rooms on his hands and at regular intervals sent out the traditional offer to "lick any man in the house".

Leonski also began to pick up girls. Not the young slips his colleagues preferred, but mature, more matronly types who were sometimes delighted at getting such a desirable escort.

"I don't know why I go for them," he confided to his tent-mate. "Their voices remind me of mom, I reckon. I like it when they talk to me. Makes me feel less homesick."

In camp he became a problem soldier; a chronic shirker and A.W.L. regular who spent more time on guard duty and k.p. than any other private in the battalion. Had anyone compared his civilian record with his army behaviour he would have noticed at a glance that something was going seriously askew with Eddie Leonski. No one realised this more than himself. Once, when a captain caught him returning to camp after an illicit outing, Eddie pleaded: "Put me in the guardhouse and keep me there, sir. Keep me there all the time – I'm too dangerous to run around loose!"

Leonski himself couldn't remember the precise date when he started to become violent. He pin-pointed it at soon after his plea to the captain; but his memory covering the entire period that followed resembled a grey fog patch shot through occasionally with blinding shafts of clarity.

He remembered assaulting three girls in quick succession, half-strangling each one, but letting go before they went limp in his grip. He couldn't recall either the localities or the circumstances of the attacks. "It had something to do with their voices," he said. "I used to feel terribly lonely and they spoke to me and I felt if I grabbed them I'd somehow be able to keep their voices for good . . ."

Two of his three early victims reported him to the police. But their statements were so vague and made so long after the assaults that they were useless in the later manhunt.

Leonski was perfectly aware that his dark urges only overwhelmed him when he drank. But he seems to have made no effort to cut down his alcohol consumption. He had been drinking heavily on the cold evening of May 2. Walking down an Albert Park street he remembered thinking of his mother, and how far he was from home. Then he saw a woman standing in a doorway . . . a pleasant-faced woman, holding a curiously old-fashioned handbag.

"I said something about that handbag, then I walked up to her and felt it. It was soft – strange and soft and it made me feel all strange inside. She stepped further back in the doorway and I followed her and grabbed her. I grabbed her by the neck . . .

"I changed the position of my thumbs so that they were at her throat and I choked her. She fell down . . . I could hear her head hitting the wall. I fell on top of her and I started to rip her clothes. I ripped them and ripped them and ripped them, but I couldn't rip her belt. I let go for a moment, then I got back to it. I felt mad and I thought I *had* to rip that belt . . . so I ripped and ripped at it . . ."

These were the words of Leonski's statement to the police. He had done his best to give an accurate account of the murder, but could not remember either how or what time he got back to camp. The following day he read that he had killed Mrs McLeod. For several nights he cried himself to sleep.

Five nights later Pauline Thompson, the policeman's wife, was stood up by her U.S. Army date and went to a café for a solitary meal. In the restaurant sat another G.I., a tall, good-looking one.

Mrs Thompson saw him looking at her across the tables. The soldier was Eddie Leonski, and Eddie was sober.

He joined her table and they ate together. The café was unlicensed and he suggested they go to a nearby hotel for a few drinks. He suggested what was tantamount to her death sentence. They walked to Collins Place, Eddie chatting in his easy-going college-kid manner. They drank – whisky with beer chasers; round after round. Eddie's voice grew softer, his smile became vapid and infantile. The woman noticed it. "Baby face," she chortled, flattening his snub nose with her finger. "But underneath – underneath you're vicious."

Around eleven o'clock Leonski ran out of funds. He was high by then, but not yet at danger pitch. Mrs Thompson paid for more drinks, inexorably pushing him towards the shadow line where the campus boy passed out and Moloch took over.

They walked to her home in Spring Street together, arm in arm through the drizzling rain. Mrs Thompson, feeling alcoholically Bohemian, sang songs in his ears; sentimental pops from her stage repertoire. She crooned softly and affectionately . . .

" . . . She was singing for me. She had a nice voice. We turned a corner and there was nobody around. All I heard was that voice of hers. I wanted that voice. We came to some long steps. Then I grabbed her. I don't know why, I just grabbed her. She stopped singing and I said to her: 'Keep singing – keep on singing'. But she wouldn't, she fell down instead. I got mad and I tore at her. I tore her apart. I kept on tearing until I heard someone coming up the street. I ducked behind the stone wall. My heart was pounding so I could hardly breathe. I thought I couldn't bear to look at her any more."

Nevertheless, Leonski remembered that he was out of

money. He took the dead woman's handbag and ran down the street. At the next corner he opened the bag, took two pound notes, and ran on. He hurled the bag away and hailed a taxi.

The next few days seem to have been a sort of waking nightmare for Leonski. He was quite conscious of what he had done – and he knew dimly that he would do it again. And he made what appeared to be an earnest effort to get caught.

No multiple slayer has ever surrendered voluntarily to the police, but a remarkable number seem to drop hints and scatter clues deliberately as if filled with an irrational desire to help fate along. Peter Kurten virtually confessed to his wife, Christie sublet the flat in which he had walled up his victims, Heath contacted the police under an assumed name, Manuel offered to investigate the deaths of a family he himself had wiped out. In the nine days between his second and his last murder Leonski literally goaded his comrades to inform on him.

He hinted that he was a "werewolf", a man with a split personality. He pencil-marked newspaper reports of his slayings and showed them to his friends, muttering "That's the doorway here." He talked and screamed in his sleep – always about women and killings, he clenched and unclenched his huge hands, gazing at them with such an expression of horror that one G.I. inquired: "What's the matter with your mitts, Eddie?"

No one informed on Eddie Leonski and like the inevitable third act of a Greek tragedy he found himself shuffling through the rain towards his last victim. The street was bleak and lonely and Leonski had been drinking all afternoon and most of the evening. He was on his way back to Camp Pell when he saw the umbrella in front of him and the small, slender figure of Gladys Hoskins underneath.

He caught up with her and smiled down from six feet. "May I walk along with you, mam? It's raining pretty hard."

Miss Hosking smiled back and nodded. She made comfortable small-talk to put the big, shy, lonely boy beside her at his ease. Her voice was soft and motherly . . . "It was a lovely voice," Leonski remembered.

They came to her home and he asked her to walk with him a little farther. "I don't know my way around here any too well." Miss Hosking nodded again.

"We came to the edge of Royal Park and she stopped and pointed and said: 'There's your camp, over there.' I knew she was going to leave then and I didn't want her to go. I wanted her voice with me. As she turned I took her by the throat. She didn't make a sound, didn't struggle, nothing. She just went limp . . . all soft. I pulled her by the armpits, pushed her under the fence. Then I climbed over and pulled her through from the other side. I carried her for a stretch but then I fell over and in the mud. She was making a kind of gurgling noise then and I said to myself 'I have to stop this'. So I pulled her dress over her face and I ripped some of her clothes."

Leonski made his three confessions willingly, halting only when his memory dimmed out. In the presence of his own officers and the detectives he signed the sheets in a curiously stilted schoolboy's hand.

From that moment he passed into the custody of the U.S. Army. Apart from presenting evidence the Australian police had nothing further to do with him. He was probably the most embarrassing accused ever to face an American Court Martial.

He had terrorised a civilian population on whose continued goodwill U.S. army operations largely depended and stretched their already hard-pressed police force almost to breaking point. He had been hunted down without the aid of American investigators and, worse, he had shown up his army's medical check as a complete farce – in spite of its vaunted accent on "psychological fitness".

Leonski was transferred to the City Watchhouse to await trial. Kept under constant observation by heavily-armed U.S. Provosts and barred from liquor he quickly regained his former good-natured placidity. Twice a day he did physical jerks "to keep in trim", he ate heartily, read whatever book or magazine was given to him, and spent happy hours sketching pretty, long-legged "Esquire Girls" on wrapping paper. Service and civilian psychiatrists eagerly scanned the drawings for some symbol of Leonski's mental kink. They found none. The sketches showed exactly the same types of chocolate-box cuties that were allegedly maintaining the morale of millions of normal Allied soldiers.

The U.S. Army authorities went to extraordinary lengths to keep their prisoner unlynched and unmolested. The location of the General Court Martial was made a top military secret – though anyone passing Melbourne's elaborate Horticultural Hall could see by the awesome concentration of armed men that something unusual was taking place there.

The incongruity that had always hung over the tear-stained mother's-boy-maniac persisted right to his end. The second-last act of his career was staged in surroundings intended for prize geraniums and seedling exhibitions.

Leonski had to plead Not Guilty, according to the Law. But since he never retracted his detailed confessions the trial became purely a matter of confirming them and deciding whether or not he was sane enough to be hanged. The question of his sanity was fascinating to the psychiatrists – for the officers sitting in judgment over him it was a source of acute embarrassment.

The fact that he had taken money from the purse of one of his victims, that he had tried to conceal the body of another, that he had felt remorse and horror for his deeds possibly made him "rational" in the strictly judicial sense. That he was utterly irrational in every other did not concern the Court Martial. But to those among us who prefer analysis – and therefore possible prevention – to legalise annihilation it is of some importance to try and fathom his motives.

The one Melbourne psychologist who had early recognised the pattern in Leonski's killings also offered the only explanation for them: "Leonski obviously adored his mother. Equally obviously he became a helpless reed when separated from her. He may have blamed her for his helplessness, bitterly resented how firmly she had tied him to her apron strings. With every middle-aged, kind-voiced woman he strangled he could have been strangling *her*."

Leonski seems to have been a creature of "Momism"

43

carried to its ultimate extreme – where it turns on and destroys the thing it loves. He was undoubtedly a fetishist; hence his preoccupation with clothes-tearing and soft handbags. He was also possibly a sadist; though of a rare "unbloody" kind who gains satisfaction not from the sights and sounds of suffering but from the *knowledge* that he has inflicted it. The only parallel to him in the history of crime would be Neill Cream, the Canadian doctor who haunted London in the 1890's killing prostitutes by means of poisoned "cough remedies". Cream was a sadist who didn't even have to be present when his victims died in agony. The realisation that the agony was happening somewhere was sufficient for him.

But all of Leonski's abberations didn't constitute insanity within the legal meaning. Even if they had it would have been very doubtful whether this could have saved his life. The pressure of public indignation on the Court Martial was tremendous; coupled with the anxiety of the U.S. Army authorities to eliminate that human blot on their escutcheon it could only result in one verdict.

After a trial lasting five days Leonski was found guilty and sentenced to death. Following the tradition of nearly all mass-murderers he took the sentence calmly. His composure lasted to the moment he died.

Back in New York his sister seemed stunned when she heard the news. "It can't be Eddie – it just can't be!" she cried. "He was the best in our family . . . the kindest, gentlest."

Old Mrs Leonski couldn't read English newspapers and was completely unaware of the fate of her favourite son. Her daughter managed to keep her so by switching off the radio whenever the news bulletins came through.

The sentence of the Court Martial had to be sent to Washington for confirmation by the President. This resulted in a delay of nearly four months; common in American legal practice but highly unusual by Anglo-Australian methods. After F.D. Roosevelt had signed his name on the document the confirmation was read out to Leonski in the death cell. He nodded pleasantly, as if in complete agreement with his President.

THE MAN WHO WANTED VOICES

At six o'clock on the morning of November 9, 1942, Edward Joseph Leonski was hanged by the neck in Pentridge Gaol. He was the first foreigner ever executed there.

John Godwin

"I Always Wanted to Torture a Girl"

The next case, hardly known outside America (for example, it is not to be found in the otherwise comprehensive *Murderers' Who's Who* by J.H.H. Gaute and Robin Odell), seems to me among the most horrific murders ever committed. The only account I could find was in an old issue of *Master Detective*, written by George Vedder Jones. I mention this to explain phrases like "shocking crime" and "the vicious depravity of his nature", for true crime magazines have always – since they began to appear in the 1920s – displayed a tendency to reassure their readers by taking a tone of high moral indignation. If the writer fails to adopt it, then I suspect it is often inserted by the editor. This has been so since the Elizabethans began producing pamphlets about the crimes of notorious criminals, which were hawked among the crowd at public executions, and it can be found in 17th century volumes on the lives of famous highwaymen and in the classic *Newgate Calendar* of the late 18th century. In fact, it is only in the last few decades of the 20th century that historians of crime have felt able to adopt the tone of scientific detachment that is, after all, appropriate to the science of criminology. I hasten to add that, in general, Mr Vedder Jones writes with admirable precision and objectivity.

At exactly 9.25 on an evening in late April, 1942 three teenage student nurses stepped from a streetcar in suburban Pueblo, Colorado. Gathering clouds obscured the moon and a few large drops of rain were splashing into the street, driven by a raw wind from the mountains. The girls were returning home from an evening nursing class. "It'll be coming down in buckets in a few minutes," blonde-haired Margaret Driscoll said. "Better stay here at my house till the storm passes." She paused before the path leading to the home of her parents.

Pretty 17-year-old Alice Porter glanced up at the blackening sky. A flash of lightning stabbed down from the clouds. She shook her head. "I only have a few blocks to go. I can get home before the storm breaks."

"I'm going to wait here at Margaret's," Eileen Muhic said. "Better stay, too, Alice."

"No, I'm going on home," Alice insisted. "So long, girls. See you at school tomorrow."

She turned and started away, her high heels clicking along the pavement.

At 9.30 that evening, Ward Lennon, who lived two blocks down the street, was sitting across from his wife in their living-room when he heard a clap of thunder.

"Better close those front windows," his wife told him. "It'll be pouring in a minute."

Suddenly a scream rang out in the night.

"What was that?" exclaimed Mrs Lennon.

"It sounded like a woman." Lennon peered out into the darkness. In the street he saw what looked like a tan-coloured car picking up speed. He listened, but heard no further sound. "The scream must have come from that car that just drove away," he concluded.

Lennon wondered if he should telephone the police, but decided that it was probably only some high school youngsters out joyriding. He closed the windows and went back to his easy chair.

At 9.45, Marvin Porter, a retired Pueblo detective, put aside the newspaper he had been reading uneasily and looked out of his front door. The rain was coming down in solid sheets, driven by a strong wind.

"I'm worried about Alice," he told his wife. "I hope she isn't out in this rain."

"She probably stopped off at the Driscolls'," his wife reassured him.

The shower passed and the moon came out again. Still Alice did not return.

At 10.15, Porter said: "I'm going to call the Driscolls and see if she's there."

He returned to the living-room a moment later. "That's strange. The Driscolls say she left for here 50 minutes ago. It's only about a five-minutes walk," he said, obviously worried.

Porter put on his coat and hat and went out. He stopped at every house on the way to the Driscolls' to inquire about Alice. No one had seen her. Ward Lennon, however, told of hearing the scream and seeing the car drive rapidly away.

At the Driscolls' house, Porter asked Margaret Driscoll if she had noticed a tan-coloured car along the street when Alice started home.

Margaret did not recall such a car. "But I wasn't noticing cars particularly," she said. "We were worried about Alice getting home before the rain."

Then she added: "I remember now! I've seen a car like that other nights, though. Eileen Muhic and I remarked about it. We saw the same car with a man in it parked near the nursing home several nights in a row. Then one night last week, after we'd got on the streetcar, the driver started up and followed along behind us. Another night, I saw that same car parked not far from Alice's house. I thought it was kind of strange."

"Did you notice anything special about the car or the driver?" Porter asked. His fears were mounting.

"No, it was too dark. I'm not even certain that it was a tan car. All I know is that it was some light colour – might have been a light grey. But I saw that same car five or six times. The driver always acted as though he was waiting for someone."

"Waiting for someone," Porter echoed under his breath. Using the Driscolls' phone, he immediately notified the police.

Picking up Ward Lennon on the way, Porter hurried home, arriving there just as a police car with Captain

Robert Pratt and a patrolman pulled up. Porter had known Pratt when both worked together at the detective bureau. The two men exchanged sober greetings.

"She simply vanished off the street," Porter said. "There's no place I know where she could possibly be." He told the captain about the car seen near the nursing school which had followed the streetcar home. Lennon told of hearing a woman's scream and seeing a similar car drive away.

"I'm certain Alice was in that car," Porter said, "and I know she didn't get in willingly. Alice is barely 17. She's had a few dates with boys. But she'd never think of getting into a car with a stranger. And this is the first time since she started nursing school that she hasn't been home promptly at 9.30."

Captain Pratt telephoned Chief of Police Arthur Grady at his home. Agreeing that the girl's disappearance called for immediate action, Grady contacted Pueblo County Sheriff Thomas Murphy and asked that county patrols be alerted to halt any suspicious-looking cars on all highways leading out of Pueblo.

When Pratt asked if there was any reason why anyone should want to harm his daughter, Porter said hesitantly: "I can think of only one reason. You remember the Dorothy Drain murder, of course. While I was working on it as a detective, I received an anonymous letter threatening my daughter with the same fate as Dorothy if I didn't lay off the investigation."

Pratt well remembered the shocking rape-murder. On a warm evening in August, Riley Drain, a Pueblo County sheriff's deputy, returned home from a dance with his wife. His two pretty daughters, Dorothy, 16, and Barbara, 14, had been left asleep in a bedroom of their modest bungalow. The Drains were startled to find the front door standing open. On the blood-drenched double bed lay the nude body of Dorothy Drain. She had been brutally assaulted, then killed by a blow on the head with an axe. An unsuccessful attempt had been made to rape the younger girl, Barbara. She lay feebly whimpering, her skull also fractured by a blow.

Prompt emergency hospital treatment saved the younger

girl's life, although months passed before she was fully recovered.

While the manhunt for the killer was in progress, Porter received the threatening letter. Police eventually tracked down two men – Frank Aguilar and Joseph Arridy. Both were convicted on the strongest evidence, including the court testimony of Barbara Drain, and were executed in the gas chamber at Canon City. Presumably the threatening letter, which was never traced, was sent by a friend of one of the slayers.

"Friends of Frank Aguilar still live here in Pueblo, so we'll certainly check on them," Captain Pratt assured Porter. "But I think we ought first to find out what men Alice knew. The man in the car may not have been a stranger to Alice. She may have gone up to the car willingly, then screamed when he forced her inside. Teenage girls sometimes keep silent about friendships with men whom they think their parents wouldn't approve of."

By this time, other detectives were arriving. Police technicians brought floodlights and other equipment. The street near the Porter home was carefully searched for some clue to Alice's abductor. Nothing was found.

Meanwhile, Pratt searched the girl's bedroom. He learned nothing from a packet of letters found in a desk. Then he came upon a diary secreted behind some books in a bookcase. Kept in a painstaking feminine hand, the last entry was for the previous day. The entries were mostly a recapitulation of everyday events at the high school which Alice attended.

Then Pratt noted the entry: "Bob drove me home again today. I think he's cute." Looking back, Pratt saw one other entry: "Bob tried to tease me again today. I believe he likes me."

Pratt asked Porter whether Alice had ever mentioned anyone named Bob.

"Not that I can recall," Porter said.

"Did she ever drive home in the car of a young man?"

Porter consulted his wife. Neither remembered Alice ever being driven home from school.

Pratt left at last. Driving to the slum area of Pueblo, he

questioned friends of Frank Aguilar who lived there. He could find nothing to arouse his suspicion, and returned to headquarters.

Chief of Police Grady agreed to assign a detective to look further into the possibility that someone connected with Frank Aguilar was involved. The chief had already called out off-duty police and detectives to visit every garage and gas station in the area in an effort to trace the missing car.

"I just had a call from Sheriff Murphy," the police chief said. "Some of his deputies near Cedarwood picked up a man driving south from Pueblo in a tan sedan. They're bringing him here for questioning."

Pratt told Grady of the "Bob" mentioned in the girl's diary. "If she'd ridden with this Bob before, she might not have hesitated to accept a ride again. The way I see it, he may have known the time Alice came home from nursing school every night and was waiting for her in the car."

"That seems to make sense," Grady said. "We'd better check up on him right away. Some of Alice's friends must know who he is."

Margaret Driscoll said that there were two young men named Bob in the crowd she and Alice went with.

"But she must have meant Bob McShane in the diary," Margaret said.

"He drives a car and he's got a crush on Alice."

The girl supplied the address of McShane's parents and Pratt went there at once.

I remember Bob speaking of Alice," the youth's father said. "He'd taken quite a fancy to her."

"Where is Bob now?" Pratt asked.

"He went to a basketball game up in Colorado Springs. He should be back before long."

"Did he drive?"

"Yes, he took the family car." McShane said the car was a tan sedan, about two years old.

"Did anyone go with him to the game?"

"As far as I know, he went alone."

Pratt asked the officer who had come with him to wait until Robert McShane returned and then bring him to headquarters, Pratt returned there himself. He found technicians examining a light tan Chevrolet sedan which stood outside the building. In his office, Chief Grady was talking to a handsome, expensively dressed man in his 30s. The man's clothing was dishevelled and the collar on his shirt was torn.

When Pratt entered, Grady told him: "Bob, this is Albert Sterling. He's the one Sheriff Murphy phoned us about. His deputies found two bobby-pins and a woman's handkerchief in his car. His clothing was in that condition when he was picked up."

Sterling, sitting tensely in his chair, pleaded: "You fellows have got to believe me. I'm a salesman and I work all over southern Colorado. I have to be in Las Animas County tomorrow, so I left here this evening, meaning to stay overnight at Trinidad. Well, it's a lonely drive, so I stopped at the bus depot to see if I could give anybody a lift in that direction."

Pausing for breath, he continued: "I found a neat little brunette who looked about 20. I got talking to her and she said she was a waitress at a place near Cedarwood. She jumped at the chance of a ride. She was so friendly that I began getting ideas. When we were about halfway to Cedarwood, I pulled off the road and started to make a play for her.

"She said no. But you know how it is with some girls. They just like to play hard to get. If a fellow's determined enough, they finally give in and like him all the better for it.

"Not this chick, though. She fought like a pack of wildcats. When I saw I wasn't getting anywhere, I finally let her alone. She wanted to get out of the car then and there, but I said I'd drive her on to Cedarwood and no hard feelings. So I did. I'd just left there when those deputies nabbed me at the roadblock."

Chief Grady asked the waitress' name.

"Her first name was Kay," Sterling said. "She told me her last name, but it was a long name and I've forgotten it."

"Where did you let her out?"

"At the bus stop. She was going to stay overnight with her brother, who lives just out of town. I offered to drive

52

her there, but she said no, she'd telephone her brother and he'd pick her up in his car."

"Then you've no idea how we could locate this girl?"

"No, but somebody in Cedarwood must know a waitress named Kay."

Sterling said that he himself lived in Denver, but came to Pueblo several times a month. He said he did not know Alice Porter and never had been in the part of town where she lived.

"We're going to have to hold you here until we can investigate this," Grady said. So Sterling was taken to a detention room, while Grady and Pratt went out to the suspect's car. A fingerprint man pointed to places where powder had adhered to the car's inner surfaces. "There are quite a lot of prints," he said, "but none so far that correspond with those we took from Alice Porter's room. Nothing else incriminating about the car, except that there was definitely a girl in it lately. You can notice a faint odour of perfume."

The handkerchief and the bobby-pins found in Sterling's car were shown to Mrs Porter, but they were of an ordinary type and she could not identify them.

Shortly after midnight, Robert McShane was brought into the chief's office. A sallow faced, blond youth, he appeared frightened. He told Grady that he had last seen Alice Porter at high school the previous afternoon.

"Did she ever ride in your car?" Grady asked.

"Yes, I took her home after school a few times."

"And she trusted you and got into your car willingly when you asked her?"

"Yes, she did."

"Where did you go when you left the house tonight?"

"To the basketball game at Colorado Springs, like my dad said."

Asked to give an account of the game, McShane said uneasily: "I didn't get there until it was half over. I ran into a regular cloud burst on the way to Colorado Springs and pulled off the road to wait. Then the car wouldn't start. I had to dry off the spark plugs and the wiring. Even then, I had trouble getting it started."

"Where were you at 9.30?"

"I must have been stuck there."

A technician examined McShane's car. "Alice Porter's prints are in it," he reported. "But it's hard to say whether they were made tonight. They look fresh."

It was decided to detain McShane for further questioning.

Grady now telephoned newspapers, urging them to publish a detailed description of the missing girl. Since kidnapping is a federal offence, he also notified the Denver office of the FBI. From then until morning, the chief remained at his desk.

Early the next morning, Sheriff Murphy stopped in at his office. "We've questioned more than 200 drivers during the night," he reported wearily. "We're holding four men till we check their alibis further, but there's no evidence against any of them. I wouldn't be surprised if the car we're looking for is right here in Pueblo, either in a public or a private garage."

A few hours later, however, Captain Pratt called in to say that the check of garages and filling stations had brought no results.

Ward Lennon viewed the cars of the two suspects, Albert Sterling and Robert McShane. He looked critically at both vehicles. "It might have been either one," he stated at last. "At that distance I couldn't see much, though I'd swear it was a tan car."

Chief Grady now called the motor vehicle bureau in Denver and asked them to list all the tan sedans registered from Pueblo County. Detectives then went from one Pueblo address another, patiently questioning car owners, while out in the county Sheriff Murphy's men conducted a similar check.

Meanwhile, sheriff's deputies in the southern part of the county located the waitress, Kay. She confirmed that she had ridden with Sterling and that he had tried to force his attentions on her. But she said he had behaved well later and she did not wish to see him prosecuted.

Grady then released Sterling, and also released Robert McShane into the charge of his parents, since there were insufficient legal grounds for holding the youth. Despite the near-certainty that Alice Porter had been kidnapped, there was still no physical evidence that a crime had been committed.

The search for the missing girl was into its third weary day when, in midmorning, Grady received a call from Sheriff Murphy.

"I'm at Johnson's Garage in Beulah, about 25 miles southwest of Pueblo," Murphy said. "Can you get down here right away?" We've found a man we think may have seen the kidnap car."

Grady picked up Earl A. Morse, a special investigator for the district attorney's office, and sped southwest along the highway. At the garage he found Sheriff Murphy with Deputies Maurice Corrister, Walter Chrisman and Undersheriff Riley Drain. The latter, father of the murdered Dorothy Drain, was taking a strong interest in trying to solve the Porter mystery.

"This is Harry Johnson, who owns the garage," Murphy told the new arrivals. "Harry, tell these men what you told us."

The elderly garage owner said that about 4 o'clock on Thursday morning, the day after Alice's disappearance, a man came to the garage on foot.

"I was asleep in my room at the rear," Johnson went on, "and he woke me. He said that his car was bogged down in mud on a back road about three miles from here and asked me to haul him out.

"I asked him why he hadn't dozed in the car till daylight, so we could see what we were doing. He said he was in a hurry to get back to Pueblo. So I got out the wrecker and we drove to a rutted, single-track road off the highway about a mile from here. It leads to an old abandoned ranch back in the hills. We bounced along a couple of miles and there was his car, hub-deep in mud.

"Well, I got him out all right, but I couldn't figure what he'd been doing in the night at that abandoned ranch. He said he'd been looking for another road and took the wrong turn. He acted very nervous and jumpy. And as soon as we got back to the highway, he hurried away towards Pueblo."

"What colour was the car?" Grady asked.

"It was some light colour. I don't remember exactly. I do recall that it was covered with mud – including the licence plates."

"Could it have been a tan car?"

"It could have been. I can't be sure."

Johnson described the driver as tall, slightly-built, thin-faced and wearing steel-rimmed glasses. "He didn't say much, and I noticed he kept his face turned away from me."

"What do you think?" Murphy asked Grady. "Does he sound like a kidnapper? Or is he a moonshiner with a still somewhere back in the hills?"

"I think he's worth investigating," Grady said. "Let's have a look along that back road."

The ground had dried out since Wednesday night's rain, and the two cars negotiated without difficulty the twisting uphill road. At the top of the hill, surrounded by desolate, barren country, was an old ranch house of crumbling abode. Its windows were boarded up, but its front door was hanging half-off its rotted iron hinges.

Sheriff Murphy pointed to fresh tyre marks in front of the ranch house. "A car turned around here," he said. "And here's a fresh oil spot, where a car had been standing for some time. Obviously, it was made after Wednesday night's rain."

The officials entered the crumbling one-room ranch building. It was littered with broken furniture and debris.

Grady directed his attention to a heavy wooden table in the middle of the room and the surrounding floor. Accustomed as he was to gruesome sights, he gasped. The table was literally covered with freshly-dried blood, some of which had dripped onto the hard-packed earth floor. On the floor were a pair of scissors, pliers, several strands of baling wire and a shoemaker's awl. All of them bore traces of blood.

"Good God!" Murphy gasped.

One by one, further evidences of a gruesome crime revealed themselves to the shocked officials. In a rude fireplace at one side of the room were the charred remnants of a woman's dress, the frame of a handbag, metal holders for cosmetics, and a number of Pueblo street-car ticket tokens. While Murphy and his deputies searched the room, Grady and Morse went outside. At the rear of the house they spotted the wooden cover of a cistern.

They lifted it aside and shone their flashlights into the murky depths below.

"Murphy, come here!" Grady's voice was hoarse with shock. The others came running from the house. In the cistern lay the nude and mutilated body of Alice Porter.

Undersheriff Riley Drain, whose own daughter had been the victim of a brutal killer, muttered: "I'm going to find the monster responsible for this, if I have to devote the rest of my life to it."

The body was covered with a cloth and lifted gently into one of the cars. Drain and Corrister volunteered to remain on watch at the abandoned ranch, while the others drove back to Pueblo. The body was taken to the mortuary, where Marvin Porter made formal identification. Then he broke down completely.

The coroner examined the body prior to autopsy. He emerged from the examination room, pale and shaken. "I've never seen anything like it, never," he said hoarsely. "Alice was bound to the table, nude, then tortured by a sex-crazed fiend. Her killer apparently heated the baling wire and used it to brand her. He stabbed her repeatedly with the awl. Then he criminally assaulted her. She bled slowly through several hours of agony, before he struck her head with some heavy object, probably to stun her. Then he shot her twice through the head."

News of the atrocity spread rapidly. Evening newspapers throughout Colorado carried the story in blazing headlines. In Pueblo, the police were swamped with telephone calls from outraged citizens who demanded that the sex slayer be found before he could attack again.

Meanwhile, Chief Grady and the Pueblo police worked on virtually a round-the-clock schedule. Robert McShane was definitely eliminated as a suspect when the garage owner stated positively that he was not the person whose car he had towed out of the mud. Nothing further had been found to connect the slaying of Alice Porter with the Dorothy Drain case.

Left with no suspects at all, Chief Grady threw himself into the task of evaluating the fresh evidence that had been found. Plaster moulds were made of the tyre marks found at the scene of the crime. The articles found in the ranch house were examined by technicians, and clear, sharp fingerprints were found on the awl. Criminal files were searched, but the prints could not be identified.

Then Grady was struck by an idea. Ward Lennon, the man who had heard the scream and seen the murder car driven away, had said repeatedly that he believed the car was tan in colour. But Lennon had admittedly seen the car only briefly and in poor light. Harry Johnson, the garage owner, had got a much better view of the car, but had observed only that it was "some light colour." Johnson had emphasised that the car was covered with mud. Perhaps Lennon had seen a car of some other colour covered with mud. Margaret Driscoll had said that the car she saw might have been a light grey one.

Grady instructed Captain Pratt to widen his search to include all light-coloured sedans. "And if the murder car was covered with mud when it was seen by Johnson, it seems to me the first thing the killer would do would be to wash it. Check up to see if it was washed in a public garage.

Captain Pratt gave the new instructions to his men early on Sunday morning. Towards noon, a detective and a patrolman walked into a garage owned by Boyd Whaley on East Fourth Street in Pueblo.

"There haven't been any new tan-coloured sedans in here since the last time you came, or I'd have got in touch with you," Whaley said.

"We're looking for something else this trip," the detective told him. "A very muddy car of any light colour that was brought in for a wash job."

Whaley stared at him. "Why, I've got a car like that here right now! I don't usually wash cars on Sundays, but the fellow said he was in a hurry, so I told him I'd have it for him. He said he'd pick it up at 6 o'clock.

"Who was the man?"

"I don't know. Never saw him before."

The detective took one look at a mud-covered grey Ford sedan and telephoned Captain Pratt. The latter was particularly interested in the caked mud adhering to the rear hub caps and rear axle. It was a car that had recently been stuck in deep mud.

The two officers waited at the garage all afternoon.

Promptly at 6 o'clock, a thin-faced, bespectacled man in his 20s walked into the garage and asked for his car.

"It's over there by the door," Whaley told him. "You can drive it out yourself."

As the thin-faced man reached for the door handle of his car, firm hands seized him by the arms.

Brought before Chief Grady, the suspect gave his name as Donald H. Fearn. "But why have you brought me here?" he demanded. "I haven't done anything. I was just getting my car to visit my wife in the hospital. She had her second baby 10 days ago."

A telephone call to the hospital confirmed Fearn's statement.

Asked if he had known Alice Porter, Fearn shook his head. "So that's what it's all about?" he said. "Well, you've made a mistake. I certainly don't know her."

"Then, if you're in the clear, you won't mind giving us your fingerprints, will you?" Grady asked him.

Fearn hesitated briefly. Then he shrugged. "Go ahead and take them if you want. Why should I mind?"

About 15 minutes after his fingerprints were sent to the laboratory, Grady's phone rang.

"The prints of the right hand match the prints on the awl," a technician said. "There's not the slightest question of it."

Grady asked for the two sets of prints. He showed them to Fearn, indicating points of identity marked by the expert.

"You're guilty and you know it, Fearn!" the chief said sharply. "You'll tell us about it sooner or later. It may as well be now."

Fearn stared numbly at the identical prints, then down at the floor. "I killed her," he mumbled.

A stenographer was summoned. For the next two hours,

the officers listened to an incredible tale of horror and depravity.

"I always wanted to torture a girl," Fearn said unemotionally. "I'd planned it several times before. I picked out the place for it and made a number of trips there to be sure it was all right. It was. No matter how much she screamed, I was sure no one would hear.

"I hung around that nursing class to pick out my victim. I'd follow the streetcar and watch where each girl lived. I decided on Alice Porter because she lived in a lonely block.

"I waited till my wife was in the hospital, so she wouldn't get suspicious if I was out all night. On Wednesday night I parked just down the street from the Porter house. When Alice came along, I drew up beside her, stepped out and pulled my gun on her. I ordered her into the car. But she screamed. I grabbed her, threw her inside and drove off."

Fearn told the officials in lurid detail of the depravity he had committed at the ranch house. After six hours of unbelievable torture, he snuffed out her life.

"I didn't want to kill her particularly," he said. "But I knew I'd have to, so she wouldn't identify me. I struck her over the head with a hammer I had in the car. Then I shot her twice and threw her body in the cistern."

News leaked out that an arrest had been made in the Alice Porter case, and reporters were soon swarming outside Grady's office, waiting for a statement. Grady knew what the temper of the public would be when the headlines hit the newsstands. To avoid any possibility of a lynching, he had Fearn driven secretly to the state penitentiary at Canon City.

Further proof of Fearn's guilt was provided when the tyres on his car were matched to the tread marks found at the scene of the crime. Alice Porter's fingerprints were also found inside his car.

Fearn was indicted for first-degree murder, tried and convicted. On October 23rd, 1942, he paid the penalty for his shocking crime in the gas chamber at Canon City.

So cleverly had Fearn hidden the vicious depravity of his nature from his family that they refused to believe the police chief's report of his confession. Not until that confession was read at the trial did they reluctantly give up their belief in his innocence.

George Vedder Jones

Harry Dobkin: The Skeleton in the Cellar

The case of Harry Dobkin is one of the classics of forensic detection, and Professor Keith Simpson's work on it ranks with that of Spilsbury on the Crippen case and Glaister on the double murder committed by Buck Ruxton. This version is told in Simpson's own words from his autobiography *Forty Years of Murder* (1978). I was acquainted with Simpson who, in spite of the rather cold and forbidding look of his photographs – that vast, egg-shaped head reminds one of Sherlock Holmes –, was a friendly man. When he sent me his book, I was excited by it, and suggested that we work together in turning it into a television series. He was enthusiastic about the idea; but alas, televison companies take years to make up their minds, and by the time things began to look promising, Simpson had died.

I was only thirty-five when I had the sort of case every young pathologist dreams of, "the case of a lifetime", Molly Lefebure called it. It certainly had all the ingredients, and, but for the heavy shadow of a war that still hung desperately in the balance, it would have hit the news headlines as Crippen did in Spilsbury's younger days.

On 17th July 1942, a workman helping to demolish a bombed Baptist church premises in Vauxhall Road, South London, drove his pick under a heavy stone slab set on the floor of a cellar under the vestry and prised it up. Underneath lay a skeleton with a few tags of flesh clinging to it, which he assumed to be the remains of another victim of the Blitz. He put his shovel under the skeleton and lifted it out. The head stayed on the ground.

Detective Inspectors Hatton and Keeling, who were called in to investigate, wrapped the bones in a brown paper parcel and took them to the public mortuary at Southwark, where I inspected them the next morning. The sight of a dried-up womb tucked down in the remains of the trunk established the sex. There was a yellowish deposit on the head and neck. Fire had blackened parts of the skull, the hip, and the knees.

Could she have been the victim of a bomb explosion? Hardly likely, considering she had been lying neatly buried under a slab of stone, neatly set in the floor of a cellar; this was no bomb crater. The detectives told me there had been an ancient cemetery on the site: could the body have been there fifty years? I shook my head. Soft tissues do not last so long. I thought the body was only about twelve to eighteen months dead. The church had been blitzed in August 1940, almost two years before.

Who was it? How had it got there? Was it murder? These questions were obviously going to take a lot of answering, and neither the cellar nor an old-fashioned mortuary was a suitable place for a scientific reconstruction. I asked the Coroner, Hervey Wyatt, for permission to take it to my laboratory at Guy's to sort it out in the only way possible – a slow step-by-step laboratory reconstruction.

The head had not broken off when the workman had shovelled up the skeleton, as he had thought. It had been cut off. Further, both arms had been cut off at the elbow, and both legs at the knee. Bomb blast could do strange things, I knew from experience, but not as strange as that. Someone had dismembered the body.

Pieces of the limbs were missing, and the first job was to try to find them. I spent two afternoons with the police sifting nearly three tons of earth from under the floor of the cellar. We found animal bones but nothing human. However, I noted two interesting things in the cellar: a yellowish powder on the earth where the body had been buried, and a wooden chest slightly less than five feet long.

John Ryffel, the Home Office analyst and Head of the

Department of Clinical Chemistry at Guy's, analysed both the powder from the cellar and the yellowish deposit on the body, and reported that she had been buried in slaked lime.

I reassembled the body and measured it. After making due allowance for missing bones and soft tissues, I calculated the height as 5 feet 1/2 inch. I checked this by reference to the well-known "Pearson's formulae" and also the less reliable Rollet's tables, both of which give estimates of height based on one of the long bones of the limbs. I had one long bone, the left humerus. Pearson and Rollet differed slightly, but the mean was 5 feet 1/2 inch.

The woman's neck was bent at a fairly sharp angle upon the trunk, and if she had been like that in life she would have been a conspicuous figure. I had X-ray photographs taken to see if there had been any disease to cause curvature of the spine. Nothing was found, and I concluded the neck had been bent after death. Why? Perhaps, at some stage, to cram the body into a space that was a little too small for it. As it was, it would have just fitted into the wooden chest. I examined this for bloodstains, but all the tests were negative.

How old was she? I had X-ray photographs taken of the skull plates, which join together at pretty constant periods between the 'teens and old age. Her brow plates were completely fused, fusion was in progress between the top plates, and there was no fusion between the two groups. That put her age between forty and fifty.

The person who had dismembered the body had evidently tried to make her utterly unidentifiable. The scalp and hair, face, eyes, hands and feet had all gone. No, not quite all: I found a fragment of hair sticking to the back of her skull. It was dark brown, going grey.

The uterus was enlarged. Another X-ray photograph, in case there was a pregnancy. No foetal bones. Instead, the swelling proved to be a fibroid tumour, three to four inches in diameter, for which she might well have sought medical attention.

Teeth? Her lower jaw had gone completely, but in the upper jaw I found as much dental information as a portrait, if her dentist could ever be found. Three molars on the right, two of them filled; the first molar on the left also filled. Marks from the metal claws of a dental plate. A high palate, and considerable thickening of the bone in the region of the back teeth. It was a mine of information. "If you trace her dentist, and he has kept proper records, you'll identify her beyond doubt," I told the police.

Inspector Keeling thought he might have found her. Working through the lists of missing persons, he discovered that Rachel Dobkin, the wife of the fire-watcher to the bombed Baptist Church premises, had disappeared after setting out to visit him to collect arrears of maintenance fifteen months previously. Her sister, Polly Dubinski, had reported her disappearance to the police.

Rachel was forty-seven, Polly said. Height about 5 feet to 5 feet 1 inch, "the same height as me". Dark hair going grey. She had been going to hospital about "something internal". Her dentist was Mr Kopkin – a strangely close spelling! – of Stoke Newington. Polly gave the police a photograph of Rachel.

Yes, said Dr Marie Watson, of the Mildmay Mission Hospital, Bethnal Green, she had examined Mrs Rachel Dobkin in October 1939, and found fibroid growths of the uterus. Yes, confirmed another doctor, at the London Hospital, fibroid growths of the uterus: an operation had been advised, but Mrs Dobkin had refused.

Yes, said Barnett Kopkin, the dental surgeon, recognizing Rachel Dobkin from the photograph – yes, she had been his patient for six years. From April 1934 to March 1940, to be precise; and Kopkin could be very precise, for his record cards were the most comprehensive that Inspector Keeling had ever seen.

"From these cards", he asked, "could you draw a picture of her upper jaw as it was when you saw her last?"

Kopkin sat down in his consulting room and drew the diagram. At Keeling's request he signed and dated it: 3rd August 1942, at 11 a.m. Then Keeling brought him to my laboratory at Guy's, where the skull of Rachel Dobkin lay upside down on the bench.

"That's my patient!" he burst out excitedly, before I had

time to greet him. "That's Mrs Dobkin! Those are my fillings!"

It was as dramatic a moment as I can remember. Molly Lefebure nearly fell off her lab stool.

Inspector Keeling produced the diagram the dental surgeon had made. It was an exact replica of the upper jaw from the cellar – teeth in the right positions, fillings just so, gap for the denture, claw marks – but also a couple of possible extra: tiny fragments of the roots of the first and second pre-molars on the left side that Kopkin thought he might have left in the jaw when extracting those teeth in April 1934. These did not appear on our X-ray photographs.

We had the jaw X-rayed again, this time by Guy's own senior dental surgeon, the famous Sir William Kelsey Fry. He found the fragments.

Meanwhile I had been feeling my way in photography myself, with the help of Mary Newman, who was in charge of the Photographic Department of Guy's. Now that we had a photograph of the missing woman, a full-face portrait, I wanted to try to superimpose it on a similar photograph of the skull. This identification technique had been used first in 1936, by Professors Glaister and Brash, in the famous case of Buck Ruxton, the Indian doctor who had murdered his wife and her maid and thrown their dismembered bodies into a ravine. Having the jumbled remains of two bodies, Glaister and Brash had been concerned with sorting out the pieces. I had only one head and one photograph, and I wanted to see how far they matched.

Miss Newman photographed the skull and photographed the portrait, and enlarged the latter to the same size. Then she made fresh photographs on X-ray film, a negative of the skull and a positive of the portrait, and placed them together superimposed. We found no dissimilarities whatever. The portrait fitted the skull like a mask.

Keeling was so pleased you would think he had caught the murderer. And in a sense he had; at least, he had him half in the bag.

Murderer? It is all very well to say you do not find yourself in several pieces under a slab of stone in the floor of a Baptist Church cellar unless something sinister has been going on, but that is not enough for a charge of murder. What evidence was there that she had been killed?

Probably there would have been none, but for a very important contribution by the murderer himself. In sprinkling slaked lime over the body he had no doubt intended to keep down the smell of decomposition and perhaps to destroy the soft tissues. Lime has a reputation for burning human flesh. But slaked lime has little or no destructive action; on the contrary, by killing maggots and beetles it acts as a preservative. Thanks to the lime, certain injuries to the throat, in part to the voice box, had been preserved in this way.

It was another dramatic moment, late in the evening, when I was alone in my laboratory and dissected out the voice box and saw that the upper horn of the thyroid cartilage on the right side was fractured. There was a little blood clot round it, so the workmen had not done the damage with their picks and shovels. It had occurred in life.

Now this little bone never gets broken, alone, except when the neck is gripped tight by a strangling hand. It is the pressure of a finger tip or thumb that does it.

"Are you quite sure, doctor?" Could I really say it was strangling without the classic signs, the imprint of fingers, the asphyxia? Both Hatton and Keeling were very tense.

"I'm certain. This means strangling. This little bone gets broken in no other way. I am quite prepared to say so in court. And if any other pathologist wants to confirm the injury for himself, well, there it is. We'll keep it and I'll have microscopic sections made to confirm the bruising."

I found another possible bruise on the back of the head. It could have followed upon the throat being gripped and the head bashed against the ground, but it might equally have followed upon a fall. This was a much less significant injury, and as there were no tissues left for microscopical examination I could not be so sure it had occurred before death.

My work was done. I had, I thought, enough evidence to convince a jury that the skeleton was Rachel Dobkin, and that she had been murdered by strangling some fifteen months previously. It was for the police to show who had killed her.

Rachel Dubinski had married the future fire-watcher in September 1920. The union had been arranged, according to Jewish custom, by a marriage-broker, and it was an immediate failure. The couple separated after three days; but nine months later a child was born, a boy. In 1923 Mrs Dobkin obtained a maintenance order. Dobkin was most irregular with payments, from 1923 to 1940 or so, and several times he served a term of imprisonment in default. Rachel had been reduced to waylaying him in the street to obtain some payment, and he had come to regard her as a pestering nuisance. On four separate occasions she summoned him for assault, but each time the magistrate dismissed the charge.

On 11th April 1941, Good Friday, the couple had tea together in a café in Dalston. They left at about 6.30 p.m., and Rachel was never seen again. Next day at 3 p.m. her sister Polly reported her disappearance to the police, saying she suspected Harry of foul play. But London was at war, the police were undermanned and overworked, and Harry was not interviewed until 16th April. Meanwhile, on the night of 14th-15th April, a mysterious fire had occurred on the Baptist Church premises.

It was mysterious because there had been no enemy action that night, and no inflammable material was kept in the cellar behind the church where the fire apparently began. Another mystery was that Harry Dobkin, the fire-watcher, did not give the alarm. The fire was first noticed by a patrolling constable, at 3.20 a.m. He summoned the Fire Brigade and went into the premises, where he met Dobkin. "I'm glad you've come, gentlemen," the fire-watcher greeted him. "It's a terrible blaze, isn't it?"

The fire was put out, and the minister, the Rev. Herbert Burgess, went round taking stock of the damage. In the cellar he saw the charred remains of a straw mattress; it appeared to have been ripped open, and straw from it had been scattered in heaps over the floor. Mr Burgess sought out Dobkin and asked him what he knew about it. The fire-watcher said he had tried to put out the fire and then called the Fire Brigade. Mr Burgess felt very strongly that the fire had been deliberately caused and he made an entry to that effect in his diary.

The next day, 16th April, there was what was officially called an "incident" at Kennington Oval, less that 250 yards from the church, killing 23 persons and injuring more than twice as many. Enemy planes had dropped a land mine. When such disasters were considered only incidental, it is not surprising that a small fire in an unoccupied cellar was just put out and forgotten. The police did not mention it when they asked Harry Dobkin that day about the disappearance of his wife. He told them he had not seen her since they had tea together on 11th April.

The police circulated a description of Rachel and inquired at hospitals and the other usual places, including the Central Air Raid Casualty Bureau. The police found out nothing more, but evidently had suspicions, for on 28th April, and again on 1st and 2nd May, they searched the Church premises, dug up the floor of the crypt, and discovered a freshly dug hole some 6 feet long by 2 feet wide. It was empty. The police finally published Rachel's photograph in the *Police Gazette* and then filed the case away.

All of which made very interesting reading for Hatton and Keeling more than a year later.

Dobkin had left his job as fire-watcher in May 1942 and was living in Dalston when his wife's remains were unearthed. Three weeks later a constable who knew him by sight saw him enter the Baptist Church premises at about 6 a.m. The constable, who was on a bicycle, stopped and watched, and presently saw Dobkin look out of an upstairs window.

Not a word about the skeleton had yet leaked into the press, Hatton waited until 26th August before asking Dobkin himself to "assist the police in their inquiries". Hatton took

Dobkin to the cellar and showed him where his wife's strangled body had been found.

"I wouldn't strangle a woman," he said. "I wouldn't hit a woman. Some men might, but I wouldn't. I didn't know the cellar was here, and I've certainly never been down here in my life." He also said he had not been back to the premises since leaving his job in May.

"I have information," Hatton told him, "that a policeman saw you going into the house on 4th August."

"Show him to me, the liar!" demanded Dobkin excitedly. "Show him to me!"

The officer, P.C. Wakeley, magically appeared. "That's the man," he said. "I've spoken to him several times at Kennington Lane about lights he has shown. I know him well."

"That's a lie!" shouted Dobkin. "I've never seen him before and I wasn't there. He's lying, he's lying!"

Inspector Hatton then formally charged him with the murder of his wife.

The trial of Harry Dobkin opened at the Old Bailey on 17th November 1942. F.H. Lawton, not yet a K.C. but later to become Mr Justice Lawton, appeared for the defence, which consulted my friend Eric Gardner on the medico-legal aspects of the case. Gardner told me later that he had advised them not to challenge the identification evidence, but Lawton chose to fight identity step by step.

"Anybody with a neck with that curvature would be a very obvious sight in life, would they not?" he asked me.

"If it was present in life."

"It would be obvious?"

"Very obvious indeed."

"If it was present in life, it could not be Mrs Dobkin, could it?"

"It was not present in life."

"That is not quite the question which I asked you: if it was present in life it could not be Mrs Dobkin?"

"But I am not prepared to consider the question whether it was present in life, because I found evidence to show it was not."

With forensic skill and remarkable medical knowledge he challenged my opinion about the dead woman's age and teeth (and gave Kopkin, who followed me, an even harder time). He also questioned me, but with an ominous lack of scepticism, about the dead woman's height.

"Taking a combination of all three methods of calculating stature, what do you say are the outside limits of stature, both up and down?"

"Working from the average height I expressed of 5 feet ½ inch, I think the possible limits are really an inch in either direction."

"So the maximum height would be what?"

"Five feet one and a half inches."

"So if Mrs Dobkin in life was 5 feet 3 inches, then this body cannot be that of Mrs Dobkin?"

"Yes." It was the only possible answer. But what was the point of the question? Counsel had something up his sleeve; he had asked Polly Dubinski at the beginning of the trial if her sister could have been 5 feet 3 inches. Why that figure? And why did counsel seem so pleased with my reply?

He left it at that for the time being, and went on to challenge the evidence of the superimposed photographs, quoting from Glaister and Brash's book on the Buck Ruxton case.

"And you are saying in this case that the photograph and the photograph of the skull together help you to make a decision as to identity?" he asked lightly, casually, as if he was not going to bother me much longer on the subject.

"Yes," I said.

"And a positive decision?"

"Yes."

The trap had closed. "Now may I turn," counsel using his heaviest voice, "to a passage on page 161 of Professor Glaister's book and see what you say about it." I waited uneasily. "'Owing to the novelty of the method and the uncertainty of some parts of the technique, a positive identification of the skulls, no matter how close a correspondence of skulls and portraits was obtained, would have been open to very grave objection.'" I had expected worse; I was relieved. "Do you agree with that?" counsel asked earnestly.

"I think it has an element of truth: it is open to objection," I said at once. "It is being used to give assistance in identification, not to prove identification."

"It is just part of the circumstantial evidence?"

"It is not circumstantial."

"You say it is direct?"

"It is scientific evidence."

"You do not agree with the words at the end of the sentence which I read to you, that this method is 'open to very grave objection'?"

"I think it is open to objection."

"But not very grave objection?"

"I should not have used those words myself."

"Now let us see why it is open to objection", and again this young barrister showed a disconcerting grasp of scientific data and technique. But I had disarmed him by conceding the limited value of the evidence.

As I had expected, counsel saved his heaviest guns for the evidence of strangling.

He asked me to imagine somebody standing in the road, or on a piece of waste land with a lot of rubble about, parts of bricks and so on, when a bomb exploded and the blast throws him violently forward so that in falling he catches his voice box on a kerb or a piece of brick or masonry or something like that. "Is it not possible – I do not put it any higher than that – that a fall under those circumstances might break the horn of the right thyroid?"

"I have seen injuries under those circumstances on many occasions," I said, "and the injuries have never been confined to a fracture of the horn, as present here."

I said I had seen the whole thyroid crushed, with fractures of both horns and both wings; I had seen only one wing and one horn broken together. But never only the horn. "In fifteen years I have personally examined over 11,000 cases, and I have never seen this injury except in manual strangulation."

"Do you say it is impossible?"

"I say that I have never seen it; and I have seen many falls and many strangulations."

Counsel asked me how many of my 11,000 cases showed any fracture of the thyroid.

"I can obtain such figures from my records, if necessary. I cannot say off-hand."

"Of course you cannot. I was wondering if I might suggest to you, then we can have a round figure" – counsel clearly hadn't consulted Eric Gardner about this – "that the number was well under fifty."

"No."

"More than that?"

"It would run into several hundreds."

It was Lawton's only slip, and at the end of the trial he gave us a bad few minutes. Harry Dobkin had spent more than a day in the witness box, largely to his own detriment, and now Counsel for the Defence was asking for one of the Crown witnesses to be recalled. "My lord, about twenty minutes ago a document came into my possession, and I wish to ask Miss Polly Dubinski a question on it. It is a matter of very great importance," he urged, looking young and guileless, "and, as I say, until twenty minutes ago I had no knowledge of it."

The document was a copy of the *News of the World* of 4th May 1941. The "Missing from Home" column included a description and photograph of Rachel Dobkin, both of which had been supplied to the newspaper by her sister Polly. Counsel began to read it out: "Height, about 5 feet 3 inches."

And he had got me to say that if Mrs Dobkin had been 5 feet 3 inches, the body from the cellar was not Mrs Dobkin!

But Polly denied she had told the newspaper 5 feet 3 inches. "I gave my evidence of 5 feet 1 inch. She was almost my own height."

Everybody was looking her up and down, literally, trying to guess her height. Dobkin would certainly be acquitted if Polly was 5 feet 3 inches. But neither the Crown nor the Defence suggested she should be measured then and there. Every pair of eyes followed her as she left the witness box and walked out of court.

Three more witnesses were called for the defence. Then Lawton: "My lord, that is the case for the defence."

L.A. Byrne, the Crown counsel, was on his feet. "Your Lordship will recall that Miss Dubinski . . . Since she was recalled I have had her measured . . ."

The judge gave permission for Byrne to call the police officer who had measured her. No witness was listened to more attentively.

What is your name . . . What are you? . . . Did you take the height measurement . . . (On and on went the preliminaries.) Is *that* the woman? . . . Was that at Snow Hill Police Station? . . .

And then, at last:

"What did you find her height to be?"

"Height without shoes, 4 feet 11¾ inches; height with shoes, 5 feet 1 inch."

And that was that. The jury took only twenty minutes to find Dobkin guilty of murder. He was executed at Wandsworth, where I had the lugubrious duty of performing the routine post-mortem that the law demanded, if only to show that the sentence had been "expeditiously carried out". It had.

Keith Simpson

The Wigwam Murder

In 1942, Simpson acquired himself a secretary, an
attractive blonde journalist named Molly Lefebure;
when she left him to get married five years later,
she wrote a book about her experiences called
Evidence for the Crown (1955), one of the liveliest
books ever written about murder. She tells the
story of the Wigwam Murder in the chapter
that follows immediately on her account of the
Dobkin case.

We must now go back to the beginning of October 1942
and those days when D.D.I. Hatton was in the throes
of arresting Dobkin, and was receiving all those wordy notes,
"Divisional Inspector, Dear Sir . . ."

That was in Southwark, among sooty warehouses and grey
old streets. In Surrey, against a background of autumn-tinted
trees and windy heathland slopes, another outstanding murder drama came to light.

On October 7th C.K.S. got a call from the Surrey police,
saying that a body had been found buried on Hankley
Common, near Godalming, and they were anxious for
Dr Simpson to come at once. We cancelled all other
appointments and by midday we were driving fast in the
direction of Godalming.

Hankley Common was a former beauty spot, all heathery
slopes, broken with graceful spinneys of birch and oak,
and surrounded by wide vistas of wooded countryside and
windswept sky. The Army, noting its loveliness, had of
course taken it over as a battle-training ground. Camps
had been built in the neighbouring woods and every day
young men were taken out and toughened up amidst a welter

of anti-tank obstacles, mortar ranges, field telephones and trip-wires.

We arrived at Hankley Common to find a large party of policemen, headed by the Chief Constable of Surrey and Supt. Roberts, and fortified by Dr Eric Gardner, the pathologist, awaiting us in a muddy hollow. Greetings were exchanged and then off we set to climb a windy ridge which reared itself, rain-swept and dismal, ahead of us.

(It is odd how it invariably begins to rain when one reaches the scene of a crime. Up till that time, for instance, it had been quite a bright sunny day.

As we struggled up the ridge, Supt. Roberts told us how the body was found. The previous day two marines, busy training, had discovered an arm sticking out of a mound of earth on the top of the ridge and had immediately reported this to the police. The body had been left buried until the pathologists should arrive.

The top of the ridge was gained and there was the mound of earth with a withered arm sticking out from the side of it. Rats had gnawed away parts of the fingers. We stood contemplating it, shivering a little in the wet wind, and trying to warm ourselves with cigarettes, while the Chief Constable, Dr Gardner, Dr Simpson and Supt. Roberts held a quick consultation. Below us a party of soldiers were busy at mortar practice, their shells whirling and whining over our heads every few minutes.

The two pathologists now took shovels and began very carefully uncovering the rest of the body. They had not been long at the job before a great stench of rotting flesh set everybody else busily judging the direction of the wind and then moving accordingly. The pathologists continued to dig, oblivious of everything but their task, and I was obliged to stay beside them, taking from them specimens of beetles, maggots, earth and heather, which I placed in the famous buff envelopes. And so the work went slowly on, until there lay exposed the sprawling, badly decomposed body of a girl.

The body was clothed in a green and white summer dress, light summer underwear, woollen ankle-socks, and a headscarf which lay loosely round the neck. The head had been battered in by some heavy, blunt implement.

It was decided to move the body to Guy's, and there was some discussion as to whether C.K.S. and I should travel back to London in a van with the body or by police-car. Much to my relief the police-car was finally chosen.

The body soon arrived at Guy's and C.K.S. had it placed in a large carbolic tank so that he might study it at his leisure, or, if you prefer it, in his "spare time".

"Spare time" mostly came at tea-time, so, for the next few weeks, C.K.S. arranged for us to take our tea beside the carbolic tank and its gruesome contents. This, I thought, was a very unattractive idea, for the smell of the body combined with the carbolic was enough to put the most insensitive off anchovy-toast and tea-cakes. However, it was not my place to complain, so there I sat with my tea-tray and memo-pad, jotting the notes which C.K.S. dictated to me as he stooped, all concentration, over the body.

Dr Gardner frequently came up to Guy's to assist with the examination of the body. The two pathologists discovered that the girl had received stabbing wounds to the left side of the top of the head, accompanied by similar wounds to the right arm and hand; these last resulting from the victim putting up her arm in an attempt to ward off the attack.

The pathologists came to a very interesting conclusion about these stab wounds. Because of certain characteristics it was clear they must have been inflicted with a hook-pointed knife. Neither Dr Simpson nor Dr Gardner had ever seen such a knife, but the nature of the wounds convinced them that such a knife must have been used.

Secondly, there were injuries to the mouth in keeping with the girl having fallen heavily on to her face, knocking out her front teeth.

Thirdly, there had been a single very heavy, blunt blow to the back of the head. Dr Simpson and I spent a whole after-noon wiring together all the fragments of shattered skull; it was like doing an exceptionally thrilling and elaborate jigsaw puzzle. When we had finished we found there was a vast depressed fracture of the skull, five inches in length and one-and-three-quarters in breadth, across the back of the head, as from a blow with a stake, or bough, or rounded bar. Such a blow would have killed the girl immediately.

A crush fracture of the right cheek-bone showed that she had been lying face downwards on the ground at the time she received this blow.

Lastly there were dragging wounds to the right leg, which had occurred after death, and which indicated that her body had been dragged over rough, open ground before burial.

So, from these tea-time sessions beside the carbolic tank, C. K. S. was able to tell the police that the girl had been stabbed at with a strange hook-pointed knife, had fallen on her face, knocking out three teeth, and while lying thus had been dealt a tremendously heavy murderous blow to the back of her head with a round, blunt instrument such as a bar, or stake, and finally, being dead, had been dragged over rough ground to the top of the ridge.

Meantime things had not been standing still in Surrey, either.

The Surrey police had decided to call in Scotland Yard, and Mr Greeno, now a Chief Inspector, had gone down to Godalming, on what was to prove one of his most exciting investigations.

It did not take the police long to identify the dead girl, through the clothes she was wearing and a portion of scalp with bleached blonde hair. A blonde girl in her late teens, wearing a green and white frock and a head-scarf, was already known to the local police; she had for some time past caused them concern by her mode of life, for she lived rough like a tramp and consorted with soldiers. She was not, the police thought, a really bad girl, but she had run away from her home, and was in need of proper care and protection, or she would, they surmised, rapidly come to grief.

Her name was Joan Pearl Wolfe, she was a Roman Catholic with a strong religious conviction and, alas, poor girl, she surely came to grief.

She had last been seen alive on September 13th, which tallied with Dr Simpson's estimate of the time which must have elapsed since death.

Mr Greeno on his arrival set his men to searching the ground round Hankley Common ridge. Day in, day out, they searched.

Bit by bit they collected clues. First they found the girl's shoes, lying some distance apart from one another, and some way from the body's burial-place. Then a bag with a rosary in it was found near one of the shoes, close by a small stream where there was a military trip-wire. Sixteen yards away was found a heavy birch stake. Clinging to this stake were a number of long blonde hairs.

Later, in a small dell up the hillside above the stream, Joan Pearl Wolfe's identity card was found, with a religious tract, and a document which was issued by the Canadian Army to men applying for permission to marry. There was also a green purse, an elephant charm, and a letter from Joan to a Canadian private called August Sangret, telling him she was pregnant by him and hoping he would marry her.

Mr Greeno learned that Joan, since July, had been living in the neighbourhood in rough huts, or "wigwams", which August Sangret had built for her, and where he had spent his leaves with her.

A deserted cricket pavilion which had also been a favourite rendezvous for Joan and Sangret was visited by the detective. Inside, Joan had drawn and scribbled all over the walls. She had drawn a wild rose, writing under it, "Wild Rose of England for ever – September 1942." And there was another sketch of a cabin, "My little grey home in the West." And a prayer written in pencil:

"O holy Virgin in the midst of all thy glory we
implore thee not to forget the sorrows of this world . . ."

There was also pencilled the address of Private A. Sangret, of Canada, and the address of Joan's mother in Kent.

The girl, at one stage, it was discovered, had been admitted to a local hospital, where she kept a photograph of Sangret, her "fiancé", on her bedside locker. From hospital she had written to tell him she was pregnant; pathetic letters explaining that the nuns at the convent where she had been brought up had taught her that an illegitimate baby was a terrible sin, but, she naïvely added, when she and Sangret were married and happy together with the baby everything would be all right.

She bought layette patterns, and people who saw this

girl-tramp in the woods in the weeks before she was murdered noticed she was knitting baby-clothes . . .

Chief Inspector Greeno now went to the nearby Canadian Army camp where Sangret was stationed. Sangret was a young man half French-Canadian, half Cree Indian. He had recently asked his C.O. for a marriage application form, but had not returned it filled in. He admitted to Mr Greeno that he had associated with Joan, but added he had not seen her since September 14th, when she had failed to keep a date with him. He had reported her "disappearance" to his provost sergeant, saying, "If she should be found, and anything has happened to her, I don't want to be mixed up in it." He had told a friend that he had sent Joan home, as she had no clothes, and he told another friend that she was in hospital. These friends of Sangret admitted to Mr Greeno that they thought Sangret's behaviour over Joan's disappearance "very strange". First he had said one thing, then he said another, and seemed very much on edge over the whole business.

While Sangret was waiting in the guard-room for this first interview with Mr Greeno he excused himself and went to the wash-house. Nobody thought anything of it, at the time . . .

Mr Greeno, after this interview, came hurrying up to Guy's. He arrived in a van, in the back of which he had what appeared to be a section of Hankley Common. There were furze and bracken, hummocks of grass, and a small tree. These were to be examined for bloodstains. There was, in addition, a Canadian Army blanket, and a battle-dress, and the birch stake that had been found by the stream.

Dr Simpson and Mr Greeno spread the blanket and battle-dress out on a table in the lab. and examined them. Both belonged to Sangret and both had recently, but not very effectively, been washed. (Sangret apparently could not, or would not, explain why he had washed them.) On the blanket, despite the washing, were faded bloodstains, distributed exactly in keeping with a person bleeding from the head and right hand that had been wrapped in the blanket. Dr Simpson decided that the body, prior to burial, had been wrapped in this blanket – and probably concealed among bushes. This would explain the very heavy maggot infestation of the body, which had clearly not been buried immediately after death.

The bloodstains on the battle-dress no doubt occurred during Sangret's attack on the girl.

The hairs on the birch stake were examined, compared with the hank of the dead girl's hair already in our possession, and proved beyond doubt to be hairs from the head of Joan Pearl Wolfe. The birch stake, too, exactly fitted the huge fracture at the back of the reconstructed skull. This was certainly the weapon with which the girl had been murdered.

"Now all we want is to find the knife," said Mr Greeno. And returned, accordingly, to searching the ground that had already been searched and searched. For it is infinite patience which so often wins the detective's day. But the knife was not lying amongst the grass and bracken of Hankley Common. Very dramatically it turned up in quite a different place . . .

In mid-November, long after all the leaves had blown down from the trees of Surrey, and Mr Greeno's investigations were plugging doggedly, but not very rapidly, along, up at the Canadian Army camp the waste-pipe of one of the wash-house basins was cleared of an obstruction which had been blocking it for the past five weeks. This obstruction turned out to be a clasp-knife; not a Canadian Army issue, but an unusual-looking knife with a hooked point; a point like a parrot's beak. And it was immediately recalled that Sangret had excused himself and gone into the wash-house while waiting for that first interview with Mr Greeno, five weeks previously. Was this Sangret's knife, and had he dropped it down the pipe in an attempt to hide it from Mr Greeno, knowing what a vital clue it would be to the detective?

It was Sangret's knife all right. One of his fellow soldiers recognised it as such. This soldier had found the knife, he said, during summer stuck in the trunk of a tree by one of the shacks Sangret had built for Joan. The soldier had pulled it out of the tree and shown it to Sangret, who had immediately claimed it as his own.

The knife was now brought to Guy's and shown to Dr Simpson. Its peculiar hook-tipped blade was, of course, precisely the sort of thing the pathologists had described after examining the stabbing wounds.

The last lap of the investigations had now been reached. C. K. S. travelled down to Surrey again and there, with Chief Inspector Greeno, made a final reconstruction of the murder at the actual scene.

It was clear now what had happened on that September afternoon when Sangret and Joan had their last date. They had quarrelled in the dell up the hillside; probably over the marriage application form which Joan was so anxious for Sangret to fill in and sign, and which he was so loath to complete. Sangret attacked the girl with his knife. She managed to escape him and, terrified, wounded and bleeding, ran down the hill away from him, but at the bottom, by the stream, she fell over the military trip-wire, landing heavily on her face, smashing her teeth. As she lay there, stunned by the fall, Sangret overtook her and murdered her by a crashing blow on the head with the birch stake, which he afterwards flung away. He then wrapped her body in an army blanket and hid it under the bushes for twenty-four hours or so, after which he dragged his victim to the top of the ridge, a distance of some four hundred yards, and buried her.

This reconstruction of the murder must have fitted the actual circumstances very closely, for at the trial Sangret's Counsel never questioned it.

It seemed odd, perhaps, that Sangret should have troubled to drag the body up a fairly steep hill for burial, but perhaps, almost unconsciously, he was following the ritual of his Indian ancestors, who always buried their vanquished enemies upon a height.

Sangret was charged with the murder on December 16th in the presence of Mr Greeno. He said, "No, sir, I did not do it. No, sir. Somebody did it and I'll have to take the rap." He added, uselessly, "She might have killed herself."

The trial was held at Kingston Assizes at the end of the following February. Dr Simpson took the skull along with him to court. We arrived just before the court adjourned for tea. Dr Grierson, then the Chief Medical Officer at Brixton prison, asked C. K. S. if he would care to take some tea down in the gaoler's room, beneath the dock. C. K. S. accepted the invitation, and I was invited too. So into the dock we climbed and thence down the short flight of steps leading to the gaoler's cellar-like quarters below.

It was a rather grim apartment, with stone floor and bare walls and several cells opening on to it. In the middle of the room was a big wooden table, laid for tea, and the gaoler, one or two policemen, two prison warders and Sangret were standing talking together. We all sat down round the table, with the exception of Sangret and the warders, who took their tea standing, buffet style; pretty obviously because Sangret didn't wish to join the tea-party. The atmosphere of the gathering was somewhat out of this world. Dr Simpson, Dr Grierson and the gaoler chatted together on the subject of juries. The policemen were discussing football. I couldn't overhear the conversation between Sangret and the warders, but it sounded amiable enough. I sat silent, eating bread-and-butter and drinking good hot thick tea from an even thicker tea-cup. Every now and again I tried to stare at Sangret without staring at him.

Sangret was a strongly-built young man of medium height, with his Red Indian blood clearly predominant. Straight features, quite impassive, cold, glittering dark eyes, straight dark hair, and a red-bronze skin. With an appetite not at all impaired by the ghastly predicament in which he found himself he enjoyed a large tea, eating and drinking noisily, holding the thick slices of bread-and-butter in both hands. Not a gracious individual with whom to share a wigwam, I mused. And not likely to make anybody a doting, devoted, baby-dandling husband, either. Did he let out a blood-curdling whoop as he crashed Joan's skull in? One could very well imagine it.

However, although he was not a very sensitive-looking man, I did not like to stare at him too much. So I sat quietly sipping tea and listening to the conversation about juries on the one hand, the conversation about who was going to be top of the League on the other, and wondering what Sangret and the warders were talking about. It was certainly the strangest tea-party I ever went to.

At length it was over, the two medical gentlemen and I returned upstairs to the court, and the gaoler and the policemen began clearing away the tea things in nice domestic style. A few minutes later Sangret was back in the dock, facing Mr Justice Macnaghten across the crowded court, and Dr Simpson was in the witness-box, telling the jury how Joan Pearl Wolfe had been murdered.

And now came an historic moment. Dr Simpson took up a cardboard box, raised its lid and lifted out the dead girl's skull, in order to demonstrate to the jury the fracture and the peculiar stab-wounds. It was the first time a murdered person's skull had ever been produced at a trial. All present craned their necks to see, including the judge; all, that is, save one, and that one was Sangret. I watched him, but only the merest twinge of curiosity flickered over his face. Indeed the impassive Redskin.

The medical and circumstantial evidence combined made an overwhelming case against Sangret and the jury found him guilty, but rather unexpectedly added a recommendation for mercy. Why they felt he deserved mercy was a bit of a puzzler to me. The girl had not been killed accidentally, during a scuffle, for the blow to her head had been a truly savage one, delivered with full murderous intent. Nevertheless, the jury felt Sangret deserved mercy.

This plea was duly considered when Sangret appealed, but it was of no avail, and he was executed at Wandsworth a week or so later.

Dr Simpson did a p.m. on him. He lay there on the p.m. table, muscular, well-built, almost good enough for one of Fenimore Cooper's novels, his handsome bronze skin marked only by the imprint of the hangman's noose around his neck, and tattooed on his arm, ironically, the name "Pearl".

Molly Lefebure

The Heirens Case

The Heirens case has intrigued criminologists for half a century – the famous inscription on the wall above a murder victim: "For heavens sake catch me before I kill more – I cannot control myself" seems the classic expression of the torment of a compulsive killer.

I wrote about the case for the first time in 1960 in *An Encyclopedia of Murder*, co-authored with Pat Pitman. It fascinated me because it seemed so typical of what I had called "the age of sex crime", discussed more fully in the introduction to this book. The first recorded sex crimes had been simply a matter of rape – like those decribed in the diary of the 16th century Nuremberg executioner Hans Schmidt, and this has continued to be true throughout most of the 20th century. Yet the Marquis de Sade, that patron saint of sex crime, had made it very clear that sexual violence is essentially a matter of the imagination.

Now pubescent teenagers have always been subject to intense sexual daydreams – even William Blake speaks of them in one of his poems; but these daydreams are seldom put into practice, at least with the opposite sex. So the sheer intensity of sexual desire tends to lead to "perversion" – the expansion of the sexual realm through "association of ideas" – that is, through daydreams and masturbation.

When *Psychopathia Sexualis*, the first textbook on sexual deviation, appeared in 1886, the Victorians were staggered by these medical revelations – sadism, masochism, voyeurism, vampirism and fetishism. It seemed incredible that anyone could want a woman so badly that he could experience orgasm while drinking her urine or licking the dirt off her shoe. These revelations made it clear that sex was no longer the straightforward "two backed beast" it had been in the age of Rabelais or Shakespeare. Frustration and social convention had lent it a morbid intensity. On the analogy of superheated steam, I once called this "superheated sex".

Towards the beginning of the 20th century, a new fetish-object made its appearance. As long ago as 1850, ladies of the upper classes had been wearing long undergarments called pantalettes, usually made of some hard-wearing material like calico and reaching down to the ankles. In 1851, a temperance campaigner named Amelia Bloomer argued that full-length skirts were unhealthy and inconvenient, and that it would be better to combine skirts that reached halfway down the shins with, underneath these, Turkish trousers, strapped around the ankles. This ensemble was known as "bloomers". At first regarded as rather indecent, they gradually caught on, until by the 1880s, most women were wearing some kind of long "drawers" (so called because they were drawn on). Oddly enough, these do not figure in Krafft-Ebing's list of fetish objects, possibly because they were so ugly – often made of red flannel – that they deadened sexual desire rather than exciting it. Little by little, the legs became shorter and the material less coarse, so that by the late Victorian age, "knickers" (the name short-ened from the male knickerbockers) were usually made of wool or cotton, and their elasticated legs reached no further than halfway down the thighs. In the 1880s, a smooth new material, rayon, was invented. Now at last knickers became the object of male fetishism – as did corsets – and in Joyce's *Ulysses*, set in 1904, the hero Leopold Bloom is a devotee of "drawers", and masturbates at the sight of a girl leaning back and displaying her underwear.

I am inclined to suspect that knickers somehow became part and parcel of western sexuality at about this time, and – against all Darwinian theory – entered the male unconscious. I can recall, in the early 1930s, being fascinated by the sight of my mother's knickers – this was long before I went to school or knew anything about sex – and even putting them on when there was nobody in the house. And when I began to experience the onset of powerful sexual desire at puberty, I found the sight of a pair of knickers in a shop window, or pictured in an advertisement, as exciting as some casual glimpse of a naked girl.

So when I read an account of the Heirens case, describing how he had begun to steal women's panties in early adolescence, and of how he eventually began to experience orgasm as he climbed in through a window in the course of a burglary, it seemed to me that this was a logical and inevitable development in the "age of sex crime".

The account that follows, from my book *The Serial Killers*[1] (1990), is based upon the only full length book on the case that existed at the time, Lucy Freeman's *Before I Kill More* (1955).

On 10 December 1945 a maid entering the Chicago apartment of a thirty-year-old ex-Wave named Frances Brown was alarmed to see that the pillow on the bed was bloodstained; in the bathroom she found the woman's naked body draped over the side of the bath. On the wall over the bed, someone had scrawled in lipstick:

> For heavens
> sake catch me
> Before I kill more
> I cannot control myself

1 Written in collaboration with Donald Seaman.

Frances Brown was kneeling beside the bath, and she was naked. A pyjama top had been folded loosely round her neck; when this was removed, police discovered a knife driven in with such force that it protruded from the other side of her throat. She had also been shot twice. The body had been carefully washed after death, and wet bloodstained towels lay on the floor.

Four weeks later, on the morning of 7 January 1946, James E. Degnan went into the bedroom of his seven-year-old daughter Suzanne, and saw that she was not in her bed, and that the window was wide open. He called the police, and it was a policeman who found the note on the child's chair; it said she had been kidnapped and demanded $20,000 for her return. Later that afternoon, Suzanne's head was discovered beneath a nearby manhole cover. In another sewer police found the child's left leg. The right leg was found in another sewer, and the torso in a third. The arms were discovered – also in a sewer – some weeks later. The case shocked the nation, but the police seemed to be unable to develop any definite leads.

Six months later, on 26 June 1946, a young man walked into an apartment building in Chicago, and entered the apartment of Mr and Mrs Pera through the open door; Mrs Pera was in the kitchen preparing dinner. A neighbour who had seen the young man enter called to Mrs Pera to ask if she knew a man had walked into her apartment. The young man immediately left, but the neighbour called him to stop. Instead, he ran down the stairs. He pointed a gun at a man who tried to stop him, then ran out of the building. Minutes later, he knocked on the door of a nearby apartment and asked the woman who answered for a glass of water, explaining he felt ill. She sensed something wrong and rang the police. In fact, an off-duty policeman had already seen the fleeing youth, and ran after him. When cornered, the young man fired three shots at the policeman; all missed. As other police answered the call, the burglar and the police grappled on the floor. Then one of the policemen hit him on the head – three times – with a flowerpot, and knocked him unconscious.

The prisoner turned out to be a seventeen-year-old youth

named William George Heirens, and he had spent some time in a correctional institution for burglary. When his fingerprints were taken, they were found to match one found on the Degnan ransom note, and another found in the apartment of Frances Brown. In the prison hospital, Heirens was given the "truth drug" sodium pentathol, and asked: "Did you kill Suzanne Degnan?" Heirens answered: "George cut her up." At first he insisted that George was a real person, a boy five years his senior whom he met at school. Later, he claimed that George was his own invisible alter-ego. "He was just a realization of mine, but he seemed real to me." Heirens also admitted to a third murder, that of a forty-three-year-old widow, Mrs Josephine Ross, who had awakened while he was burgling her apartment on 5 June 1945; Heirens stabbed her through the throat. In addition to this, he had attacked a woman named Evelyn Peterson with an iron bar when she started to wake up during a burglary, then tied her up with lamp cord; he had also fired shots through windows at two women who had been sitting in their rooms with the curtains undrawn.

The story of William Heirens, as it emerged in his confessions, and in interviews with his parents, was almost predictably typical of a serial sex killer. Born on 15 November 1928, he had been a forceps delivery. He was an underweight baby, and cried and vomited a great deal. At the age of seven months he fell down twelve cement steps into the basement and landed on his head; after that he had nightmares about falling. He was three years old when a brother was born, and he was sent away to the home of his grandmother. He was frequently ill as a child, and broke his arm at the age of nine. The family background was far from happy; his mother had two nervous breakdowns accompanied by paralysis, and his father's business failed several times.

Heirens matured very early sexually – he had his first emission at the age of nine. Soon after this, he began stealing women's panties from clotheslines and basement washrooms, and putting them on. (After his arrest, police found forty pairs of pink and blue rayon panties in a box in his grandmother's attic.) He came to think of sex as something "dirty" and forbidden. This was confirmed when, at the age of thirteen, he walked into the school washroom and found two boys playing sexually with a mentally retarded boy; he refused to join in. Being a good-looking boy, he was attractive to girls; on eight occasions he attempted some form of sex play, touching their breasts or pressing their legs, but this had the effect of upsetting him so much that he cried. There was a deep conflict between his sexual obsession and his rigid Catholic upbringing. He found normal sexual stimulation repellent. From the age of thirteen he had been burgling apartments, entering through the window, and experiencing sexual excitement – to the point of emission – as he did so. After this, he lost interest in underwear, and began to experience his sexual fulfilment by entering strange apartments through the window. He often urinated or defecated on the floor. He also began lighting small fires.

He was arrested for the first time in the same year – 1942 – charged with eleven burglaries and suspected of fifty; in many of them he had stolen guns and women's dresses. He was sentenced to probation and sent to a semi-correctional Catholic institution. After a year there he transferred to a Catholic academy, where he proved to be a brilliant student – so much so that he was allowed to skip the freshman year at the University of Chicago. Back in Chicago, the sexual obsession remained as powerful as ever, and led to more burglaries. If he resisted for long, he began to experience violent headaches. On one occasion, he put his clothes in the washroom and threw the key inside in order to make it impossible to go out; halfway through the night, the craving became too strong, and he crawled along the house gutter to retrieve his clothes.

Once inside an apartment, he was in such a state of intense excitement that any interruption would provoke an explosion of violence. This is why he knocked Evelyn Peterson unconscious with an iron bar when she stirred in her sleep. On another occasion he was preparing to enter what he thought was an empty apartment when a woman moved inside; he immediately fired his gun at her, but missed.

None of the victims was raped – the thought of actual

sexual intercourse still scared him. Sexual fulfilment came from the "forbiddenness", the excitement of knowing he was committing a crime. After the ejaculation, he felt miserable; he believed that he was a kind of Jekyll and Hyde. He even invented a name for his Mr Hyde – George. Although he later admitted that the invention of an alter-ego was partly an attempt to fool the psychiatrists, there can be no doubt that he felt that he was periodically "possessed" by a monster. This is why he scrawled the message in lipstick on the wall after killing Frances Brown. It may also explain why he eventually courted arrest by wandering into a crowded apartment block in the late afternoon and entering a flat in which a married woman was cooking the dinner as she waited for her husband to return from work. Dr Jekyll was turning in Mr Hyde. In July 1946 Heirens was sentenced to three terms of life imprisonment in Joliet penitentiary.

In August 1991, I saw an advertisement in an American bookseller's catalogue for a new book entitled *William Heirens, His Day in Court*, by Dolores Kennedy, published by Bonus Books of Chicago, and sent off for it. To my astonishment, the author argued that Heirens was innocent. Dolores Kennedy had been legal secretary to the lawyer who represented the Degnan family – although, oddly enough, he believed that Heirens should be released. In 1983, a federal magistrate ordered the release of Heirens – after thirty-seven years in jail – because the parole board had failed to comply with his parole requirements. There was immediate uproar, and the Attorney General declared: "I am going to make sure that kill-crazed animal stays where he is." The magistrates's decision was reversed.

The father of Dolores Kennedy began to work for Heirens's release, and when her father died, she went to see Heirens in the Vienna Correctional Center in Illinois to discuss what could be done. She found Heirens likeable – as did most people who had met him – and helped to form a committee for his release. But Heirens himself presented a curious obstacle. He argued that he did not want to be released on parole – or at least, that he was not willing to pacify the parole board by taking what they regarded as the essential first step in considering him for parole: admission of guilt. He declared: "In 1946 I had to plead guilty to live. I was 17 years old and I wanted to live, and sometimes I wanted to die. I am 60 years old now and I will never admit to murders I did not commit." In other words, he had been forced to plead guilty only because the alternative to this "plea bargain" was the electric chair. As Dolores Kennedy looked into the case, she began to "uncover the magnitude of the misrepresentations connected with his conviction", and decided to write a book about it.

My immediate reaction to her book was scepticism. At least fifty per cent of criminals claim they have been "framed". Where Heirens was concerned, the case against him seemed to hang together so well that I found it virtually impossible to believe in his innocence. And as I read the book, it seemed to me that Dolores Kennedy deliberately underplayed the most powerful evidence – the box of knickers found in the house of Heirens's grandmother. I wrote to her to tell her so. She replied politely, declaring that Heirens had concocted the fetishism story because he hoped to be found insane. She said that Heirens himself would write and confirm this.

In March 1992, I received a letter from Heirens in which he did exactly that. He pointed out that although he had twice been arrested for burglary in his early teens, there had been no suggestion of stealing panties. "None of these examinations remotely indicated fetishism." He also pointed out that, when he was arrested, it was the police who fired the three shots, not he.

He went on to explain how, when he was nine, he had found a trunk of old clothes on a garbage dump near his grandmother's home, and had taken from it various items, which included women's underwear – bloomers and slips – as well as some men's swimming trunks. He put these in a cardboard box and hid them behind the chimney in his grandmother's house. "None of the underwear was of the frilly sort common with panty fetishism." In fact it was made of cotton and was of the pre-war variety. There were no semen stains, as there would have been if it had been used in masturbation. And, according to Heirens, it was only after he had agreed to the plea-bargaining, which included the fetishism story – that he told the police of the whereabouts of the box, which had been there for almost ten years.

On the whole, I was not convinced. Yet I had to admit that his refusal of parole *unless* he was given the opportunity to establish his innocence was a persuasive argument in his favour. My wife suggested that perhaps he didn't really want to be released. After all, a man in his sixties is likely to find the modern world a bewildering place after forty or so years in jail. He replied to this comment by pointing out that his prison "is not as comfortable as you seem to believe . . . it is still a prison where you are told what to do and when . . ."

I asked if there was any documentary evidence indicating that the box found in his grandmother's attic contained a mixture of male and female clothing; he replied that, as far as he knew, no inventory had been made.

When the publisher of this present volume asked me to compile an anthology of murders of the 1940s, it was obvious to me that Heirens had to be included, and that I had to make some mention of Dolores Kennedy's belief that he was innocent. That is why I decided to write to Heirens and ask him to write me a simple and brief account of his own side of the story, which I would print alongside my own account of the case. This is it.

> My name is William Heirens. I have been imprisoned in Illinois for 47 years for murders I did not commit. Many of you over the age of 50 will remember the murder and dismemberment of six-year-old Suzanne Degnan in January of 1946. If you are younger, you may have read about it in crime anthologies or studied the case in classes. And, based on your reading, you may have been satisfied that the person responsible is paying for the crime.
>
> I did not murder Suzanne Degnan. I did not murder Frances Brown and Josephine Ross – two women whose unsolved murders I was also forced to take the blame for to save my life.
>
> Over the years many writers have canvassed my case in crime anthologies. Almost without exception they have been carelessly written with no regard for the facts and

aimed at titilating the reader. A hallmark of such articles state that the lipstick message left by the killer in the Brown case was found on a mirror when it was actually found on the apartment wall. For the first time a crime anthologist has asked me for the truth of what happened in 1946.

Chicago, January 6, 1946 – midnight. On this clear, cold winter night, blond, blue-eyed Suzanne Degnan was taken from her bed in a house on the north side of Chicago and murdered. The next day her dismembered body was found in catch basins near the family residence.

Investigation disclosed that the child had been strangled. She had not been raped. Her body had been expertly dismembered into five pieces and distributed among various catch basins in the area. The dismemberment had taken place in the laundry room of an apartment building near the Degnan home. On the floor of the child's bedroom a ransome note was found.

The horror of the crime swept through the nation. The murder of a child is not uncommon, but decapitation is unusual, and dismemberment is rare and unthinkable. The effort made by those responsible for the crime suggested that the creation of horror was intentional. How much easier it would have been to dispose of the body in nearby Lake Michigan. One catch basin would have held the child's body without dismemberment. The scattering seemed to invite discovery.

The crime created dread and fear among Chicago parents. Emotions surplanted rational thinking. And, of course, the Chicago police were under enormous pressure to solve the crime. The case was ripe for a quote from Oscar Wilde: "It matters not if one is guilty as long as someone is found guilty."

The police arrested hundreds of suspects, grilled many and brutalized several in an effort to secure a confession.

The five Chicago newspapers, freed from the incumberance of wartime newspaper rationing, vied with each other for circulation by reporting every detail of the crime and the investigation that followed. I remember reading daily accounts of the Degnan murder, little suspecting that one day I would be held responsible.

Six months after the murder of the little girl, on June 26, 1946, I was arrested for burglary. Detected in the act of burglarizing a north side apartment, I fled the scene, but the police cornered me. A struggle followed during which I was severely beaten over the head, rendering me unconscious. I was taken to a police hospital where suspects were held. Almost immediately a newspaper reporter suggested to the police that I might be guilty of the Degnan murder. Before I regained consciousness, I was strapped spread-eagle to a bed in solitary confinement. For the next six days, without benefit of counsel, I was accused, questioned and threatened. I was 17 years old.

During those six days and nights of police grilling, I continually denied murdering Degnan. I was illegally questioned under the "truth serum" and denied murdering Suzanne Degnan. I was forced to undergo two lie detector tests that confirmed my denial. The police, however, claimed my prints matched a partial fingerprint found on the ransom note. The state's attorney announced to the press that the killer of Suzanne Degnan had been found.

My parents hired attorneys to represent me and I was finally released from police custody, charged with a couple dozen burglaries, not murder, and put in the county jail where I spent a week in the jail's infirmary recovering from my ordeal with the police.

On July 7th my attorneys were summoned to the prosecutor's office. They were told that the prosecution was anxious to settle the case on a plea bargain. In exchange for confessions to the murders of Suzanne Degnan, Frances Brown and Josephine Ross (two women whose murders had not been solved) and pleas of guilty to the murders and all other charges brought against me, the prosecution would guarantee one life sentence with all sentences running concurrently. If the offer was not accepted, the prosecution would seek the death penalty in the Degnan murder and, even if no conviction was obtained, sentencing for the burglaries would be so contrived that I would be imprisoned for life.

The attorneys informed me of the offer and I refused it. I had not murdered anyone and had no intention of taking the blame for it.

During this time, the Chicago newspapers, in the midst of a circulation war, printed everything they could to convince the public that I was responsible for the murders, even manufacturing "evidence" of guilt in order to "scoop" the other papers. Defense counsel kept me informed of what was appearing in the newspapers and discussed the effect of the publicity on my trial.

On July 16th, three weeks after my arrest and before I was indicted for any murder, the Chicago Tribune manufactured and printed my "confession" to the three murders. Only *after* I was sentenced did the newspaper boast:

For the first time in newspaper history, the detailed story of how three murders were committed, naming the man who did them, was told before the murderer had confessed or was indicted . . . So great was public confidence in the Tribune that other Chicago papers reprinted the story solely because the Tribune said it was so. Never have a newspaper's contemporaries and competitors paid a higher tribute to its reputation for veracity . . . For awhile, Heirens maintained his innocence, but the world believed his guilt. The Tribune had said he was guilty.

The possibility of a fair trial was now impossible, defense counsel told me that it looked "very likely" that I would get the electric chair, and so I agreed to accept the plea bargain offer.

The problem was that all I knew about the murders resulted from what I had read in the newspapers and what I had been told by others. The Tribune's fake confession could be followed to some extent. I found myself in the position of Scheherazade, a spinner of tales to save my life. I knew I could make up a story; after all, our librarys' fiction shelves are filled with credible but untrue stories. However, I had a problem other story tellers did not face – my story was to be presented to a prosecutor who would renege on the plea bargain if he did not find it plausible.

During those long days and nights in jail, my seventeen-year-old mind constructed a substructure, an easel, to hang my story on. It had to be something that was self-effacing, certainly not self-serving. In those days sex was a taboo subject and I thought that its interjection into the confession stories would upset the interrogation so unanswerable questions would be abandoned. It would give me some control over the questioning.

On one of my burglaries I had obtained some books on sexual dysfunctions, read them and became intrigued with the practice of fetishism. I decided to use what I had learned and selected women's underwear, which was very common, as the fetish that I would claim. The police had removed everything from my living quarters and examined the contents. Not one item of women's underwear was found to support fetishism and to get around that I would claim I stole women's underwear eight years previously and the act transferred itself into the act of burglary instead. I didn't know if the psychology of transferrence worked that way but expected nobody else would know either.

Once it was decided that I would accept the prosecution's offer of a plea bargain, defense counsel began rehearsing the confession story with me. They corrected me when my account didn't check with the facts and I changed my story accordingly. Finally, defense counsel had the confession typed and presented it to me and my parents in the jail chapel to be signed. Even at that stage counsel had me change the typed version because of inconsistency. In spite of the rehearsal, I later learned that many aspects of the confession were at variance with the facts.

The murder of Frances Brown had occurred on December 10, 1945, between the hours of 4:00 and 5:00 a.m. She was 33 years old and was shot to death with a .38 caliber gun in her apartment. It was a bizarre murder during which the killer had written on the wall in lipstick: "For heaven's sake catch me before I kill more. I cannot control myself." A smudged partial fingerprint was found on a door jamb. After my arrest, the police announced that this print did not compare with my fingerprints. Ten days later they claimed there was a match.

Josephine Ross, 43, was stabbed to death in her apartment on June 5, 1945. Although there was no evidence of any kind to link me to the crime, the prosecution insisted that I confess and plead guilty to this crime.

The authorities attempted to establish a pattern between the three murders but it was difficult. The three females were in different age groups, did not look alike, were killed at different times of the day and by different methods (strangulation, knife and gun). In my confession story I tried to link them by saying the victims had surprised me in the act of burglarizing. It was a weak motive but never questioned. I had been interrupted in burglaries many times and instantly fled the scene, harming no one. Furthermore, I had my own modus operandi which included making certain no one was at home before I broke in. Burglary hours always occurred in the early evening before people went to bed. That way I could tell by the lights inside whether anyone was at home. None of the murders occurred during that time. And lastly, despite my "pack rat" habits, not one item taken from the scene of the murders was found in my possession. Few of the facts matched my confession, but no one cared.

Once defense counsel felt that I could hold my own, I was taken to the prosecutor's office which was filled with more than 30 officials. The prosecutor had newspaper reporters waiting outside in the hallway for copies of the confession stories as they unfolded. After some preliminary discussion, the prosecutor made a statement I hadn't heard before. He said he wanted the "truth" and I responded with "Do you really want the truth?" He replied "yes". Questioning about the murders began and when I was asked if I had murdered Suzanne Degnan, I responded by saying that I had no memory of killing her. Questioning ceased and my attorneys took me in another room. They were angry and asked me what happened. I explained that the prosecutor was insisting on the truth and that's what I gave him. I reminded my attorneys that they never asked me for the truth themselves. My parents were called to persuade me to go along with the agreement and I told them the same thing. I was taken back to my cell.

Several days later my attorneys again talked to me in jail and by this time I had gotten over my anger about the "truth" issue. For weeks I had lived in fear for my life with no other emotion. The "truth" demand had gotten me angry, an anger that swept away my fear. No longer scared, I reacted as I had. By the time my attorneys saw me the anger had passed and I was back to being scared and compliant. One British reporter covering the case wrote home in the London Sunday Pictorial under the headline "Condemned before his trial, America calls this justice", and discussed my conviction in the Chicago press.

I finally agreed to go through with the plea bargain and another date was set. However, by this time the prosecutor was angry because I had embarrassed him in front of his colleagues and the newsmen he had assembled in the hallway. Now the plea bargain became three consecutive life sentences if I went through with it. At this point there was no longer a choice and I gave my confession to the three murders as rehearsed.

As I had anticipated, difficulties arose about matters I didn't know the answers to and I could see that the prosecutor was getting angry about my "don't remember" and "don't know" answers. It was then I volunteered the sex angle, and, as expected, the prosecutor abandoned the line of questioning and asked for more sex input. I was then taken to the scenes of the murders for a reenactment and did exactly what I was told to do. I made many mistakes when asked questions at the scenes.

The next phase of the agreement was a psychiatric examination limited to finding out if I were sane enough to plead to the charges. This was merely a continuation of the confession phase because if there was a sanity question it would have been looked into before the plea bargain was accepted. The psychiatrists never considered my sanity at the time of the crimes.

The psychiatric examination was exhaustive. The psychiatrists didn't believe the fetishism and wanted proof. My family regularly visited my grandparents on weekends and they lived in the suburbs of Chicago. The area hadn't yet been built up and there were open fields for my brother and I to play in. There was a lot of landfilling going on and we examined the dumps for toys and other interesting things people threw away. There was a huge dump, a former clay pit, at some distance that we would visit in the evening on our bike to hunt for junk. I was alone at the big dump when I found an old trunk somebody had thrown out. I opened it hoping to find a treasure but all it contained was old clothes.

I sorted out the cotton items, which were mostly women's undergarments and put them in a small cardboard box. The items were clean but frayed. I also found a clean bedsheet that wasn't badly torn and put that in the box too. I took the box to my grandmother's house. I removed the sheet and my brother and I made a sail out of it which we mounted on our wagon so the wind would give us a ride down the empty streets (it didn't work well as we could only go with the wind and then had to walk back). The rest of the box I secreted in my grandmother's attic with the intention of making guncotton out of the material once I could get the acids needed for the process. At the time I was interested in Chemistry and read about making explosives in a chemistry book I got from the library. I was only nine years old at the time and my brother was six. Needless to say I couldn't obtain the acid – too young. So I forgot about the box in the attic. But I remembered it in 1946 when I was considering using the fetishism story. I told the psychiatrists where to find the box and they recovered it, supporting my claim of fetishism.

We also got into dual personality because the newspapers were playing up the Jekyl-Hyde angle. When the police used sodium pentothal on me to make me talk, I was unconscious most of the time but when I was coming out from under the drug I remembered talking about a George and saying that maybe George did it. At the time a common saying was "Let George do it" when passing off a job to someone else. I knew very little about dual personality, only common knowledge gotten from magazines of the time. The psychiatric report had a lot of material on the George alter ego. As to the murders, the psychiatrists recorded one statement I made to them: "I still believe yet that I didn't do it". After I was sentenced one of the doctors came to my cell and asked some more questions. The doctor reported what I said to the newspapers and that was: "As far as the murders are concerned, I don't know whether I did them or not."

About the only thing of merit that came out of the psychiatric examination was their finding that I was unusually susceptible to suggestion but then all immature people are to one degree or another.

On September 4th I was taken to court and pleaded guilty

to all charges. The police fingerprint expert testified to the fingerprint match in the Degnan and Brown cases.

We've tried to get copies of the fingerprint evidence so we could have it examined by independent experts. The state's attorney has refused to comply with this request. Modern fingerprint expertise could well tell a different story than was told in 1946. The prosecutor's handwriting expert, Herbert Walters, testified my handwriting matched that on the ransom note and lipstick message. Incidently, before my arrest, this same expert had compared the lipstick message and ransom note and declared they were not written by the same person. Recently five independent handwriting experts reexamined the same material used by Walters and determined that the messages were written by different people and neither matched my writing.

The confessions were read into the record and the psychiatrists made their report to the court.

Then the prosecutor rose and told the court how grateful he was to the newspapers and to my attorneys for helping resolve the case. He explained that without the cooperation of defense counsel in obtaining my confession, a conviction would have been impossible in the Ross case and a sincere public doubt would exist in the Degnan and Brown murders.

My attorney then rose and told the court that although at the outset he thought he had a duty to me and to me alone, he ultimately determined that his public duty was greater. At that point he cooperated with the prosecution to secure my convictions. I have since learned that my attorneys failed to investigate potential alibis (which people volunteered later) and gave confidential information to the Tribune in order to encourage my confession.

And that is why I have spent 47 years, from ages 17 to 64, in prison. Since that time, I have continually sought the fair trial denied me in 1946 through our appellate courts. One such appeal is pending now. So far our judicial system has denied me the opportunity for an advesarial trial before an unbiased jury. One attorney appointed to help me in an appeal commented: "When William Heirens stands before a court of law, justice peeks."

I was wrong to be burglarizing in my youth but I never

thought it would get me into so much trouble. If it wasn't for that, I would not have been in a no-win situation.

My sentence includes provisions for parole as part of the sentence I received under the plea bargain contract. The day after I was sentenced the prosecutor breached the plea bargain by sending a "Pen Letter" to the prison, telling the parole board not to parole me. Although the parole board has unfettered discretion, the board has admitted they do honor such pen letters. Several other breaches have occurred since then. In 1946 my attorneys told me that I would have the same chance for parole as any other prisoner that behaves himself in prison. This assurance was made to give me hope of a future in order to encourage me to accept the plea bargain. At the time it wasn't much of an inducement because parole eligibility was 20 years in the future but as time passed it became something to look forward to. 30 times parole has been denied.

Needless to say, over all these years I've learned more about the murders in a quest to establish to everyone's satisfaction that I did not murder anyone. The rational approach to solving any murder is to look for the cause; every event has a cause. The cause may be in the past, in the present, or in the future. Revenge is a cause out of the past. I knew none of the murder victims or those close to them, eliminating the revenge motive in my case. A common "present" cause is a reaction to a threat; rape-murders fall in this category because the victim's survival threatens exposure. I always fled when detected burglarizing. Neither Suzanne Degnan, Francis Brown or Josephine Ross were raped so they weren't killed under that scenario. A "future" cause is often for remuneration of some sort so that some murders occur for insurance money. Very often the one who profits from the victim's death is the murderer. In the Degnan case there was a bid for a ransom but the police, by immediately publicizing the discovery of the child's body, thwarted a follow-through in apprehending those who collect the ransom. I was a petty burglar, not a kidnapper.

I thought I had a hot clue some years ago. In the Brown murder, ballistics matched the bullet to one fired at another woman a month before. Two published accounts had the police recover the gun under the woman's window so that the Brown murder weapon was last known to be in police custody. One published account of finding the gun said the writer relied on the other published account.

The writer of the first account said she got the information from police reports or somebody told her and couldn't remember which. A search of old police reports was futile, they had been destroyed over the passage of time. In my confession story, though I complied with the demand to show where the Brown murder weapon was the police didn't find the weapon there.

William Heirens: *His Day in Court* by Dolores Kennedy, a book published by Bonus Books of Chicago in 1991, covers my case thoroughly and I commend it to the reader.

Am I convinced of the innocence of Bill Heirens?

Let me put it this way: I am now far less certain of his guilt than I was a year ago.

In the *Encyclopedia of Murder*, I also wrote an account of the Lindberg kidnapping case. There again, it seemed abundantly certain from the evidence presented in court, that Bruno Richard Hauptmann was guilty of the murder of the Lindberg baby. The chief evidence consisted of the various bills of the ransom money which were found in Hauptmann's house – which, after all, looks quite conclusive. (He was arrested when he used one of the ransom bills to pay a garage.) But the main back-up was the evidence of a piece of board which was missing from Hauptmann's attic. The prosecution alleged that one of the rungs of the ladder which was found below the window of the kidnapped baby was made from this piece of board. The ladder itself was made of yellow pine, and an eighteen month search of timberyards finally established that the pine might have been bought at a yard in the Bronx; this yard later proved to be the one used by Hauptmann. Another convincing piece of evidence of Hauptmann's guilt was a telephone number written on a closet door in his house – the telephone number of "Jafsie" Condon, the doctor who acted as contact-man between Lindberg and the unknown kidnapper.

Between the Lines

HANDWRITING AND DOCUMENT EXAMINATION
115 NORTH ARLINGTON HEIGHTS ROAD
ARLINGTON HEIGHTS, ILLINOIS 60004
(708) 255-5855

ELIZABETH M. BIESTEK

Statement of handwriting experts attending
workshop on May 9, 1992

Based upon our examination of the handwriting as
presented in the book, <u>William Heirens, His Day in
Court</u>, it is our preliminary opinion that the
handwriting on the Suzanne Degnan ransom note and
the handwriting on the Frances Brown wall do not
compare favorably with the handwriting sample
attributed to William Heirens and most probably
were written by someone other than William Heirens.

Elizabeth M. Biestek

Diane Marsh

Marie Gerage

Frederick G. Dudink

inter-graph associates, inc.

4020 West 111th Street
Suite 202
Oak Lawn, Illinois 60453
(708) 424-4443
(708) 424-4447

MR. PAUL LAURENT
Assistant Public Defender
Cook County Public Defender
2650 S. California
Chicago, IL. 60608

April 14, 1990

Re: William Heirens

Dear Mr. Laurent,

On April 12, 1990, photocopies of script were delivered to my office via U.S. Mail. Enclosed were exemplars of Mr. William George Heirens. Also enclosed were documents of questioned origin.

Please refer to the attachments. The page marked "A" are taken from the ransom note. The letters underlined in brown are from the questioned document. Those underlined in blue are from exemplary material offered by Mr. Heirens. These are all comparisons of indivdual letter structures.

The page marked "B" show comparisons from the note written on the wall. The letters underlined in brown are of an unknown origin. Those underelined in blue are from exemplary material offered by Mr. Heirens. These are all comparisons of individual letter comparisons.

The page marked "C" show word grouping comparisons. The words were taken from the ransom note. The words underlined in brown are of an unknown origin. Those underlined in blue are from exemplary material offered by Mr. Heirens.

The samples provided were subjected to all the measuring prescribed by our profession. It is the finding of this examiner none of the questioned material matches the writing of Mr. Heirens. So different is the script that no comparisons could be found.

Sincerely,

R.W. Hellstrom

R.W. Hellstrom
Certified & Licensed
Examiner

Hauptmann protested that the ransom bills had been left in a box in his house by a business associate named Fisch, who owed him money. Fisch had died after his return to Germany, so when Hauptmann found that the box contained "gold certificates", he felt he had a right to help himself. In fact, Hauptmann's story about Fisch checked out in every detail. So is it possible that Fisch was the kidnapper? Possible, but unlikely. Bills of the ransom money were on sale in New Yorks underworld at a heavy discount long before Hauptmann was caught; Fisch, who was a dubious character, may well have purchased some of them.

As to the ladder, Hauptmann pointed out that it was such a botched job that any professional carpenter – such as he was – would have been ashamed of it.

Then what about the rung made from wood in his attic? In fact, Hauptmann's wife had made the mistake of moving out of their house soon after her husband's arrest, giving the police and reporters free access. One reporter admitted that it was he who wrote Condon's phone number in Hauptmann's closet. In *The Airman and the Carpenter*, Ludovic Kennedy has argued that it is likely that Detective Bornmann, in charge of the case, prised up the board from the attic floor and sawed out the telltale rung. After all, why should Hauptmann, who had plenty of timber at his disposal, prise up a board from his own attic?

Moreover, the footprints found below the baby's window were definitely not Hauptmann's. *If* he was involved in the kidnapping, then he was not alone . . .

In short, there is a very strong possibility that Hauptmann was not guilty, and that some of the evidence presented in court was fabricated.

What Dolores Kennedy's book makes quite clear is that William Heirens did not receive a fair trial. Just as in the Lindberg case, the police were feverishly anxious to charge someone with the crime, and a powerfully-built seventeen year old burglar seemed the ideal suspect. He was pressured until he confessed, and then told that unless he entered into plea-bargaining and pleaded guilty, he would receive the death sentence. Under such circumstances, most of us would agree to plead guilty.

There is also the fact that Heirens has pressed hard to have the fingerprint evidence – on which he was convicted – re-examined. If, in fact, such a re-examination showed that the fingerprints found at the scene of the attack on the nurse *were* his, this would obviously badly damage his case. This has been pointed out to him by his legal representatives, yet he still persists in asking for the fingerprint evidence to be re-examined.

But for me, the most powerful piece of evidence in Heirens' favour is the two documents reproduced here, in which handwriting experts testify that the writing found on the bedroom wall and the writing of the ransom note was not that of Bill Heirens. Like the "wrong footprints" in the Lindberg case, it is the piece of evidence that has the effect of throwing doubt on the whole prosecution case.

In a sense it is all irrelevant. Heirens has served a far longer term in prison than most people sentenced to "life". If he is a killer, then he has paid his debt to society. Yet for some reason, he declines to plead guilty – which would probably lead to parole – and quietly slip into obscurity; he insists that he is innocent and that his case should be re-examined. I do not know how you, the reader, feel after reading his statement – you may be totally unconvinced and pity my gullibility in even accepting the possibility that he may be innocent. But surely there can be no one who would disagree that, under the circumstances, he at least deserves what he is asking for: a re-examination of the evidence against him?

Colin Wilson

Neville Heath: The Sadist

June 21, 1946 – the day Margery Gardner's bruised and lacerated body was found in the Pembridge Court Hotel, Notting Hill – was five days before my fifteenth birthday, and I can still recall the sensation caused by the discovery. The police were already looking for the man with whom she had spent the evening, Neville Heath, for his "help in the murder enquiry". At that time, the British public knew little about sadistic murders – the trial of Gordon Cummins had been rushed through with such speed that no one had noticed it. But a woman found naked and dead in a hotel room with lash marks all over her body was the kind of material that tabloid editors dream about – particularly in the "silly season" – and the search for Heath received maximum publicity. Three weeks later, after Heath had been detained by the police, the naked body of another girl was found lying in undergrowth near a Bournemouth hotel, again horribly mutilated.

Heath's trial, which took place two months later, was probably the great British murder sensation since Jack the Ripper. I can clearly remember the general reaction to it – a kind of shivery horror, incredulity that human nature could be so depraved. There was nothing quite like it until the Christie trial in the following decade.

I recall meeting a journalist who had known Heath, and whose theory was that Heath was so good-looking that he could virtually take his pick of pretty women; this, the journalist thought, had led to a kind of Byronic boredom which in turn led to experiment in sado-masochism. I find this hard to accept. All the evidence is that sadism starts fairly early, in childhood, and develops if and when it is given the opportunity. But Heath certainly strikes me as an interesting example of the con-man killer – Ted Bundy is a modern example – whose murders spring out of a low sense of self-esteem, a desire to be a Somebody with a capital S. "Group Captain Rupert Brooke" was fundamentally a man who was unsure about his own identity, and who suddenly felt he knew "who he was" when he allowed himself to turn into a monster and abandoned himself to an orgy of beating and slashing.

This account is taken from *The Sound of Murder* (1973) by *Daily Express* crime reporter Percy Hoskins.

The Heath case presented the authorities with a terrible dilemma. Sadist and pervert Neville George Clevely Heath had already committed one murder in London, during which he flogged, bit, suffocated, beat and savagely mutilated a young woman.

He was a monster, wild with desire after gorging on one murder and clearly capable of, and likely to commit, murder again soon. It was absolutely vital to warn the public to be on their guard. The best way of doing that, in 1946, was to issue his picture to the newspapers.

The police were able to do it: Heath had a record and they had a photograph of him in the files. *But* the only positive evidence they had that Heath had accompanied the woman to the hotel where she was murdered came from a cab driver who took them as fare. And here was the dilemma: if Heath's picture appeared in the newspapers before the trial, the defence would almost certainly maintain the taxi driver had been unduly influenced by its publication. In plain English, defence counsel would infer he was claiming to recognise a face he had only seen in the newspapers. On that, a case could founder.

So a calculated gamble was taken that Heath's photograph would be circulated to the police only, in the hope and belief that someone, somewhere in uniform would pick him up before he murdered again.

The gamble failed. That decision cost another life, for Heath did murder a second time. No-one knows if that life would have been spared had the alternative course been taken – of saying, publish and be damned! – but it is possible, even likely. That was a hideous dilemma for all those CID chiefs saddled with the responsibility of decision. Their feelings when the news of the second murder broke can be imagined.

A curious-sideline to the Heath case is that Fleet Street's reporters knew Heath well, under one name or another, long before the murders. We didn't like him whatever the label he wore. Incidentally, one world famous figure who thoroughly distrusted him is Denis Compton the former international cricketer and footballer, born – like me – at Bridport. Denis, who of course is now a colleague of mine on the *Sunday Express*, rated Heath a dangerous phoney.

World War 2 had just ended. Millions were still in uniform, and it was fashionable in many quarters for temporary officers and gentlemen to cling to their wartime rank even when demobbed. The pubs were packed with returning warriors, and the hangar doors were open in every saloon bar every day. In Fleet Street we suffered "Group Captain Armstrong" almost daily. The dashing Groupie, alias Heath, was such an obvious exhibitionist, such a patent fraud to us old cynics. It has always been a source of amazement to me that women should fall so easily – and fatally – for his brittle, surface charm.

Our instinct was right, our suspicious noses had caught the right scent. Ladies' man Heath was in fact a brute, a sadist, and quite horrific killer. Now his blood was roused, and he was prowling through the hotels and pubs of London like any animal in the jungle looking for prey.

On the night of 20 June, 1946, Neville Heath was drinking and dancing with thirty-two-year-old Mrs Margery Gardner at the Panama Club in South Kensington, in London. Mrs Gardner was an experienced young woman who liked men. Heath fascinated her, with his crinkly blond hair, pale blue eyes and baby-smooth skin. Around midnight they left the Panama, with many a drink on board, and took a cab to the Pembridge Court Hotel in the Notting Hill district. Heath had booked in there some days before with another girl friend, whom he allowed to leave quite unharmed, and had signed the register "Lt. Colonel & Mrs N. G. C. Heath".

He still had a front door key to the hotel from that booking, so on the night he arrived late with Mrs Gardner no-one in the hotel ever heard them or saw them together. *The only witness to their arrival together was the taxi driver who brought them from the Panama Club.*

At two o'clock the next afternoon the chambermaid used her master key and went into the bedroom they had used after knocking two or three times without answer. One twin bed was soaked in blood. In the other lay the body of Mrs Gardner, with sheets drawn up to her neck. The "colonel" was missing.

Detective Inspector Shelley Symes and pathologist Dr Keith Simpson were called to the hotel. It was clearly a sex murder and the work of a maniac. Her ankles were still tied together, and her face and body, front and back, were covered in bloody weals. They appeared to have been made with a metal-tipped cane or riding crop. Her face was severely bruised consistent with blows from a clenched fist, and there were more bruises on her throat, as though strangulation had been attempted. (It was later proved that suffocation with a pillow was the actual cause of death.) Her face had been washed before the killer left – why was never clear.

A hunt was started for "Colonel Heath". His background was interesting. His schooldays were shared between a Roman Catholic school and grammar school, which he left at the age of seventeen. Date of birth: 1917. Place: Ilford, Essex.

In February 1936 he obtained a short-service commission in the Royal Air Force. He won his wings as pilot, but the next year he was dismissed the Service for a number of civil offences. He stole an NCO's car, went absent without leave and "bounced" a few cheques. After he was dismissed from the Air Force, he went around posing as "Lord Dudley" – rank and title always seemed to fascinate Heath – and bounced more cheques, whereupon he was placed on probation for two years. In the summer of 1938 he was sent to Borstal for housebreaking.

He was sentenced to three years there, but was released on the outbreak of war so that he could volunteer for the Armed Forces. He did so at once. He joined the Army this time, and by March 1940 he was once more an officer and a gentleman (so much for Selection Boards!) and was posted to Cairo. But Heath just could not keep out of trouble. There followed one escapade after another. Then, in July 1941, after swindling the Paymaster into paying him two salaries as Captain and disappearing without leave into the fleshpots of Egypt, Heath was courtmartialled and dismissed the Service *a second time*!

Most Armies would have flung a man in jail for this, but not ours: not an officer. On 27 October, 1941, *Mister* Heath, civilian, sailed from Egypt (second class, naturally, following his disgrace and dismissal) on the s.s. *Mooltan*, bound for Old Blighty's shores via Durban. Life on board ship clearly agreed with Heath. I have a sharply descriptive eyewitness report from Wing Commander Johnny Johnston, who sailed with Heath on the *Mooltan*. Wing Commander Johnston wrote to me about Heath in April, 1970:

"Heath was a handsome young man at that time, and it was obvious that some women on board were attracted to him. It may have been his good looks and aloof manner which attracted *them*, but he struck me at the time as being a very suave and plausible rogue.

"He left the ship at Durban, driven off in a large car by a well-dressed and attractive lady. The ship stayed there for three weeks, *and during that time we had inquiries from the South African police about Heath*.

"As far as I can recall now, their inquiries concerned a road accident where the body of a woman had been found in a burned-out car.

"Heath never joined the ship for the rest of the voyage."

* * *

Incredibly, Heath enlisted again. This time he volunteered for the South African Air Force, where he served for a trouble-free rest-of-the-war record. He collected a wife on the way. Neville Heath married in South Africa in 1942. Very little is known about the marriage. But Mrs Heath divorced him in October 1945, while he was away serving with S.A.A.F.

Heath was by all accounts a good pilot and aircrew officer: but he could not stay out of mischief on the ground. On 4 December, 1945, the South Africans made it number three – and cashiered him for a number of offences. I don't know if Heath's is a unique military record, to be thrown out of the service of the Crown three times in eight years, but it certainly is unique in the criminal world.

He came back to England in February 1946. Two months later he was in court. He was fined £10 by the Wimbledon magistrates for wearing uniform and ribbons he had no right to wear. Now he was officially a phoney, and it was at this time that "Group Captain Armstrong, D.S.O." was trying to strike up friendships in Fleet Street.

Now there was a naked, mutilated body lying in a bed in the Pembridge Court Hotel, and Heath had committed murder.

And now it was that the authorities had to make that fateful decision: to issue his picture to the newspapers or not. They did not. Instead they put out a statement and his description, saying the police were anxious to contact him "in case he could help their inquiries".

Heath was moving quietly around the southern seaside resorts, Brighton, Angmering, Worthing. He booked into the Ocean Hotel in Worthing. Then, cool as you like, he rang the same young woman who had spent the night with him at the Pembridge Court Hotel four days before the murder.

Naturally, she raised the subject of murder – in their hotel, *in their room*. The story was in every newspaper. She could talk of little else. "Colonel Heath" said yes, indeed, it was awful, but you see he had simply lent his door-key to a couple who wanted privacy and had slept elsewhere on the night himself.

Colonel Heath called on the girl at home. The visit was

not an unqualified success. Her parents did not care much for him. And when they too read in the newspapers that Heath was wanted – merely for questioning in case he could help inquiries – they made their daughter *insist* he contacted the authorities. Perhaps by so doing they saved her life. Perhaps the Fiend of Notting Hill intended her no harm: who knows? But either way there walks a lucky, lucky woman today.

Heath said goodbye to her. He never went to London. Instead he went to the Tollard Royal Hotel in Bournemouth and registered as "Group Captain Rupert Brooke". However, before he left Worthing, he sat down and wrote a long letter to the CID chief in London who was directing the manhunt for him. It was a curious thing to do. It was a curious letter, too, tantamount to an invitation to the police to pull him in for questioning. He even told them how to get in touch with him: via the personal column of the *Daily Telegraph*.

He may have written because the young lady had urged him so strongly to get in touch with the police. It may have been intended as another lie, another red herring. There may have been, though personally I doubt it, a noble motive behind the letter. Eminent counsel certainly thought so. After his trial Joshua Casswell, K.C., for the defence, said he believed Heath wished to be prevented from killing again.

Heath wrote to Det. Superintendent Tom Barratt:

"Sir,
     "I feel it to be my duty to inform you of certain facts in connection with the death of Mrs Gardner at Notting Hill Gate.
     "I booked in at the hotel last Sunday, but not with Mrs Gardner, whom I met for the first time during the week. I had drinks with her on Friday evening, and whilst I was with her she met an acquaintance with whom she was obliged to sleep.
     "The reasons, as I understand them, were mainly financial. It was then that Mrs Gardner asked if she could use my hotel room until two o'clock, and intimated that if I returned after that, I might spend the remainder of the night with her.
     "I gave her my keys and told her to leave the hotel door

open. It must have been almost 3 a.m. when I returned to the hotel, and found her in the condition of which you are aware.

"I realised that I was in an invidious position, and rather than notify the police, I packed my belongings and left. Since then I have been in several minds whether to come forward or not, but in view of the circumstances I have been afraid to.

"I can give you a description of the man. He was aged approx. 30, dark hair, black, with small moustache. Height about 5ft. 9in. slim build. His name was Jack, and I gathered he was a friend of Mrs Gardner of some long standing.

"The personal column of the *Daily Telegraph* will find me but at the moment I have assumed another name. I should like to come forward and help, but I cannot face the music of a fraud charge which will obviously be preferred against me if I should do so.

"I have the instrument with which Mrs Gardner was beaten and am forwarding this to you today.

"You will find my finger prints on it, but you should also find others as well.

signed,
N.G.C. Heath."

He never sent the riding crop to Superintendent Barratt or anyone else at the Yard. The letter was interesting: Heath was sounding out the police with an alibi. There is no sign of insanity, read it how you will.

The letter was received in London on 24 June. From then until 3 July, while his picture was circulated to every police station in the country but none shown to the unsuspecting public, Heath lived quite openly as Group Captain Rupert Brooke at the Tollard Royal. Down on the front he found his next victim, an ex-Wren called Doreen Marshall.

Doreen was a fine young woman, pretty, well brought up, and on holiday alone because she was recovering from a bad bout of 'flu. There was no mystery about how she met Heath: a smile from the dashing blond young man, a casual word on a sunny morning, a date for dinner that night – and murder.

He entertained her to dinner at his hotel and they had drinks in the lounge afterwards. As on the night he murdered Mrs Gardner, Heath was drinking hard all night. Miss Marshall tried to get a cab back to her own hotel, Heath insisted they walk – and he would escort her. She agreed. She was never seen alive again.

Before they left, Heath told the night porter he would be back shortly. He did not use the hotel entrance, but climbed a builder's ladder instead and got into his room unseen by the staff.

The night porter, a conscientious man, kept an eye on the clock. At 4.30 a.m. he went into Heath's room – and saw him asleep in bed. He noted that Heath's shoes were in the room, by the bed, and caked with sand, instead of being out in the corridor for cleaning. Heath admitted coming in by ladder, next morning.

Two days went by before Miss Marshall was missed at her hotel. The manager made inquiries. Someone remembered she had a dinner date at the Tollard on 3 July. When *his* hotel manager questioned him, Heath denied his guest had been Doreen Marshall.

Her body was discovered by a woman, out with her dog in the bushes and flowers of Bournemouth's Branksome Chine. She was naked. Her dress and underclothes were placed on top of her body. Her stockings were found yards away. She had been badly beaten, stabbed, and disgustingly mutilated. The worst mutilations were made after death. The police believed Heath stripped naked himself before the attack and that this explains the lack of bloodstains on his clothing. And that he washed himself clean in the sea after the murder, dressed and walked back to his hotel.

Heath had physically to walk right into a police station and confront a man in uniform before he was recognised, but by then it was too late to prevent another murder, too late to help poor Doreen Marshall.

All my life as a crime reporter I have tried to see the police point of view and I do not criticise them now: I merely question, as I have always done, the decision to withhold general publication of his picture.

Apart from the letter to Det. Superintendent Barratt,

there was no clue to Heath's whereabouts. Heath put his own head in the noose. When Doreen Marshall was still officially missing he rang the police in Bournemouth (as Group Captain Rupert Brooke) and offered to help them in their inquiries.

They accepted. When the handsome, blue-eyed Group Captain strolled round to the station, a sharp-eyed young detective thought he bore an uncanny resemblance to a wanted man called Heath. He held him pending further inquiries and called the Murder Squad. When they found the body next day, Heath was already in the bag.

Spooner of the Yard (a Detective Inspector in 1946) questioned Heath. On his arrival Spooner had been handed a statement Heath had written and again it was interesting, fascinating even – he was accused of nothing yet here he was offering another alibi.

He wrote that Miss Marshall (*on the dinner night, at the Tollard*), – "told me she was considering cutting short her holiday in Bournemouth and returning home on Friday. She mentioned an American staying in her hotel, and told me he had taken her for car rides. She also mentioned an invitation to go with him to Exeter but I gathered – although she did not actually say so – that she did not intend to go.

"Another American was mentioned, I believe his name was Pat, to whom I believe she was unofficially engaged some while ago.

"At 11 p.m. Miss Marshall suggested going away but I persuaded her to stay a little longer. About 11.30 the weather was clear and we left the hotel and sat on a seat, overlooking the sea.

"From this stage onward my times were vague because I had no wristwatch. We must have talked for at least an hour, probably longer, and then we walked down the slope to the Pavilion. Miss Marshall did not wish me to accompany her but I insisted on doing so at least part of the way.

"I left her at the pier and watched her cross the road and enter the gardens.

"Before leaving I asked her if she would come round the following day, but she said she would be busy for the next few days, but would telephone me on Sunday, if she could manage it.

"I have not seen her to speak to since then, although I thought I saw her entering Bobby's Ltd. on Thursday morning.

"After leaving Miss Marshall, I walked along the seafront in a westerly direction and up the path from Durley Chine, and to the clifftop, and so back to the hotel where I went to bed.

"It rained heavily before I reached the hotel."

Spooner took Heath back to London. After attending an identity parade he was picked out by the cab driver who had taken him and Mrs Gardner to their Notting Hill Gate hotel. Heath was then charged with Mrs Gardner's murder. He made no reply.

He was tried at the Old Bailey in September that year, before Mr Justice Morris. Heath's counsel pleaded insanity and called Dr William Hubert, psychiatrist and former psychotherapist at Broadmoor, for the defence.

Heath himself would have none of it. Halfway through the doctor's evidence Heath scribbled this note from the dock to his counsel: "It may be of interest to know that in my discussions with Hubert I have never suggested that I should be excused or that I told him I felt I should be, because of insanity."

Very few madmen, of course, believe themselves insane so Heath's protest was not inconsistent with his counsel's plea.

Joshua Casswell pleaded that Heath was "as mad as a hatter". And there are those who believed Heath actually murdered Doreen Marshall in a deliberate attempt to escape the hangman (for the Mrs Gardner murder) by being sent to Broadmoor.

The judge had this to say:

"The tests as to insanity to which I have referred are the tests which have in all criminal cases to be applied in regard to this matter. Whether medical men might wish from a medical point of view to frame other tests is not a question with which I need trouble you.

"We are here to administer the law.

"Equally you will see that insanity is not to be found merely because some conduct might be regarded as so outrageous as to be wholly unexpected from the generality of men.

"Strong sexual instinct is not insanity: a mere love of bloodshed or mere recklessness are not in themselves insanity: an inability to resist temptation, the satisfaction of some perverted impulse, is not, without more, to be excused on the ground of insanity.

"The plea of insanity cannot be permitted to become the easy or vague explanation of some conduct which is shocking merely because it is startling.

"The law of insanity is not to become the refuge of those who cannot challenge a charge which is brought against them."

I sat in the court and listened to the Judge very carefully. Already we were moving into the fringe battlefield of the capital punishment issue, though none of us realised it so clearly then, and I would have liked his words to be hung on the wall of every defence counsel and psychiatrist in the land.

Heath was sentenced to death. He was hanged at Pentonville, on 16 October, 1946.

Heath died coolly enough. When the prison Governor paid his final call and offered this fresh-faced, scrubbed-looking, so-handsome young man a last drink (of brandy), Heath rustled up a grin from somewhere and jokingly asked for a double. He got it. And went straightway to his death on the scaffold.

I shed no tears for the sadist Heath. But still, today, a quarter of a century later, I could weep at the decision that had to be made within the requirements of the law and led directly to the murder of Doreen Marshall. If the public had been warned, she need not have died: the likelihood is that Heath would have been recognised by some member of the public long before he could have killed a second time.

I had long talks with my friends in the CID over this (Spooner was one of them) and I know how they grieved over the Marshall murder. But is there a dry-as-dust official mind that could not care less as long as the letter of the law is obeyed?

After the case was over, I published the official picture of Heath as it appeared in the *Police Gazette*. I said this was the picture every policeman carried in his uniform pocket – but none of the public were allowed to see.

I was later told that the Director of Public Prosecutions had "seriously" considered summoning me for "publishing an official document". For the sake of the police and the reputation of the Yard, I am glad he did not. That would have made a bad decision contemptuous.

Percy Hoskins

The Porthole Murder

When I first came to live in Cornwall in 1957
– fleeing from the publicity that followed my
first book *The Outsider* – I became acquainted
with Dr Denis Hocking, the Cornwall county
pathologist, and heard from him some interesting
tales of murder and suicide. Ten years ago, when
Denis was already in his mid-eighties, he sent me
the typescript of his autobiography, and asked
me if I could recommend a publisher. In fact,
it was soon accepted, but after a delay of two
years or so, the publisher went bankrupt. Denis
persisted, and a few days before writing these
words, I attended the launching party of *Bodies
and Crimes* in a hotel in Carlyon Bay, St Austell.
Among the guests was a scriptwriter who was
beginning to script a series based on the book
for Anglia Television, and Dennis Herbstein, who
had written a book about Dr Hocking's favourite
case – the one that follows.

As we discussed the porthole case, Dennis
Herbstein made an intersting point: that James
Camb might well have been telling the truth when
he claimed that Gay Gibson simply died in his
arms while having sex. Herbstein had interviewed
many doctors, who had told him about similar
deaths – in one case, a husband and wife came
back from a party and were in the process of
making love when the wife simply expired. The
post mortem revealed no cause of death.

I am inclined to doubt this version of events,
simply because it seems to me that if this had
happened, Camb's first reaction would have surely
been (a) to report the death to the captain – which

might have involved his being disciplined, but not the risk of being charged with murder, (b) simply left the body where it was and made his way back to his own cabin. Having said which, I just admit that *Porthole* is an impressive piece of crime writing, and that the notion of an officer losing his head in sheer panic when he finds himself embracing a corpse is by no means inconceivable.

Bodies and Crimes is published by the Book Guild.

What I have always regarded as my most interesting murder concerned the disappearance of the actress Gay Gibson from the *SS Durban Castle* on the night of 10 October, 1947, on her passage from Cape Town to Southampton. It was intriguing because we had no body and so could let our imaginations run riot – a favourite pastime of mine. Dr Donald Teare of St George's Hospital, London, thought that she had been strangled. Prof. Webster and I thought that she had died from natural causes, possibly associated with sexual excitement.

This case has been recorded elsewhere as "The Porthole Murder' in *Facets of Crime*, published by Bossiney Books along with ten other stories. It is reproduced here by kind permission of the proprietor of Bossiney Books, Mr Michael Williams. Incidentally, the cover of his publication, depicting the victim as she would have appeared after having been thrown to the sharks is well worth the price of £1.50.

To whet your appetites, not all the evidence obtained by the Defence from South Africa was allowed to be given at the trial. We were limited to three witnesses from that country, but we had significant affidavits from a number of others. As their testimony, however, tended to attack the morals of the dead girl, it was thought that the Judge would probably disallow it. From his conduct of the trial, I felt certain that he would most certainly have done so. The significance of this unrecorded evidence was that the girl had been in the habit of indulging in unusual sexual exercises, and there was a possibility that she had lost her life during one of these adventures.

This is from memory; unfortunately the original documents have disappeared after being sent to Prof. Webster.

Amongst her sexual perversions, it was stated that "she sucks a cock".

Only one person knows exactly what took place in cabin No. 126 in the Union Castle liner *Durban Castle* on the night of 17th–18th October 1947.

This is James Camb, a one-time Promenade Deck Steward who was tried for the murder of the occupant of that cabin, Miss Eileen Isabella Ronnie Gibson, at Winchester Assizes between 18th March and 22nd March 1948.

The case is cited by Mr Justice Humphreys as "yet another instance of convincing proof of the guilt of an accused person being afforded by circumstantial evidence". Yet, to the minds of many lawyers, and even more medical experts, there was equally compelling proof of the Defendant's innocence. A great many of the known facts were not in dispute, and readily admitted by the Defendant. There is no doubt that the girl died in her cabin that night; it is how she met her death that is so intriguing.

Eileen Isabella Ronnie Gibson, quiet and friendly in manner, was just over twenty-one years of age when she boarded the *Durban Castle* on 10th October at Cape Town, bound for Southampton. The ship was practically empty, there being only fifty-seven first class passengers, most of them elderly, and apparently most of them rather bored. Gay Gibson's two main companions, with whom she usually dined, were an elderly Mr Hopwood and Wing-Commander Bray.

Her background suggested a desire for much more lively companionship. She did most of her war service in a touring company of Service personnel, having a taste for the theatre, although probably not brilliant. She was described as having been a beautiful girl, slim built with dark hair and large, dark, almond-shaped eyes. An outstanding feature was her white skin, likened by her theatrical producer to alabaster. She had the grace and poise of a good, professional actress.

She left the Forces on compassionate grounds, and when medically examined on her discharge, was graded AW1, but it was also noted that she had a chronic ear infection and she was marked as "non-tropical". After her release from the Forces, she toured South Africa with a repertory company, playing a leading part with considerable success. It was whilst engaged in this way that she met, amongst others of the cast, three people who were to give evidence of the greatest significance on behalf of the Defendant at his trial.

Through no fault of the repertory company, the play in which she was taking the leading lady's part, Clifford Odet's famous play *Golden Bay* came to an abrupt end in Johannesburg, but the producer made plans to take it to Pretoria. But Gay Gibson suddenly threw in her part and announced her decision to return to England by the next available boat, which in fact she did.

Life on board with only elderly companionship must have been dull for her, and it is therefore no surprise to find her, even when only two days out from the Cape, having chatty conversation with the young and good-looking Promenade Deck Steward, James Camb. He was rather thick set, with bright eyes and a good complexion. Confident in manner, he looked attractive and dashing in his white Steward's uniform. But nobody could say that Camb was an exemplary character. Aged thirty, with a wife and daughter of three, he enlivened his life as a first class Deck Steward by having sordid little affairs with unattached female passengers. He even boasted that "some of them like us better than the passengers. I have been with them several times on other trips." This was said during an early interview with the police (Detective Sergeant Quinlan) at Southampton; and then he added a most significant phrase – "Of course, if I was found out, I would get the sack."

This was confirmed by the Master of the ship, Captain Patey, who said at the trial that Camb, as a Deck Steward, had no right to visit any cabin, and that if found in one, he would have been logged, his book endorsed, and finally he would have been dismissed. He would find it very difficult to get another job.

Gay Gibson was presented as a young woman of impeccable character. Her mother, quite properly, said that she was one of the finest types of English womanhood, physically, mentally, and morally. One of the South African witnesses, Dr Schoub, the wife of the producer of the play *Golden Boy*, said that she liked her very much: "she was a nice, charming girl."

And yet a very different picture developed as a result of inquiries instituted by Camb's solicitor, Mr Geoffrey Wells of Southampton. Camb told him of many personal and intimate details of the girl's past life that he could have got only from the girl herself. Only three or four days out from Cape Town, in conversation with Miss Gibson's Stewardess, Miss Field, he said that Gay Gibson had told him that she was three months pregnant. Asked why she did not marry him, she replied that he was already married, but she was crazy about him. In any event, she suddenly decided to throw up her job and return to England. She had travelled out to South Africa in an emigrant ship. She was returning as a first class passenger, and there was no dispute that her fare was being paid by a Mr Charles Sventonski. In all, Miss Gibson received something like £500 from this man, but it was with the knowledge and approval of her mother, who said that it was a proposition by a wealthy and successful man who was ready to back Gay's career as a business proposition. Although, as far as was known, he had never been in England, he gave Miss Gibson a letter of introduction to the Abbey Theatre, Dublin.

A contraceptive was found in her cabin. One other thing that came out of these apparently intimate conversations was that Miss Gibson told Camb that she had gone to South Africa for her health as she suffered from asthma.

As a result of the information obtained from these conversations, Mr Wells went to South Africa and interviewed members of the cast of the repertory company, run by a Mr Gilbert, in which Miss Gibson had played the leading lady. Three of these were brought over by the Defence to give evidence on behalf of the Defendant. They were Mike Abel, Henry Gilbert, and his wife Dr Schoub.

Mike Abel testified that Miss Gibson had told him that

she had come out to South Africa because she had a chest complaint, and mentioned asthma. She often behaved in an hysterical manner, and on one occasion she collapsed, became blue about the lips, and in the corner of her mouth there was white saliva. There were times when she fainted, when she coughed a great deal, and when her breathing was laboured. On occasion, she complained of pains in her tummy and left arm – a sort of shooting pain coming right down into her fingers. These are all possible symptoms of lung and heart disease. Mike Abel went on to say in his evidence that Miss Gibson had told him that she was pregnant, and asked him for £200 to get to England to get a doctor to take care of her; she said she had no faith in South African doctors and wanted to get to England.

Henry Gilbert, also of Johannesburg, testified that he was an actor-manager, and had produced Gay Gibson as "Lorna" in *Golden Boy*. He often found her distraught and highly strung, tiring easily, sometimes drinking too heavily and becoming highly emotional. He also said that she had come to South Africa for health reasons, as she suffered from asthma. She also said, "I cannot love like other people" and "I am not like other girls".

Dr Ina Schoub, the wife of Henry Gilbert, in her evidence also said that Miss Gibson had told her, too, that she had come to South Africa because of her health, as she suffered from asthma. She tired easily and became short of breath on exertion, but the doctor said she had never seen her in an actual asthmatical attack. Miss Gibson discussed sex rather intimately, said that she had had sexual experience, and later became worried as she thought that she had become pregnant – a thing apparently known to the whole cast.

This was the background to the subsequent tragedy. A young actress of possibly dubious morality, not averse to the attentions of a very presentable and highly-sexed young man who risked his career in order to be with her in her cabin.

The Crown called compelling circumstantial evidence to prove that James Camb strangled Miss Gibson in her cabin on board the *Durban Castle* at about 3 a.m. on the morning of 18th October 1947; afterwards, he threw her body out into the shark-infested sea through the porthole of her cabin, in order to conceal evidence of his crime. It was alleged that he raped, attempted to rape, or attempted to sexually assault the girl; that she resisted and raised the alarm, and in order to preserve his job and prevent her giving evidence against him he killed her – by strangulation.

The Defence admitted that the girl died in her cabin at the material time, and they called equally compelling medical evidence that her death could have been due to natural causes. The Defendant was there at the time of her death, but because he had been disturbed and possibly recognised, he panicked and threw the body of the girl out of the ship hoping that her disappearance would be put down to suicide or accident.

The trial opened on Thursday, 18th March 1948 in the Assize court at Winchester. The court was a temporary one, formed of plywood partitions in the Great Hall of Winchester Castle, and presided over by King Arthur's Round Table.

Going into the witness-box was physically very similar to "walking the plank" of old, and felt very much like it. One mounted some four or five steps, walked six to eight feet along a narrow rail-guarded walk, and then found oneself perched four or more feet high up in the middle of the court, completely isolated. The Judge was on one's left, the Defendent on the right, the Jury in front, and Counsel seemingly lost around their table on a much lower level.

Counsel for the Crown was that able, and to a guilty prisoner, dangerous KC, the late Mr G.D. (Khaki) Roberts, with Mr H.H. Elam as his junior. The Defence was led by the equally able Mr J. D. Casswell, KC, with Mr T.J. (now Sir Joseph) Molony to assist.

The Judge was the late Mr Justice Hilbery, and in this choice Camb was unfortunate. The Judge's attitude throughout the whole of the trial was clearly against the Defendant, as was his summing-up. So much so, that one of the grounds of the ultimate appeal was that the Judge's summing-up was too unfavourable to the prisoner. But the Lord Chief Justice, Lord Goddard, sitting with Mr Justice Pritchard and Mr Justice Humphreys dismissed this argument, saying, "Undoubtedly the learned Judge's summing-up was not favourable to the prisoner," and he went on to quote an earlier judgment given in the Appeal Court to the effect that a Judge is bound to give some assistance to the Jury on questions of fact as well as on questions of law.

In the court, in full view of everybody there was the bed from cabin 126 of the *Durban Castle*, a porthole of the size of the one in the cabin mounted in a wooden frame, and the bell-push in the cabin; this was at the head of the bed, and in a narrow opening beside the bed was a small chest. Other exhibits included plans of the cabin and cabin deck, bedding and pillows from the bunk, and photographs.

On the night that Gay Gibson disappeared, she had dined as usual with her friends Mr Hopwood and Wing-Commander Bray. She danced a little afterwards, and then as it was a very hot night she left her companions to look for her swimsuit to go bathing in the liner's swimming pool. She returned about half an hour afterwards, saying that she could not find it. It was during this half hour that the senior night-watchman saw Miss Gibson and Camb talking together, and he overheard a very significant remark made by Camb, *viz*: "I say, I have a bone to pick with you, and a big one at that." This was the first of two remarks of supreme significance in this case. The obvious inference drawn by the Crown was that Camb had indeed a grudge to be paid off. His own explanation was a perfectly rational one. There was no question of these two people being on very friendly terms from almost the beginning of the voyage. As a Deck Steward, Camb was not allowed in the cabin area. Orders had been given by Mr Hopwood that Miss Gibson was to have her tea every afternoon in her cabin. These trays were prepared by Camb and left out for the Stewardess to take down to the cabin. On the 17th, orders were given for a special tea tray to be prepared. This was done, but the tray was never collected. He was angry: hence his remark. Could anything be more rational?

After his remonstrance, Miss Gibson said that she was sorry, and then asked him to leave out a rum for her to collect later in the evening. Pushing his friendliness a little further, probably with obvious intentions, he asked her if she would like him to prepare a supper tray or bring her some lemonade, adding that he had a good mind to bring a drink down and join her. Her reply was, "Please yourself. It's up to you," or words to that effect. At 12.45 that night, he noticed that the glass of rum had been taken, and in its place there was Miss Gibson's alarm clock, normally kept on the dressing-table top. That clock appears never to have been seen again.

At about 12.40 a.m., Mr Hopwood escorted Miss Gibson back to her cabin; but it was a very warm night, and some twenty minutes later, the boatswain's mate saw her leaning over the rail at the after end of the Promenade Deck. She must have made an attractive picture on this her last appearance in public around midnight, in her long black evening dress, her feet in silver dancing shoes. The boatswain's mate was in charge of a party cleaning the decks, and asked her to move on, otherwise she would get wet.

This was the last that was ever seen of her by anyone – excepting James Camb.

The subsequent tragedy was heralded in by the ringing of bells. At night-time, the bell-pushes in the cabins are switched through to the night-watchman's galley. At 2.58 a.m. on the 18th, Murray, the senior night-watchman and his assistant Steer, heard the bell ringing above their heads. Following a trail of lights, Steer arrived at cabin No. 126.

The light was on, coming through the fanlight; and – most surprisingly – both red and green lights were showing, indicating that both bell-pushes had been pressed at the same time, as there was only one ringing of the bell. One bell would have called the stewardess, the other the night-watchman.

Something very peculiar had happened, something probably of great urgency, as emphasised by the Crown; but, as always in this curious case, there was an alternative explanation as will be revealed later.

Steer said that it would take him under a minute to reach the cabin from his galley. There was no noise coming from the cabin when he reached it. He knocked on the door and tried it; it was not bolted and he opened it a couple of inches. It was immediately slammed in his face, but not before he had seen the face of James Camb, who said,

"All right." Returning to his senior, Murray, Steer told him that he had seen Camb in the cabin, and then they both went back. They found the cabin in darkness, with all lights, including the indicator lights, extinguished. Both men then decided to report the matter to the officer on the bridge, but not wanting to get a colleague into trouble, they merely reported the matter. Believing that it was probably another passenger in Miss Gibson's room, the officer said there was nothing he could do about it, and that it was not for him to interfere with the passengers' morals.

Four hours later, at 7.30 a.m. Miss Field, the Stewardess knocked on the door of cabin 126; there was no reply, and she found the door unlocked. This was unusual, as Gay Gibson invariably bolted her door at night. It was also of great significance, because whoever, including Camb, might have been with the girl in her cabin that night was obviously there with her consent, if not by her invitation. Miss Field entered the cabin and found it empty. Thinking that the occupant might have gone to the bathroom, Miss Field was not alarmed. She found the bed a little more disarranged than normal and there were some stains on the pillow and sheets, but she did not take particular notice of these. The bedclothes had been pulled back. The porthole was open, but this would be natural in tropical seas; Miss Gibson's evening dress was hanging in its usual place at the foot of the bunk; her dressing-gown, and black pyjamas were missing. Miss Field tidied up the cabin, and it was only a little later after she had asked the Bedroom Steward if Miss Gibson had had a bath, and was told "No" that she became alarmed, and reported her missing. Her disappearance was broadcast over the whole ship, but without response. Captain Patey reversed course for over an hour, but realising the futility of any further search in shark infested waters, he resumed his course at 11.40 a.m. Incidentally, amongst many other wild rumours in this case, there was the report of a shark caught off the West Coast of Africa shortly afterwards, having a woman's painted fingernail in its stomach.

Captain Patey immediately set inquiries afoot. Steer told him that he had seen Camb in Miss Gibson's cabin early that morning, and Camb was sent for. Camb, thinking he had not been recognised, immediately embarked on a series of lies designed to protect his job. He said he was nowhere near any passenger cabin, since retiring at 12.45 a.m. He continued on this course, until his line of defence was broken by the police after arrival of the ship at Southampton. He got himself into serious trouble by this line of conduct, and the first devastating question asked in crossexamination at his trial by Mr Roberts was, "Would you describe yourself as a truthful man?" He obviously was not, at that time, anyway.

Captain Patey, at the first interview, did not tell Camb he had been recognised in Miss Gibson's cabin. He merely suggested that Camb was suspected of being in the neighbourhood of the cabin at about 3 a.m. Camb's reply was a flat denial. The captain then sent for William Pott, a steward who shared a cabin with Camb. Pott said that contrary to normal practice, Camb turned up that morning wearing Steward's full dress, a long-sleeved jacket, to do the ordinary routine work of cleaning-up. Was there something on his arms that he wanted to conceal?

Captain Patey decided that Camb should be medically examined. By this time Camb's nerves were becoming somewhat frayed, but he agreed to be examined by the ship's doctor, Dr Griffiths.

Dr Griffith's findings were of the most importance. He gave evidence at the trial that he found three main groups of injuries on Camb. First, there were some scratches over the back of the right shoulder, quite recent, and similar to those made by a cat's claws. The inference was that they could have been done by a woman's finely-pointed fingernails. Camb explained these away by saying that he had done them himself with a rough towel – a quite reasonable explanation. Secondly, there were some rather old scratches on the left collar bone, obviously of no recent significance except that they did bear out Camb's contention that he had recently been scratching himself rather severely with rough towels. The really important group of injuries was the third, on the front of the right wrist. These injuries were of intriguing interest. There were about twelve of them, some linear, some crescentic, running more of less horizontally across the inside of the right lower arm, commencing some four to five inches above the wrist. Dr Griffiths described these injuries as having been done probably by digging with finger-nails into the flesh. This was an important feature in the evidence, but as usual in this trial, there were divergent opinions as to how they might have been caused. The Crown said by Miss Gibson, who being manually strangulated, had attempted to tear away the hand of her assailant by pulling on his arm, digging her nails into him in the process. The Defendant offered an alternative and completely acceptable explanation as will appear later. These marks, however, had obviously caused Camb to wear his long-sleeved jacket on the morning of Gay Gibson's disappearance.

Camb, now thoroughly rattled, then wrote two notes to his Captain. In the first, he denied again having been anywhere near the girl's cabin on the night, and in the second he gave rather unconvincing explanations as to how he came by his injuries – mainly by scratching himself with his nails or with rough towels.

On the morning of 25th October, the liner steamed into Southampton and at 1.25 a.m. Detective Sergeant Quinlan boarded the ship; at 5.25 a.m., after preliminary inquiries, he interviewed Camb. Camb continued to deny that he had ever been near Miss Gibson's cabin on the fatal night, but after a while, he sensed that the night-watchman Steer had given away to the authorities the fact that he had been recognised in her cabin, and he made the not unexpected remark, whether he was innocent or not: "That puts me in a tight spot."

Later the same day, Detective Sergeant Quinlan decided, quite properly, to increase the pressure, saying that he had definitely established that Camb had been in Miss Gibson's cabin at about 3 a.m. on the night of her disappearance. A very worried Camb then confessed that he *had* been down to the cabin that night, asking Miss Gibson if she wanted some lemonade with her rum; she was looking for a swim suit – confirmed by her friend, Mr Hopkins. She asked Camb to leave her rum in its usual place. He still denied having gone later to the cabin. Later Detective Sergeant (Acting Inspector) Gibbons said to him, "You are being given an opportunity to make any explanation you may care to about this. That explanation, so far, has been a categorical denial that you know anything about the death of Miss Gibson. You may find that such a complete denial will be difficult to explain if later you are called upon to explain it." Camb replied: "Does that mean I murdered her and that I shall be charged with murder?" Gibbons said that he could not say whether or not a charge would be preferred. And then there occurred a conversation which set in train all the investigations that became the basis of the evidence for the Defence.

Gibbons said: "We have to give particular care to any explanation which you may put forward. You may be able to give a reasonable explanation of the cause of her death and her disappearance." Camb replied: "You mean that Miss Gibson might have died from some other cause, other than being murdered? She might have had a heart attack, or something?"

How does one interpret such a remark?

One explanation, put forward by the Crown, was that it was a heaven-sent invitation to Camb to adduce a heart attack as the cause of Miss Gibson's death. The other is that it is equally consistent with the mental attitude of a worried man who had racked his brains to find some explanation as to why a woman should suddenly die in his arms, and, in a flash, the explanation comes to him. After only a short while, during which he boasted that he and other members of the crew were often preferred at night-time by female passengers, he elected to make the following statement:

"I have already stated to you that I went to Miss Gibson's cabin at about eleven o'clock, and during the course of conversation with her I made an appointment to meet her that night. I knocked at the door after I had finished work at about one o'clock, but there was no answer. I opened the door of her cabin and found it empty. I then went forward to the well deck, where I sat for about half an hour smoking. I then returned to Miss Gibson's cabin at about two o'clock and found her there. After a short conversation I got into bed with her consent. Intimacy took place. Whilst in the act of sexual intercourse she clutched me, foaming at the mouth. I immediately ceased the act, but she was very still. I felt for her heart beats, but could not find any. She was at that time very still, and I cannot offer any explanation as to how the bells came to be rung, as I most definitely did not touch them myself. Thinking she had fainted, I tried artificial respiration on her. Whilst doing this, the night-watchman knocked at the door and attempted to open it. I shut the door again, saying it was all right. Then I panicked, as I thought he had gone to the bridge to report to the officer of the watch, and I did not want to be found in such a compromising position. After a few minutes I could not find any sign of life. After a struggle with the limp body – by the way, she was still wearing her dressing-gown – I managed to lift her to the porthole and push her through. I am fairly certain that at the time she was dead, but I was terribly frightened. I then went forward and turned in. The time would be about 3.30 a.m."

After saying that he was glad to have got the matter off his mind, Camb then added: "What will happen about this? My wife must not know about this. If she does I will do away with myself." Camb's Counsel, Mr Caswell, believed that this was absolutely true and proved his innocence. He had lied like a trooper up to this point to save his job, but it still did not occur to him that he might face a murder charge.

Camb is then alleged to have said something to a Detective Constable, unconfirmed, which no man in his senses (anticipating that he was about to be charged with murder) would make. The Detective Constable said that when he was alone with Camb, the Steward said to him, "She struggled. I had my arms around her neck and when I was trying to pull them away she scratched me. I panicked and threw her out of the porthole. It was a hell of a splash when she hit the water. I can't understand why the officer of the watch did not hear something." This was manifestly ridiculous. The porthole was some twenty-five feet above the water line, there was backlash from the bow wave immediately below, and machinery in the dummy funnel above all would have drowned any sound of splashing, as was confirmed by Captain Patey. The Detective Constable who made the statement had "left the Force before the trial to better himself, but was still unemployed".

The Prosecution produced two more important witnesses.

The first was Dr Montgomery, a senior Scientific Officer at the Metropolitan Police Laboratory at Hendon. He had received various exhibits in the case for scientific examination. The only things of any significance that he found were:

On the top sheet, two small blood spots, each about the size of a sixpence. The blood was of Group "O". This was not the group of Camb, which was Group "A". On the bottom sheet, there were faint blood spots, too small to group. No hair from the accused was found, and nothing of significance was found in scrapings from around the porthole, or elsewhere in the room. It was obvious that no fight had taken place there.

I later examined all the exhibits with important results that will appear later.

The last, and very important witness for the Crown was Dr (now Professor) Donald Teare, then Assistant Pathologist and Lecturer in Forensic Medicine at St George's Hospital, London.

Dr Teare described the signs he would expect to find in a case of death by strangulation, the most important relevant to this case being probable slight haemorrhage from the lungs or upper air passages due to constriction of blood vessels by pressure on the neck, and hence in this case, the possible explanation of the blood on the sheets. The blood might also have come from scratch marks by the victim injuring her throat during attempts to relieve the pressure. Unconsciousness would supervene in a matter of only a few seconds, probably not more than fifteen, and death would be within a minute. Dr Teare refused to express any opinion concerning the scratch and other marks on the body of Camb. He agreed that signs of muddiness in Miss Gibson's finger-nails, noticed by her friend Mr Hopwood, would indicate that the girl was suffering from some circulatory defect, confirmed by pains down the left arm, and that she was possibly suffering from some form of heart disease associated with asthma. On balance, however, he felt that what had been found was more in keeping with death by strangulation than death from a heart attack, although in all conscience what had been found was very little.

Dr Teare concluded the evidence for the Prosecution, and then came the turn of the Defence.

This was outlined at the beginning by Mr Casswell. His main contention was that Miss Gibson was a young woman not at all averse to the attentions of a presentable young man, even to the extent of not opposing his visiting her in the early hours of the morning in her cabin, more or less naked. There was a well-authenticated history of longstanding illness, though not by any means of a serious nature; also very experienced medical evidence that the girl could have died in exactly the way described by the Defendant, and with signs exactly as were found. Camb knew nothing about the significance of Miss Gibson's past medical history. Indeed, it was remarkable that he should have told a story about what happened on the fatal night, so close to what might have been *expected* to happen in the circumstances. Confirmation was surely almost complete.

The first witness for the Defence was the accused himself.

He outlined the increasing friendliness that grew up between himself and Miss Gibson during the early days of the voyage, and confirmed his part in preparing tea and drinks for her, to be taken down to her by the night-watchman. He explained, too, his use of the phrase: "I have a bone to pick with you."

He then went on to detail the events of the fateful October night.

After the episode of ordering the rum for the night, he went to the cabin soon after 2 o'clock. The door was not fastened. As, according to Miss Field, Miss Gibson invariably bolted her door after retiring to her cabin, Camb's advent in the early hours of the morning cannot have been a surprise to her. She was wearing nothing underneath a yellow quilted dressing-gown. Camb was emphatic, and could not be moved, that she was not wearing black pyjamas. There were no black pyjamas in the room, and he did not throw them out of the porthole after the girl when he put her through. Much was made in cross-examination of the loss of these pyjamas. The Crown contended, most reasonably, that they were missing because the girl was wearing them and was therefore not inviting intercourse. They were never found. Rumour again had it that they were, in fact, in the cabin of a distinguished male fellow-passenger who is alleged to have said that he would come forward if there was any danger of Camb's being hanged – which there was not, as capital punishment was in abeyance, fortunately, at that time. There is indeed an interval of time, from about 1 a.m. to 2 a.m. completely unaccounted for, but of course the girl could have gone back at once to her cabin after being moved on by the crew swabbing decks.

However that may be, the couple talked, for some time, about the dullness of the dance. Then almost inevitably Cambs climbed on to the bed beside her. Raising no objections, she unzipped her dressing-gown, revealing her nakedness beneath. He then went on to describe exactly what he mentioned in his statement to the police. He added, however, that she had her right hand round his neck with her left hand holding his right arm. When her body stiffened as she was gasping for breath, her right arm was still round his neck, and her left hand holding his forearm, gripped tightly. Of course, a perfectly rational happening, which would account for the nail mark injuries seen in his neck and arm. Verbally he added somewhat to the content of his written statement to the police – and it was of significance. In his own words: "I immediately got off the bed. She was completely relaxed, as though she was in a dead faint. One eye was just slightly open. Her mouth was a little open too. There was a faint line of bubbles, which I assumed to be froth, just on the edges of the lips. It was a muddy colour and appeared to be slightly blood-flecked. I was rather stunned for the moment. First of all I listened and felt for her heartbeats. I could not find any and I attempted to massage the stomach towards the heart to bring back circulation." It was at this stage that in all probability Camb pressed his thigh against the bell-pushes, and set off the alarm that was his undoing. He swore that Gay Gibson herself did not ring the bells, nor did he know how they had been rung. Confronted by Steer, he panicked and thought only of destroying any evidence. His whole career was now in jeopardy. He hoped people would presume that she had fallen overboard. It was at this point that Camb had a gruelling cross-examination by Mr Roberts, who quite rightly said that he had wilfully destroyed the only positive evidence. If there were no marks on her body, and other things were found out by a postmortem examination showing that she was not a healthy girl, then his story would have been proved to be correct, and he would have been completely exonerated. This was a point hammered home by the Judge in his charge to the Jury. It was certainly a very valid point, but one can perhaps visualise the man in his dreadful predicament behaving as he did.

The whole of Camb's cross-examination was a testing experience, but he stood up to it superbly, without being shaken or departing in one detail from his account of the way in which the girl died. So composed was he that the point told rather severely against him in the eventual final speech to the jury by Mr Roberts. Mr Roberts said: "Camb says he threw her through the porthole in panic. Did he panic? Panic? Do you think he is the sort of man to panic? Did you see any sign of panic at all? Did you see any lack of poise, or composure, or full control of the thinking facilities?" The same point was also pressed home by the Judge.

The main plank in the evidence on behalf of the Defendant was the medical evidence.

Professor Webster, Professor of Forensic Medicine at Birmingham University and a Home Office Pathologist, had been asked by the Director of Public Prosecutions to review the medical evidence and give his opinion as to the possibility of Camb's statement being correct. He did so in characteristic no-nonsense terms, saying that, in his opinion, Camb's statement was perfectly possible. On this account Professor Webster was naturally offered to the Defence. What impressed him most was the detailed description of the way in which Gay Gibson died, by a man without any possible medical knowledge. Professor Webster said: "The account given by Camb of this girl's death could have occurred." He instanced three cases in his experience in which death had occurred during sexual intercourse, when there was no question of any violence. In none of them had the dead person shown any previous sign of any disease. Death could occur from the rupture of a small aneurysm in the brain, or from heart disease, the latter either primary or secondary to some other condition, including asthma. (An aneurysm is a thin-walled dilatation of a blood vessel. It is not unusual, and rupture frequently occurs. Such rupture in the brain can cause instant death in many cases, an occurrence which is by no means rare in young people, and more likely to occur under strain or excitement. With regard to heart disease this can, of course, be primary, due to some affection of the heart itself, or secondary. Secondary causes of degeneration of the heart muscle include chronic infection resulting in bacterial poisoning of the tissues, or such conditions as asthma, which throw an increasing strain on the heart to pump blood through increasing resistance in the lungs.)

He thought that in Gay Gibson's case it could have been heart disease associated either with asthma, or her chronically septic ear. Professor Webster's conclusion was that the chances of natural death were equal with those of strangulation. Dr Teare put the chances of strangulation as greater than those of natural death, but admitted to the latter possibility.

I was called in to the case on two grounds. Firstly to help assess the possibility of natural as opposed to violent death; and here I agreed entirely with Professor Webster. I assessed the chances as about equal. Secondly, I had been asked to re-examine the bedding. This revealed something of very great importance which had hitherto been overlooked.

On the top pillow, I found a light smear of blood mixed with cells from the mouth, and digestive ferments found in saliva. This was proof that the blood had come most likely from congestion in the respiratory tract, and not from any external damage that might have been done to the girl. Something of much more importance was evident: on the top sheet, not visible in ordinary light, but showing up quite clearly when examined in ultra-violet light, was a stain, roughly oval in shape, measuring fifteen inches by six inches. It was dried urine.

This finding set off a whole chain of examination and cross-examination questions. In the first place, it provided the Prosecution with a missing link in their evidence. It was almost certain proof that Gay Gibson had died in her cabin, and that she was dead when thrown out of the porthole. This apparently was a great relief to public opinion. Mr Roberts seized on this additional information at once, as confirmation of strangulation. Voiding of urine almost inevitably occurs when a person is strangled, but it occurs equally in many cases of sudden death by natural causes, so that its occurrence is no actual proof of strangulation. Mr Roberts also argued that urine on the top sheet showed that the girl was lying on her back at the time of her death, covered by the sheet. Urine voided by a female lying on her back, of course, goes upwards. This finding, according to Mr Roberts, was also proof that Camb could not have been lying on top of the girl, as he said, at the time of her death. But, unfortunately for Mr Roberts, this finding completely destroyed his previous contention that, at the time of her death, the girl was wearing her black pyjamas. He obviously could not have it both ways. Furthermore the finding of the urine on the top sheet did not mean that the girl was covered by the sheet. If she and Camb were lying on the top of the bed together, and she passed urine this would run down on to the uppermost, i.e. the top sheet, as was found – again confirming Camb's statement. It does not seem reasonable to suppose that these two, having intercourse, would have covered themselves with a sheet.

That, then, was the evidence in the case.

The trial had lasted for four days. The Judge's summing-up lasted about four hours, and the Jury brought in their verdict of Guilty after a retirement of only forty minutes. Mr Casswell complained bitterly about the Judge's summing-up, reminding him of many matters in favour of the Defendant which he had not mentioned, but Mr Justice Hilbery, brushing this aside, said: "I have not attempted to mention everything, and I am not bound to do so".

The case naturally went to Appeal. It was dismissed without even calling on the Crown to answer Mr Casswell's arguments.

At the commencement of the trial, the Clerk of Assize read out the indictment: "James Camb, you stand charged upon the indictment with murder, and the particulars state that, on the 18th of October last year, on the high seas, you did murder Eileen Isabella Ronnie Gibson; to that charge do you plead Guilty or Not Guilty?"

Camb replied: "Not Guilty."

After conviction, the Clerk of Assize asked him, as is usual, if he had anything to say before sentence of death was passed upon him. His reply was not unworthy of note: "My lord, at the opening of this case I was asked to plead Guilty or Not Guilty; I pleaded Not Guilty, and I repeat that statement now."

Guilty or Not Guilty?

Mr Casswell thoroughly believed in his innocence, as he repeats in his own account of the affair in his book *A Lance for Liberty*. Professor Webster and I thoroughly believed that Camb's account of the happenings on that tragic night was medically possible and reasonable, with at least a fifty-fifty chance of being correct. Dr Teare agreed, but put the chances considerably less in favour of the accused.

Camb's neat appearance and supreme confidence in himself never left him throughout the whole ordeal of his trial, but in many ways he was his own worst enemy. He completely lost any sympathy the Jury might have had for him by his own utter selfishness in putting his job and future before the life of a young girl. He "concluded that she was dead" but was not certain, and he made no attempt to summon any medical aid for her. He thought only of himself. He denied that he could have inadvertently rung the bells, although it was quite possible, and denied that he had received any injury from the girl which was one of the main planks of his defence.

To Mr Casswell's mind, the Jury convicted him because they could not forgive him for his brutal and callous action.

The case has often been debated by lawyers, pathologists and medico-legal experts. On balance, I would say that generally the legal minds supported the conviction, whilst the medical men supported the opinion of Professor Webster and myself. After all, why kill the goose who is laying the golden eggs?

Mr Justice Humphreys, one of the judges who sat in the Court of Appeal is alleged to have said afterwards: "That man wasn't given a chance".

Nobody knows what he meant by that remark.

A full account of the trial was published in the series of *Notable British Trials*, edited by Geoffrey Clark, William Hodge & Co.

It even attracted interest in the United States, where a transcript was published under the title *The Girl in the Stateroom* by Charles Boswell, Louis & Louis Thompson.

The most fascinating account, however, has been written by Denis Herbstein in his book *Porthole*, published in June 1991 by Hodder & Stoughton. He not only gives a complete account of the Court proceedings, but also most skilfully analyses all the aspects of the case.

I have suffered remarkably little abuse during my career, in fact really only on one occasion connected with this case of Gay Gibson.

One newspaper reported a short paragraph recording my evidence that this girl might have died from natural causes. The reader wrote "liar" across the paragraph and sent it to me.

The other incident was an anonymous letter sent to me in the following terms:

"Dear Sir,

"I see by the enclosed press report you said in evidence in the Camb trial that it was perfectly possible for Miss Gibson to die as you say. Well now, you being a pathologist should know that what you said was a lot of damnation rot and many thousands are of the same opinion as myself that you was a Bluddy old waster to give such evidence to try and influence the Jury on the verdict they come to a right conclusion for Camb was nothing more than a blasted rotten blighter; what about the other 3 young women who he tried to strangle the same as he did what did the Judge say about her epitaph.

"What Camb did was to enter Miss G's cabin with

the intention of criminally assaulting her and when she objected he seized her around the throat with his hand his own words and thereby strangled her to hide his result and put her out of the porthole but what about the blood on the bottom sheet does this not prove her to have been a virgin as her mother said you ought to know but it appears you know Bugger all about it and so the sooner this dirty rotten Bugger is *hung* the better it will be for the general public and as for you you are too a rotten dirty, Bloody old waster, there was no need for you to have poked your nose on the case at all so once more to Hell with such a rotten old Bugger for you are nothing more I wonder what you would have said if it had been *your* Daughter its a pity it wasn't you rotten old scoundrel and Bugger you once more."

It was not signed.

Dennis Hocking

Marcel Petiot: Murder for Profit

In post-war France, the Petiot trial was the most sensational since that of "Bluebeard" Landru in 1921. Petiot was another "con-man killer", like Heath and Haigh. According to Pat Pitman's article on him (in our *Encyclopedia of Murder*) he had been stealing since his schooldays, and even when he became mayor of Villeneuve in 1928, was in trouble with the police for robbing a gas meter. An attractive housekeeper became pregnant and then disappeared – but of course, she may simply have gone back to her parents. But when a patient called Madame Debauve was robbed and killed in 1930, and another patient went around accusing Petiot, this man also died suddenly. Petiot ceased to be mayor when he was sent to prison for theft.

This account of the case, from Alister Kershaw's *Murder in France* (1955) originally struck me as too long for this book, but after looking at a few more, I decided that Kershaw was far and away the best.

A mong other aspects of a lunatic world, the German-controlled Paris press for Saturday, 11th March, 1944, reported heavy and successful Nazi counter-attacks in the Ukraine and the sinking by Japanese naval forces of two U.S. destroyers off New Guinea. At Limoges, a group of "terrorists" had been variously sentenced to death or to forced labour, and British air losses over Germany were mounting daily.

All this was the press of any country at that time, differing only in accent.

More specifically local notes were struck elsewhere in the exiguous news-sheets, combining to form an impressionist glimpse of a Paris at once astonishingly transformed and essentially unchanged. Yves Montand and Edith Piaf were singing at cabarets which bore familiar names but were required to close at the uncanonical hour of midnight. On that day all but a few especially favoured restaurants and hotels were prohibited from serving wine. The inevitable news of current literary events was juxtaposed with angry accounts of Jewish perfidy.

There was no reference to the bitter ersatz coffee, the stodgy yellow bread which had replaced the traditional crisp French loaf or to streets given over almost entirely to bicycle traffic except for an occasional German staff car going about its owner's secure and weighty business. Yet these, in all likelihood, were the colourings of their world which Parisians found most irksome, and probably more relevant than the immense events taking place in Russia or the Pacific or the skies above the Reich. For "the French character" – if one dares to make another generalisation on the subject – is stubbornly and admirably concerned with the tiny important assaults on individual life. Complaints of ill-cooked meals, unsmokable cigarettes or the scarcity of wine, never seem incongruous to a Frenchman merely because there is a war in progress or because the Gestapo is questioning "doubtful elements" (that sinister abstraction!) around the corner in the rue de la Pompe. This loyal preoccupation with the minutiae of man's existence is another of France's contributions to the human heritage: a Frenchman stands for individual man and his pitiful, vital rights.

M. Jacques Marçais, living at 20 Rue Lesueur, was a Frenchman and his neighbour's chimney was smoking. The official horrors of 1944 made this no less objectionable and constituted no sort of reason for tolerating it any longer. Rue Lesueur is a sober and dignified street near the Etoile, running between the avenue Foch and the avenue de la Grande Armée; No. 21, which annoyed M. Marçais, was, until its recent demolition, a good, grey building of the sort which the French call a *hôtel particulier*. The whole atmosphere fairly forbids chimneys, or anything else, to misbehave themselves. Since the first Thursday of this particular March, however, the furnace at 21 had been emitting singularly unpleasant and acrid fumes; by Saturday the thing had become insupportable. In the absence of the guilty proprietor – who seemed not to live on the premises but only to cycle over from some other address in order to light the troublesome fire – there was nothing for M. Marçais to do except telephone a complaint to the local police station. This he did and was assured that the police would attend him immediately.

The arrival of these officials in so select a quarter caused some excitement and the local residents were only too happy to give what sparse information they had on the shadowy owner of No. 21. His pyrophiliac activities, it was explained, had not previously caused annoyance; but for the last few days, possibly due to some unusual movement of the wind or to an alteration in the fuel employed, the chimney had made life intolerable. Beyond this nothing was known of the man, but a card affixed to the front door invited inquirers to address themselves to 66 rue Caumartin. The Paris directories enable one to locate a telephone number from the address, and a call was therefore made by one of the police to Pigalle 77–11. A Mme Petiot answered, brought her husband to the telephone, and Dr Marcel Petiot was duly informed that a fire had been notified at his house in rue Lesueur.

The doctor replied that he would present himself at that address forthwith and in point of fact did so. Not, however, quite quickly enough. The smoke continued to pour oilily from the chimney, the police became apprehensive that a fire had started in the building, and, before Dr Petiot had appeared, the fire brigade was summoned to make an entry. Firemen accordingly broke into the house without delay, and with still less delay broke out again, crying (as recounted dramatically in the following Monday's *Matin*): "This is no job for us! The place is full of corpses!" It was a pardonable exaggeration. Not altogether full, perhaps, but certainly well-stocked. A number of human heads were scattered about the dark congeries of cellars beneath the ponderous, respectable building – a smouldering corpse explained the loathsome smoke – and a body had been literally split from skull to groin in order (it was presumed) that it might more easily be added to the reeking contents of the furnace. These scraps, littered among various wretched bits of clothing, were the gruesome advance-guard of the twenty-seven men and women with whose deaths Dr Marcel Petiot was to be charged within a year, representatives of the sixty-three people he himself insistently asserted he had destroyed.

While the local police were contemplating this abominable handiwork the artist himself arrived. He even descended into the cellar for a last look round, although it is hard to account for such foolhardiness, and then turned casually to leave. The police thought differently, but the doctor, with his unvarying sense of expediency, muttered in a convincing undertone that he was "a patriot – risking his head – on business for *la Patrie*". Hadn't they understood? They had uncovered an execution chamber of the resistance movement.

Fortunately for Petiot, the policemen were also patriots and made no further effort to hinder him. Dr Petiot thanked them on behalf of the French underground forces and vanished into the dusk. He was not seen again by any of those most anxious to confer with him for eight months.

Organised society's task of trapping its deviationists would be immeasurably facilitated if every murderer revealed himself in his childhood by some ugly and unmistakable tic of behaviour. Such tics actually are evident, but they are shared by those children destined to become acceptable members of the tribe. In Petiot's case, as in so many others, much has been made of an early taste for deliberate cruelty to animals, and no doubt this disagreeable trait did exist in his make-up; at the same time, a close investigation of the childish diversions of a bishop or businessman would reveal identical enthusiasms. Indeed, a murderer can be roughly written down as merely one who fails to shed (or conceal) on reaching manhood the instinctive criminality of the child. Childish ruthlessness, childish egotism, a childish belief in the basic rightness of any act which begets his own pleasure or profit – these are the qualities which lead a man to the death-cell unless he applies them to such morally unexceptionable forms of personal satisfaction as social-climbing or floating bogus companies. In *Murder for Profit*, a title too suitable for the present study to be resisted, William Bolitho suggests that, stripped of the "mountainous trappings" bestowed on them by self-justifying society, murderers would "dwindle to homunculi, perhaps no bigger, no wickeder, no redder even, than new-born babies, kicking and screaming to have their will" – in a word, men who at no age reach years of discretion.

At all events, it is certainly impossible to detect in the earliest youth of Marcel-André-Henri-Félix Petiot even the tiniest quirk which might have marked him out from any potential lawyer or functionary. He was born in Auxerre (Department of the Yonne) on 17th January, 1897, the son of a minor postal official, and led the normal existence of a French provincial child. Until middle adolescence, the solitary variation from the average lot was his becoming an orphan when only thirteen years of age, his father dying in 1905 and his mother in 1910.

It has, inevitably, been suggested that this early disappearance of parental control may have been responsible for the later horrific performances of the man, and parental admonitions, it is true, do tend to inhibit some of the less attractive attributes of children; Petiot's guardian, his aunt, may well have been less worried by his young waywardness than his own parents would have been, and less solicitous to check it. But the idea of any murderer, let alone the colossal Petiot, being so merely because he was too seldom cuffed over the head as a child is comically unconvincing. True, if an exploit which he carried out when aged sixteen had been adequately punished, it might have caused his happy-go-lucky (so to speak) self-confidence to diminish, but one can hardly say more than that. It was a trivial business – a matter of robbing letter-boxes in the district – but it was leniently viewed, and this may have implanted in Petiot his lifelong conviction that he could get away with things.

The war of 1914–18 provided evidence in support of his theory. He had begun studying medicine in 1916, but he patriotically interrupted his course (French mobilisation laws are impartially severe) in order to join the army. Characteristically, his first thought, even in the midst of the surrounding horrors, was to find some profitable side-line, and in due course he was arrested and tried for having stolen drugs from the casualty clearing stations in order to retail them to those whose need was not officially recognised. (It would be interesting to know how many of the 22,000 known drug-addicts in France in 1918 had dealt with Marcel Petiot.)

Men were shot at that strange time for a variety of strange offences: an enthralling list might be compiled of the artificial crimes which have been codified by our masters since 1914. But the large-scale creation of new wickednesses has called a resistant strain into being among the human race, and Petiot was the classic representative of this immune group. While such dark army malefactions as sleeping or running were punished with death, Petiot's trafficking in narcotics was not only mildly judged but actually rewarded. He had been wounded earlier in the war, and the ludicrous logic which rules in the army decided that his grenade-shattered foot had somehow caused a condition of "mental debility". Consequently, while tired or terrified human beings were stood against the brick wall, Marcel Petiot was given a spell in the psychopathic ward to recuperate, an honourable discharge from the army, and a pension for life.

This surely was the moment when he decided that the imbecile contemporary world was worth dicing against. Intelligent and, above all, endowed with a positive genius for knowing a good thing when he saw it, he must have appreciated that he ran small risk in gambling with such simpletons. He had twice broken the law (perhaps more often than that) and in the first case had been treated with forbearance, in the second and more serious case had been rewarded. Everything, including his indifferent acceptance of his own death, indicates that at some point he adopted a deliberate philosophy of crime and was prepared for the returns and hazards equally. Unless one has been completely conditioned by this our age, one cannot help but take an immoral satisfaction in the triumph of the unrighteous, and it is essentially amusing to reflect that but for the irrational leniency of the military mind, those charred corpses might never have lain in the cellar of 21 rue Lesueur.

The war over, Marcel Petiot emerged into the helter-skelter of peace with his sturdy notions of self-interest unimpaired. By way of having something to fall back on, he resumed his medical studies, and in 1920 was working at the Sainte-Anne lunatic asylum, the *médecin-chef* of which, Professor Bessières, more than twenty years later was to discover that the provincial intern had possessed an "unstable temperament". This notwithstanding, the young man's thesis – *Contribution à l'étude de la paralysie ascendante aïgue* – was sufficiently esteemed to earn him his doctorate; and he managed to retain this honourable status despite subsequent spells in prison, in the midst of amorous scandal, and in the face of general suspicion (long before it was proved) that he was a murderer.

Dr. Petiot set up practice in 1921 in Villeneuve-sur-Yonne, not far from his birthplace of Auxerre, having first circular-ised the district with a remarkable document setting out his powers and attainments in the fashion of eighteenth-century apothecaries. He was handsome in a dark heavy way, and had considerable charm, as well as that genial manner which persuades the great self-doubting majority that so much self-assurance must be based on solid merit. His practice soon became extremely satisfactory.

Like many provincial doctors, he also participated in the social and political life of the neighbourhood, and here too with a good deal of success. During his twelve years in the Yonne, Marcel Petiot held office variously as Councillor, General Councillor, and Mayor of the canton. A convinced socialist, he was a frequent and appreciated speaker at the League for the Rights of Man. He was married, in 1927, to the charming and attractive Mlle Georgette Lablais of the same district. They had one son, Gérard.

Certain incidents intrude discordantly on this gentle biog-raphy. In the doctor's early years of practice, for example, he employed a servant girl whose physical charms seem to have been more noteworthy than any intellectual or spiritual qualities she may have possessed. Her presence in the bachelor household need not itself have caused any scandal – might even have been welcomed as a juicy subject of conversations; and even the fact of her becoming pregnant need not have been disastrous had the doctor elected to change her status to that of permanent and unpaid house-keeper. What did happen, however, was that the girl simply disappeared, and the manner of her disappearance – with not one farewell made – occasioned much regrettable specula-tion. She has still not returned to clear the doctor's name.

Further unpleasantness resulted from the death of Mme Debauve. This lady, coincidentally one of the doctor's patients, was the manageress of a local shop and known to have substantial sums of money very often in the place. In 1930 she was murdered and the establishment robbed, and certain enemies of socialism and the rights of man spread the astounding rumour that Dr Petiot had been guilty of this unprofessional conduct. He bore these slanders with almost Christian resignation, even going so far as to offer to treat one of his chief accusers who was suffering from rheumatism. With remarkable lack of dignity, the man accepted and within a few hours of swallowing the doctor's tablets was dead. The autopsy, conducted by Dr Marcel Petiot, revealed that this sudden death had been from natural causes.

No aspect of the man's background is more intriguing than that, in spite of all this, he nonetheless continued to hold political office, and it is reasonable to explain the fact by there having been somebody who was solicitous to protect him. Whoever this mysterious good fairy may have been, it is clear that the influence was powerful as well as benign, for in 1944, when a Paris journalist remembered the theories about Mme Debauve's murder and went to check the police dossier of the affair, he announced that it had completely disappeared.

Not long after Mme Debauve's death, Petiot was again in trouble, and this time there was no room whatever for speculation. There had been a whole series of thefts from the municipal stores and eventually the Mayor himself, Dr Petiot no less, was caught in the act. For this application of his socialist principles he was sentenced to three months' imprisonment and removed from office.

The doctor could tolerate this pharisaic hostility no longer and, in 1933, he and his wife were installed at 66 rue Caumartin, a populous street near the Madeleine and distinguished by the quantity of unusually attractive prostitutes who make it their promenade. Still in the boisterous eighteenth-century tradition, the doctor had a broadsheet distributed in which it was announced that he had opened consulting rooms "using the most modern and highly perfected equipment, with X, UV and UR rays, faradisation, ionisation, cryotherapy, diathermy, electric scalpel, ozonotherapy, aerotherapy, etc." "Dr Petiot," the pamphlet added, "ensures painless childbirth; he also gets rid of pain in cases of cancer, ulceration, neuritis, etc."

For three years after his arrival in Paris, Dr Petiot, as far as is known, applied himself exclusively to the mysteries of faradisation and aerotherapy although, remembering his past, it seems probable that he managed to fit in one or two unofficial diversions which were never recorded in his dossier.

In 1936, he was arrested for stealing from a bookshop in the Boulevard St Michel. What book? It was said to have been a "technical" work, and it would be interesting to know what technicality was then occupying him but, unfortunately, the fact is not at this date discoverable. Petiot himself always asserted that he had pocketed the volume in an unaccountable spasm of absent-mindedness (he, the least scatter-brained of men!) but one may be forgiven for believing that a natural taste for criminality was finding renewed expression. It is perhaps significant that a number of his offences were oddly motiveless, as if the enjoyment of cocking a snook at the upright world were a reward in itself. However this may have been, a liberal court, having heard the opinions of Dr Ceillier, decided that Petiot could scarcely have so manifested his contempt for the ethical system which they represented unless he had been insane, and the accused was therefore discharged along with a recommendation that he submit himself to some form of psychiatric treatment.

As a reasonable precaution against possible mishaps, medical men suspected of insanity are customarily dissuaded from practising; but still no medical board saw fit to remove this errant creature from its rolls. The *Conseil des Médecins de la Seine*, it was later explained by the President, Professor Balthazard, was never so much as informed by the responsible authorities of its wayward member's defections. Was this also attributable to the beneficent fairy's magic wand?

There is no limit to the number of sterile speculations which one can make in regard to Marcel Petiot, of all famous killers the one in whose history there are most lacunae; and, for just this reason, the guessing-game is irresistible. What, for instance, were his thoughts on 3rd September, 1939? Was he one of those haggard men who gathered in otherwise empty Paris along the boulevards, waiting for the next bulletin to be posted up outside the newspaper offices? Absurd rhetoric! He was egotistical to the uttermost extent – an individual being, never a social one – and he had learned by direct experience that international conflicts could be of very considerable use to the adroit man on the spot. There is no way of knowing and it is, of course, possible that he shared his compatriots' tragic apprehension of doom; it is possible, but the chances are rather that there and then he looked about for a method whereby he might personally take advantage of the chaotic future which was so clearly imminent. And, into the bargain, there are grounds for supposing that he may even have contemplated the world ahead with considerable satisfaction.

What is certain is that either just before or just after the war began, he utilised his professional standing (yet another example of his gift for making the most of circumstances) to set up as a drug-peddler – a means of livelihood very possibly held in mind since 1917.

It may be worth while at this point to dispose of a proposition sometimes put forward that he was an addict himself. For a number of reasons this is unlikely. To begin with, it is almost never the case that a trafficker becomes an addict; he knows too much about the consequences of such distractions. Then, again, there is no record of Petiot during his various incarcerations, when presumably narcotics were not available to him, having shown the least need of them. Lastly, it was not in his psychological structure to submit to any authority – whether that of society, or individuals, or hypodermics.

Sooner or later the inspectors of the Narcotics Squad intrude on the sub-world for which Petiot was catering at this time; and the very basis of these men's work consists of patiently linking the first transgressor whom they discover to his nearest associate, that associate to the next in the chain, and so inexorably back until they locate the chief begetter of so much pleasure, so much pain. Early in 1942 a young female drug-addict was picked up by the Paris police; under interrogation she involved her lover, Jean-Marc Van Bever; he, in turn, charged Dr Petiot with having provided the means for his mistress's melancholy diversion. The doctor rejected the slander with weary urbanity.

Released on bail, the young man made no effort to conceal his determination to sustain this allegation, and it can hardly surprise anyone who has followed Petiot's career up to this point that Van Bever, like the servant girl at Villeneuve, abruptly disappeared.

In the same year Mme Kahid died. This lady's daughter, Mlle Baudet, had been under treatment by Dr Petiot for drug-addiction, and Mme Kahid held that there were better ways of curing her offspring's unfortunate quirk than by supplying her with morphine and heroin at something over normal retail prices. Believing this, she announced her intention of interviewing the doctor and threatening him with exposure unless he employed a more conventional technique of disintoxication, and, as far as is known, she did set off on this pious jaunt. Once again, one is simply guessing as to what happened after the devoted parent left for her meeting with Dr Petiot; all that one can assert is that she was never again seen by her family. M. Kahid was later to depose that he had made inquiries of the doctor and had "read in his eyes that he had killed my wife". He may even have communicated this alarming discovery to the police, who certainly interrogated Petiot regarding the lady's disappearance, but there was no evidence which might have proved his involvement in the affair.[1] A certain consistency was beginning to emerge in respect of the fate of those acquaintances whose continued existence was likely to embarrass the doctor.

Other events occurred in 1942 to strengthen this tradition. There was, for instance, a young provincial housewife on whom Petiot performed an abortion, who, when the countryside gossips guessed all too well the reason for her trip to Paris, had the weird idea of demanding a certificate from Petiot – a certificate which would attest that she had required an altogether different medical treatment and which would thus confound the neighbours.

Under Marshal Pétain's benevolent régime, abortion had been declared a capital offence (five abortionists were guillotined during the Occupation) and the young woman's request revealed to Petiot that she was a possible, a probable threat to his security. The consequence was therefore foreseeable: she disappeared. According to a letter received by her husband, she had crossed into the Free Zone of France (M. Kahid had had a similar note from his wife) but, like Mme Kahid, like M. Van Bever, she has still to return to liberated Paris.

Petiot's solitary vexation as a result of these incidents was a (suspended) sentence of one year's imprisonment plus a fine of 10,000 francs in connection with Van Bever's mistress's drug-addiction.

Two years prior to all this, the Wehrmacht had entered Paris and had instituted just such conditions as Marcel Petiot found most suited to his undoubted talents. Under German governorship, both Jews and those sworn friends of European civilisation, the Communists, were submitted to severe control. Even though the latter were at this time disposed to view Nazi triumphs in a tolerant light – M. Molotov was actually moved to send his personal

---

1 It may be noted that Mlle Baudet testified at the time of Petiot's flight that her mother had previously had an interview with the doctor, and in the presence of Mme Petiot. If true, this would establish that the latter was aware of at least one aspect of her husband's activities. But, as she was later to point out in another respect: "My husband was not the sort of man of whom to ask questions."

felicitations to the Führer on the entry into Paris – yet their situation was a hazardous one. Like the Jews, they lived in unceasing expectation of more aggressive treatment. Understandably, then, they preferred to carry their concept of European culture to greener fields, while others, less politically enlightened, had in mind London and the slowly-gathering army of General De Gaulle. To meet the needs of this ill-assorted group, a low-voiced travel agency came into being, its branch offices located in scores of Paris cafés. Here, to the accompaniment of a coffee-substitute decanted from the familiar complicated mechanism which dominates all French bars, men with names like *"Roland le Roi de l'occase"* and *"Georges Bras de Fer"* whispered suggestions as to the whereabouts of people able to arrange conducted tours of South America or the United States. Among the principals so recommended was Dr Marcel Petiot, to be seen by appointment only at 21 rue Lesueur in the 16th arrondissement.

Petiot had bought this house (sufficiently grandiose to have been at one time the residence of Cécile Sorel) in September of 1941 with a definite object in mind. That it was no haphazard purchase is proved by his having in the following month engaged builders to effect some curious (but plausibly explained) alterations to the place. One room was to be windowless and as far as possible sound-proofed (it was to be used for the installation of a rather noisy transformer); a magnifying spy-glass was to be imbedded in the wall of this chamber (in order that the scientist might study the workings of his contraption without the fatigue of entering); and from this small cell a passage was to lead to his consulting-room, a passage traversed by three doors (that the racket of his transformer might not disturb the thoughtful fellow's neighbours). In contrast to this considerate move, he gave instructions for the building of a high wall which completely obscured the view of any nearby residents who might be curious as to what went on in the courtyard. Finally, a block and tackle was set up over a pit beside the garage in the courtyard (whatever explanation he gave for this arrangement has not been revealed) and, naturally, a check was made to ensure that such a feature of a respectable establishment as the furnace was in proper working order.

At 21 rue Lesueur he interviewed the clients whom he discovered for himself or who were sent along by his agents. One such, who had second thoughts about accepting help from a man he found inexplicably disquieting and who stayed alive in consequence, has recorded his meeting with the doctor, and doubtless it represented a standard form. Petiot, it seemed, confirmed that a trip to the appropriate country could be promptly arranged at a cost ingeniously calculated in relation to the applicant's known means; and he recommended (what more reasonable?) that the victim should gather together all his or her available cash or jewels and bring them along to the subsequent rendezvous. He was prodigal in his counsels and explanations; uniquely he hesitated to provide any details as to the port of departure, the port of arrival.

No one has survived to provide an account of the second – and crucial – encounter, but one may reasonably guess that the genial medico insisted then on rendering yet another service: this was the inoculation of the would-be traveller against those diseases notoriously prevalent in foreign countries. That Hippocratic civility performed, a last, never-to-be-realised meeting was fixed and the visitor shown to a door which led, the doctor observed casually, more conveniently and discreetly to the street. *A demain.*

How many wretched men and women, a burden at last removed from their anguished minds, passed through that innocent-seeming door? Impossible to know; but each and every one found him- or herself eventually in a tiny triangular apartment; the door by which they entered slammed behind them and was bolted; the door ahead was a fake, masking a brick wall. Here, while Petiot contemplated their writhings through his spy-hole, the "inoculation" took effect and they died.[1]

---

1 This is supposition: Petiot's method of killing was never definitely proved. A high police official, who had been directly concerned with the case, has told me of the possibility that a toxic gas was pumped into the "death room" and certain wall-fittings give some support to this theory.

Their bodies were carted out into the courtyard and low-ered into the pit. It was filled with quick-lime, and whatever scraps remained after this treatment were consigned to the furnace.

Petiot's first known victim was acquired by his own unaided efforts. This was one of the doctor's neighbours in the rue Caumartin, a middle-aged Polish furrier named Joachim Gusbinov under treatment by Petiot for some unspecified illness. He confided his anxiety to quit France, obtaining in return the gratifying news that this could be arranged for no more than the 25,000 francs needed to sweeten certain intermediaries.

Wonderful and efficient machinery! Joachim Gusbinov kept his appointment at rue Lesueur and was duly shep-herded to the quick-lime. In addition to the original down payment, this operation netted the doctor 2,000 U.S. dollars and 2,000,000 French francs.

Gusbinov was killed in January of 1942, but no one can imagine that Petiot waited so long before putting his ingenious business into profitable operation. Some evidence for this belief is to be found in the fact that, even before he had bought the house in rue Lesueur, a number of corpses had been located around Paris, for whose presence none of the official extermination squads could be held responsible. Moreover, these bodies had all been dismembered in a manner identical with that observed in the case of several of the corpses located at 21 rue Lesueur. It is probable that Petiot bought that property when he felt it to be increasingly risky to scatter his handiwork in the parks and vacant lots of the city.

In the tradition of modern business, Petiot even trans-formed social encounters into profitable deals. At a bridge-party given by his wife's cousin he made the acquaintance of a Jewish colleague, Dr Paul Braunberger, and within a few days the latter was making and receiving mysterious telephone calls, waiting vainly at pre-arranged meeting places, settling on code-words, being whirled faster and faster in the mad helterskelter which Petiot seemed gleefully to impose on his clients as if in deliberate mockery of the Resistance Movement's tragic complexities. When at last the game became wearisome, a final appointment was fixed from which Dr Braunberger never returned.

Simultaneously and under the name of Dr Eugène, Petiot was investigating prospects among quite a different social class. Less imaginative than himself, such men as "Jo the Boxer" and "François the Corsican" had carried on with their peacetime trade of theft, assault, armed robbery and similar banalities. They, too, had their reasons for desiring to quit France; they, too, made and kept their appointments at rue Lesueur; and, apparently, were crammed into the furnace as expeditiously as elderly doctors and ailing furriers.

It is typical of Marcel Petiot's epic opportunism that he did not initiate his business of large-scale murder until conditions seemed wholly favourable; and it is a mark of his intelligence that he judged conditions so well. Never in the twentieth century had there been a time when individuals, even those with families and friends, could vanish in a great city with so few inquiries resulting. The French police might reasonably surmise that any such disappearance was by the wish of the Gestapo; the Gestapo itself, less satanically well-informed than is popularly believed, might interpret it as another escape from occupied territory. Resistance groups and Fascist militia complicated the situation still further, and for mere individuals with some interest in the whereabouts of a friend or relation, it was only sane, not craven, to avoid asking questions.

Even if not omniscient, the Gestapo was nonetheless a notably efficient organisation. One by one, criminals, shopkeepers, merchants, Frenchmen, Dutchmen, Poles, men, women, and children, Petiot's clients vanished; and as steadily, Dr Yodkum, chief of the Gestapo's Section IV B, added to his dossier on the adroit and notorious "Dr Eugène". The link with Dr Petiot was easily established and the minor question of proof was entrusted to a wretched Jew blackmailed into the service of the Germans. This man was instructed to present himself to Petiot as one desiring, for obvious racial reasons, to get out of France; in this way he was to acquire evidence in support of their suspicions and then report back to his superiors. He obeyed orders, interviewed Petiot in the cunning guise agreed on, was

accepted by the doctor as being what he claimed to be
– and left by the same door as so many others, after
sardonically submitting to the obligatory inoculation.

This sinister and unconscious joke had less serious consequences for Petiot than might have been anticipated. When
their agent failed to report to headquarters, the Gestapo
concluded that he had taken advantage of his contact with
Petiot in order actually to leave the country, nobody having
any reason to suspect the real destination of the doctor's
visitors. It was therefore on a charge of having for payment
aided the departure of "those having an interest in leaving
France" (the terminology of police-states ranges from the
brutally insulting to the venomously discreet) that Petiot
was arrested by Dr Yodkum's men.

It was in May of 1943 that he was imprisoned by the
Gestapo, and he remained in their care for eight months.
At the end of that period he was released – an unusual
termination to such a history – and was able to resume
his career without, apparently, any apprehension. Had the
Gestapo visited 21 rue Lesueur immediately on arresting him
(he was picked up at his home in rue Caumartin) they would
have discovered some significant bric-a-brac. As it was, they
never called on that atrocious building at any time, so Petiot
need not have ensured, as he did, the speedy transfer to the
country of the miscellaneous garments and suitcases which
had accumulated as by-products of his monstrous trade.

"This is no job for us." The firemen's concept of where
their duties ended was a reasonable one, and the question of the unconventional fuel in the furnace of 21 rue
Lesueur became the concern of another department of
the Republic. Commissaire Georges Massu, Chief of the
Brigade Criminelle, arrived at the unholy crematorium
of the 16th arrondissement without delay. Passing from
room to room on his preliminary inspection, he found the
building unfurnished, dust-covered, unused except for the
little cluster of rooms on the ground floor: the doctor's
consulting-room, the passage, the execution chamber.

The Constitution of the French Republic holds that a
private house is "inviolable", and expressly prohibits anyone

from entering uninvited at night except in the case of fire
or flood. This proscription is equally binding on the police
as on any other citizens, and it was therefore not until
the legal hour of 6 a.m. on Sunday, 12th March, 1944,
that Commissaire Massu's inspectors were able to enter
Dr Petiot's residence at 66 rue Caumartin. Here they
discovered every evidence of a hurried departure, but
no evidence whatever of anything else – unless one is
disposed to regard the presence of an "erotic statue" (a
homely feature of so many worthy households) as being in
any way noteworthy.

On Tuesday the investigation shifted to the vicinity of
Petiot's earlier life and works, to Auxerre where his younger
brother, Maurice, had a radio repair shop which apparently
provided him with a most satisfactory income. He had even
been able to purchase (for 130,000 francs) a house in the rue
des Lombards large enough for the overnight entertainment
of any friends who might call. One such had clearly passed
Monday night there, and the police were interested enough
to ask the identity of the guest. It was, Maurice explained,
a friend from the nearby town of Courson and, on the
insistence of the officials, he provided the friend's name.
Seemingly, there was some confusion in his mind, as the
friend, when questioned in turn, had no recollection of
the event, and Maurice Petiot was arrested on a charge of
making a false statement. Two hours later the doctor's wife,
Georgette, was likewise arrested in Auxerre. The doctor
himself remained invisible.

Interrogated the following day in Paris, Mme Petiot was
willing to be communicative. After the doctor's departure
from the rue Caumartin in response to the telephone call
made by the police on Saturday evening, she had awaited
his return all night. On the Sunday she concluded that he
had made a sudden trip to his brother in Auxerre, having
forgotten (perhaps in a fit of absent-mindedness such as
had afflicted him while browsing among the bookstalls in
1936) to let her know in advance. Equally impulsive, she
decided to follow him, but the improved conditions of
daily life so characteristic of wartime included an absence
of trains to Auxerre that day. She attended church, strolled

along the boulevards, and, being disinclined to return to rue Caumartin, passed Sunday night at yet another of her husband's properties, 52 rue de Reuilly. On Monday evening she took the train for Auxerre. She knew nothing of Marcel's present whereabouts, knew nothing of his activities at rue Lesueur. Being assured, however, that these had taken place, and being given some idea as to their nature, she volunteered an interesting observation: "It is possible that at rue Lesueur my husband got rid of people who had been reported to him as traitors." She gave no hint as to which of the many currently offered causes these persons might have betrayed.

For Maurice the *juge d'instruction* had prepared a "*coup de théâtre*" of the kind most appealing to officials with a dramatic sense. Police inquiries had established that the quick-lime which was so essential a commodity in Marcel's business had been transported from Auxerre by his brother. After listening patiently to Maurice's flatly persistent assertions that he knew absolutely nothing of the doctor's pursuits, the *juge d'instruction* suddenly revealed that the tie-up was known. Maurice clearly lacked the appropriate feeling for theatricality. In the face of this announcement he limited his response to an indifferent: "It's up to you to prove it."

The inculpation of Maurice and Georgette Petiot represented no more than the modest beginning of a lavish series of arrests. On 21st March, three of the leg-men who, in bars and at street corners, had conducted their discreet publicity campaign for Dr Petiot's dark profession, were arrested; and a fourth joined them next day. These men were a mixed lot, but all inhabitants of a twilight world in which they met with the sort of people eager – and able to pay – for a quietly-arranged trip. And all told a similar story: they confessed that for a percentage of the fares (50,000 francs for Spain, as much as 200,000 for South America) they had conducted the prospects to 21 rue Lesueur; but none of them guessed that the voyage came to an end there. They were tidied away into the cells.

The gathering-up of such riff-raff was small compensation for the continued coy seclusion of the man they served, nor were their protestations of virtuous ignorance of much service. But on 24th March a better-informed witness was added to the group, one who gave the first hint as to the scale of Petiot's operations. Réné Nézondet had known both Marcel and Maurice for some considerable time and was for this reason required to make a statement. It was rather more than anyone had bargained for.

Long before M. Marçais had been bothered by his neighbour's smoking chimney, Réné Nézondet had enjoyed a confidential chat with Maurice Petiot, in the course of which the latter had given the disturbing assurance that "My brother has killed at least fifty or sixty people". Nézondet had felt free to discuss this intelligence with the doctor's wife, but an understandable delicacy had withheld him from passing on his knowledge to the police. For this failure to report a crime as required by law, he was added to the slowly-mounting number of prisoners. It must be added that both Maurice and Georgette disclaimed any recollection of these startling conferences having taken place but, even so, Nézondet's revelation of the extent of Petiot's private war obtained far more public interest than did the "massive new raid on London" which official German sources stated to have occurred the previous day.

Nearly a week passed without there being any development, the police continuing their search for Marcel Petiot, whose ubiquity, as always in these affairs, was downright uncanny. Reports of his presence in all parts of France – sometimes simultaneously – arrived incessantly at the Quai des Orfèvres and were each checked, but the doctor had caused himself to disappear almost as completely as his various victims.

Another search was taking place concurrently for the odds and ends – mostly suitcases – known to have been removed from rue Lesueur at the time of Petiot's seizure by the Gestapo. These were located, with aid from Maurice, at the end of March: they had been confided (by Maurice) to the care of a certain M. Neuhausen of Auxerre. M. and Mme Neuhausen followed their friends to prison.

There is something almost piteous in the determination of the police, deprived of the one captive they really wanted, to imprison *faute de mieux* whoever came their way: the number eventually reached fourteen and even included such cousins-german to the case as the former servant of the doctor's late father-in-law.

As from 7th July, however, official enthusiasm seems to have been superseded by official despair. On that date two of the leg-men were released, Mme Neuhausen was set free on 12th August, and Mme Petiot on 1st October; the others followed them, and with their emergence from behind bars, they step from the midst of this ghastly history into their private ambience of assumed names and hateful recollections.

In the outside world, whose stupendous actions Petiot so deftly parodied, immense events were taking place which could yet not wholly drive the doctor's already legendary name from the front pages. In the early morning of 6th June, 1944, the Allies had effected landings on the French coast and begun their advance across Europe. On 20th July, at the Führer's headquarters, a bomb exploded within feet of Hitler, who stepped from the room unhurt to direct the liquidation of those who had sought his death. On 24th August, the first detachment of General Leclerc's armoured division entered Paris where civilians sniped the retreating Germans or, in the name of patriotism, executed men and women against whom the patriots had a private grudge. Ramshackle barricades had been thrown up in scores of streets, there were collaborators to be judged and summarily executed, women to be dragged naked through the city for having possibly slept with German soldiers, accusations to be made and refuted. There was work for all.

Somewhere amongst this mingled squalor and splendour moved Dr Marcel Petiot, appraising conditions as dexterously as ever, considering how best to take advantage of them, acting on his decisions, preparing a new rôle for himself.

Not altogether new, perhaps; merely an elaboration of one which had already proved ideal. In the circumstances, what could be better than a full-blown performance of The Resistance Leader? He did not, however, come before the public in this guise until after repeated allegations in the daily press that he had all along been a Gestapo agent. The slight was insupportable; and he addressed a letter to the newspaper *Résistance* insisting that he had throughout been – as who at that time had not? – a loyal worker for the Underground, and was currently an officer in the F.F.I. He evinced no eagerness, even so, to leave his patriotic duties and set the police right on one or two points about himself which continued to puzzle them.

But his handwritten note was the clue for which the searchers had waited. It was passed on to Colonel Roll, chief of the Parisian sector of the F.F.I., with the request that it be compared with the handwriting of all the officers under his command. The idea was sound. After a fortnight's work, the author of the letter was identified as Captain Henri Valéry, stationed at Reuilly. Captain Valéry had been a member of the F.F.I. for just six weeks.

On 31st October, 1944, as he left the métro station of Saint-Mandé-Tourelle, Dr Marcel Petiot, alias Dr Eugène, alias Captain Valéry, was arrested.

In spite of a newly-acquired beard (which gave him an unfortunate facial resemblance to his less-gifted predecessor, Landru) and in spite of his newly-acquired name and title, Marcel Petiot was essentially unchanged. At the preliminary interrogation he was relaxed, affable – a little condescending, perhaps – as he recounted his career in the Resistance Movement; and he ended his statement with a dignified observation, reminiscent of (and possibly recollected from) his electioneering days: "I have nothing with which to reproach myself. Speaking as a patriot, I am proud of everything I have done." It was presumably as a patriot that he carried membership-cards for the Communist Party, the Franco-Soviet League and a Communist-controlled militia corps. Such documents at that particular moment were almost of themselves a guarantee of respectability (the Party's recommendation of loving co-operation with the invaders had been forgotten) and it was correspondingly inevitable that Petiot, so sensitively alert to prevailing moods, should possess them.

There were other discoveries made: a ration card belonging to a Jewish child who had vanished with his parents some time previously; numerous *laissez-passers* and requisition forms: parodist of his age even there, Petiot's pockets were stuffed with almost every lunatic document which bureaucracy and political fanatics had been able to dream up.

From the day of his arrest until the day of his death, Petiot held consistently to two main claims – that since the beginning of 1941 he had served in the Resistance, and that he had only "executed" traitors or Germans. No one could deny that he had indeed participated in the Underground Movement – in fact Captain Valéry had so impressed his companions at Reuilly with tales of his own ardour and courage that many of them remained convinced of his disinterested patriotism until the end. They were ready, even eager to testify on his behalf, but not one witness could be found to bespeak the doctor's devotion to the Allied cause prior to September of 1944.

Petiot himself named various men (all of them dead) as one-time superiors of his in the Resistance; but he was oddly unable to give any details about them other than those splashed in the exultant post-liberation press. And he spoke readily of his own underground organisation, known, he revealed, as *Groupe Fly Tox* – but known to whom? None of its other members came forward to claim the distinction of having served with Petiot. Then there was a "secret weapon" invented by himself and handed over to the Americans, but Washington had never heard of it. The Argentinian diplomat who, by Petiot's account, had helped smuggle those victims of Nazism from France (for the doctor candidly admitted that he had indeed arranged such trips) was sought in vain.

He was, however, no more elusive than the clandestine travellers themselves. What had happened to them, Gusbinov, Braunberger, and the rest? Petiot could not help: his job, he made clear, had finished once the clients were outside France; if then they took it into their heads to change their itineraries, that was no concern of his.

Nonetheless, it was a teasing mystery and led inevitably to some scepticism in considering his claim to have killed none but the enemy and the enemy's friends. Were the owners of such Hebraic names as Wolff, Marx and Kneller likely to have been serving in the Wehrmacht or on terms of jovial familiarity with the Gestapo chiefs of the rue Lauriston and the rue de la Pompe? And if not, and their undeniable visits to Petiot made in the course of escaping from the occupation – then where were they? Petiot shrugged.

Considered from another viewpoint, who were the collaborators whom he had executed, who were the German soldiers? Again Petiot proved unhelpful. It was felt that if he had from time to time – in the course of business, so to speak – included a Gestapo man or collaborator among his victims, it must have been due more to a genial lack of selectivity than to nationalistic fervour. But it should count in his favour, for all that; one name, just one.

There was no answer to be had from him, but he did provide one piece of information which may or may not have caused some official embarrassment: during all the time when he was being sought in the provinces, he had been installed in Paris. The old Resistance trick had worked again, Petiot having persuaded a M. Georges Redouté that he was hiding from the German or German-dominated authorities.

Whether this revelation upset officialdom or not, the dominating mood was one of understandable satisfaction and this benevolence expressed itself on 4th January, 1945, when eleven persons implicated in the affair, including Maurice Petiot, were discharged in consequence of a finding of Not Proven. As to the doctor, the *Chambre des Mises en Accusation* three weeks later remanded him for trial before the Assizes Court of the Seine. The date was set for 18th March of the same year, and the defence was entrusted to Maître René Floriot.

Petiot appeared at his trial shorn of his beard but, by way of compensation, endowed (it was noted by the press) with a pair of strange and hypnotic eyes. These terrifying organs are obligatory on all mass murderers, but Petiot's photographs hardly help to support the legend. On the other hand, it must be admitted that it would have been in keeping with his sardonic character to have affected a glare of that sort in mere derision of commonplace concepts of the Typical Killer. This ironic streak in him had already been remarked and, after the charge had been formally read, President Leser referred to the "Accused's disquieting fits of temper". Petiot eyed him with derisive reproachfulness. "Ah, now come," he said gently, "if we start off like this there's bound to be trouble."

He was right; but most of the trouble was created by himself. Alternating with his blithe jests were outbreaks of querulousness, rage, bitterness, as he sought to maintain the familiar thesis that he had been a selfless patriot and had all along acted as such. He did not deny that he had killed a number of people (himself raising the estimate to sixty-three) but the issue was whether they had been legally despatched (for the benefit of a particular social system) or illegally (for the benefit of an individual). Petiot held to the former view. Collaborators and German soldiers had been his meat, no one else. He knew nothing of those antique mysteries – the murder of Mme Debauve, the disappearance of his maidservant, M. Van Bever's abrupt and permanent departure. He had found the human debris in the cellars of rue Lesueur when he returned from the prison of Fresnes where the German authorities had kept him; he presumed that it had been piled there by fellow-resisters; and he had no comment to make on the government pathologist's conviction that the morsels bore unmistakable signs of having been sliced up by a practised professional hand.

Most damaging of all to Petiot's cause (if he can be said to have had one) was his austere refusal to name his companion-in-arms in the Resistance cell whose sentences he claimed to have carried out. They were all, he affirmed, yearning to give evidence in his favour but he himself would not permit them to be implicated in such a sordid business. One would have thought that these daredevils who had helped Petiot capture German soldiers from crowded streets in full daylight would have come forward despite this prohibition, but none did so – a fact which did not inhibit the doctor from demanding on their behalf, as well as his own, that they be decorated with the Cross of the Liberation – presumably in absentia.

The first day's hearing ended as it had begun with a cheerful quip from the man in the dock. "Oh, you can keep going," he announced when, at 6.30 p.m., the court was adjourned, "personally, I'm not at all tired."

Most of the debates during the succeeding days were boring even to the person most concerned. Petiot slept, or affected to sleep, through much of the most damaging evidence, and diverted himself by writing little poems of which one is remarkable for its ferocity if not its technical skill. Very roughly translated:

Ah! It is fine to see, haphazardly assembled
In one or another of these adjoining rooms,
The black birds of the night preparing their meal –
Three judges and a prosecutor drawn up in a square.

It is fine to see within this confined court
The heavenly crew juggling the law at will,
Sticky with ambitions and carrying in their faces
All the hidden vices by which they are devoured.
But it would be better still to see the city in arms,
Crying "Down with the rogues!" or fearlessly
Sacking the court; but best of all,

Hacking at this one and stringing up that,
It would be fine to see them die a slow death
And to see ten judges' skins for sale at ten sous.[1]

Little poems and little jokes are poor substitutes for a

---

1 This was not his only literary achievement. While in prison he completed a curious work entitled *Le Hasard Vaincu* (Imprimerie Roger Amiard, Paris, 1946). Sub-titled *Les Lois des Martingales*, the volume is decorated with several odd and possibly significant designs by the author. The text is printed in a facsimile of Petiot's manuscript and consists largely of elaborate mathematical propositions and columns of figures. It is sardonically dedicated "*à vous – qui m'avez fait ces loisirs*" and as an additional jest it is recorded that "the researches have been executed by Dr Eugène, ex-chief of the Fly-Tox Resistance Group; the columns of figures have been drawn up under the command of Captain Valéry of the 1st Army, 1st Paris Regiment; the mistakes in the operation have been committed by Dr Marcel Petiot . . ."

The book gives additional and superfluous proof of Petiot's preoccupation with chance and the avoidance of its ill results; and it is unnecessary to point to the irony of his having seen all his carefully-planned activities ruined by the sheerest hazard – a smoking chimney and a testy neighbour.

strong defence, and even the fabulous Maître Floriot could hardly create that out of Petiot's unsubstantiated claims and provable lies. Witness after witness demonstrated how tenuous were the Accused's connections with the Resistance; while Petiot himself could manage no more than a sequence of grateful clients and childhood friends. It was evident from the beginning that the Cross of the Liberation would not be awarded this time.

Yet somehow a vague, unhappy notion grew up that Petiot *had* been in one way or another involved in patriotic endeavour – but then he had been involved in everything. And whether or not some of his murders had benefited his country, the fact remained that some had benefited Petiot and were therefore criminal. At ten minutes to midnight on 4th April, 1946, the jury, after two and a half hours' deliberation, returned a verdict of guilty and he was sentenced to death. "Let me be revenged!" he called to the public.

Marcel Petiot was awakened at dawn on 26th May, 1946, and told he was to die that morning. The bitter, intelligent face showed no sign of fear, but when, as called for by tradition, he was adjured to have courage, he snarled an exasperated vulgarism which might be translated as "Get the hell out of this." His wife had brought him some clean clothes the previous night and he dressed himself with care; then he borrowed a pencil to write a last letter to his wife and, having finished it, turned to the waiting officials with: "And now, gentlemen, I am at your disposal."

It is some distance from the condemned cell of the Santé Prison to the courtyard where the guillotine is erected when an execution is to take place, but Petiot walked unperturbedly all the way to his destination. He stopped *en route* in one of the corridors where a temporary altar had been set up. He declined to hear Mass but, after a moment's hesitation, decided to pray "to please my wife". He refused a glass of rum but smoked a final cigarette.

In the courtyard he contemplated the guillotine without apparent emotion but muttered that he wanted to urinate. The executioner was in a hurry; he begged the doctor to control his bladder for a moment, adding consolingly that it would not be for long. Petiot nodded in acquiescence.

One last effort was made to persuade him to confess and to elucidate the mysteries still surrounding those vanished travellers and their heaped suitcases. Nothing could have been more apropos than Petiot's reply: "When one sets out on a voyage," he remarked, "one takes all one's luggage with one."

Monsieur de Paris's work was done by five minutes past five in the morning.

As a character Petiot seems, at first glance, to have no more interest than is attached to him by his awe-inspiring massacres. The reports from his schools fail to single out any notable quality in him; the psychiatrists charged with the task of examining him were unable to do better than record their conviction that the murderer of sixty-three people was "morally retarded"; he evinced no precocious inventiveness as did Troppmann, nor had he that terrible and tawdry sense of theatre which was one of Landru's fascinating quirks. The solitary surviving example of his verse is not impressive, and his wit was impudent rather than epigrammatic. For the rest, he struck all except those who had a few moments for reflection before dying at his hands, as a charming and worthy fellow, extraordinary only in the degree of his amiability.

The servant at 66 rue Caumartin (even when given a perfect chance to claim premonitory sapience) asserted that she had never remarked any oddity in his behaviour or manner; and Mme Legros, a neighbour in rue Caumartin who had some acquaintance with the Petiots, deposed in the course of a newspaper interview that "so pleasant a man could not possibly have committed such crimes". His electoral triumphs in Villeneuve indicate that he was respected and liked in the district, and there were even those who maintained ever after that there must have been some mistake in the matter of the servant girl, the municipal funds and all the rest.

Yet there is a definite interest in Marcel Petiot's character, and the reason lies perhaps in the fact that he hideously caricatured the world in which he lived. Modern bureaucracy has created in people a sense of wary opportunism; Petiot perfected this sullen defence and applied it to his own better-ment with absolute logic and completeness, transforming it in the process from defence into aggression. His abominable trade was scarcely a distortion of the brutish techniques of big business, and his killings a tiny imitation of the Gestapo and the MVD. What was his drug-trafficking but an individual parallel to government hand-outs designed to keep the slaves quiet? And what were his thefts but insig-nificant personal equivalents to the organised gangsterism of mankind's masters?

The war, with its mass executions, obliteration bomb-ings, its evil underground manœuvrings and employment of decoys and spies, was a thing too vast in its horror to be understood; it enveloped everything so utterly as to seem almost normal and beyond questioning. In Petiot's actions the whole complicated foulness was seen reduced to comprehensible dimensions. He needed only to have made a private *Baedeker*-raid on the Louvre to have completed the analogy.

The great puzzle in the Petiot case is the identity of the person or persons who throughout a period of nearly twenty years would seem to have been concerned with his well-being. That he did in fact enjoy some sort of powerful protection becomes, at the very least, a reasonable supposition if certain questions are posed. Chronologically, these are as follows:

1. How was he able to retain political office despite the widespread local suspicion that he was guilty of having murdered his servant girl, Mme Debauve and the chief unofficial prosecutor in respect of that case?

2. How was it possible for Petiot to conduct the autopsy on a man who had died under his treatment?

3. Why was he never interrogated regarding the murder of Mme Debauve? And how did the dossier on this case, believed to have contained the murderer's fingerprints, come to vanish from the files?

4. Why did no report of his various court-room convictions

and sojourns in psychopathic wards ever reach the Medical Council?

5. How did he come to be released by the Gestapo in 1943 on the grounds (ludicrous for such an organisation) that there was insufficient evidence? Petiot claimed that he had purchased his release for 100,000 francs; but in every other such case the figure was considerably higher – and why did the negotiations take so long to complete?

6. Was it a mere coincidence that his eventual arrest, so long delayed, followed quickly on the liberation of Paris?

All these questions may, of course, be explicable on depressingly commonplace grounds; but it is also possible to answer them by presuming the existence of a protection more powerful and far-reaching than any individual could provide. In short, it is a fair guess that some organisation was looking after Petiot.

As already mentioned, various Resistance newspapers, shortly before his arrest, argued that the doctor was a Gestapo agent. The charge at that time was a not uncommon one and Petiot's membership of the Communist Party by no means conclusive proof to the contrary: the theory was, at any rate, more applicable to his case than to thousands of others similarly accused. There are, however, serious objections. If he was one of their employees, why was Petiot ever arrested by the Gestapo at all? And surely the Gestapo, if they employed him, would have known all his addresses, so why did they not visit 21 rue Lesueur at the same time that they were busily searching all his other properties?

Another proposition sometimes put forward is that, while politically innocent at the time of his arrest by the German police, Petiot subsequently obtained his release by agreeing to become one of their undercover men. But this would not account for whatever protection he may have enjoyed extending back to 1930.

If, then, he was in fact the protégé of some powerful group, it must have been one of the several German secret services which functioned independently of the Gestapo and long before that malignant force came into being, allowing nonetheless that initially Petiot may not have known who or what was behind his immediate benefactors. There was some measure of rivalry and a very spasmodic co-operation between the various German intelligence services,[1] and this lack of liaison would account for his arrest by the Gestapo and, assuming that his own superiors later made representations, his eventual release.

Further, it is quite possible that the German authorities learnt at some point of his murderous activities and, believing them to involve only "persons having an interest in leaving France", gave their unofficial blessing to the enterprise.

M. Marçais having brought the French police into the business, even the occupying Power would have hesitated to side publicly with Petiot; but they might (and it has been alleged that they did) attempt to abort the French efforts to locate him, hamper the inquiry in a variety of ways, and it is worth noting that the German authorities insisted on receiving a detailed daily report of the progress of the hunt. Such weighty interference (perhaps applied deviously, without the police even realising what it was that hindered them) might well have kept Petiot at liberty until such time as the Germans were no longer in Paris to obstruct the traditional skill and patience of the Police Judiciaire.

All of which is the sheerest supposition: Petiot took all his luggage with him.

Alister Kershaw

As a footnote to this case, it is worth mentioning *Petiot, Victim of Chance* by Ronald Seth. Seth was in Paris at the end of the war as a member of Military Intelligence, and argues persuasively that Petiot *was* a member of the Resistance, and that his defense may have been basically true. Seth argues that the evidence in the case was so

1 Cf. H.R. Trevor-Roper's *The Last Days of Hitler* (Macmillan Ltd., London): "In Nazi Germany neither war production, nor manpower, nor administration, nor intelligence was rationally centralised; and Ribbentrop's protest at Nuremberg that foreign intelligence was not supplied by the Foreign Ministry but by thirty competing agencies is substantially true. The structure of German politics and administration . . . was in fact a confusion of private empires, private armies, and private intelligence services."

complex that no jury – "even a jury of geniuses" – could have grasped it, and that even though Petiot lied and repeatedly changed his story, he was probably telling the truth when he declared that he was in the Resistance. The reason, Seth thinks, is that Petiot could never have dealt with so many bodies without some help. He often had two bodies to dispose of, and sometimes as many as six. Yet before March 1944, when the smoke from his chimney caused his downfall, no one had noticed heavy smoke – even though Petiot had been killing since January 1942. Seth suggests that Petiot was a member of a Communist group, and that he was afraid to speak out because they would have killed his wife and son.

Seth seems to believe that the Communist group killed the victims to raise money for the Resistance. If this is correct, then Petiot was not innocent; he was a kind of hired killer, and deserved to go the guillotine with his co-conspirators.

At all events, I must confess that, having read three books on the case, I find it very hard to feel much sympathy for Marcel Petiot.

C.W

The Black Dahlia

Like the case of Donald Fearn, described earlier, the Black Dahlia case has always struck me as one of the most horrific in the annals of sex crime. When I first read it – in this account from David Rowan's *Famous American Crimes* (1957), I remember feeling utterly shocked and nauseated; I recall that it was the account of suspending her upside down and burning her with cigarettes that so revolted me.

The crime writer James Ellroy has written a powerful novel called *Black Dahlia* that suggests, probably correctly, that Elizabeth Short was involved in drugs and porn movies. In Ellroy's novel, the killer is an extremely sick sadist with a badly disfigured face. It sounds appropriate, yet somehow I doubt it. Few sadistic killers look like the hunchback of Notre Dame.

It has been suggested that Elizabeth Short's murderer was the killer known as "the mad butcher of Kingsbury Run", who killed and dismembered a dozen or more victims between 1935 and 1938 in Cleveland, Ohio. (An account of the case – by my son Damon – will be found in my *Murder in the 1930s*.) It is an interesting speculation, but seems to me unlikely. The mad butcher killed both men and women – often two at a time – and dismembered their bodies. All the evidence indicates that he was a homosexual sadist – I suspect the women were killed because he hated women, but that there was no kind of sexual motive. Such a man would hardly have travelled to Hollywood nearly a decade later to kill one would-be film actress. Only the horror of the cases serves as a connection.

Down in the heart of Hollywood, well away from the much-publicised glamour of the film stars' mansions, some of the side streets tell a sad story. Here is all the cardboard tawdriness of the disused film sets stacked behind the big studios. Here, a short ride from the world's most expensive hotels, the cheapjack stores shriek a thousand vulgar boasts, in garish neon lighting. But when the lights are out, little is left but the dirt on the plaster façade – and for hundreds of the pretty girls who arrive each year in search of a Hollywood fairy-tale, this is the reality . . .

Nobody cares. The masters of the film studios may be among the richest and most powerful men in the United States, but Hollywood is only a suburb of Los Angeles. And who notices what becomes of a pretty girl in a city with more than one and a half million inhabitants?

In the normal way, nobody would have noticed what happened to Elizabeth Short. She was just another of the countless failures, the forgotten souls sacrificed on the altar of a gaudy myth. Yet she, alone, broke through the callous flow of public indifference.

Elizabeth Short was murdered. That, too, was of little moment in a city which has an average of one murder a day. But the manner of her killing has ensured that her name will be remembered when those of the lucky few – the ones for whom the Hollywood fairy tale came true – have sunk into oblivion.

A tall, unusually beautiful girl, Elizabeth Short had several of the qualities which can make for renown in the extravagant, nerve-stretched capital of make-believe. In her personal appearance, she adopted a peculiarity of dress well calculated to attract the attention of a passing film producer. To emphasise her milk-white complexion and striking head of raven hair, often set off by a white flower, she rarely wore anything but black. Tight-fitting black dresses, the sheerest black underwear, black court shoes, even a jet ring on her pale hand. The habit had quickly earned her the nickname of "The Black Dahlia" – and possession of a nickname like that is another useful means of standing out from the ordinary film crowd. In her origins, she conformed with the favourite version of the studio publicity men in that she was born as far from Hollywood as possible, and in a small town or village rather than a big city. Miss Short, in fact, had come right across the continent, more than three thousand miles, from her home in the little manufacturing town of Medford, Massachusetts.

Finally, in her private life, "The Black Dahlia" had traits which, though morally reprehensible, testified to her high spirits and guaranteed her a solid basis of experience. Despite her stern New England background, she was wild and independent. Early in the war, she had been arrested as a juvenile delinquent, for drinking with soldiers in a café. When she gravitated to Hollywood a couple of years later, she loved to be taken to night clubs frequented by the film stars. It was not long before she fell in with a certain section of the film colony, whose morals were in inverse proportion to their potential influence. Although one may condemn her, it has to be admitted that quite a few young actresses, now famous, have won their first screen part by similar means . . .

For a while, Elizabeth Short did manage to find regular work as an extra, but that was all. There were so many girls like her. And soon after the war, when the studios went through a bad period, even that work dried up. Facing the facts of life, she moved out and got a job in San Diego, the booming seaport town a hundred-odd miles to the south. It was near enough for her to return to her old haunts for a day or two, every now and then, in the faint hope that one of her old film friends would remember her.

Yes, there were so many girls like "The Black Dahlia" – until a bleak, windy morning in Los Angeles in mid-January, 1947. Somewhere behind that wretched, grubby little pattern of her life is the clue to a discovery which, when they saw it, made hardened detectives vomit where they stood.

On that morning, alerted by a passing motorist, police rushed to a vacant building site beside a local "lovers' lane". There they found two halves of a female corpse.

It was nude. It had been cut in two at the waist. It had been hideously mutilated, beyond recognition. As a last refinement, the murderer had carved the initials "B.D." deep into one thigh.

Worse was to come. Pathologists who examined the body established that most of the bestial injuries had been inflicted *before death*. From their reports, police deduced that the victim had been overpowered and suspended by her ankles. Her legs, hands and feet had then been bound with wire or rope. In this position, head downwards, she had still been alive when the killer began mutilating her with a knife.

In its unspeakable sadism, I can think of only one comparison in recent criminal history – that of Neville Heath, the British sex murderer who was hanged the previous year. It happens that I was among the first newspapermen on the scene of Heath's first murder, a Notting Hill boarding house, just after the body was discovered. One of Britain's most famous detective chiefs told me then that, throughout his twenty-five years in the police, this was the only time that the sight of a murder victim had made him physically sick. The men of the Los Angeles Homicide Squad suffered a similar revulsion with the "lovers' lane" victim. On reading the medical reports, one of them muttered: "I hope to God she died of shock first – before the bastard had finished." Unhappily, the reports showed that, when the passing motorist saw the severed body, the victim had not long been dead. From the place where the murder was committed, wherever that might have been, the killer had taken the body and dumped it on the vacant site only a short while before it was discovered.

At this stage, the initials "B.D." cut into the body conveyed nothing to the police. Because of the obliteration of any recognisable features, it seemed likely that identifying the victim would be a long business, if not impossible. Experts were able to take impressions of some of the dead woman's finger-prints, however, and these were sent out for nation-wide checking. It was purely a routine measure. Unless she had been a criminal or an alien, or perhaps had worked in a confidential government job, there was little hope that her prints had been recorded. But now the police had the first of their very few breaks in the case. From the vast finger-print files of the Federal Bureau of Investigation, one punched card dropped into place. By a chance that could be reckoned in millions, the victim had given her finger-prints – *voluntarily* – to the F.B.I. while working during the war as a clerk in the U.S. Post Exchange (roughly the equivalent of the British NAAFI). She was, of course, Elizabeth Short, "The Black Dahlia". At the time of her death she was just twenty-two years old.

It had taken only a few hours to overcome this first hurdle, and the Los Angeles police made good use of their luck. Under Captain Jack Donohue, of the Homicide Squad, detectives rapidly traced the dead girl's mother, Mrs Phoebe M. Short. Her daughter's body had been cut up so terribly that she was unable to confirm the identification, but she did give the police a new lead. After quitting Hollywood, she told them, Elizabeth had written to her from San Diego, saying that she had found work there in an Army hospital or in some connection or other with the armed forces.

A hurried call to San Diego established that Elizabeth Short had left her room there six days before her death. She had taken no luggage with her – so it seemed possible that she had been planning to stay in Los Angeles with a woman friend, who could provide her, if necessary, with extra clothes and make-up. Meanwhile, other detectives scoured the less savoury back streets of Hollywood in search of anyone who had seen "The Black Dahlia" during her last visit. At one period one hundred policemen were engaged on different aspects of the case.

They found two bartenders who said that they had served drinks to Miss Short two or three days before the murder. Each time, she had been accompanied by one or more women friends.

They built up a description of "a man with red hair", who was believed to have been the last to see the victim alive. At the same time, they sought one of her former room-mates, who had disappeared on the very day the body was found.

All the time, too, they were building up a strangely mixed picture of the dead girl's character. Neighbours told them that she was "crazy about clothes" but that otherwise "she seemed to be a nice girl". A woman with whom she had once lived in Los Angeles said that Elizabeth had described herself as a friend of Ann Todd, the British film actress. When police checked the story, however, Miss Todd denied that she knew her. Next day – only three days after the crime was discovered – they made their first arrest.

The suspect, a thirty-eight-year-old cook named Edward Glen Thorpe, of Laramie, Wyoming, was handed over to them after fellow-passengers in a long-distance bus had heard him mumbling in his sleep – apparently about the murder. He was alleged to have muttered: "I forgot to cut the scar off her leg." Thorpe denied all knowledge of the crime but was said to have been unusually nervous during interrogation. Police also stated that they found what appeared to be blood-stains on his jacket. There was all the tense expectancy which immediately precedes the solution of a major crime . . . and then, as suddenly as it had begun, the enquiry fizzled out and the "Man from Laramie" was released. His description, it was announced, did not fit that of the "man with red hair" for whom the police were looking, and he was in the clear on other counts.

Only a few hours later, detectives brought in a man who did answer the required description. He was Robert Manley, a twenty-five-year-old salesman, formerly a musician in the U.S. Army Air Force. He had red hair – and he admitted that he had had a "flirtation" with Miss Short. But Manley, who had a wife and four-month-old child, denied any connection with her death. Lie-detector tests showed that his conscience was clear, and his wife supported his statement that he had been visiting friends with her on the night of the murder. Once again, the enquiry had come to a dead end. Before his release, however, Manley gave the police one hopeful lead. At one of his meetings with "The Black Dahlia", he recalled, he saw scratches on her arms. When he asked her about them, she explained that she had a friend who was "intensely jealous."

Despite these two setbacks, the hunt for the killer was proceeding along lines which could normally be expected to produce a solution within a week or two. The "Dragnet" series of television films has given many people an excellent insight into the methods of the Los Angeles detective force – and, for that matter, of detectives throughout the world. It is all a matter of routine thoroughness, of unending questioning, the elimination of each name on a list which may run into the thousands, the constant checking and cross-checking of every statement, every rumour, every known activity of the victim throughout his or her life. And all backed by scientific experts who can deduce a man's appearance from two short lengths of hair, or his job and probable home town from a speck of dust. No detail is too small to neglect. Intuition and inspired hunches, with which the detective-thriller sleuths are so gifted, do play their part in real life, but not often. One of Scotland Yard's greatest detectives, Mr William Rawlings, Deputy Commander of the C.I.D., has estimated that 97 per cent of all successful solutions are reached solely by the method of infinite pains.

So it was with the murder of "The Black Dahlia". Unmasking the culprit seemed only a matter of time. Under Captain Donohue, detectives questioned literally thousands of people. They came to know every place where the victim had ever worked, her likes and dislikes, her personal habits. They spread out from her known friends and began to amass a list of her more casual acquaintances, one link in the chain leading to the next. It was not easy, for her circle of acquaintances was large and indiscriminate, although the job appeared to have been simplified by another stroke of luck – in the shape of an anonymous letter received by a local newspaper in the week after the murder. The letter contained Elizabeth Short's birth certificate, social security card and address book. The envelope was addressed with portions of newspaper headlines relating to the case, crudely pasted together. A terse note inside said: "Here are Dahlia's belongings. Letter to follow." Exceptionally clear finger-prints were obtained.

But there the Homicide Squad's good luck ran out on them. This time, there was no record of the finger-prints in the files of the F.B.I. or anyone else. Nor did a minute scientific examination of the headlines and paste on the envelope yield anything of immediate use. The police laboratory experts could identify the newspapers (down to the exact edition) and the make of paste, but both could have been bought almost anywhere in the city, and Los Angeles covers a bigger area than any other city in the world. Even Miss Short's address book, in which she had written the names of her many men friends, produced little but hard work and disappointment. Several detectives were assigned to the sole task of tracing each name (a few of them surprisingly prominent and one of them actually a Hollywood millionaire). Occasionally they turned up somebody who gave them reason for suspicion; always, after further enquiry, they had to give him a clean sheet – so far as the killing was concerned, anyway. When the long, tedious job ended, it was as if they had never begun it . . .

Apart from their misfortune in being unable to uncover a vital lead, the men of the Homicide Squad were hampered by two factors beyond their control. The first was that, in addition to their usual one-a-day murder rate, they now had to contend with a whole series of brutal killings closely resembling that of "The Black Dahlia". Murderers are notoriously imitative, and detectives always know that if, say, a woman has been asphyxiated with a pillow and considerable publicity is given to the case, somebody else is sure to try the same method within the next few weeks. The death of the young film extra, and the enormous amount of space devoted to it in American newspapers, sparked off at least half a dozen sex killings of a similar type in the Los Angeles area. One came only three days after the Dahlia murder; the victim, Mary Tate, was savaged and then strangled with a silk stocking. Next month, the body of Mrs Jeanne French was found, atrociously mutilated; obscenities had been written on the corpse with lipstick. On March 11th, Mrs Evelyn Winters was slashed to death; she, too, had been slowly mutilated beforehand. Throughout the summer, as the Dahlia investigation dragged on, three more women suffered exceptionally gruesome deaths. Rosenda Mondragon was clawed and strangled with a silk stocking; Mrs Dorothy Montgomery was stripped bare and mutilated; Mrs Laura Trelstad was ferociously beaten and then strangled. In each of these six murders, there were other features, best left unmentioned, which suggested that they had been inspired by the manner of Elizabeth Short's death. Not only did these crimes have to be solved, but detectives had to make sure that there were no direct links between them. It was always possible that one or more of the six had been committed by the original Dahlia killer.

The second big obstacle to police progress turned out to be even more serious. From the start, Homicide Squad detectives were bedevilled by fantastic interference from ordinary members of the public. Day after day, an unending stream of misleading information and dubious "tipoffs", mostly motivated by a desire for publicity or personal revenge, poured into police headquarters. Yet, inside the framework of essential thoroughness, each one had to be examined closely before it could be rejected.

Above all, there were the false confessions. In the early days of most sensational murder cases, one or two cranks can be sure to give themselves up, wildly confessing their guilt of the crime; it is a common phenomenon. The Dahlia murder attracted at least *twenty-eight* of these claimants – far more than for any previous killing in U.S. criminal history.

Despite its gruesome nature, Elizabeth Short's death might long have been forgotten by now; but the phoney confessions have ensured it a place among the classics of American crime. For their character, the reasons behind them and behind the other forms of public interference in the case, lifted the stone and exposed an ugly growth: the hysterical unbalance affecting a wide section of the community.

A fortnight after the murder, Captain Donohue revealed that a thirty-three-year-old man had telephoned the Homicide Department to come and pick him up, saying: "I can't stand it any longer – I want to confess to the murder of Black Dahlia." In the patrol car which brought him in, he mumbled continually: "I killed her . . . I killed her." At police headquarters, the man, Daniel S. Voorhees, a former restaurant employee, signed a statement which was displayed to the waiting newspapermen afterwards by one of the detectives who questioned him. On the sheet of paper, above his signature, was written simply: "I did kill

Elizabeth Short." Voorhees, the detective said, had refused to give any details but denied having written any of the many anonymous letters and postcards received by the police – notably one which had stated that the murderer would surrender that very day. In passing, he had revealed that he had a wife and nine-year-old daughter at Phoenix, Arizona. Another detective said that Voorhees would not be given a lie-detector test "until he recovers from his bewildered and befuddled state". Unhappily, his recovery was immaterial. As detectives grew more insistent, pressing him to elaborate on his story, he became increasingly sullen. Eventually he growled: "Ah, I'm not going to talk to you any more. I've talked too much already. I want to see my attorney." Voorhees remained in custody – as a mental case.

Ten days later, Captain William Florence, of the U.S. Army Criminal Investigation Department, announced the arrest of twenty-nine-year-old Corporal Joseph Dumais, a combat veteran of Fort Dix, New Jersey. He was convinced, the captain said, that Dumais was involved in the crime. The curly headed, moustachioed young corporal, who had just returned from forty-two days' leave, was reported to military police by another soldier with whom he had quarrelled over money. He volunteered the information that he had known Miss Short and had been out with her on January 9th – only six days before her body was found. Investigators found bloodstains on his clothing and, among his possessions, a batch of newspaper cuttings about the murder. In an alleged statement running to 50 pages, Dumais was reported to have said that his first wife, by whom he had one child, died in 1937 in mysterious circumstances (which he did not elucidate). He was then 19. His second wife bore him three children, two of whom died. While serving overseas, he married a Czech girl in 1945 and adopted two children; he did not know her present whereabouts. The alleged statement then described his supposed association with Elizabeth Short. The presence of certain marks on her body which he mentioned was said to have been corroborated. Dumais himself admitted: "It is possible that I could have committed the murder. When I get drunk, I get rough with women . . ." Yet again, however, the whole edifice collapsed when the Los Angeles police came to give it a close inspection. They merely checked his story against facts known only to themselves – then sent Dumais, too, to a psychiatrist.

Experienced detectives can usually spot a false confession in a matter of minutes, if not seconds, by asking trick questions. In the Dahlia case, their task was made easier by the fact that many details of the murder were unprintable. Even the most uninhibited American newspaper draws the line at telling its readers the exact nature of the sadistic wounds inflicted by a sex killer. Accordingly, detectives seldom had any trouble in establishing that the would-be suspects knew nothing more about the murder than had actually appeared in the Press.

Some of the confessions arose from the misinterpretation of individual boasting. In a Long Beach bar, a U.S. naval man, Chief Pharmacist's Mate John N. Andry, talked long and loud about his skill at cutting up bodies. The police were informed and Andry, aged 30, was taken into custody. There he sat back and calmly insisted that it was he who had killed "The Black Dahlia". Tripped up during interrogation, he said sulkily: "Well, I'm *capable* of doing it." Finally he admitted that he had just been "kidding". The police said that there was some suspicion that he had shortly been due for an unwanted draft overseas . . .

Men were not alone on this exhibitionistic roundabout. Back in San Diego, a tall young woman, formerly in the Women's Army Corps, walked into a police station and announced: "Elizabeth Short stole my man, so I killed her and cut her up." When she, too, stumbled over essential questions about the location and method of the murder, she agreed reluctantly that she had "made the whole story up". In Barstow, California, a bartender reported that a beefy woman customer had told him: "I know who killed Beth Short and if the reward is big enough, I'll talk." Two plainclothes men rushed out from Los Angeles to question the woman, a twelve stone brunette. She alleged that two of her men friends had been involved in the murder. They had since walked out on her; so, to get her own back, she had decided to "shoot off her mouth". Although her story was patently phoney, the detectives' journey was not wasted. They took her two friends back to Los Angeles with them and "booked" them as suspects – not for murder, but in connection with a car theft!

Such attempts to lay information for reasons of personal revenge – an unpleasant trick known to the police as a "roust" – were always treated with severity. At least three Los Angeles landlords will think carefully in future before worrying the Homicide Squad with their troubles. Each of them, soon after the murder, reported the actions of certain tenants as suspicious. And each landlord, it transpired, had been trying unsuccessfully to evict those particular tenants . . . A blonde dancer telephoned police headquarters one evening and, with an air of great secrecy, whispered: "I'm meeting a man at First and Temple Streets at nine o'clock and I've reason to believe he is the 'Black Dahlia' killer." Captain Donohue sent detectives to the rendezvous to arrest both the girl and her suspect. They found that the man was a harmless business executive, innocent of all knowledge of Elizabeth Short or her murder. He had met his accuser during the war, quite fortuitously: they had been placed in the same "share-the-ride" group – a patriotic wartime scheme to save petrol, under which car owners gave regular lifts to people along their route. She had "dogged, threatened and slightly blackmailed" him ever since. His temporary arrest was a blessing in disguise; the blonde dancer is most unlikely to pester him again.

The task of sorting out the false confessions, "rousts" and other misinformation fell mainly on two veteran Homicide detectives, Harry Hansen and Finis Brown. "Most of them were exhibitionists and publicity seekers," Lieutenant Hansen said. "One man who confessed eventually admitted that he had done so because he and his wife had separated and he could not find her. He thought that, if he confessed, he would get his picture in the papers." It must have been hard to raise a laugh, yet the flood of strange tip-offs and offers of outside assistance, made for whatever reasons, sometimes had its amusing side – tragi-comic, anyway. The Homicide Squad men themselves figured in a typical incident. A few days after the murder, two of them were in a restaurant near police headquarters, discussing the case over coffee. They returned to their office at the very moment a frantic telephone call came through from somebody who thought he had just seen the killers. The caller proved to be a waiter in the restaurant. His "suspects"? The two detectives!

Another caller, telephoning with great anxiety from a public call-box, urged the police to pick up a man who had been sitting on the stool next to him in a nearby coffee shop. The informant explained: "I'm certain he's the murderer. He had an apprehensive look and ordered only a half-cup of coffee." One old lady walked five miles to tell the police that, if Elizabeth Short's body were buried with an egg in one hand – the way they did back in Alabama, the old lady's home State – the killer would be found within a week. An astrologer from the little town of Altadena, near Los Angeles, asked for the date and exact hour of Miss Short's birth, also promising (through the resultant astrological chart) to produce the murderer's name within a week. An amateur photographer, scorning both superstition and stars, requested the loan of the dead girl's right eyeball; he would photograph the last image reflected in it, he explained, and return with a picture of the killer.

Local drunks and petty criminals soon learned to turn the case to their own advantage. The former found that, by spinning a plausible yarn to suggest that they knew something about the murder, they could avoid, for a day or two, the discomfort of their regular cure in the city's "drunk tank". One habitual inebriate thought up an uproarious game; his system was to telephone the police from one bar, saying that he wanted to confess to the crime, then move on quickly to another bar from which he could see the fun – and then repeat the process all over again. He did it six times altogether before the overworked patrol car caught up with him. Public fear, meanwhile, made easy pickings for small-time footpads and hold-up men; where before some people might have resisted them, now all they had to do was to warn their women victims to keep quiet "or you'll get what the 'Black Dahlia' got."

Since it was always possible that one of these threats or

drunken jokes might provide a genuine lead, the police could never treat them at their face value. In December 1947, for instance, the Homicide men were informed – though it would not normally have concerned them – when a pretty, nineteen-year old wife, Mrs Helen Miller, complained that a man had scarred her with a knife. The man, Donald Graeff, aged twenty-eight, had offered her shelter when she was penniless, she said, but afterwards he had held her prisoner in his hotel room for a week. Two days before she escaped, she alleged, he had decided to brand her. He had thrown her on a bed and cut his initials in her hip with a sharp knife. Mrs Miller's story appeared to be true; police found three-inch letters carved deep into her flesh. Remembering the "B.D." cut in Elizabeth Short's thigh, they subjected Graeff to an intense grilling about the coincidence. On his treatment of Mrs Miller he admitted readily: "When I get drunk, I don't know what I'm doing." But on all questions concerning "The Black Dahlia", his denials were firm. He had been strangely imitative, hadn't he? Perhaps, but he hadn't consciously been so – and he still didn't know anything about the murder. For hours the questions kept coming; for hours he shook his head stubbornly. When at last the interrogation ground to a halt, it had failed to uncover a single direct link between Graeff and Elizabeth Short.

Slowly, as the months passed, the stream of "rousts" and busybodies began to dry up – but not the false confessions, although there were now long periods of quiescence. In September, 1950, police at Oakland, California, were suddenly reminded of the case by thirty-four-year-old Mrs Christine Reynolds. She committed the murder, Mrs Reynolds told them, when Elizabeth Short left her for the company of another woman. Because of this unpleasant new twist, her story took a few hours longer to disprove than most of the others.

The police were equally careful, though equally sceptical, when a man named Max Handler, also known as Mack Chandler, gave himself up to them only eleven days later. For among Miss Short's papers, they remembered, was the card of a company for which Handler had once worked. Moreover, Handler named two places to which he claimed to have accompanied the dead girl – and she was known to have been at both places. Once again, however, there was nothing to it.

Just how deeply the Dahlia killing has exerted its unholy grip is indicated by the fact that the 28th "confession" (and the last at the time of writing) came no fewer than nine years afterwards. The claimant, Ralph von Hiltz, a forty-four-year-old dishwasher, emerged in New York on January 5th, 1956. For a change, he did not announce himself as the culprit, but merely asserted that he had been a witness to the murder. Hiltz told detectives that he saw his friend kill Elizabeth Short and that afterwards he helped him to cut up her body. Unfortunately, most of the details he provided were at variance with those in the police dossier, and his friend's identity remains a mystery.

The cranks who tried to implicate themselves in the crime faced two big traps. The first, of course, was their ignorance of several basic facts. The second, known to few people outside the police, is that detectives have long had a good idea of the type of person actually responsible. And that, I can disclose, is not a man but a *woman*.

This theory was formed by Captain Donohue within two weeks of the murder. Although he could not be absolutely sure, and the male suspects were interrogated as thoroughly as ever, he was led to the belief that the killer was more likely to be a woman for a number of reasons. Primarily, the nature of the injuries – the peculiarly vicious spite with which they had been inflicted – pointed to the "deadlier of the species". Many of the wounds, Captain Donohue noted, were similar to those found in other mutilation murders in which jealous women had hacked their rivals to death.

Various points of circumstantial evidence supported his belief. Looking back over the case, it may be remembered that when Elizabeth Short left San Diego, she took no extra clothes or make-up with her – meaning, most probably, that she intended to stay with a woman friend who could lend her some. Who was the woman? The police never found out. Again, the two bartenders who reported serving drinks to her, a day or so before her death, both said that she was in the company of one or more women at the time.

Finally, might not the "intensely jealous" friend mentioned by former suspect Robert Manley – the one who, she had told him, had caused the scratches on her arms – have been a woman, too?

Whatever the murderer's sex, there can be little doubt that the principal motive for the crime was jealousy. The stories thought up by the few women who made false confessions – to the effect that "The Black Dahlia" was killed by a woman she had deserted or whose man she had stolen – may have been nearer the mark than their perpetrators imagined. But the police have not discounted another possibility. In certain details, there is a marked similarity between the Dahlia murder, and the unsolved sex killings which followed it, and the notorious "Jack the Ripper" killings in London towards the end of the last century. Among the innumerable legends about the Ripper, the only certain facts are that he had expert surgical knowledge and that his victim – six in three months – were all poor street walkers. As a result, the most widely accepted story is that he was a doctor, who launched his terrible campaign against that class of women because one of them had caused him (or, in the more fanciful version of the story, his son) some serious harm. In other words, he sought revenge against prostitutes as a whole and not merely against the specific individuals he happened to catch. Were Elizabeth Short and some of her fellow-victims caught in a similar vendetta? One or two of them were known prostitutes; others appear to have been enthusiastic amateurs. It is at least feasible that some person whose son had been ruined by such a woman might have wreaked indiscriminate vengeance on others of the same type. And that person, to return to Captain Donohue's theory, might well have been a woman herself . . .

The murder of "The Black Dahlia" remains unsolved. But even after this length of time, there are still grounds for believing that the killer may yet be found. The grounds are psychological – developing, strangely enough, from the string of false confessions. They were first expounded by Dr J. Paul de River, black-bearded staff psychiatrist of the Los Angeles police. In March, 1947, he told detectives that the confessions did not arise just from a lust for publicity, as they thought, but could spring from masochism, exhibitionism or a guilt complex engendered by some forgotten incident of childhood. He predicted, therefore: "The confessors will keep coming." As we know now, he was right. By the same token, Dr de River concluded, the type of mind which conceived the Dahlia murder "will one day have to boast about it". We can only hope that eventually he will prove to have been right about that, as well.

David Rowan

John Haigh:
The "Vampire Murderer"

The sensation caused by the Heath murders was eclipsed three years later by the case of the "vampire murderer" John George Haigh. On Sunday 20 February 1949, a man and a woman arrived at the Chelsea police station and explained that they wanted to report the disappearance of an elderly lady, Mrs Durand-Deacon, who was a fellow guest at the Onslow Court Hotel in South Kensington. The man – dapper and well-dressed, with a neat moustache – explained that he had arranged to meet Mrs Olivier Durand-Deacon two days earlier, to take her to his place of business in Sussex, but she failed to keep the appointment; now, with her friend Mrs Constance Lane, he had come to alert the police. When the police checked on him at the Criminal Records Office, they discovered that John Haigh had been in prison for swindling.

Crime reporters flocked to the Onslow Court Hotel, and Haigh gave a kind of impromptu press conference, emphasizing his own concern for the missing woman. But the West Sussex Constabulary was already looking at Haigh's "place of business", Hurstlea Products, at Crawley. He rented a two-storey brick-built storehouse from the firm, using it for "experimental work". The police broke in, and found a revolver, and a receipt for a Persian lamb coat from a firm of cleaners. The coat proved to belong to Mrs Durand-Deacon, and further enquiries revealed that her jewellery had been sold by Haigh to a jewellers in Horsham. Haigh was arrested and taken to the police station. At first he told obviously concocted lies about his relationship with Mrs Durand-Deacon, hinting at blackmail. Then he suddenly asked the police inspector what the chances were of anyone being released from Broadmoor, the criminal lunatic asylum.

Inspector Webb was non-committal. "Well", said Haigh, "if I told you the truth you wouldn't believe me . . . Mrs Durand-Deacon no longer exists . . . I have destroyed her with acid!" He gazed at the incredulous policeman with a bland smile. "How can you prove murder if there is no body?" Like many murderers, Haigh made the mistake of believing that the phrase *corpus delicti* means the corpse, without which murder cannot be proved; in fact, it means the body of the offence or crime. Fellow convicts who knew Haigh in his earlier days in Dartmoor had nicknamed him "old *corpus delicti*" because he liked to expound his view that a killer could not be convicted so long as there was no body.

Haigh added: "You'll find the sludge that remains at Leopold Road [Crawley]. I did the same with the Hendersons and the McSwanns."

Haigh had decided that his best means of escaping justice was a defence of insanity; he continued to pursue this objective by telling the police that the motive for the killings had been a desire to drink the blood of his victims; he had an insatiable lust for blood, and after each murder, filled a glass with his victim's blood and drained it. (In fact, blood is an emetic, and a glassful would undoubtedly have made him vomit.)

Haigh had embarked on his career of mass murder with the deliberation of a businessman. After a number of spells in jail for petty fraud, he decided that the best way to avoid being caught was to kill his victims and dispose of their bodies. In 1936 he had been employed by an amusement arcade owner named McSwann; after coming out of prison in 1943, he had met their son Donald again, and proposed a business partnership. Donald was lured to Haigh's basement "workshop" at Gloucester Road in September 1944 and bludgeoned to death; then Haigh dissolved his body in a vat of concentrated sulphuric acid – he had already experimented on mice in the prison workshop and decided that this was the perfect method of destroying corpses. He emptied the "sludge" down the drain. McSwann's parents were told he had gone off to Scotland on business. Ten months later, the elder McSwanns were lured separately to the basement and disposed of in the same way. Haigh then disposed of their considerable property, forging the necessary documents, for about £4,000.

By September 1947, Haigh had spent the £4,000, and looked around for more victims. He saw an advertisement for a house, and introduced himself to its owners, Archie and Rose Henderson, and offered them £10,500 for it. The deal "fell through", but Haigh continued to see the Hendersons, posing as a rich businessman. On 12 February 1948, Archie Henderson accompanied Haigh to his "workshop" at Leopold Road, Crawley, and was shot in the back of the head. Haigh then went and collected Rose Henderson, telling her that her husband was ill, and killed her in the same way. Various letters were despatched to relatives of the dead couple, explaining that they had been close to a "bust-up", and were travelling while their relationship was repaired. Haigh forged these letters so expertly that all suspicion was finally allayed. Then he disposed of their property, collecting some £7,700.

Other possible victims – including the widow of a Wakefield business-man – slipped through the net. By February 1949, Haigh was again in debt, and realized that he had to find a victim within the next week or so. To Mrs Durand-Deacon, who always dined at the next table at the Onslow Court Hotel, Haigh suggested a business deal involving the manufacture of plastic fingernails. And on 18 February 1949, Mrs Durand-Deacon made her fatal visit to the Crawley workshop. Twelve days later, on 2 March, Haigh was charged with her murder.

When Professor Keith Simpson travelled down to the Crawley workshop on 1 March, he had little hope of finding evidence of murder; Haigh had already told the police that he had poured the "sludge" over the ground several days earlier. The sludge was lying on an area of ground about six feet by four, and was about three inches deep. Simpson was staring intently at this sludge when he exclaimed: "Aha, gall-stones." He had seen an object about the size of a cherry, lying among some pebbles that were, to the inexpert eye, indistinguishable from it. After this find, the police carefully shovelled the sludge into boxes, to be removed to the Scotland Yard laboratory. There it was searched by spreading it thinly in steel trays; because the acid was so strong, the searchers had to wear rubber gloves. But the effort was worthwhile: the sludge proved to contain a partially dissolved left foot, and intact upper plastic denture, a lower denture, three gall-stones (easy to distinguish at close quarters by their facets), 28 lb of greasy substance, 18 fragments of human bone, the handle of a red plastic handbag and a lipstick container. Haigh had left more than enough of Mrs Durand-Deacon to hang him.

Simpson took the bones to his laboratory at Guy's. He discovered the presence of osteo-arthritis in some of the joints – Mrs Durand-Deacon suffered from osteo-arthritis – and was able to identify most of the bone fragments as human. Meanwhile, the police had made a plaster cast of the left foot, and checked it against Mrs Durand-Deacon's left shoe; the fit was perfect. The plastic dentures were identified by Mrs Durand-Deacon's dental surgeon as having been supplied to her two years earlier. Haigh had no way of knowing that the false teeth were of plastic, and therefore would not dissolve in acid, nor of knowing the gall-stones cannot be dissolved in acid.

Bloodstains found on the whitewash of the storeroom were tested and found to be human. Bloodstains were also found on the Persian lamb coat, and on the cuff of one of Haigh's shirts. The handbag strap was identified as belonging to the handbag Mrs Durand-Deacon had carried when she drove with Haigh down to Crawley.

Haigh's major mistake had been in confessing to the murders, and trusting to a defence of insanity. If he had said nothing about the "acid bath", the sludge might not have been examined for many weeks, and Simpson later admitted that by that time, the acid might have consumed everything but the gall-stones and the human fat. And in themselves, these would not have constituted sufficient evidence of identity.

In prison, Haigh continued to build up the notion that he was insane, claiming that there had been three more victims – all penniless – whom he had killed for their blood alone. He explained that the urge to drink blood developed after an accident with a lorry in 1944, when his car overturned. After this, he said, he began to have a recurrent dream of a forest of crucifixes which turned into trees that dripped blood . . . He also claimed that the murders were divinely inspired. When aware of being observed, he drank his own urine.

All this was useless. A number of doctors and psychiatrists examined Haigh, and all but one concluded that he was perfectly sane. A woman friend who visited him in prison observed that he was playing the role of mass murderer with tremendous gusto, delighting in his belated "fame". The newspapers were full of accounts of the "vampire murderer" – probably no case of the century has received so much publicity – and one of them, the *Daily Mirror*, went too far and was fined £10,000, while its editor was sentenced to three months in prison. But at the trial, which began on 18 July 1949 at Lewes Assizes, all the evidence revealed Haigh as a calculating killer who had murdered for gain, and who was shamming insanity. Dr Henry Yellowlees, for the defence, argued that Haigh was genuinely paranoid, but the jury was so unimpressed that they took only 15 minutes to bring in a guilty verdict. Haigh was executed at Wandsworth on 6 August 1949.

Simpson, who was responsible for the medical evidence that convicted Haigh, later commented on the absurdly small profits that Haigh had made from five years of murder – a mere £12,000. The last murder, of Mrs Durand-Deacon, would have brought him only about £150 for the coat and the jewellery. He could have made more money in almost any honest occupation.

Keith Simpson died in 1985, at the age of 78. Like Spilsbury, he was inclined to overwork, and his publisher J. H. H. Gaute remarked in an obituary that this was the cause of his death. But his enthusiasm for his gruesome occupation was so great that he was unable to stay away from the morgue and the "path lab". Gaute recalls how, after lunching with Simpson at Guy's, Simpson asked him if he would like to come down to the mortuary, and seemed surprised when the publisher declined. "Not the keen type, eh?" he remarked drily.

The present writer did not decline a similar invitation,

and was taken into the mortuary to view the body of a male child of about 7, who had – according to a teenage baby-sitter – died after a fall downstairs. Simpson expertly opened the body in a few minutes, then, as if he knew exactly what he was looking for, plunged in his hand and drew out the liver, which was broken in half. "That wasn't caused by a fall downstairs. It's an impossibility. He must have been kicked in the stomach." Since the baby-sitter had been alone with the child at the time of the "accident", the evidence suggested that he was the culprit. I never found out the sequel to the story. But I retained the impression that Simpson had known intuitively that he was looking at a case of murder.

Colin Wilson

AFTERWORD

The crime writer Nigel Morland once told me that he had received a phone call from someone who gave his name as "Hay", and who enquired about how long it would take to dissolve a body in acid; Morland told me that Haigh pronounced his name "Hay."

For me, perhaps the most interesting story about Haigh is told by Blanche Patch, who was Bernard Shaw's secretary. Shaw and Miss Patch were eating a meal in the Onslow Court Hotel, and a child in the dining room was being a nuisance. The man at the next table – whom Blanche Patch later recognised as Haigh – suddenly snarled: "If that child doesn't shut up I'll murder him." At this, Shaw told Miss Patch: "That man is going to be hanged one day." I would like to think that this indicated some profound psychological intuition on Shaw's part, but the truth is probably that Shaw was simply reacting to Haigh's sudden loss of control, and his remark indicated distaste rather than precognition.

The Lonely Hearts Murders

The Lonely Hearts murder case caused an understandable sensation at the time; Ray Fernandez
and Martha Beck were regarded as inhuman
monsters. I was always fascinated by the case
because it involved the syndrome psychologists
call "folie a deux" – and because this so often
reveals an interesting pattern of dominance of
one character by the other. It was the psychologist
Abraham Maslow who discovered that all human
beings fall into one of three "dominance groups"
– high, medium and low. He preferred to study
women – because he thought they were more
truthful than men – and concluded that the female
high dominance group is always 5% of the total –
one in twenty. High dominance women tended to
be highly promiscuous, often had experience of
lesbianism (without necessarily being lesbians),
and were only interested in high dominance males
who liked fairly rough sex. (Interestingly enough,
even for high dominance females, the male had
to be slightly more dominant than she was.)
Medium dominance women, the largest group,
were basically "one man women", who liked the
kind of lover who wooed them with soft lights
and flowers. Low dominance women disliked sex
and thought the male organ downright ugly (high
dominance women thought it beautiful; medium
dominance women didn't take either view.)

What I found interesting was that both men and
women usually preferred long term sexual relations with someone in their own dominance group.
But sometimes, a high dominance character and a
medium dominance character became involved by

chance, and then there was potential for a violent explosion.

In such circumstances, the dominant partner often seems to be carried away by a recklessness that is based upon the joy of ego-assertion, and is prepared to commit acts of which he would be incapable alone. Leopold and Loeb, the homosexual killers of the 1920s, were such a mixture, Leopold referring to himself as Loeb's "slave". Ian Brady and Myra Hindley, the "moors murderers", were another example in which the male exercised almost hypnotic dominance. When I first wrote about them, Fernandez and Beck struck me as another example, except that, oddly enough, Martha Beck seemed to me the dominant partner.

When asked to write up the case for a partwork called *Murder Casebook* (on which the following account is based), I changed my mind; closer study of the case made it clear that Fernandez was the dominant partner, and that he was changed from a medium-dominance and basically honest person into a high-dominance crook by a head injury. Blows on the head often seem to play an important part in criminality; others who developed criminal tendencies after a head wound were Earle Nelson, the "gorilla murderer", Albert Fish, the American child killer, Alfred Rouse, the burning car murderer, Henry Lee Lucas, the serial killer, and a Chinese man called Lock Ah Tam, who can be found in the *Encyclopedia of Murder*. It is worth commenting, in parenthesis, that the painter Augustus John was a second rate artist until he dived into the sea and smashed his skull on a rock; from then on he became a painter of genius.

But there are, I think, few cases in which a violent blow on the head produced such bizarre and unexpected results as in that which follows.

*　　*　　*

It was a head injury that turned Raymond Fernandez into a monster. The accident happened at sea in December 1945; a falling hatch struck him on the forehead with such force that it made a dent in his skull. He spent four months in hospital, and it was later revealed that his brain tissue had been scarred. Before that, Raymond Fernandez had been a mild, unaggressive character, a hard worker and a faithful husband. The accident turned him into a criminal and a sex maniac.

Not that Fernandez was a sex criminal in the usual sense – even after the accident he would have been incapable of trying to take a woman by force. But he suddenly became possessed of such an overwhelming sexual urge that his only aim in life was to seduce women. It made no difference if they were young and attractive or middle aged and overweight. Anything female aroused his lust. He later estimated that in the next two years he seduced over a hundred women.

But first he spent time in jail for a minor offense whose irrationality baffled the court. In Mobile, Alabama, he tried to walk through customs with a huge packet of soiled linen, all marked with government stamps. It was worthless anyway – with luck he might have received a dollar for the lot. Pleading guilty to attempted theft, he was sentenced to a year in the prison in Tallahassee, Florida. And here occurred another event that was to exercise a baleful influence on his life. There were large numbers of West Indians in the jail, and much talk of voodoo and black magic. Fernandez was fascinated – particularly by tales about hypnotism. He became convinced that he possessed magical powers, and in order to test them out, wrote a letter to the judge who had sentenced him, complaining that his punishment had been too severe. Then he spent days concentrating on the judge, and trying to influence him by a kind of distant hypnosis. Incredibly, it worked. When the judge asked for guidance on the case, court officials agreed that there *was* room for leniency; they had advised Fernandez not to secure himself a council, thus depriving him of skilled advice. The judge decided to cut the sentence to six months. To Raymond Fernandez, this was a revelation. If he could infuence people from a distance, nothing was impossible. He could become rich and famous. Or, more important, have all the women he wanted . . .

Raymond Fernandez was born of Spanish parents in Hawaii in December 1914; his father was a labourer, and he treated his children harshly. Raymond, who was small and weak, was never a favourite. When his father began running a farm in Connecticut, the boy was always given the most unpleasant tasks. Raymond was highly intelligent – a later test showed that his I.Q. was 135, near genius-level; but his father refused to allow him to go to college. At sixteen, anxious to provide the family with a bird for Thanksgiving, he and two friends stole some chickens. They were caught red handed. The fathers of the other two boys offered sureties for their future good conduct; Raymond's father refused, and he went to prison for two months.

During the American depression of the '30s the family moved back to Spain; Fernandez senior became a successful businessman and mayor of the town. At the age of twenty, Raymond married, and went on to father four children. During the Second World War, he went to Gibraltar, where he worked as an ice cream vendor, picking up information for British intelligence. Many writers on the case have assumed that Fernandez's stories of being a spy were pure invention; in fact, they were confirmed by his biographer Wenzell Brown.

At the end of the war, Fernandez decided to return to America to seek his fortune. But on the voyage, he was struck on the head by the falling hatch, and his whole life changed . . .

Back in New York Fernandez went to stay with relatives. They found the change incomprehensible. The Raymond Fernandez they had known had been a shy, reserved young man with impeccable manners. This hollow-cheeked, balding man boasted and ranted like a madman, always dwelling on his favourite subjects – magic and hypnotism.

And now it was time, he felt, to put his newly-discovered powers into operation. According to the doctrines of voodoo, all he needed was some small item belonging to any woman

– a lock of hair, a fragment of clothing, even a letter – to entangle her in a web of magical desire. New York was full of potential conquests – lonely middle aged women hoping to find romance. Many of them belonged to the "Lonely Hearts Clubs" that advertised in cheap magazines, and from one of these, Mother Dinene's Friendly Club, Fernandez obtained a list of addresses.

Most of the replies that poured in were gushingly senti-mental – these women were crying out to be seduced. And Fernandez was well equipped to do it. The child of Spanish parents, he had an old world courtesy combined with charm and self-confidence. At the age of thirty-one, he was far from unattractive, being tall and thin, with a gaunt face and dark eyes – some pictures make him look rather like Henry Fonda. With a toupee covering the scar on his forehead, he was a highly presentable male. And even if he had lacked these advantages, the man-shortage in post-war America would have made up for it (there were one and a quarter million more women than males.) Soon he was writing to several women at the same time. Most of them fell in love with him at the first sight, and many of them – even respectable matrons – allowed him to make love to them at their first meeting. Fernandez, of course, attributed all this to his hypnotic gaze (and he may not have been entirely wrong). His sexual appetite was omnivorous: old women, young women, thin women, fat women, rich women, poor women – he even seduced a woman who was badly deformed. In cases where the lady proved more difficult, he performed various occult rituals, such as scattering his letters with a magic powder (bought at a Jamaican shop in Harlem) and putting spells on dolls. Few women resisted for long. He was soon having affairs with a dozen at the same time – his average turnover was one a week. The sheer complexity of such an existence would have deterred most Romeos. Fernandez seemed to be driven by some obsessive compulsion, a desire to prove something.

He soon discovered that there were concealed benefits in the life of a sex maniac. Many of the women were well off, and they were anxious to press money on him. It seems fairly clear that obtaining cash was not a part of his original intention. But since it was freely offered, it seemed absurd to refuse it. And since his life was so complicated it was obviously impossible for him to bestow himself completely on any one of his mistresses. If the lady had no money, he stayed a few days. If she was rich and generous, he might stay a week or so. But his compulsion forced him to keep moving on.

In the late spring of 1947, he embarked on one of his longer affairs. The lady was a middle-aged cook named Jane Lucilla Thompson, and she lived with her mother in a large apartment on West 139th Street. She also had a few boarders, and Fernandez soon left his sister's home in Brooklyn to move in with her. By August they had decided to take a holiday in Spain. They sailed in October, travelling as man and wife, then visited Madrid, Granada, and Malaga, with Fernandez acting as guide to his own country – for although he had been born in Hawaii, he had spent most of his adult life in Spain. In fact, he had acquired himself a wife there, a girl named Encarnacion, and she had presented him with four children. Driven by the strange irrationality that had made him steal the soiled linen, he now visited La Linea, where his family – and his wife's family – were living, and actually introduced his wife to his latest mistress. It is not known how he succeeded in persuading the two women to be polite to one another – as they were for several days. But a point came where Lucilla Thompson felt that she was sharing her "husband". Or possibly Encarnacion revealed that Fernandez was *her* husband. For whatever reason, on the evening of November 7, 1947, Lucilla Thompson exploded – servants later described her screaming at Fernandez – and undoubtedly threatened to return to America alone. Since she had been footing all the bills, this would have caused her gigolo severe inconvenience. But the crisis was averted, for the next morning, Lucilla Thompson was found dead in her room. The local doctor diagnosed a heart attack brought on by gastro-enteritis. Since there were no suspicious circumstances attached to her death, Fernandez was allowed to leave town the next day.

A few months later the police of La Linea received a disturbing communication via the American Consulate. An

English lady named White had reported her suspicion that Mrs Thompson had been murdered. She had met her on board ship, and noted that her "husband" was many years her junior, and that he seemed to want to prevent her from talking with other passengers. She suspected that his interest in Lucilla was purely financial. Mrs White and Mrs Thompson had subsequently kept in touch by letter, and when Mrs White heard of her friend's death, she was shocked and suspicious. The police of La Linea soon discovered that Fernandez had purchased a bottle of digitalis from the hotel pharmacy two days before Mrs Thompson's death, and it was found, half empty, in her medicine cupboard. This would certainly have caused symptoms like those from which she died. Unfortuntely, it was now too late for an autopsy; the body proved to be too badly decomposed.

Meanwhile, Fernandez had hurried to Lucilla Thompson's New York apartment, and presented her mother, Mrs Pearl Wilson, with a document that made made him sole heir to Mrs Thompson's property. The feeble old lady was too shattered by her daughter's death to object; besides, Fernandez told her she was welcome to stay on. A closer examination would have revealed that the "will" was a forgery; it later became clear that Fernandez had simply obtained Lucilla's signature on two sheets of blank paper, then filled them in to make himself her legatee.

Now once again Raymond Fernandez took up his career of seducing lonely widows and divorcees whose addresses had been provided by Mother Dinene. His attention was immediately drawn to one woman who was far younger than the rest – a mere twenty-six. Moreover, she held a responsible position as the superintendent of the Pensacola Crippled Children's Home in Florida, and apparently had her own apartment. She sounded ideal. Her name was Martha Seabrook Beck. Fernandez lost no time in sending her a telegram announcing his imminent arrival.

Martha Beck's childhood had been even more difficult than Raymond's. She was the first child of a highly dominant mother, with whom she spent much of her life quarelling. Her mother went on to marry a man named Holland Seabrook, and Martha adopted his surname. She was born in Florida in

1920, and from the beginning had a deep attachment to her strong-willed mother; her feelings veered between love and hatred. She was a sullen child, overweight and either ignored or disliked. Other children tormented her. At the age of nine her breasts began to develop, and older men began making passes at her. Her glandular disorder filled her with violent sexual cravings, but her mother's watchful eye made any gratification impossible. At the age of twenty-two she passed her nursing exams, but failed to find a job – her physical appearance was against her. Eventually, she went to work for a local mortician, washing and laying out bodies. She spent all her spare time devouring cheap romantic magazines. Sheer frustration brought her to the edge of nervous breakdown, and she decided to get away to California. There she found employment in a large hospital. She also found sexual gratification – of a sort – picking up men around bus stations. One of these, a bus driver, made her pregnant. She pressed for marriage, and he reluctantly agreed. When he tried to drown himself, Martha was shattered, and had a nervous breakdown with amnesia. She decided to go back to Florida, where her mother was living in Pensacola; there she told everyone that she had married a naval officer named Joe. When she announced that he had been killed in action, all her acquaintances were deeply sympathetic; after the birth of her baby she obtained a job in the local hospital. (Later investigation revealed that the marriage was a figment of her imagination.) She met a local bus driver named Alfred Beck, and soon persuaded him into marriage. By May 1945, after less than six months, she was filing a suit for divorce. Now pregnant for a second time, she obtained a job in the Crippled Children's Home in Pensacola. Six months later, she was appointed superintendent.

Her major problem was her immense sexual appetite. Moreover, normal sexual intercourse gave her little pleasure; she needed a man who was rough and demanding. She began going to parties and drinking heavily. At this early stage, the home had no suspicion that its superintendent was a nymphomaniac who was fast becoming an alcoholic.

Then, in November 1947, an acquaintance from her schooldays played a cruel practical joke: he replied to a

Lonely Hearts Club in her name. Her first response was to burst into tears. Then she decided to forget caution and write an application . . .

Fernandez's first sight of Martha Beck was something of a shock. To describe her as fat would have been an understatement. She was positively gross. But Raymond Fernandez had never yet failed to provide satisfaction. Besides, she might be rich. Showing no sign of his lack of enthusiasm, he accompanied her back to her apartment, and sat down to an elaborate meal. Neither was he alarmed to discover that she had two children, and had been married twice. And when they retired to bed he was in for another surprise. The gross-looking nurse responded with immense passion. What was more important, she displayed no aversion to some of the minor sexual abnormalities that Fernandez had developed of recent years – and which many of his more demure conquests had found unutterably indecent. Full details of their sex life – which emerged during their trial – have never been published, since they were regarded as too vile. In our less inhibited age, it is probably safe to say that they amounted to bondage, sodomy, oral sex, and simple variations on these three. What we *do* know is that Martha Beck not only consented to these experiments, but suggested a few of her own. Fernandez, accustomed to prudish American ladies, and to even more prudish Spanish ones, found it an incredible experience. Each of them ended that night in a state of total sexual exhaustion.

Yet for the seducer of more than a hundred women, alarm bells were ringing. It was obvious that Martha Beck was madly in love; she felt that her good fairy had at last provided her with something she had craved all her life: a truly romantic lover. As she assured him of her undying devotion, he inwardly cringed. This one was going to be difficult to get rid of. Moreover, she was obviously as poor as he was. So after two days, he made flowery and regretful farewell speeches, and fled back to New York. The lovelorn Martha bombarded him with adoring letters, but recieved no reply. Then, one day, she received a letter with his writing on the envelope; she tore it open ecstatically. But she found what he had to say was shattering and unbelievable. She had, he assured her, mistaken his feelings for her, which were of deep respect rather than passion. They must never see one another again.

Martha escorted her children to a neighbour's house, then put her head in the gas oven. But the neighbour had noticed her distraught state, and went to investigate; when she smelled gas, she called the police. A farewell note to Ray Fernandez was lying beside her. A few days later, Fernandez received it in the post, together with a letter describing the suicide attempt. And either from motives of remorse or of prudence – at the prospect of being involved in a scandal which might alert other prospective victims – he lost no time in writing her an affectionate letter, inviting her to New York. Martha paused only to obtain a two week's leave of absence from the children's home, then caught the next train.

For Martha the next two weeks were a dream of bliss. Fernandez seemed cool, but she realised that she had to win him all over again; she cooked him huge meals, ironed his shirts and cleaned the flat. She slept in Lucilla's old bedroom; but since Fernandez experienced powerful and abnormal sexual urges several times a day, their love life was soon as passionate as ever. Yet even the insatiable Spaniard was beginning to realise that sex was not everything. He simply did not want to be tied down. So when he finally waved goodbye to the train, he heaved a sigh of relief.

Back in Pensacola, Martha had a shock awaiting her. She was told that she was fired from the crippled children's home. No reasons were given, but it was obvious that in a place as small as Pensacola, news of her torrid liaison was causing scandal. She had been fired from a previous job in a maternity hospital for promiscuity. Martha railed at the injustice, then set out to cause a scandal by taking her case to the local newspapers. The attempt backfired; it only guaranteed that she would find no other work as a nurse in Florida. Now there was only one thing to do: move in on Raymond, complete with children.

Fernandez was stunned to find her on his doorstep. He needed freedom for his complicated love life – a love life that was now his sole means of livelihood. He began by telling her sternly that he could not accept the children. Martha found this shattering, but knew she had to give in. With the aid of the Welfare Department, her mother was persuaded to take charge of the children. Martha never saw them again, nor showed any inclination to do so.

As on the previous occasion, she strove to make herself useful. It was Martha who sternly told the bewildered old lady that she would have to move, since Fernandez intended to sell the apartment. She was sent off to live with one of her sons. And now they were alone in the place, Fernandez decided to play for all or nothing. He told Martha frankly that he could not marry her, because he made his living by seducing middle aged women, and she would cramp his style.

It would be untrue to say that Martha did not turn a hair – she was deeply shocked. But her passion was so deep that it finally made no difference. He was her man, her hero, her god – a man who could seduce women from a distance by hypnosis. What did it matter if he was a petty crook? She could never leave him. The feelings of the trapped gigolo are not recorded. But since he was basically a far weaker character than Martha, he conceded defeat.

The next victim on the list was a retired teacher named Mrs Esther Henne of Pennnsylvania. Fernandez had already met her when she was on holiday in New York. Now he arrived at her home with a proposal of marriage. Yet even on a mission as delicate as this, Martha was too jealous to allow him to go alone. She was introduced to Mrs Henne as Fernandez's sister in law, and she drove down with them – in Mrs Henne's car – to Fairfax, Virginia, where they were married, then back to the New York apartment. Now Raymond applied himself to the main part of the enterprise, parting her from her cash and property. But Mrs Henne proved to be cautious and hard-headed. When she declined to sign over her insurance policies and pension fund, Fernandez ceased to be an attentive husband, and became rude and irritable. He succeeded in obtaining possession of her car and extracting five hundred dollars. By then, Mrs Henne had heard rumours from other tenants in the block about the sudden death of his previous "wife" in Spain; she lost no time in hurrying back to

Pennsylvania. She even instituted legal proceedings against him, and succeeded in recovering her car and three hundred dollars.

Fernandez was already finding life difficult. One of his mistresses was pregnant and wanted him to marry her. He decided to sell the apartment and go in search of fresh dupes. One of these – supplied by the Lonely Hearts Club – was a lady named Myrtle Young, of Greene Forest, Arkansas. When Fernandez arrived with his "sister in law" in Arkansas, Mrs Young was swept off her feet, and lost no time in accepting his proposal of marriage. But during their honeymoon – in a cheap Chicago rooming house – she became increasingly impatient as Raymond failed to consummate their marriage. The jealous Martha was doing everything to prevent it from happening. On the third day, the new Mrs Fernandez announced that either Martha should go or she would. The result was a screaming row that ended with Martha persuading Myrtle Young to swallow a sleeping draught of barbiturates. And since they now had four thousand dollars of her money, and no further use for her, they put her on a bus for Little Rock, Arkansas. On the journey, the groggy Mrs Young collapsed, and had to be taken into hospital, where she died. Her death was ascribed to a cerebral haemorrhage.

It was becoming plain to Fernandez that Martha was something of a jinx. Their next enterprise confirmed this view. The "mark" was a young and relatively rich woman in New England, and she succumbed readily to the Fernandez brand of Spanish courtesy. Unfortunately, she found his sister in law intolerable. Martha had quickly recognised that Fernandez found his new conquest attractive and suspected that he was wondering whether it might be time to settle down. Martha displayed such jealousy that Fernandez lost his temper and gave her a beating. Finally, cowed and contrite, Martha agreed to go away and visit relatives. But by now the wealthy lady had seen through Fernandez and told him to go away. Back in a newly rented apartment in Queens, Raymond could no longer stand the loneliness, and sent for Martha. She was there as soon as he beckoned.

*   *   *

It was a gloomy Christmas. The money they had obtained from Myrtle Young was almost finished. But at least there was a new quarry in sight. She was a sixty-six-year-old widow from Albany, New York, named Janet Fay. She belonged to many Lonely Hearts Clubs and kept up a wide correspondence. She was a Catholic, and her letters were full of religious sentiments. When a correspondent who called himself Charles Martin told her that he was also a Catholic, she entered enthusiastically into religious discussions. And when he proposed to come and visit her, she lost no time in extending a warm invitation.

On New Year's day, 1948, "Charles Martin" arrived at Mrs Fay's small apartment in Albany, together with a large woman whom he introduced as his sister. He began by explaining that he had lost his wallet in the course of the New Year's Eve celebrations, and would be grateful if they could stay there until he could send for more. In fact, Fernandez and Beck were penniless. They *had* to make this con-trick successful.

Mrs Fay was delighted with her religious pen-pal. Three days later, she was so much under the spell of the thoughtful and charming Spaniard that she agreed to marry him. The following morning, they visited various banks and Mrs Fay drew out six thousand dollars. Then they all drove back to New York, in the car that had belonged to Myrtle Young, and to a new apartment on Long Island.

The marriage was to take place almost immediately; meanwhile, Raymond suggested a delightful way of informing her relatives. They would receive sheets of paper containing the word "Surprise!", with Mrs Fay's signature. Mrs Fay not only signed the papers, but also two blank cheques. Her trust in Charles was total.

That night, apparently, she began to suspect it was misplaced. This was not due to any oversight on the part of Raymond Fernandez, but to Martha's jealousy. Mrs Fay and Martha slept in the same bed, and Mrs Fay plied her future sister in law with probing questions about her fiancé's childhood. Martha grew taciturn, then angry. And when Mrs Fay lost her temper and told her that after the marriage she and Charles were going to live alone, Martha realised that she was jinxing their latest swindle. Mrs Fay stormed out of the bedroom – in a pink chenille bath robe – and woke Charles, to explain her grievances. She was obviously hoping to persuade him that his sister had to leave in the morning. Before the discussion could reach that stage, Mrs Fay was knocked unconscious by a hammer wielded by Martha Beck.

Typically, Fernandez was thrown into a state of panic – so much so that he suggested calling the police. At which point, Martha knelt beside Mrs Fay and announced: "She's dead."

Mrs Fay was bleeding all over the carpet. Numbed with shock, Fernandez helped Martha to clean up the blood and bind a towel round the dead woman's head to stop further bleeding. When there was time for calm discussion, Martha admitted that she had struck Mrs Fay out of sheer jealousy. But that was now an academic point. How could they dispose of the body?

They devised an answer that has suggested itself to many murderers. The next day they purchased a large trunk, and Raymond's sister was persuaded to allow them to store it for a few days in her basement in Astoria. Then came a frantic search for a more permanent disposal site. Eight days later they found a house in Queens. The trunk was transported there in a jeep, and lowered into a hole in the cellar. When it was cemented over, and dust rubbed into the surface, the grave was indistinguishable from the rest of the floor. They then told the agent that the house would not be suitable after all, and left without demanding a return of their advance rent.

With such a traumatic experience behind them, it might be supposed that the homicidal lovers would think twice before embarking on another scheme of a similar nature. In fact, Fernandez's conviction of his magical powers probably sustained him. On the day of Mrs Fay's murder, he had received a letter from another likely prospect, a forty-one-year-old widow named Delphine Downing, who lived in Grand Rapids, Michigan. And although Martha was in favour of relaxing for a while on their ill-gotten gains – they had even gone back to Mrs Fay's home and stripped it bare – he was now ready for fresh adventures. Or perhaps he simply liked the idea of moving as far away as Michigan.

Delphine Downing was a young widow with an infant daughter; her husband, a war hero, had been killed in a railway accident two years earlier, just before the birth of Rainelle. When "Charles" arrived on her doorstep with his sister, she made him welcome. He was grave, thoughtful and good-looking – as well as being nearly a decade younger than she was. She even liked his sister Martha, who struck her as "loads of fun". When Charles and Martha moved in, Delphine Downing told her neighbours that Martha was the nurse who had delivered her baby.

Raymond was getting tired of not being allowed to have sex with his conquests, and he was determined that this rather attractive woman would be the exception. He told Martha so sternly, and she sullenly agreed – after all, her last fit of jealousy had cost them a great deal of inconvenience. Within days, Raymond was sleeping with Delphine, and Martha was doing her best to hide her misery and rage.

Martha's later story of what led to the murder seems somehow inadequate. She claims that Delphine walked into Raymond's room and discovered him without his wig. This led to accusations of deceit and quarrels. The story seems unlikely – a woman in love does not quarrel with a new lover because he has thinning hair. The truth is probably that Fernandez and Beck decided to kill Delphine Downing for her house and her bank account. It is also possible that it was Martha who killed her, as she killed Mrs Fay, out of an uncontrollable jealousy which erupted when Delphine Downing confessed that she thought she was pregnant. The stories they told later were understandably designed to make the crime seem less horrific.

All that seems fairly certain is that on the morning of Sunday February 27, 1949, Martha offered her rival some pills to bring about an abortion; they were actually sleeping tablets. Then, when she was in a deep stupor, Raymond Fernandez wrapped a blanket round her head, and shot her with a service pistol that had belonged to her husband.

As soon as he had done so, his nerve went. The truth was that, in spite of the things he had done, Ray Fernandez was not a bad man. Now he was sickened and demoralised by what he had done. It was Martha, the efficient nurse, who had so often laid out corpses, who thrust him aside and took over the operation. She began by tying the blanket round Delphine's head to prevent further bloodstaining, then ordered Fernandez to take the shoulders while she took the feet, and help her carry the body down to the cellar. The rest of the day was spent burying the body and cementing it over. The fact that the cement was already in the basement suggests that the murder had been planned well in advance. Then, in the evening, they went to call on neighbours with whom they had become acquainted, and explained that Mrs Downing had been called away to see a sick relative, and that they were staying in the house and looking after the child.

They spent the following day preparing to leave, and having minor repairs made on their car. It was their intention to take Rainelle back to New York – although what they then intended to do with her is not clear. But Rainelle cried incessantly. It was Fernandez who announced that she would have to be killed. At first Martha objected; but she had become accustomed to obeying her lover, and finally agreed. She carried Rainelle over to a large washtub of water – which had been bailed out of Delphine Downing's grave – and immersed the child's head. After that they dug another grave, buried Rainelle, and cemented her over.

Back upstairs, more neighbours dropped in, and were told about the planned departure – which was fairly obvious, since a car with a large trailer was standing outside the door. They left an hour later, apparently convinced by the story they had been told. In fact, they were deeply suspicious. It seemed unlikely that a woman would leave her home – and child – in the hands of strangers. And they found Fernandez's story about being a wealthy businessman highly improbable – he simply didn't look the part. That evening, Ray and Martha went to the cinema. They had only just returned home when the doorbell rang. It was the police, asking questions about Delphine Downing and her daughter. When the couple repeated the story of a sick relative, they politely insisted on searching the house. Deputy Sheriff Clarence Randle had a hunch that the bodies would be buried in the basement, and when he saw the damp cement, he knew he was correct. Within hours, Delphine and Rainelle Downing had been exhumed.

At the police station, Fernandez seemed relieved to confess. The next morning, headlines all over the country announced the arrest of the "Lonely Hearts Killers". Mrs Fay's step-daughter saw them, and suddenly knew with horrible certainty what had happened to Janet Fay. Police soon traced the house in Queens, and found the cemented grave in the basement. When news of the arrest reached La Linea, in Spain, the police re-opened the question of the death of Lucilla Thompson.

The story of how Rainelle had been drowned like a kitten shocked America; Fernandez and Beck were labelled "America's most hated killers". This repugnance was so strong that it even affected the Michigan judiciary. Michigan had no capital punishment; New York had. So when Michigan decided to hand the killers over to New York, it was with the proviso that if they were not sentenced to death, they should be handed back.

There was little chance of that happening. If the lovers had been sentenced to life imprisonment, lynch mobs would probably have broken into the jail. It was leaked to the press that the police were investigating the possibility of twenty murders, but all the law had to do was to prove one of them: that of Janet Fay.

The defense – conducted by attorney Herbert Rosenberg – was hardly convincing: that Martha was insane, and that Fernandez had no foreknowledge that Martha would kill Mrs Fay. It would have been far more plausible to argue that Fernandez had been insane ever since his head injury. Much sensational evidence about their extraordinary sex lives was offered as further proof of insanity. It was all to no effect. On July 17, 1949, after a forty-four day trial, they were both found guilty. Appeals were exhausted two years later, and on March 8, 1951, the Lonely Hearts Killers went to the electric chair in Sing Sing. Martha, taken into the death cell twelve minutes after Raymond, had to squeeze her huge bulk into the chair. It had taken only one shock to kill Raymond; it took four before Martha's body sagged against the straps.

Colin Wilson

The Cleft Chin Murder

As Edgar Lustgarten remarks in the following account, the Cleft Chin murder is not of special interest to criminologists. But it is a typical case of "folie a deux", and in that sense affords an interesting parallel with the Lonely Hearts case, and the Moors case of the 'sixties. Told in detail, the story would make a good novel – the American Walter Mitty, Karl Hulten, and the wide-eyed little Welsh nightclub stripper whose admiration led him to play out his dangerous fantasy of robbery and murder. In that sense it is the perfect example of the high-and-medium-dominance syndrome discussed in connection with Fernandez and Beck.

Perhaps because the case holds relatively little interest for criminologists, it has been difficult to find an account of it that would be suitable for inclusion in this volume. Lustgarten's is perhaps too short and too lacking in detail, but it catches something of the essence of London in the last days of the war.

This account is from Lustgarten's book *The Murder and the Trial* (1960.)

During 1944 I was working at the B.B.C. and my duties often took me to the Service ministries. To avoid the crowds in Regent Street, I made a habit of using the narrow lanes lying parallel as a quick walking route from my office to Whitehall.

About three o'clock one bright spring afternoon, I had got within a long stone's throw of Golden Square when I heard the sounds of an approaching rumpus. Presently an American soldier came round the nearest corner at a lurching trot. It was obvious from a glance that he had been drinking heavily. His head was bandaged and there were fresh bloodstains on his tunic: traces of some brawl or scuffle earlier that day. In his arms he carried several unopened liquor bottles. Behind him, at a distance, followed a shouting crowd of Soho Italians, Cypriots, and Greeks, presumably led by the owner of the shop that had been robbed. They made no attempt, however, to overtake the thief, for a good reason that was soon apparent. Every few yards, he turned unsteadily and hurled one of the bottles back at his pursuers. They jumped and dodged in terror as the glass cracked and the wicked fragments flew.

I stepped into a doorway and waited for this perilous operation to pass by. When the soldier was level with me, though, he threw into the air his last remaining bottle, and the exultant crowd now rushed swiftly forward. But still more swiftly did they halt and dive for cover. Because, deprived of simpler weapons, the soldier drew a gun and aimed it at them sightlessly as he went lumbering on.

Whether it was loaded or not, I never knew. In due course the soldier disappeared from view, the hue and cry was cautiously resumed, and I continued on my way towards Whitehall as if nothing in the least out of the ordinary had occurred. In a sense, nothing had. For this was London's West End during those hectic months when the American military invasion reached its peak, and the atmosphere prevailing in some respects resembled that of a Yukon boom-town in the gold rush of the 'nineties. This atmosphere affected, in varying degree, elements of both invaders and invaded. It generated a racing pulse of unhealthy excitement. It imparted a contempt for civilized conventions. It prompted countless minor sins of recklessness or licence. And it gave rise to at least one major act of evil – that which was popularly called The Cleft Chin Murder, but which legal records less dramatically designate the case of The King versus Jones and Hulten.

Karl Gustav Hulten was twenty-two years old. Swedish by birth but American by upbringing, he was trained as a paratrooper in the United States and ultimately dispatched with his regiment to Britain in order to assist in liberating

Europe. Instead he preferred the path of a deserter. Wearing an officer's uniform (to which his rank did not entitle him), using the bogus name of "Lieutenant Ricky Allen", driving about in an army truck he had contrived to make his own, Hulten on the run possessed in goodly measure what he afterwards described as "a build-up" for himself.

The precise form of his "build-up" – *anglice*, shooting a line – depended on his estimate of persons that he met. But as he carried a fully primed revolver at the ready – that is, with both the safety catch and the hammer back, so that it could be fired at once at any time – it was easiest for him to sustain the role of desperado, whenever that might seem advantageous or attractive. Thus his "build-up" was predetermined when he fell in with the girl whose name is now forever linked in infamy with his.

Elizabeth Marina Jones (the Marina had been Maud) was still younger than Hulten – a few months past eighteen. Most of her life had been spent in the Neath district of South Wales, against a drab background of industrial depression. Eventually she escaped to London where she worked in turn as barmaid, waitress, cinema usherette, and what is euphemistically termed a strip-tease artist (in which capacity she performed at several third-rate nightclubs for an average reward of four pounds ten a week). She lived in one small room in King Street, Hammersmith, and took most of her meals at a local eating-house. London hardly gave her the flamboyant life she craved – neither the colour not the throb nor the sensation – but at least it was not Neath, and at least she could assume a smart name like Georgina Grayson, and at least there was the shoddy glamour of the dancing floor. Above all, there were the Yanks. To the little striptease artist, as to countless other girls, America was identical with glittering Hollywood, and every farmer's boy from Tennessee or South Dakota appeared potentially a Gable or a Crosby. Better still, perhaps, a Cagney or a Bogart; the romance of brutality was very much in vogue, and Georgina Grayson responded to it ardently. Thus her course was predetermined when she fell in with the man whose name is now forever linked in infamy with hers.

Their first encounter, so powerfully charged with ruin and

not only for themselves, took place on October 3rd, 1944. They were introduced to one another in a café. This is Georgina Grayson; Georgie, this is Ricky. Pleased to meet you, Ricky. Hiya doin', babe? All right, how's yourself? Okay, okay; like to take a ride tonight? What you got to ride in? I got it, don't you worry; pick you up eleven-thirty, by the cinema. Where'll we go, Ricky? Most anywhere you like . . . Each kept the appointment, and shortly before midnight they were speeding in the stolen truck along the Great West Road.

As they drove they talked, finding out about each other. Hulten, as always, was eager to show off, and he very quickly sized up his new acquaintance. He remarked in casual fashion that he was a gunman, and that back home in Chicago he ran round with a mob; then noted complacently how his callow lie immediately won the girl's naïve admiration. You a real gangster? Sure I'm a real gangster – why, if you wanna know, I'm boss of a gang that's operating over here right now. What, over here in London? Yeah – but take it easy, Georgie; don't you go round telling no one about this . . . He took a hand from the wheel and groped inside his belt; the striptease artist gasped and thrilled – she saw the gun.

Interactions became fast. The man's conceit was flattered by the girl's enraptured awe, the girl's imagination stirred by the man's parade of toughness. To feed his conceit and her imagination further, by separate process each conjured up the same unreal world; a world that they undoubtedly derived from the same sources, a world where they were partners – a gunman and his moll. It was a platitudinous fancy, and had it ended there – he concocting tales and boasting, she receptive and enthralled – the phenomenon need not have been malignant; it would not even have been especially unusual. Make-believe is a more common adult pastime than is supposed, and play-acting the part of villain may be harmlessly cathartic. What made this pair remarkable and dangerous, forcing society to strike out in self-defence, was the way they translated their conception of themselves from the plane of air-drawn fancy to the plane of solid fact. For although neither had previously committed an offence involving any kind of physical assault, within a few hours of their meeting in the café they embarked on a positive debauch of violent crime.

Later, when each of them came to tell the story of the ensuing orgiastic days, their two accounts did not wholly correspond. The girl maintained that she was terrified of Hulten, and had only done the things she did from fear: Hulten maintained that it was she who made the pace, she who urged him on. Their respective defences were shaped accordingly and, as a result, at their subsequent joint trial at the Old Bailey, the two prisoners set about attacking one another with far more ferocity and far more virulence than a rightly temperate Crown exhibited in attacking either. Their mutual hostility was indeed so marked, and the effort of each to destroy the former ally so relentless, that they almost invited comparison with the classical "cut-throat" cases; Millsom and Fowler, for instance, or Browne and Kennedy. Such behaviour on the woman's part was at any rate comprehensible in perpetration – as distinct from inception and idea – she, it was not gainsaid, acted merely as auxiliary; making things as black as possible for Hulten offered her, albeit faintly, a prospect of escape. Hulten, however, had not even this practical excuse. On his own admission, his was the active hand; if – which he denied – criminal intention lay behind it, he was doomed; by implicating the woman, he stood to gain precisely nothing – except the doubtful luxury of malice satisfied. Nonetheless, his inculpations surpassed hers. Between the two conflicting and irreconcilable versions, that of the timid girl bullied by the brutal male, and that of the simple boy made the designing female's puppet, the jury of mankind is left to choose one – or neither.

The trial, therefore, is a dubious and indeterminate guide to the development of their personal relationship during the period in which they ran amok. But concerning broad essentials there can be no real dispute. They turned into a pair of vicious, predatory beasts. They made expeditions almost nightly in the truck, with highway robbery as their express object. They offered lifts to unsuspecting walkers; they molested cyclists on lonely country roads; they tried to hold up cars. They were absolutely ruthless and cold-blooded.

One girl, whom Hulten had struck with an iron bar and afterwards half-strangled, they threw like a discarded dummy into the Thames to drown. That in fact she survived they neither knew nor cared. There could be no looking back as their wild campaign of banditry tore towards the inevitable climax.

It came on the fourth night of their association. At half-past eleven, Hulten whistled outside the girl's lodging. She came downstairs, and joined him in the street. Where's the truck, Ricky? Ain't brought out the truck. What we going to do, Ricky? Let's go get a cab . . . She had no doubt about the underlying innuendo. "I knew the meaning of his words," she admitted to the police. "He wanted me to go with him to rob a taxi-driver."

They walked along Hammersmith Road and stood together in a doorway. A grey Ford car leisurely approached. Hi, taxi, taxi. The grey Ford pulled up opposite. You a taxi? Private hire; where d'you want to go? What d'you say, top of King Street? That'll be ten bob.

Strictly, a private hire car should not pick up casual fares. But the driver of the grey Ford was not punctilious. He had had a slack night – and didn't everybody dodge the regulation anyway? So when the American officer agreed to his somewhat exorbitant demand, he grinned affably, emphasizing the hollow in his chin – a feature that was shortly to fascinate the head-line writers, after his corpse had been discovered in a ditch near Staines.

Hulten and the girl got in, and sat in the back seat. The car moved off. Nobody spoke a word. Bored by the silence, the driver whistled softly through his teeth. He didn't specially like the look of his two passengers, and wasn't sorry when they reached their destination. Here's the top of King Street. Yeah, that's right, bud, but I wanna go further on. You said top of King Street; further on'll cost you more. Take it easy, bud; I don't mind what I pay.

On they went again, past the darkened houses, over the round-about, into the open road. The driver grew irritable, even a shade uneasy. This near where you want, guv'nor? Yea, it's near; go slow. We come a tidy way, guv'nor. Okay, we'll get out here . . . As the car came to a standstill, Hulten was holding in his hand the fatal gun.

The driver leaned across to open the nearside door. Then the final madness supervened. Without warning, without prelude, Hulten fired into his back. The driver moaned, and slumped over to the left. Hulten jumped into the front, and drove rapidly away. The driver ceased to moan and his breath came chokingly. As he died, the girl was going through his pockets.

The Cleft Chin murder – for which Hulten was hanged and the girl, reprieved at the eleventh hour, condemned to a life sentence – is not of special interest to criminologists; the minds of both criminals were crudely commonplace. It is, however, of surpassing interest to social chroniclers, for no murder has ever been more firmly rooted in its age. At any time Frederick Seddon might have poisoned his lodger. At any time Jack the Ripper might have slashed his prostitutes. At any time Alfred Rouse might have kidnapped his unknown. But for the Cleft Chin crime there could be only one occasion; the occasion when it happened; the occasion when the characters responsible had been transported by events and transformed by one another.

The brash American, physically strapping but of stunted mental growth, consigned by army order to an unfamiliar land, sought to impress the natives with his own superiority by aping the habits of a gunman or a thug. The poverty-stricken adolescent refugee from Neath, frail alike in body and in mind, vaguely aspiring but completely talentless, sought a pitiable escape in fantasies inspired by the spurious appeal of gangster films. A world convulsion brought this pair together, at a moment when life was cheap and violence sanctified; under such conditions the union was deadly. It was like holding a lighted match to dynamite, having first ensured that the latter was exposed.

And so the hapless car driver, whose facial marking gives the case its name, may be written down no less a casualty of war than those who met a death more orthodox from shell or bomb.

The Blackburn Child Murder

The Blackburn case is one of the true classics of crime detection, an example of what happens when both the police and the public become obsessed with catching the perpetrator of a crime that has caused a sense of outrage. This account of it is by a man who was deeply involved in the manhunt, Detective Chief Inspector Tony Fletcher, of the Fingerprint Bureau of the Manchester Police. His book *Memories of Murder* (1986) is, in my opinion, among the best of all autobiographies by a policeman – I can especially recommend the chapter in which he describes trying to take the fingerprints of a ghost at a seance.

The Second World War was a time of hardship, death, disaster and yet of enormous public spirit and great self-discipline amongst most people. As always after a war, a new world had to be built. The men in the forces, coming home after demobilization, voted in the general election for the first time for many years, and they put a Labour Government in power. The Government chose to retain rationing, believing it to be the fairest system until a free market with ample supplies could be established. Some resentment about this was certainly felt by many, because in what had been Occupied Europe free markets began almost immediately, their belief apparently being that supplies would rapidly reach demand, if demand were not restricted. They may have been right.

It was against this background that in May 1948 there occurred in Blackburn a most brutal murder. It resulted in what is arguably one of the finest enquiries involving finger-prints in the history of criminal investigation.

Policing goes back over 600 years in this country, but it developed in a somewhat piecemeal fashion. Indeed, in the mid-nineteenth century many local police forces had as few as fifty men. One thing about them is certain; the force would know its own villains. Thieves have always travelled, but mobility has been relative to the times. If a man with stolen property hitched a lift on a slow-moving wagon he could be caught by a rider on a faster horse. A thief on a fast horse, knowing his own moors and by-ways, could get away.

It is also startling to remember that the first juries were composed specifically of men who knew the offender, because they alone were in a position to judge whether he was guilty and whether anything could properly be said in his defence. Nowadays, of course, every endeavour is made to collect a jury which does not know any of the contenders in a case and can therefore be impartial. Even magistrates are supposed to declare any private interest that might cloud their judgment. Things change but slowly, and it is only in looking back that change can be properly assessed.

In 1969 a Royal Commission on Local Government reported that "England needs a pattern of local authorities with clear responsibilities big enough in area, population and resources to provide first-class services." Thus came the death knell for several (in most cases efficient) small police forces. They were soon replaced by fewer but larger, if not more efficient, police forces. As technology has developed, so police forces, fire brigades and local government have increased their equipment; there has not been any alternative. But such expertise has to be shared and its use cover a wide area. Where expenditure is heavy, the huge police forces we have today do in fact share facilities. This is a responsible and sensible approach.

Prior to this reorganization, if a murder occurred in a small borough and the Chief Constable decided that he did not have the necessary resources to deal with the situation he would seek assistance from New Scotland Yard or from a larger neighbouring force. How the newspapers loved it when the "Yard" were called in! The placard writers worked overtime, and outside all the newsagents' shops would be the enticing words "Murder – Yard Called In". How many thriller writers have made a decent living out of the intrepid "Yard" man, whizzing up (or down) from London to take charge. What calling in the "Yard" usually meant was the arrival of two experienced officers, one of whom would be senior and expected to control the investigation, and the other his reliable right-hand man. They would need to be pretty diplomatic, too, because the local Chief Constable, having called them in, had probably offended his own head of CID. If a neighbouring force gave help, it was usually by way of extra manpower or some equipment.

Whilst not denigrating this kind of help in any way, it must be emphasized that it is the local policeman with knowledge of the area, the nature of the community and its criminals, the reaper of casual information, known and it is hoped respected by the local populace, on whom the success of the enquiry depends. In the case of the Blackburn murder, such a man was Inspector William Barton.

Blackburn has always been important to Lancashire, being a mill town with a skilled labour force, turning out high quality goods for export all over the world. Manchester is surrounded by a network of such towns and, when their goods were technically finished, they would come into the big Manchester warehouses to be run through the measuring machines, checked for faults, labelled and packed according to each customer's requirements, and shipped overseas. Blackburn, Bolton, Oldham, Burnley and the rest had been busy during the war years, and whilst some man-made fabrics had been invented and more were yet to come, cotton was still important. But like so many other places, these towns had suffered bombing and house repairs had had to go by the board because the men and materials necessary were not available. By 1948, however, a start had been made on bringing about the improvements we all hoped for, but it was not always easy.

Blackburn lies in a hollow, though it is higher above sea level than one might think, not far from windy moorlands. There were still cobbled streets here and there, and some gas lighting. Clogs were still being worn because they were practical for many trades. Blackburn was noted for good weavers and in 1948 there were about 110,000 inhabitants in the town. Most of the 35,000 houses were of the working-class type, set in compact terraces. A large proportion were two-up-and-two-down, with a backyard and an outside lavatory, though in some cases a small row would have their lavatories set next to each other in a common courtyard. On high ground, South-East of the town, stands Queen's Park Hospital overlooking Blackburn itself. It was in this hospital, on 15 May 1948, that the events which caused so much public interest, concern and co-operation took place.

Like most of the public hospitals built in Victorian times, Queen's Park consists of several buildings in grounds covering some seventy acres. A high stone wall surrounded most of it except for a small portion in the North-West corner, where there was a disused quarry. Part of the wall had collapsed at this point, but to serve as a protection a six-foot high chestnut paling fence, with interwoven wire, had been erected. The main entrance had a porters' lodge where legitimate callers entered, stating their name, address and business.

In accordance with the custom of the times, the local public assistance committee controlled the hospital's affairs, catering for mental patients, aged and infirm persons, maternity cases, general illness cases – and children. Naturally, separate wards were maintained for dealing with these specialities. Emphasizing the role of the public assistance committee was the continuing presence of a casual ward, where vagrants or tramps were accommodated for the night – mostly around ten on any one night. In all the hospital housed about 1,200 people.

The events of the day in question revolve around ward CH3, which was a children's ward at the furthest point of the hospital from the lodge entrance. There were twelve cots in it, though only six were occupied, and June Anne Devaney, almost four, was in fact the oldest patient.

She had been admitted to the ward ten days earlier, suffering from pneumonia. The only child in the room who could talk, she was a big girl for her age, and when seen in bed she could have been taken for six or seven years old. June had recovered well in the hospital, and her parents were expecting to take her home during this particular Saturday.

225

About twenty minutes after midnight the night nurse in charge, Gwendoline Humphreys, went round all the cots, saw their occupants were safely asleep, and then went to the kitchen near the ward to start preparations for their breakfasts. She had been in the kitchen about twenty minutes when she heard a child's voice. She went quickly back to the ward, but found nothing amiss, so she returned to the kitchen – little children quite often call out in their sleep. At twenty minutes past one she noticed a draught. She went to the porch doors and found them open, but did not worry about it because the outer door had a faulty catch and a strong gust of wind could have opened it. Then she went into CH3 ward to see to one of the babies. She saw that June was not in her cot. The drop side of the cot was still in its raised position and, as it was about four feet above the ground, it was not likely she would or could have climbed out. She appeared to have been lifted out, very neatly.

On the floor, by the side of June's cot, was a Winchester bottle. This kind of bottle comes in several sizes and this particular one was quite large. When the nurse had last seen it, an hour earlier, it had been in its usual place on a trolley at the end of the ward some six yards away. A quick glance round showed some footprints on the polished floor, one near June's cot – and they seemed to Gwen Humphreys to have been made by someone in bare feet. This was a frightening situation for her.

A quick alarm and a rapid search by hospital staff of adjoining wards and the hospital grounds did not reveal anything useful. At five minutes to two the police were told. A squad of officers carried out a systematic search of the grounds and one hour and twenty-two minutes later, at 3.17 am, June's body was found lying near the boundary wall some 283 feet away from the ward. The Chief Constable, the police surgeon and Detective Superintendent Woodmansey of Lancashire Constabulary arrived at 4 am. They saw little June lying, face down, in the grass. Her nightie was lifted a little and was dirty as though she had been rolled about on the ground. It was obvious she had been brutally raped, her left buttock had been severely bitten and she had been battered to death by being swung against the stone wall by her ankles.

The hospital area was sealed off. The immediate help of New Scotland Yard was sought and the Chief Constable of Lancashire placed the whole of his large force and its equipment at the disposal of the Chief Constable of Blackburn. The Assistant Chief Constable of Lancashire and officers manning radio cars arrived quickly. Even hardened officers can be deeply moved by the killing of a young child, and this abduction of a three-year-old girl from her bed, and her violent and nasty death, were worse than most.

A bloodhound was brought to the hospital. It was given the scent from the child's bed and the footmarks on the ward floor. It sniffed around a bit and then led its handler to the child's body; no further. Police officers followed the trail directly to where the boundary wall joined the paling fence, where there was a small gap. It was possible to climb through this gap and to reach a small ledge skirting the edge of the quarry. It needed careful manoeuvring not to fall sixty feet into the quarry before reaching Queen's Road, but somebody had done it, and got away.

A forensic scientist joined the team; he came from the Home Office Laboratory at Preston, which now operates from Euxton, near Chorley. Colin Campbell, Officer in Charge of Lancashire Constabulary's Finger-print Department, also arrived. The usual photographs were taken of the child's body and its immediate surroundings, and she was then taken to the police mortuary. At that time Colin Campbell was one of this country's foremost finger-print experts, a man of vast and useful experience.

An ordinary chap cannot imagine himself taking a little girl from a hospital cot, carrying her outside the building and killing her. Nevertheless, any investigating officer has to imagine himself doing just that; to cast round for the slightest disturbance, scratch, scuffmark, fibre, that will throw any light on the actions of the intruder.

Together with Mr Looms, the Chief Constable of Blackburn, Colin Campbell stood outside the children's ward. Both men peered through a window near the cot which had been occupied by June Anne Devaney. As they did so,

Mr Looms briefed the Chief Inspector as to all known human circumstances in the case, particularly drawing his attention to the Winchester bottle standing on the floor near June's cot.

The ward, about forty feet long and eighteen feet wide, had in it twelve empty cots. Once the murder was discovered the remaining children had been moved to another ward. A quick tour of the outside of the building showed there was a verandah on the West side of the ward; on the East, a concrete path. In each of the West and East walls of the ward were three glass doors that were never locked. At the ward's northern end was a small office containing three windows, and two of these were left open for ventilation. At the southerly end was a corridor which gave access to bathroom and kitchen, and another short corridor, at right-angles, led to the ward where toddlers were accommodated.

Obviously, there had been many open doors and windows available to the intruder, so it wasn't surprising that Colin Campbell didn't find any signs of forcible entry on which attention could be concentrated.

After this quick tour Campbell and Looms stood in the corridor at the southerly end of the ward. They stared in to the ward, looking particularly at what seemed to be a trail of bare footprints which had been made on the wax-polished floor. On more detailed examination it was seen that the foot had not been bare, as the nurse had thought, but had been stockinged, the pressure of the foot making shallow impressions in the thin layer of wax polish.

This trail appeared to begin at the door leading from the office at the North end of the ward. It travelled to the first cot on the West side, then to an instrument trolley standing against the North wall, recrossed to the West side of the ward and to the second cot from the door. At this cot the footprints were implanted side by side on the floor, as if made by a person standing alongside the cot, looking at its occupant. Similar footprints were found alongside the third and fourth cots, this latter being the one from which June had been taken. The toes of these footprints were at right-angles to the cot side and actually under its edge, showing their maker was standing very close to the cot. From there the footprints went down the ward and stopped about two feet from the South door. There, they seemed to turn round and traverse the entire length of the ward in a straight line right up to the North door. There were no footprints on the East side of the ward. It was pretty clear what this evil human being had done.

Colin Campbell selected the most distinct right and left footprints and asked for them to be photographed.

Now it was time to concentrate on the Winchester bottle found near June's cot. It was labelled "Sterile Water". It also bore twenty finger and palm impressions.

Some of these impressions appeared to have been made recently, whilst others seemed fairly old. And if you ask me now, after so many years of experience of my own, how a finger-print officer can tell the age of a print, I have to confess it is almost impossible to put into words. A print can have a "new" look; the sweat which has made it somehow looks fresh. It has not been changed by atmospheric dust molecules. One can be wrong in this judgment of a "fresh" print, but it's rare. Most important in the case of this Winchester bottle was that the recent impressions were much larger than the other, older ones. Colin Campbell took the Winchester bottle back to his own force headquarters and in the Finger-print Department the impressions were quickly photographed. After the smaller, older impressions had been eliminated as those of nursing staff (their prints having of course been obtained for comparison) a large-scale search began in the department's files.

Whilst the Detective Chief Inspector had been examining the Winchester bottle in the ward, the Home Office forensic scientist, Mr Jones, had also been busy. He scraped the wax from the floor where the footprints were implanted. Certain fibres, invisible to the naked eye, were later found embedded in these scrapings. He also measured the footprints. They were ten and a quarter inches long: not a small foot. The next examination he made was of one of the three windows which formed the bay in the small office at the North end of the ward. It had been left open, and it overlooked a concrete area at the rear of the ward. There were marks on the window which were consistent with a person having climbed through it. Adhering to the wooden window frame the scientist found fibres. He collected them, and with the other specimens took them back to the laboratory.

A special squad of officers had been established in the hospital, under the control of Detective Chief Inspector Bob McCartney. They screened the movements of all inmates, staff and patients alike. All persons who had legitimate access to the ward were finger-printed and the finger-print forms were given to Colin Campbell for elimination purposes. And providing an extra bit of news for the papers, Detective Chief Inspector John Capstick of New Scotland Yard, a name well recognized now, came with Detective Inspector Daws. Mr Capstick took control of the enquiries.

There had to be a post-mortem examination. Although it can be very distressing to relatives, it is an essential part of the enquiry. The pathologist found that June's death was due to shock caused by a fractured skull and extensive injuries. The bite on her buttock had been made before death, as had a bruise in each groin. Internal injuries were consistent with rape. Specimens were taken not only from the body but also from various places at the scene of the enquiry. Those which proved vital were:

Fibres from the window of the room adjoining the ward.
Blood and hairs from the boundary wall of the hospital.
Fibres found on the child's body.
A single pubic hair found on the child's body.
The child's nightdress.
Various swabs.
Fibres taken from the footmarks in the ward.

Add to these the finger-prints on the Winchester bottle and the footprints found in the ward, and you have an idea of the material on which the police had to work.

The hospital staff and local people were much concerned. They began to think, and think hard. Quickly came the news that at about a quarter past eleven on the night of Friday, 14 May, some nurses in the nurses' home about a hundred yards from ward CH3 saw what tradition describes as a Peeping Tom peering into a window on the ground floor. When a nurse told him to go away, he put a finger to his mouth and said, "Hush, don't tell anyone." Naturally, this looked helpful, but on the 19th of May he was traced and interviewed, showing that though he might have been up to no good he was not the man who had left the finger-prints on the Winchester bottle.

On the 18th of May a taxi driver came forward to say that just before midnight on the 14th he had picked up a man in the town centre on a road which leads to the hospital, and had set him down in Queen's Road near the quarry. When he got out of the taxi, the man had run across the quarry and was last seen going in the direction of the hospital. The taxi driver could not describe the man in any detail, but thought he had a local accent.

After giving a great deal of thought to the evidence in the ward itself, Detective Chief Inspector Campbell deduced that the murderer had entered the ward by the North door and had peeped into the first cot; he had then crossed to the instrument trolley, where he had picked up the Winchester bottle, before crossing to the second and third cots, where he had gazed at the sleeping children. He had then walked to the fourth cot, put the Winchester bottle on the floor, lifted June from her cot and had carried her to the South door. He had there presumably heard a noise and had turned and retraced his steps, walked the length of the ward and carried the child out through the North door.

A conference was called on 18 May at the Central Police Office. All officers concerned in the investigations were present.

Chief Inspector Campbell gave his assessment of the situation. He said that after the most exhaustive comparisons with both finger and palm prints of all persons who had access to the hospital, all the finger and palm impressions found at the scene had been eliminated with the exception of ten prints found on the Winchester bottle. These ten were the fresh marks which had been made by a person with a large hand.

He believed these impressions consisted of a left thumb print, a sequence of left fore, middle and ring finger-prints and a left palm print. There were two impressions which appeared to have been made by right middle and ring fingers. The remaining three were partial finger-prints which could not be allocated to any particular finger. Whilst he would not make a guess as to the murderer's age or as to whether he was right- or left-handed, Campbell did say that having regard to the span of the sequence of finger-prints left on the bottle, the clarity of the ridge detail and the absence of coarseness or temporary injuries, he believed they were made by a biggish man who was not old and did little or no manual work.

For some hours all the available evidence was discussed by those present at the conference and eventually the following four conclusions were arrived at. Firstly, the finger-prints on the bottle were undoubtedly those of the murderer, as all males in the hospital and all persons with legitimate access to CH3 ward had been eliminated. Secondly, the wanted man was someone living locally, who knew the hospital and its surroundings, particularly in view of the taxi driver's evidence. Few people could take off into the darkness and successfully negotiate the edge of this quarry; and it seemed a return trip had been made the same way. Thirdly, the man had to be reasonably tall. A small person could not have lifted June cleanly out of the cot without dropping the cot sides, and there was no evidence that this had been done. Furthermore, a small man would not be likely to have feet ten and a quarter inches long. Fourthly, the person's clothing would be bloodstained.

The big question now was how the finger-prints could best be used to trace the murderer. All prints filed in the bureaux were being examined, but this would take several weeks and, in any case, the wanted man might not have been recorded in general criminal files; and whilst this search was proceeding the trail would be going cold.

The problem was huge. A bold and courageous decision was taken to deal with it. All male persons of sixteen years or over known to have been in Blackburn on 14 and 15 May 1948 would be finger-printed. The manpower, the time and the paperwork could be provided; a matter of logistics. What was disturbing was the knowledge that at least one person in Blackburn had a good reason for not having his finger-prints taken and might be expected to do whatever he could to avoid putting himself on record. Of course many men could have left Blackburn for perfectly legitimate reasons: to work elsewhere, join the army, or even to die and be buried in the cemetery or be cremated. All these things can be checked, but it takes time.

Inspector William Barton of Blackburn Borough Police was allocated the most demanding task of all, that of ensuring that no man in the town of Blackburn slipped through the net of the finger-printing officers. It was an enormous responsibility, though he was comforted by the fact that the finger-prints on the Winchester bottle were clear and could be matched without difficulty if their maker were traced. If and when the time came there would not be a grain of doubt. Inspector Barton picked his small staff and gave them a simple instruction: "No adult male must be missed."

On occasions such as this the newspapers can be particularly helpful and through them the Mayor of Blackburn appealed for men over the age of sixteen to volunteer their finger-prints. Alongside this the Chief Constable assured everybody that such prints would not be used for any other reason and that when they had served their purpose they would be publicly destroyed. Public feeling was running very high indeed. The nation had just come through a long and bloody war which had been impossible to avoid; the hospital incident was an unnecessary and evil thing, and people were quick to help. When the special squad of finger-print officers made their first visits to houses in the vicinity of the hospital on Sunday 23 May, eight days after the killing, they found everybody on their side. This is a heartening feeling for any officer of the law.

Plans were made to obviate overlapping of visits. Thoroughness was essential. The electoral registers were used to ensure that every house in Blackburn, some 35,000 dwellings, was visited. Not every house is on the roll, but as one goes round a street armed with such a list any omissions are obvious. The registers at that time recorded all those over the age of twenty-one and thus entitled to vote. When visiting a house an officer could ask about other, younger members of the family. You might think to yourself that a member of a household could easily suspect a brother or son and omit him deliberately. True enough, but a check with neighbours either side will reveal discrepancies.

Armed with the Blackburn registers, divided into fourteen

voting divisions, subdivided into sections and then alphabetical street and road order, the finger-print squad went
into action. Carrying finger-print cards and inked pads they
worked to a predetermined pattern until every house in every
street was covered. Whilst doing this, enquiries were made
to obtain information about persons not normally resident
in the town but who were there on the night in question.
Public co-operation was truly magnificent. Each night all
the gathered information was handed in to Inspector Barton
along with completed finger-print cards.

This mass of detail meant enquiries had to be made in
all parts of the United Kingdom via local police, and to
forces in Australia, Singapore, India, Egypt, South Africa,
Canada, the USA and almost every country in Europe.
People were located in all these places, and finger-printed
for elimination.

The finger-print cards were cancelled against the appropriate entry in the electoral roll and then sent to Chief
Inspector Campbell for comparison. It didn't take long to
check an individual card, but it took a long time to examine
all the thousands. After checking, each card was stamped
"Cancelled" and filed in strict alphabetical order at police
head-quarters in Blackburn.

At the same time Detective Chief Inspector Capstick of
New Scotland Yard was seeing that other lines of enquiry
were being pursued regarding the peculiar nature of the
crime and its implications. You will realize how extensive
these enquiries can be when you study the following types
of people who were seen and finger-printed. Much of this
line of enquiry is not pleasant, but it has to be done. The
human psyche is a complex and often secretive thing.

1 About 3,600 persons discharged from mental institutions
in the northern half of the country, the nature of the crime
suggesting a person of low mentality. Many of these persons
had been convicted of offences involving indecency.

2 About 3,000 male persons of uncertain nationality; prisoners of war and Polish Army men living in camps within
twenty miles of Blackburn. This line of enquiry arose from
the biting of the child, not normal in Great Britain, but fairly
often committed on the continent in crimes of indecency.

Lancashire Constabulary officers conducted this part of the investigation.

3 Epileptics and sufferers from schizophrenia who might have committed such a crime during a temporary black-out.

4 Persons suffering from venereal disease, so far as the confidential treatment of such persons would permit. Some sufferers from this kind of disease believe, wrongly of course, that sexual intercourse with a virgin or young child will effect a cure.

5 Persons known to commit or suspected of committing sexual offences contrary to nature, that is homosexuals and the like (though the phrase "contrary to nature" would now be hotly disputed, I don't doubt). Many people in this category were the subject of anonymous letters to the police.

6 All persons having recently committed suicide and remaining in mortuaries, and those who had recently attempted suicide.

7 Casuals and other people forming the moving population of the district, who might have stayed at the casual ward on some previous occasion and thus be familiar with the hospital.

8 All persons missing from home at the relevant period.

Working on these eight groups was quite an undertaking, and indeed it is likely that some people came into more than one category. Assaults on young children are, regrettably, not uncommon and it is carefully amassed local knowledge about the kind of people who commit such crimes which can be helpful not merely to trace a wrongdoer but also to eliminate the rest.

After about eight weeks of intensive finger-printing work most of the houses in Blackburn had been visited, but no clear lead had as yet been established.

There was another source of information in 1948 which would not, so far as I know, be available to us now, and Inspector Barton did not hesitate to take advantage of it. To do whatever was possible to ensure that every person in the borough would be finger-printed, the records already obtained were compared with the records kept by the local registration officer for the issuing of food ration books. In 1948 these would be reasonably up to date, because between 30 June and 18 July 1948, new ration books had been issued to everybody in response to the completion by each person of a reference leaf from the previous year's books. If this was not done, a new ration book was not issued. The reference leaves gave the name, address, date of birth and national registration number of the holder, all filed in strict alphabetical order of surname at the registration office.

On 18 July finger-printing was suspended. The next three weeks were spent by Inspector Barton and his squad in the registration office. They compared each finger-print card with its counterpart in the registration files. When this had been done, the remaining ration book reference leaves showed the balance of the population which still required to be printed. A good deal of clerical work followed, producing new lists, separated into the sub-divisions of the borough wards.

House-to-house finger-printing restarted on Monday 9 August, but now the officers had lists giving particulars of specific persons whose prints were needed to complete the check.

On the night of Wednesday 11 August one of the squad obtained the finger-prints of Peter Griffiths, aged twenty-two, at his home, 31 Birley Street, Blackburn. His card, with others obtained that day, was sent in the normal way to Chief Inspector Campbell at the Lancashire Constabulary Finger-print Bureau, arriving at about 3 pm on Thursday 12 August 1948.

One of the experts, making the comparisons, spotted on Griffiths's card the finger-prints exactly as they appeared on the bottle. It was quite a moment. He could hardly believe his own eyes. He double checked and then exclaimed, "I've got him! It's here!"

In addition to his name and address, there was national registration number NBA 6917–188, indicating he was an ex-serviceman. News of the identification quickly went to the Chief Constable of Blackburn. His name would not have been found in the electoral register, as he had not qualified for inclusion when the last list was prepared on 30 June 1947.

Friday 13 August 1948 was not Peter Griffiths's lucky day, but it was a good one for the police. He was arrested near his home and brought to police head-quarters. He admitted his guilt in the following statement:

I want to say that on the night the little girl was killed at the Queen's Park Hospital, it was on a Friday night, the Friday before Whitsun. I left home that night on my own about six o'clock. I went out to spend a quiet night on my own. I went to the Dun Horse pub or hotel and bought myself about five pints of bitter beer. Then I went to Yates' Wine Lodge and had a glass of Guinness and two double rums. I then had another glass of Guinness and then went back to the Dun Horse again. I then had about six more pints of bitter. I was on my own and came out of there at closing time. I walked down to Jubilee Street off Darwen Street and I saw a man smoking a cigarette sitting in a small closed car with the hood on, with wire wheels, they were painted silver. I did not know him. I had never seen him before. I asked the man for a light as I had no matches to light my cigarette. I stayed gabbing to him for about fifteen minutes. He said to me, "Are you going home?" I said, "No, I'm going to walk round a bit and sober up first." He asked me where I lived and I told him. He said, "Well get in, open the window and I'll give you a spin." He took me to the front of the Queen's Park Hospital and I got out opposite to the iron railings. I don't know what happened to him, I never saw him again. I must have got over the railings, for the next thing I remember was being outside the ward, there were some children. I left my shoes outside the door, which had a brass knob. I tried the door and it opened to my touch and I went just in and heard a nurse humming and banging as if she was washing something so I came out again and waited a few minutes. Then I went back in again and went straight to the ward like, I think I went in one or two small rooms like, like a kitchen, and then I went back into the ward again. I then picked up a biggish bottle off a shelf. I went half way down the ward with it and then put it down on the floor. I then thought I heard the nurse coming, I turned round sharply, overbalanced and fell against a bed. I remember the child woke up and started to cry, and I hushed her. She then opened her eyes, saw me and the child in the next bed started whimpering. I picked the girl up out of the cot and took her outside by the same door. I carried her in my right arm and she put her arms round my neck and I walked with her down the hospital field. I put her down on the grass. She started crying again and I tried to stop her from crying, but she wouldn't do, like, she wouldn't stop crying. I just lost my temper then and you know what happened then. I banged her head against the wall. I then went back to the verandah outside the ward, sat down and put my shoes on. I then went back to where the child was. I like just glanced at her but did not go right up to her, but went straight on down the field to the delph. I crossed over the path alongside the delph leading into Queen's Park. I walked through the park and came out on Audley Street. I went down Cherry Street into Furthergate, then I went down Eanam to Birley Street and got home somewhere around two o'clock on Saturday morning. It would be somewhere about that time. I went into my house, took me collar and tie off and slept in me suit on the couch downstairs. Mother and father were in bed and did not know what time I came in. I woke up about nine o'clock, got up, washed and shaved, then pressed me suit because I was going out again after I had had my breakfast. I went out then down the town, had a walk round, then went to the Royal Cinema in the afternoon, came out of the pictures at five o'clock, went home and had my tea. I looked at the papers and read about the murder. It didn't shake me, so that I just carried on normally after that. My mother and father asked me where I had been that night and what time I came home and told them I had been out boozing and had got home at twelve o'clock. This is all I can say and I'm sorry for both parents' sake and I hope I get what I deserve.

Shortly before midnight on Friday 13 August 1948, he was charged with the murder of June Anne Devaney. His finger-prints were again taken, and also palm prints and impressions of his stockinged feet. A comparison resulted in ten of the twenty finger-prints found on the bottle being identified as his.

There was more to come. All possible samples were taken and examined by forensic scientists. Certain clothing was removed from his home. His suit, which he had worn on the night of the murder, was recovered from a pawnbroker's pledge office, where he had pawned it on 30 May. Tests showed that fibres from the window were identical with those of the suit. Fibres taken from the child's body were found to be made of wool ranging in colour between blue and violet, and agreeing exactly with the threads from which the suit cloth had been woven. Other wool fibres agreeing with those of the suit were found on her nightdress. And fibres taken from the footprints in the wax on the floor of the ward were found to match a sock taken from Griffiths's home.

Human bloodstains, sufficient for grouping purposes, were found on the lining inside the trousers at the bottom of the fly. This blood was of group A, the same as that of the child. There were more blood-stains on the linings of both trouser side pockets, on the lining at the bottom of each jacket sleeve, on each lapel, on the right front above the top button and inside the right edge, on the top button and near to the right shoulder, and inside the right bottom front.

It was interesting that the speculative conclusions arrived at during the conference had proved substantially correct, because Griffiths was not only local, and five feet ten and a half inches, but also had a good knowledge of the hospital grounds as between the ages of ten and twelve he had been a patient in the very block of buildings from which he had taken the little girl. And he was later identified by the taxi driver as the man set down near the quarry on the fatal night.

The due processes of law followed: first the magistrates' court and then on Friday 15 October 1948, he entered a plea of "not guilty" before Mr Justice Oliver at Lancaster Assizes. Many people not versed in law may wonder why anybody, having admitted guilt, pleads not guilty. In fact, this plea ensures the hearing of all evidence during the trial and a jury verdict, followed by sentence if found guilty. If a guilty plea is entered, even though a jury may be present, the judge conducts proceedings rather differently: an outline of the evidence is given, the judge makes sure that the prisoner has full knowledge of the circumstances in which he is placed, and then sentences him.

On the first day of Griffiths's trial the prosecution evidence was presented in total. It was pretty damning and the defence appeared to accept it almost without question, because there was little or no examination of the Crown witnesses. The case was then adjourned until the following Monday.

From the defence point of view the case was desperate, but Griffiths's counsel was honour bound to try and find a way out for him. An attempt was made, using medical witnesses, to prove that he was schizophrenic and therefore insane when he committed the crime. It was also given in evidence that Griffiths's father had been an inmate of a mental hospital for six months after the end of the First World War and that young Peter's condition could have been inherited. However, a medical officer from Liverpool Prison said he had had Griffiths under almost continual observation since his admission there on 14 August and his conclusion was that Griffiths was sane when he committed the crime.

On the second day of the trial, after only twenty-three minutes, the jury returned a verdict of guilty. It had been a short trial, but it was not surprising in view of the forensic evidence.

When pronouncing sentence, Mr Justice Oliver addressed Griffiths thus:

> Peter Griffiths, this jury has found you guilty of a crime of the most brutal ferocity. I entirely agree with this verdict. The sentence of the court upon you is that you be taken from this place to a lawful prison and thence to a place of execution and that you there suffer death by hanging and that your body be afterwards buried within the precincts of the prison in which you shall have been confined before your execution. And may the Lord have mercy on your soul.

The sentence of the court was carried out at Liverpool Prison at nine o'clock on the morning of Friday 19 November 1948.

The people of Blackburn had co-operated magnificently in this enquiry and the promise of destruction of finger-prints was kept: on 3 November about 46,500 finger-print cards, several hundred finger-print forms and numerous other documents were pulped at a local paper mill. The destruction was an event of great local interest, attended by the Mayor of Blackburn, journalists, press photographers and a newsreel cameraman. There had been a press announcement that if persons applied for their finger-print cards to be returned to them this would be done. Some five hundred people did so. No doubt many of these are still preserved in sideboard drawers and the popular old wooden document boxes as a memento of an event in which thousands of innocent people were caught up.

Most murders are of a domestic nature and quickly detected, and do not arouse much discussion amongst the general public. This case was different. Griffiths, of course, knew what he had done, and many people unversed in the ways of criminals thought he had been stupid to remain in Blackburn and risk detection by being finger-printed. It may be of interest to readers to outline what police reaction would have been to some of the things he could have done.

Firstly, he could have refused to have his prints taken. It will be appreciated that there are people who, being innocent and uninvolved in an event, will refuse to have their finger-prints taken on the grounds of it being their legal right. I do not think Peter Griffiths had this sort of intelligence. If he had refused, his movements on the night in question would have been very carefully looked at. If, in the likely event of his saying he was at some place other than the hospital during the relevant time, he would certainly have qualified as a major suspect when this proved false.

Secondly, he could have left the district. This again would have meant he would come under strong suspicion.

Thirdly, he could have committed suicide, but you will remember that bodies were examined and finger-printed.

Fourthly, he could have engineered an accident to his fingers. Local hospital staff were aware of this possibility and, if he had gone for help having injured the inner surfaces of his hands, subsequent enquiries would have raised suspicion. In any case his normal finger-prints could most likely have been obtained from surfaces in his home. Peter Griffiths took a chance when he volunteered his prints, and lost. He may indeed not have been bright enough to know exactly what he was risking.

A few more thoughts may occur to the reader when considering what Griffiths actually said in his statement and what came out in the course of the enquiry. He may or may not have been confused about the identity of the vehicle in which he was taken to the quarry. He says he had eleven pints of beer, two glasses of Guinness and two double rums between 6 pm and the closing time of local pubs; quite an intake, if it were true. If it were so, could he have negotiated the quarry edge so easily? When interviewed after his arrest he would have been closely questioned in great detail. In his statement he glides over the actual attack on the child, probably preferring to push it all to the back of his mind. This is not uncommon in sordid crime.

The vast majority of murder enquiries are solved by team-work. This Blackburn investigation is a perfect example. Each officer, from the highest rank down to the beat Constable and the Detective Constable, was but a small cog in a powerful machine. Each officer played his or her part to the full and in so doing gained tremendous support from the entire population of a town.

Tony Fletcher

1949

Howard Unruh: The First of the "Crazy Gunmen"

The Unruh case deserves inclusion here, towards the end of this volume of murders of the 1940s, because it can be regarded as the predecessor of a new type of murder. In the introduction to *An Encyclopedia of Murder* (1961) I pointed to the appearance of a new type of crime: the apparently motiveless murder, which might be labelled "the crime of boredom." In March 1959, after a man named Norman Smith had been watching television in his caravan in Sarasota County, Florida – a programme called "The Sniper" – he took his revolver and went out with the intention of shooting someone – anyone. His victim, Mrs Hazel Woodard, was chosen at random, and shot through the window as she watched her TV set.

Since then, "crazy gunmen" have become a feature of crime in the late 20th century: in 1966, Charles Whitman shot nineteen people from the tower in the University of Texas; in 1974, Mark Essex killed nine people on a shooting spree in New Orleans; in 1975, James Ruppert killed eleven relatives in Hamilton, Ohio; in the same year pro-Nazi Frederick Cowan went on a shooting rampage and killed five strangers; in Ottawa in October 1975, teenager Robert Poulin raped and murdered a local girl in his basement room, then went on a shooting rampage at his school, killing one and wounding seven; in 1983, another pro-Nazi, James Huberty, killed twenty-one in a shooting rampage in San Diego, California; in 1989, Patrick

243

Purdy walked into a schoolyard in Stockton, California, and opened fire on Asian children, killing five and wounding thirty; in August 1987, nineteen-year-old Julian Knight opened fire on a busy highway in Melbourne, Australia, hitting twenty-six people, of whom seven died; also in 1987, in Hungerford, England, gun enthusiast Michael Ryan killed sixteen in a shooting spree; in December 1989, Mark Lepine took a repeating rifle to the University of Montreal and killed fourteen, wounding another thirteen; in April 1989, twenty-two-year-old Robert Sartin opened fire at Monkseaton, near Newcastle on Tyne, killing one and injuring fourteen. This list is by no means complete.

And so Unruh may be seen as the first of a long line of "crazy gunmen", and an ominous portent of things to come.

This account is from Brad Steiger's *Mass Murder*.

Perhaps because it was hard to believe that with each shot someone was dying, the Camden, New Jersey, residents, who lived near the intersection of 32 Street and River Road, were at first slow to take cover. Some of them heard the gun ring out five times before they believed anything extraordinary was happening.

At the sound of the shots customers in a grocery store across the street and the people in a neighboring bar-restaurant crowded to the windows to see what was going on. The setting in front of them appeared exactly normal. The relatively busy intersection carried the usual amount of mid-morning traffic, and a few cars were on 32 Street waiting for the traffic light to change. It looked like the beginning of a beautiful late summer day. The sky was clear and the morning sun was warming the air. Even the tall man who emerged from the barber shop across the street seemed to move casually, walking at an easy pace in spite of the sound of the shots.

Eyes followed the man as he walked out of the barber shop that had just been vacated by a woman carrying a little boy and girl. When the tall man reached the corner, and the entrance of the drugstore, they could see that he carried an automatic pistol. Then, as if it had been pre-arranged, out of the drugstore walked another man who practically bumped into him. There was a short pause during which the two men seemed to be exchanging words. Then two more shots rang out, and the man from the drugstore crumpled and rolled toward the street.

The observers had seen enough. The proprietors of the two establishments locked their doors, and the customers fled to the back. As the stunned and frightened people waited, they heard more shots and wondered who the gunman had killed. Although they could not have known it at the time, the killer, who moved calmly through the business establishments across the street, was in the process of setting an all-time high in rapid-fire killings. The quick action of the managers of both the grocery store and the bar-restaurant probably saved the lives of their customers. When the toll was finally taken, the methodical killer had taken twelve lives in twelve minutes, fatally wounding number thirteen, who would die before the day ended, and wounding three others who would survive.

Howard Unruh had been considered a gentleman throughout his adult life. People who came in contact with him believed him to be one of the most mild-mannered young men they had ever met. Unruh seemed to be the kind of man who would go out of his way to avoid trouble. His fellow employees, his former Army buddies, the members of his church congregation, all confirmed Unruh's quiet and responsible nature. Yet, on September 6, 1949, the twenty-eight-year-old ex-GI descended the steps of his mother's apartment, walked out on the streets of Camden and started to kill in what seemed an indiscriminate pattern of murder.

Nobody could understand what had made the quiet young man go off the deep end. But later the investigation revealed that the black day had been festering in the young man's mind for a long time.

Although it is impossible to say when Howard Unruh first began heading for that day of violence, certain factors of his personality had remained constant throughout his entire life. Even as a schoolboy he was described as quiet, although he could hardly have been classified as abnormally passive. A better-than-average student at school, Unruh went in for activities on a scholarly level. He seems to have been well received in spite of the fact that he did not participate in athletics. As a boy, he had been just another kid. Quieter than some, but still just an average boy.

His parents were middle-class working people, and even though they had begun living separately during Howard Unruh's adolescence, their separation did not change Howard's life significantly. Although still on friendly terms with his father, Howard lived with his mother. The boy's only brother was married and lived in the suburbs.

While in high school, Unruh decided to become a pharmacist and was preparing to study for that career when his plans – like those of many others – were interrupted by World War II. There was probably some speculation among Unruh's acquaintances about the kind of soldier the quiet lad would make, but to their surprise, Unruh became a very efficient fighting man.

Howard Unruh's superiors rated him a top-notch soldier. When the ground got tough to gain, the lanky boy from New Jersey performed surprisingly well from his position as a tank gunner. As part of a tank command, he took part in the Battle of the Bulge and earlier had participated in the trek up the length of the Italian peninsula.

Unruh was also accepted by his fellow GIs, even though they gave him a hard time about his refusal to drink or to go out with girls. Unruh preferred to remain by himself and read his Bible. As often as his buddies tried to set him up with an Italian or French girl, he always turned them down.

The man who was Unruh's sergeant for most of the European tour of duty said that in tense situations Unruh's demeanor never changed. He coolly did his duty at all times. The only time that the sergeant ever recalled the soldier laughing was when another GI mounted a Naples balcony and did an imitation of Il Duce. Unruh was not unfriendly, and even though he abstained from all the customary pleasures of the soldier, he never preached at his barrack mates, nor held himself above them. He was given an honorable discharge at the end of the war, and returned to his New Jersey home, eager to get back into civilian life.

But military life and World War II did have an effect on the quiet man. One of Unruh's buddies was surprised to glance at a page of Unruh's diary and find that Unruh had written with delight of the Germans that he had killed. This ex-GI – who later became a New York police officer – said that after the mass murder, it had been his suspicion that Unruh had had the soul of the murderer all along and that the Army had merely channeled his killer instinct for the duration of the war. The Army had also introduced Unruh to firearms, and he had used them well. During training, Unruh had been ranked as a sharpshooter, and his accuracy did not diminish under combat pressure.

In civilian life, Unruh continued to be fascinated with firearms. He had picked up a couple of souvenirs during the war, and he purchased other pistols to add to his collection. Unruh set up a firing range in the basement of his Camden apartment, and he spent hours there, improving his already excellent marksmanship.

Like many other GIs, Unruh had become a little rusty on his high school subjects, so he took several refresher courses in preparation for entering the university. Once again he wanted to study to become a pharmacist. Unruh was consistently at the top of the class in the preparatory courses, but when he finally enrolled at Temple University in Philadelphia, he had lost much of his ambition. He found the adjustment to civilian life less easy than he had expected. He complained to his mother that he could not concentrate sufficiently to get anything from the courses he was taking. His mother tried to reassure him by telling him that it would require patience to attain his goal.

Though things began to lose meaning for him, Unruh and his mother continued to attend a nearby church regularly, and Howard also participated in a Bible class. The only girlfriend that he was ever known to have had was a member of the church.

But Unruh's benign appearance masked an inner turmoil that was eventually to climax in twelve minutes of death for his neighbors. Howard Unruh had become what psychiatrists term a paranoid schizophrenic. He had begun to view the world around him as an alien place, its inhabitants as his enemies. This mental trauma was not something that had happened suddenly. The new Howard Unruh was the result of many years of mounting suspicion, which his twisted personality had turned into a violent hatred of his fellow men.

There were signs of the impending disaster, but the young man was so unobtrusive that it barely jogged anyone's memory when his name was mentioned. Early in the summer of 1949, Unruh ceased to attend the church he had gone to faithfully since his return from Europe. Although several members of the congregation were aware of this, no one thought it worthy of extensive consideration. About the same time, Unruh stopped dating the girl he had been seeing.

Authorities were later to discover that it was at this time that Unruh was going through some radical adjustments in his sex life and had begun to seek sexual gratification from other men. It was a crucial time in his paranoia, and Unruh felt as though the entire world was peering at him.

Unruh always left his mother's apartment by the rear door and cut through the backyard of his next-door neighbors, the Cohens. Mr Cohen was the owner of a drug store which adjoined the flat where he, his wife, son, and mother lived. On one occasion Cohen's mother had yelled out a window at the passing young man.

"Hey, you," the elderly lady said from behind her screened window. "Do you have to go through the yard?" Irritation rang in her voice.

It was not the complaint that hurt Howard Unruh so much as the fact that she had not called him by name. Back in his room he added the incident to a list of grievances that he had already recorded against the Cohens. His expression never changed as he wrote, in a very legible hand, concise statements of complaint. He listed the violation just as impassively as he had listed the bugle that the Cohens had given their 12-year-old son the Christmas before. Higher up on the list was a phrase that told of a screen door that banged late at night. A number of other seemingly insignificant incidents were also marked on the list, and behind each one was the concise abbreviation, "retal."

But the Cohens were not the only people against whom Unruh intended retaliation. He had complaints written against nearly all of his neighbors. Each of these "violations" would have been considered insignificant by a normal person, but to Unruh, they had acquired tremendous significance – for each notation marked or confirmed an individual for killing.

Unruh had begun his planning two years earlier. With each added irritation, he would revamp his plans. His weapon collection grew. He paid $40 for a 9mm German Luger, which seemed to be his favorite. His suspicions that the neighbors were talking about him behind his back mounted to the point that any time Unruh saw them in conversation, he felt certain they were speaking of him. Actually, Howard Unruh seldom entered the conversation of his neighbors. He simply was not that interesting to them.

Unruh continued to plan. He finally arrived at the conclusion that he would have to kill his mother in order to spare her the agony of the killings he would later perform. The chief target of his reprisals would be the Cohens, and his special plans for them were the most hideous of all. A machete had been added to Unruh's collection of weapons. After the crime, Unruh told investigating psychologists that he had planned to use the machete to behead Mr and Mrs Cohen.

In back of the Unruhs' apartment was an extremely small yard that was completely enclosed by a fence. On September 5, 1949, Howard Unruh sublimated his anger for one more day by installing a gate in that fence. This would allow him to get in and out of the yard without crossing anyone else's property. It was one way to prevent the prying eyes of the neighbors from falling on him. He worked industriously through the day. In the afternoon his father stopped by to give Howard a hand in fashioning the crude gate that was to hang in the middle of the back fence and open to the alley. It was not a work of craftsmanship by any standard but, to Howard Unruh, it represented a personal victory over the neighbors.

What Howard Unruh did on the night of September 5, is not known. At about 3:00 a.m., however, traveling a path that would take him through the newly constructed gate, Unruh came home. He was surprised and angered to find that the gate had disappeared, leaving only a gaping hole in the fence where it had been. As always, his calm demeanor remained, but the incident became the proverbial back-breaking straw. Though pranksters had taken the gate away, Unruh was positive his neighbors were to blame.

He walked into the apartment and began to review the plans he had made, revising and bringing them up to date. Later, the only complaint Howard Unruh had about the night was that he had had trouble falling asleep. Although he had no proof of who actually had taken the gate, there was one way in which he could be certain of punishing the true culprit – he could kill everybody.

The following morning, his mother made eggs and cereal for Howard's breakfast. Mrs Unruh was disturbed by the wild look in her son's eye, but nothing prepared her for what was to come. Howard Unruh made a quick trip to the basement and returned carrying a chromeplated wrench. His expression, and the way he handled the wrench, so terrified his mother that she ran from the house. Nearly hysterical, Mrs Unruh finally stopped at the house of a friend. When she began to tell of the hatred she had glimpsed in her son's eyes, she fainted.

Howard Unruh was a little upset by his mother's reaction. It threw his schedule off and forced him to start earlier than he had planned. He went to his room, loaded the Luger and another pistol, and put a knife in his coat pocket. All the extra clips for the Luger were loaded also, and he shoved them into the other pocket of his coat. Deciding to leave the unwieldy machete behind, Unruh picked up a tear-gas cartridge before he left the room, then walked outside and vaulted the fence instead of walking through the gateless hole in it. He made his way over a neighboring yard and then through an alley that brought him to the sidewalk on River Road, between a cleaning establishment and a shoe repair shop. Unruh's first stop on one of the deadliest walks in history was at the shoe repair shop. The time was 9:20 a.m.

Cobbler John Pilarchik had opened his shop as usual that sunny September day. He was particularly busy working on children's shoes that the youngsters would need for the beginning of school the next week. He had just purchased the shoe repair shop and business was expanding. He looked up from his work as Howard Unruh entered the store, and was met by the barrel of Unruh's Luger. Unruh's expression never changed as he squeezed off two quick shots. The blasts echoed through the little shop, and Pilarchik pitched headlong to the floor.

Taking his time, Unruh walked out of the cobbler's shop and turned to his left, heading for the corner of the block and the Cohen drugstore. But before he got there, he turned into the first door past Pilarchik's, a barber shop owned and operated by Clark Hoover.

When Unruh entered, the barber was busy giving six-year-old Orris Smith a pre-school haircut. Mrs Edward Smith, Orris' mother, was standing next to the boy, who had mounted the plastic horse on which the barber trimmed young would-be-cowboys. Mrs Smith's eleven-year-old daughter and two boys from the neighborhood were also in the barber shop. The most that could be said for Unruh's expression was that it was impatient. Unruh had come after Hoover, the barber, and the Smith boy was in his way. He shot the boy in the head, then leveled the gun at the barber himself, shooting him once in the body and once in the head. Unruh paid no attention to the other people in the barber shop. Mrs Smith snatched up her son's body and, together with her daughter and the neighborhood boys, scrambled out of the place.

The buildings leading to the corner of 32 Street and River Road are sandwiched together with hardly any space between them. Therefore it was only a short stroll for Howard Unruh to reach the corner and the entrance to the drugstore. He moved unhurriedly and was about to go in when a man stood in his way. He was the Unruhs' insurance agent, James Hutton, a man with whom Howard Unruh had no quarrel at all.

"Excuse me," Howard Unruh said.

But James Hutton stood stock still, astonished at the sight of the gun in the other man's hand.

Because the man was in his way, Unruh fired the gun twice again, one slug in Hutton's body, the other in his head. The insurance man fell to the sidewalk.

Having disposed of this temporary obstacle in his path, Unruh entered the drugstore to search for the chief targets he wanted to place in front of his Luger. But Cohen had observed what had happened at the entrance of the store and had run upstairs to warn his family. When the gunman could not find anyone in the store, he, too, walked slowly up the stairs.

Mrs Cohen had hidden her son in one bedroom closet, while she, herself, had hidden in the other. Unruh entered the bedroom and shot through the closet door before he opened it and watched the woman's body fall to the floor. He shot her again, this time in the head, apparently unaware of the footsteps of the escaping boy.

Leaving Mrs Cohen's body on the bedroom floor, Unruh walked out of this room and into the next, where he found the druggist's mother on the phone, trying to call the police. The Luger banged twice again, and the woman dropped the phone as she crumpled to the floor.

While the killer was occupied with shooting the women, the druggist and his son climbed out a window, onto the sloping roof of the building. Unruh moved to the window and picked off the man with a shot in the back. The druggist's body fell to the sidewalk. Cohen was one man Unruh did not want to miss. Taking careful aim, Unruh shot through the window again. The bullet entered the man's skull and ended his life. Of the four people who had been in the building when Unruh entered, only one remained alive.

But the gunman was far from finished. The Cohens had been his prime targets, to be sure, but there were other neighbors who had to be repaid for the stabs in the back that Howard Unruh had imagined they inflicted on him. As if he were some grim avenger measuring out justice, Unruh retraced his path, his footsteps slow and deliberate as he traversed the stairs and then the length of the drugstore. Outside, the body of James Hutton still sprawled on the sidewalk. A car had stopped on River Road, apparently to aid the luckless Hutton. Without hesitation – and again with deadly accuracy – Unruh leveled the Luger and fired. In his attempt to aid a man beyond help, Alvin Day had forfeited his life.

With practiced smoothness Unruh reloaded, then walked across the street to where a car waited for the lights to change. A woman sat behind the wheel. Before she could pull away, Unruh shot her in the head through the open window. In the car with her were the woman's ten-year-old son and aged mother. Unruh poked the barrel of the gun through the car window and blasted until the boy and the older woman were also dead.

The tall, taciturn murderer walked on as if nothing extraordinary had occurred, then attempted to enter the supermarket and the bar-restaurant. Unruh fired two shots into the locked door of the bar-restaurant before recrossing the street on a diagonal that brought him back to the shoe repair shop where the carnage had begun. Down River Road, a truck driver was climbing from his cab. It was a long shot, but Unruh proved his marksmanship once again when he hit the driver in the leg.

On the other side of the cobbler's shop, was a tailor's establishment. Tom Fegrino, the owner, was out, but Unruh entered the shop and proceeded to the back room where he found Fegrino's terrified wife.

"Oh, my God, don't," the woman sobbed. Mrs Fegrino's pleas had absolutely no effect on the killer as he impassively triggered the two shots that ended the woman's life.

Outside again, Unruh chanced to see a movement in a nearby window. Most of the residents had sought cover, but three-year-old Tommy Hamilton had wandered to a window and was looking curiously through it when the glass shattered in front of him and the boy fell to the floor, dead.

Unruh left River Road by way of an alley running between the tailor's shop and the cobbler's shop. Knowing that he was low on ammunition, Unruh walked to a house that opened to 32 Street and entered it.

Mrs Madeline Harrie was at home with her two sons, Leroy, fourteen, and Armond, sixteen. Though Mrs Harrie's first thought was to retreat, she decided that she was not going to be driven out of her own home. She turned and held her ground in the kitchen. Her older son went further, however, and rushed the gunman. Perhaps because of the body flying at him, Unruh's aim was, for the first time, inaccurate. He shot twice and only wounded both Mrs Harrie and her son. He would have shot again, but, mercifully, he had run out of bullets.

For the first time that morning, Howard Unruh seemed to be in a hurry. He trotted lightly back toward the apartment where he lived, vaulted the fence, and ran inside. The thin wail of police sirens was heard. Unruh had barely climbed the stairs when the first police car arrived at the intersection. The time was 9:32 a.m. Only twelve minutes had passed since life on the street had first been interrupted in its normal routine! Soon the entire area swarmed with law enforcement officials.

The news spread quickly and, at the office of the Camden *Courier-Post*, city editor Phillip Buxton had a hunch that he felt compelled to follow. He had heard the killer's identification reported over the police radio and had quickly snatched up the Camden telephone listings to look for a name. When he had located the only possibility, the editor dialed the number, hoping that the deranged killer would answer the phone.

Barricaded in his apartment, Howard Unruh still acted unconcerned. Even while the bullets of the police tore through the plaster walls, he calmly answered the phone. The story of this incredible telephone interview was carried on the front page of the *Courier-Post*.

"Hello," Unruh said into the receiver. His voice was calm.

"Is this Howard?" Buxton asked.

"Yes, this is Howard," the man answered with his usual courtesy. "What is the last name of the party you want?"

"Unruh."

"Who are you and what do you want?"

"I'm a friend," Buxton said, trying to win his confidence, "and I want to know what they're doing to you."

"Well, they haven't done anything to me, yet, but I'm doing plenty to them." He sounded as if he might have been describing a shopping trip.

"How many have you killed?"

"I don't know yet – I haven't counted 'em, but it looks like a pretty good score."

"Why are you killing people?"

"I don't know. I can't answer that yet – I am too busy. I'll have to talk to you later." He hung up.

Unruh was indeed very busy. The police had begun heaving tear gas through the shattered windows, and, almost immediately, the killer lost interest in returning their small-arms fire. He could have retaliated with the tear gas he also carried, but instead he chose to give himself up. Fifty guns were trained on Howard Unruh as he walked out of the back door with his hands in the air. He was frisked and handcuffed immediately.

"What's the matter with you?" someone demanded as they led him away. "You a psycho?"

"I'm no psycho," Unruh replied calmly. "I have a good mind."

Howard Unruh was never brought to trial. A team of over twenty specialists were unanimous in their determination that he was insane. Not many people wanted the twenty-eight-year-old man on the loose, however, and it is doubtful that he will ever leave the New Jersey State Mental Hospital at Trenton.

During one interrogation he told psychiatrists: "I'd have killed a thousand if I'd had bullets enough." Fortunately, Howard Unruh had run out of ammunition.

Brad Steiger

A Mixed Bag

As in the previous volume, *Murder in the 1930s*, I conclude with some shorter accounts of cases that deserve at least a mention.

Although I have avoided political murders in this "Murder File", the assassination of Leon Trotsky deserves to be the exception, since it is one of the few murders of this period which is also a "historical event". This account is from the *Encyclopedia of Murder*, as are all but one of the others that follow.

The brief account of Bruno Lüdke is included because Lüdke was undoubtedly one of the major German sex killers of the 20th century; if his confession to eighty-five murders is accurate, then he is *the* major German sex killer. But since he was summarily executed without trial, no full account of his crimes survives.

I include the unsolved case of the Texarkana Moonlight Murderer because, together with the Black Dahlia case, it may be regarded as *the* unsolved sex crime of the 1940s.

The odd case of Ley and Smith is included in the *Notable British Trials* and must inevitably figure in any list of British crimes of the period.

The classic British murder mystery of the 1940s is undoubtedly the Lower Quinton "Witchcraft" murder. I was torn between whether to include the account by Fabian of the Yard, or the chapter from *Perfect Murder* by Bernard Taylor and Stephen Knight; however, space was running out, and this short account is by Rowan Wilson, from a book on unsolved murders I co-authored with my sons Damon and Rowan.

Finally, we end as we began, with a typical American sex murder of the forties. Like most sex killers, Charles Floyd was an inadequate personality. And, like so many sex killers, he began simply as a voyeur, watching girls undress through uncurtained windows. Twenty years later, a far more intelligent killer, Ted Bundy, would begin his career of crime in the same way – catching a casual glimpse of a girl removing her clothes, and then turning voyeurism into a "project", which ended – inevitably – by breaking into houses.

From the point of view of the history of crime, the lesson of the 1940s seems to be that the Second World War served as a catalyst, leaving no doubt that the Age of Sex Crime – which began so hesitantly in the last quarter of the 19th century – had finally come to stay.

The Assassination of Leon Trotsky

In the afternoon of 20 August 1940 exiled Russian Communist leader Leon Trotsky received a visit from a man known to him as Frank Jacson, 26, journalist, whose mistress, Sylvia Ageloff, was a devoted supporter of Trotsky's political creed. Few people gained admittance to the Mexican fortress (a villa in Coyoacan, a suburb of Mexico City) where the 61-year-old revolutionary lived, still regarded as a deviationist and potential menace by Russian dictator Stalin and his satellites. An abortive attempt on Trotsky's life had been made on 24 May, when twenty men, disguised as policemen, had gained admittance to the villa (through the gullibility or possible collusion of secretary Robert Sheldon Hart, a 23-year-old American, found days afterwards shot dead in a bed of quicklime), had machine-gunned Trotsky's bedroom and thrown incendiary bombs as their target and his wife Natalia cowered under the bed. Four days after this incident Frank Jacson paid the first of many visits, and on this hot August day Natalia Trotsky expressed amazement that her guest should be carrying a raincoat. Left alone with Trotsky (Jacson said he wished to consult him concerning an article draft) the younger man produced from the raincoat pockets a fourteen-inch dagger, a .45 automatic pistol, and an ice pick, which he rammed into Trotsky's head. Jacson, bludgeoned by guards summoned by Trotsky's screams ("Who made you do it? The Soviet Secret Police?"), was taken into custody muttering, "They've got something on me. They are keeping my mother as a prisoner." Trotsky died next day, his brain ($3^1/2$ lb. in weight) having been pierced to a depth of three inches. In Jacson's pocket was a letter expressing disillusionment with Trotsky, who, he said, was only motivated by the desire for personal revenge and who had instructed him to assassinate Stalin. He was sentenced to Mexico's ultimate penalty, twenty years' imprisonment; he proved a model prisoner, teaching illiterates to read, setting up a prison electrical repair shop (employing twenty-six men), and even taking a beautiful Mexican woman, Roquelia Mendoza, as his common-law wife, a practice permissible in Mexico prisons.

This assassin's true identity remains in doubt. He had been introduced to Sylvia Ageloff in Paris in 1938 as Jacques Mornard, a Belgian reporter; he joined her afterwards in New York as Frank Jacson, explaining that he had used a forged passport in order to avoid the Belgian call-up. Jacson-Mornard himself said he was Jacques Vandendreschd, born in Teheran, son of that country's Belgian ambassador, but this story was found to be false. As he could speak a Barcelona dialect, one investigator looked up Madrid police fingerprint files on Civil War political prisoners, and found that Jacson-Mornard's prints tallied with those of anti-Franco fighter Ramon Mercades del Rio, born 1914, whose mother had been a member of the Barcelona Communist Party and later an agent of the Russian Secret Police, fleeing to Moscow with some of her children in 1937 after Spanish forces were routed.

On his release from jail on 6 May 1960, Jacson-Mornard had a passport issued to him by Czecho-Slovakia, and was last seen in Havana.

Bruno Lüdke

Lüdke was born in 1909; he was definitely mentally defective, in the same way as Earle Nelson. He began his murders at the age of 18. During the war he found it easy to kill. He was arrested for a sexual assault and sterilized by order of Himmler's SS. He was a petty thief (like Kürten) and a sadist who enjoyed torturing animals and (on one occasion) running down a woman with his horse-drawn delivery van. (He worked as a laundry roundsman.)

On 29 January 1943, a 51-year-old woman, Frieda Rösner, was found strangled on the outskirts of a wood near Berlin where she had been collecting fuel. Kriminal Kommissar Franz, in charge of the case, examined all the known criminals in Köpenick, the nearby village. These included Lüdke, who lived at 32 Grüne Trift. When he was asked if he had known the murdered woman, Lüdke admitted that he had, and that he had last seen her in the woods. Asked if he had killed her, he sprang at his interrogator and had to be overpowered; he then admitted he was the murderer, and added that under Paragraph 51 (concerning mental defectives) he could not be indicted for the crime. Lüdke went on to confess to killing eighty-five women throughout Germany since 1928. His normal method was strangulation or stabbing with a knife, and although he stole their belongings, rape was the chief motive. Franz investigated the murders and after a year, reported that it seemed to be true that Lüdke was responsible for all the crimes he confessed to. But it is also true that local police chiefs blamed all their unsolved murders on Lüdke, the ideal scapegoat.

Lüdke believed that he could never be indicted because he was insane. In fact, the embarrassment of various police forces who had arrested innocent men for Lüdke's crimes led to the case being hushed up and treated as a State secret. Lüdke was sent to a hospital in Vienna where he was a guinea-pig for various experiments, and one of the injections killed him on 8 April 1944.

The Texarkana Moonlight Murderer

On the night of 20 February 1946 a young couple were seated in their car near Texarkana, Texas, listening to the radio, when the door was swung open, and the man was struck on the head with a revolver. The girl was also knocked unconscious as she attempted to run away, and was raped. It was daylight when the man regained consciousness, carried his fiancée to the car, and drove to the nearest house for assistance. Six men were arrested almost immediately, following the description given of the attacker by the young couple, and tyre-tracks were noticed close to the spot where the assault had taken place. However, no positive evidence could be obtained, and the men were released. Towns within two hundred miles of the Texas-Arkansas border were alerted to be on the lookout for the criminal.

A month later, on 24 March, Richard Griffin and Polly Anne Moore, a 24-year-old salesman and his 19-year-old girl-friend, parked their car only a mile away from the spot where the previous couple had been assaulted. Griffin was shot through the head; the girl was shot twice, mutilated with a sharp knife, and sexually assaulted. Evidence showed that Griffin had been murdered two hours or so before the girl. Tyreprints near the murder site were identical with those found near the scene of the previous assault. The bullets came from a .32 revolver.

On both occasions a bright full moon had simplified the sex-maniac's search for victims.

Again, many suspects were arrested and released.

On 13 April a 15-year-old girl, Betty Jo Booker, had been playing a saxophone at a local dance. She left the dance after midnight with her boy-friend, 17-year-old Paul Martin. The next morning, both bodies were found a mile away from the car. The youth had been shot in the back three times. The girl had evidently been dragged away from the car, and was shot and mutilated about four hours after the death of her boy-friend. She had been tortured for some time before she was killed; she was also raped.

Scores of suspects were interviewed, and all available police in Texas and Arkansas were used on the case, without result. The newspapers headlined the unknown killer, and a "reign of terror" began in the area of the murders.

On 3 May 1946, again on the night of a full moon, a wealthy farmer, Virgil Starks, was shot as he sat reading a newspaper at ten-thirty. His wife, rushing into the room, was also shot. She managed to run to the house of a neighbour, A.V. Prater, and gave the alarm. This crime had occurred within the state of Arkansas.

Evidence showed that the murderer had killed Virgil Starks with a .22 rifle, and had entered the house immediately after Mrs Starks ran for help. His intention was probably to assault the housewife in his usual manner; the familiar tyre-tracks were found near the house. Mrs Starks recovered from her wounds a few weeks later.

Measures for discovering the criminal were on the enormous scale that is usual in such cases. Hundreds of men were interviewed in towns for a hundred miles around. All military personnel were investigated. A detective with a dummy dressed like a woman sat in a car for night after night in the murder area, but the murderer ignored the bait.

After the murder of Virgil Starks, the crimes stopped. In 1954 a man confessed to being the killer, but careful investigation revealed that this was impossible.

There seems one likely explanation of the sudden cessation of the murders. A few days after the death of Virgil Starks, a man committed suicide by leaping under a train near Texarkana. His description fitted that of the murderer; he was obviously not the hobo type; but he was unknown in the vicinity. His identity was never established. But at the same time that he committed suicide a small car was found burning in a heavily wooded area near the site of the murders. It was definitely a case of deliberate arson, but the tyres had been destroyed, and the ground was too hard to show tracks. It seems remotely possible that the murderer was a Jekyll and Hyde character who was affected by the full moon, and who may have committed suicide in a fit of remorse.

Ley and Smith

If I had more space, I would have liked to include an account of another of Simpson's classic cases, the Chalkpit Murder. As it is, a brief summary will have to suffice.

The case is a curious one; Thomas Ley was certainly insane, and developed a strange obsession about Mudie; he then hired Smith to murder him. But the obsession had no relation whatever to reality.

The career of Thomas Ley had been in many ways remarkable; in New South Wales he had once been the Hon. Thomas Ley, Minister for Justice, but a charge of bribery, and two suspicious deaths – business associates of Ley who were in his way at the time of death – brought his political career to an end. Ley was a grossly fat man, whose fortune had been made by many dubiously legal activities. He returned to England in 1929.

A few weeks after he returned to England, Mrs Maggie Brook followed him; she was a widow of a Perth J.P., and had been 40 when she met Ley in 1922. She became his mistress, and it was because of Ley's jealousy of her that the murder was committed.

Mrs Brook had a daughter, who married a man named Barron and went to live in Wimbledon. When the daughter was ill in hospital, Ley suggested to Mrs Brook that she should go and look after her son-in-law. This was in May 1946. On 12 June 1946, at 10 p.m., Ley telephoned Mrs Brook and accused her of having sexual relations with her son-in-law. (Mrs Brook was 66!) At two-thirty in the morning he arrived in a car and insisted that Mrs Brook return with him to his house in Knightsbridge Court.

There is no explaining Ley's strange jealousy obsession about Mrs Brook – they had ceased to have sexual intercourse ten years before. But there can be no doubt of his madness. He went to Mrs Brook's landlady in Wimbledon and declared that Mrs Brook had asked him to take her away because she was being pestered by the men in the house.

He asked the names of the male lodgers, and Mrs Evans (the landlady) gave them. They included John Mudie, a 35-year-old barman and a decent young man who had only once ever spoken to Mrs Brook. Mrs Evans assured Ley that it was unlikely Mudie had slept with Mrs Brook. Later, Ley called again, saying he wanted to apologize to Mudie. Mrs Evans gave him Mudie's new address at Reigate, where he had become a barman.

Ley moved into a new property at 5 Beaufort Gardens. One day Mrs Brook's son-in-law received a phone call asking him to have tea with Mrs Brook at Beaufort Gardens. He was suspicious and checked with Mrs Brook, who knew nothing about the invitation. Barron was lucky, for Ley was waiting for him at Beaufort Gardens with hired thugs, who might very probably have killed him as Mudie was later killed.

After this failure Ley turned his attention to Mudie, and on 19 June tried a curious trick to find out if Mudie was associating with Mrs Brook. He sent some cheques to Mrs Brook care of Mudie; Mrs Brook's counter-signature was needed on them. Naturally, Mudie had no idea where Mrs Brook was, and returned the cheques to the firm directed by Ley and Mrs Brook. Ley then had his solicitors write to Mudie demanding the return of the cheques, and finally went to see Mudie himself; Mudie satisfied Ley that the cheques had been returned and, after confirming this, Ley apologized. The reasons for his conduct are mysterious.

Ley now contacted John William Buckingham, a car-hirer, and invited Buckingham to a meeting. At this meeting, attended by Ley, Buckingham, and John Lawrence Smith, a joiner, Buckingham was told that Mudie was a black-mailer who must be decoyed to London and forced to sign a pledge not to bother Mrs Brook and her daughter again. A friend of Buckingham's, a Mrs Bruce, was also brought into the conspiracy. Her job was to go to the Reigate Hill Hotel and make Mudie's acquaintance. Smith hired a car, a Ford 8, number FGP 101, and on Wednesday 27 November 1946 drove down to a chalk pit situated on the Slines Road, leading from the main Croydon – Westerham road to Woldingham in Surrey. At about four-forty on this date, two labourers saw Smith standing on the edge of the chalk pit; when he saw them he ran away to the car, which was parked behind some trees, and drove off fast; they noticed the 101 in the number of the car, and also its make.

Mrs Bruce made Mudie's acquaintance according to plan, posing as a wealthy lady, and invited him to come and mix cocktails at a party to be given by her in London. Mudie accepted. On 28 November Mrs Bruce and Buckingham's son went to Reigate to pick up Mudie, and drove him to Beaufort Gardens, where Mrs Bruce let him in by a side door. She then closed the door and went off with Buckingham junior; this was the last she saw of Mudie. For this service she received £30. She had, of course, no idea that Mudie was to be murdered.

Inside the house, Smith and Buckingham pounced on Mudie and threw a blanket over his head, then tied him up with some clothes-line which Buckingham had bought. Buckingham was then given £200 – thirty of which were for Mrs Bruce – and told to go, and not to contact Ley again. (A few days later he was told that Mudie had signed the agreement, and had left the country with £500 given him by Ley.)

Now either Ley or Smith, or both, administered a brutal beating up to Mudie – probably Ley, in view of his motives. Then one of them strangled Mudie and the body was taken out to the chalk pit and dumped.

Two days later, on 30 November, the body was discovered by Mr Walter Coombs. A rope was tied around the throat, and there was signs of violent blows on the head, chest, and stomach. He was soon identified as Mudie, and among his possessions at the hotel were letters relating to his dealings with Ley. The police soon had Ley, Smith, and Buckingham under arrest and charged Ley and Smith with murder. Buckingham had gone to Scotland Yard of his own accord on 14 December, two weeks after discovery of the body, and made a statement.

Smith was an evasive witness who made a bad impression. He declared that he had left Mudie bound and gagged and alone in the house with Ley. He admitted his indifference to Mudie's fate, but claimed he did not believe Ley intended to murder him.

The trial opened on 19 March 1947 at the Old Bailey before Lord Goddard, Lord Chief Justice. Mr Anthony Hawke and Mr Henry Elam prosecuted; Sir Walter Monckton led Ley's defence, and Mr Derek Curtis Bennett defended Smith. Both pleaded not guilty, but Ley simply disclaimed all knowledge of Mudie. This was stupid, and it gave Ley's counsel an extremely difficult task.

An interesting witness for the defence was an ex-convict named Robert Cruikshank, who had been in Australia in 1929 (and so may have known Ley) and who was living in Switzerland at the time of the murder. But Cruikshank claimed that he had flown to England on the afternoon of the murder on some smuggling venture, and had a few hours to kill before flying back the same night. He decided to call on Ley, whom he claimed he did not know, hoping that Ley, as a rich Australian, might help him to get back to Australia. He also claimed that at 8 p.m. he found the house in darkness, and decided that it might be worth burgling. He let himself into the basement, and saw a man tied into a chair. His lighter failed at that moment, but he went to the man and pulled on the ropes. However, he abandoned any intention of freeing the man and made off. The whole point of Cruikshank's evidence seemed to be that he *might* have strangled the man by pulling on the ropes. Lord Goddard asked if he meant to confess to killing the man, and Cruikshank replied that it was only a possibility. In his summing up, Lord Goddard made no bones about the possibility that Cruikshank had been bribed to confuse the prosecution with a possibility that Mudie had died accidentally.

Both Ley and Smith were sentenced to death, but on May 5, after an examination by three specialists, Ley was declared insane and moved to Broadmoor. A month later he died of a seizure. Since it would have been hardly fair to reprieve the master and not the man, Smith's sentence was also commuted to penal servitude for life.

The Lower Quinton Witchcraft Murder

Charles Walton was practically retired from labouring by the spring of 1945. He had worked on the local farms all his life and now, in his seventy-fourth year, was afflicted with crippling rheumatism. Despite this he still insisted on doing some work around farmer Albert Potter's farm when the weather allowed him.

St Valentine's Day, 14 February 1945, was a clear and sunny day in Lower Quinton when Charles Walton took up his walking stick and made for Meon Hill on Potter's farm to do some hedge cutting. Walton lived with his niece Edith who had a war job in a nearby factory. When she got home at 6 o'clock that evening, her uncle had not returned. Normally he was back from work around 4. Edith was anxious, worried that he had fallen and, unable to stand up, was lying out in the open in the approaching darkness.

Co-opting a neighbour to help her search, Edith made for Potter's farm. Accompanied by the farmer, Edith and her neighbour hunted through the fields by torchlight. Their shouts brought no reply. Edith was beginning to fear for her uncle's life. Suddenly, in the beam of the torch, they saw a body. Charles Walton was pinned to the ground with his own pitchfork. Edith, stunned with shock, returned to her cottage escorted by the neighbour while Potter remained with the body.

Only when the police arrived with spotlights did it become clear how violently Walton had been butchered. His throat was slashed with his own hand scythe, which had been left jutting from the wound. His arms were criss-crossed with cuts where he had evidently tried to defend himself. The pitchfork that fixed him to the ground took two policemen to remove – Potter had tried and failed. Cut into the wrinkled skin of Walton's neck and chest was a cross.

Superintendent Robert Fabian, known as Fabian of the Yard, one of Britain's most celebrated detectives, took over the case after local police failed to uncover any leads. A tin watch had been removed from the corpse, and Fabian enlisted the help of the Royal Engineers equipped with mine detectors to search the surrounding countryside for it. Meanwhile constables took statements from the village's 493 inhabitants.

The crime should have been easy to solve. The murderer must have been someone with a grudge against Walton. In a small community, such a motive would be difficult to hide. This was the rational view. The terrible violence of the attack and the superstitious silence of the locals suggested a more ritualistic cause for Walton's death.

The pinning of a witch to the ground in order to destroy her power is a ritual dating from Anglo-Saxon times. The villagers tacitly implied that this is what happened to Walton. In 1875 a man called John Haywood had murdered an old lady named Ann Turner because he believed her to be a witch who was persecuting him. In his statement to the court he said that it was common knowledge that most of the misfortunes suffered by the local community were inflicted by a small coven of witches. He had merely taken his revenge. He had stabbed her with a pitchfork and cut a cross into her neck.

Fabian uncovered only one other lead. A villager had made a statement to the effect that a POW from the nearby camp was seen wiping blood from his hands in a ditch on the day of the killing. The camp inmates were all searched and an Italian was found to have bloodstains on his coat. He refused to answer questions. The coat was sent, along with other samples taken from villagers, to the forensic lab. The Royal Engineers were despatched to search the ditch. They found metal. It was not however the tin watch, but a rabbit snare. The blood on the coat also proved to be that of a rabbit. The POW had declined to talk because he was scared that he would be punished for poaching.

There the investigation ended – it remained one of Fabian's few total failures. But in their book *Perfect Murder*, Bernard Taylor and Stephen Knight claim to have learned the solution to the mystery. In "The Mysterious Death of Charles Walton", Knight alleges that Fabian was certain of the identity of the killer, but simply lacked the evidence to prosecute. The murderer, Knight says, was Farmer Potter himself. His motive had nothing to do with ridding the countryside of a witch, but was purely financial. Walton was an obsessive saver, and he had lent Potter a large sum when Potter was on the brink of ruin. The money became due; Potter was unable to pay it back, and on that St Valentine's Day, he chose a violent solution to his problem. Potter may not have intended to kill Charles Walton when he went to talk to him about the debt – or to ask for an extension. Perhaps Walton threatened him with court action, or flourished the receipt under his nose. Whatever the reason, Potter killed the frail old man, then mutilated the body to suggest a witchcraft connection.

Knight's evidence for this theory tends to centre upon Potter's conflicting statements to police and the ease with which he found Walton's body in the dark that February evening. His attempts to pull the pitchfork from Walton's chest were, according to the theory, attempts to cover his fingerprints from the time of the murder.

Whether or not Potter killed Walton, the aspect of the story that intrigues is the idea of a well hidden group of Satan worshippers at the heart of a seemingly tranquil English village life. Even if Potter did kill Charles Walton and mark the body with pagan symbolism, where did he learn the pagan symbolism? It would seem that the more comfortable, greed-based explanation of Charles Walton's murder merely leads to more questions.

Rowan Wilson

Charles Floyd

No full account of Floyd's case history has been given; his first victim may have been Mrs William C. Brown, the 20-year-old wife of a Tulsa truck-driver, strangled and raped in her flat at 825 North Main Street on 10 July 1942. She was pregnant and only six days away from delivering the child when she was murdered; the unborn baby was also killed.

Less than six months later, 6-year-old Clara Stewart and her daughter, Mrs Georgina Green, were battered to death and raped in their apartment, again on the north side of the city. Mrs Green's husband was in the army. All three victims were redheads.

Two and a half years went by before the next attack, on 15 May 1945. Panta Lou Liles, the redheaded wife of a sailor, returning to her ground-floor room at 501 Cheyenne Street, undressed without drawing the curtains. The "peeping Tom" outside watched her undress, waited until she was asleep, and clambered over the windowsill into the room. He knocked the girl unconcious before she woke up, and went on to batter her to death. He then wrapped her head in a sheet, and raped her. Several hours later he was still in the room when Mrs Liles" room-mate, a night nurse, rang up to wake the girl in time to be at her work at a nearby aircraft plant. A man's voice answered; and the nurse called the police.

A man named Henry Owens was arrested on suspicion; he was known to be weak-minded, and had been booked before on a charge of molesting women. A lie-detector test was inconclusive; although the graph jumped when Owens was asked about the murders, it seemed possible that he might be deluding himself by a kind of wishful thinking. The lie-detector operator told of an interesting case, when a lunatic who claimed he was Napoleon was given a test. When asked if he was Napoleon, he denied it, but the detector showed he was lying!

While Owens was still in custody, the murderer had another outburst, this time wounding three girls and killing a fourth. This was on 1 July 1948. The murderer broke into the flat of a woman on North Cheyenne Street, and attacked the woman and two children who were sleeping in the flat – her daughter and a friend, aged respectively 12 and 14. The woman was knocked unconscious and an "unnatural sex act" committed on her. The two children were knocked unconscious and partly undressed, but the killer was disturbed by a neighbour who had been roused by screams and escaped by the back door before he could complete the assault. Two blocks away, at 11 East Cameron Street, the killer found another redhead, Ruth Norton, whom he bludgeoned while she was still asleep and then raped. Ruth Norton died of her injuries. The killer had apparently forced his way in by cutting a hole in the back door – a method reminiscent of the New Orleans Axe Man.

A description of the murderer came from a woman who

had been awakened by the barking of a dog on the night of the Ruth Norton murder. She had seen a man standing outside and flashing a torch; he was more than six feet tall and looked like a truck-driver.

The police began a careful check on all trucking companies in Tulsa, and finally discovered that a tall man named Charles Floyd had left his job on the day after the murder of Ruth Norton; Floyd was known to have a passion for redheads. It took some time to find Floyd, but he was finally arrested a year and a half after his last murder. Floyd seemed to be tired and confused, but he was able to supply details that would be known only to the murderer. He admitted to being an inveterate "peeping Tom" who had killed when the sexual excitement became too overpowering.

In some ways, the case fails to conform to the usual pattern of the sexual murderer, whose crimes tend to become more and more frequent. After the three murders in 1942, two and a half years elapsed before the next, then a period of three years.

It has at least one feature worth commenting on. From Floyd's confession, it emerged that he was in the habit of watching Panta Lou Liles undressing through her window. In a sense, therefore, the girl was partly to blame for not drawing her curtains. One of the causes of the increase in sexual crime is certainly the increase in stimulation.